The Art of State Persuasion

The Art of State Persuasion

China's Strategic Use of Media in Interstate Disputes

Frances Yaping Wang

Oxford University Press is a department of the University of Oxford. It furthers
the University's objective of excellence in research, scholarship, and education
by publishing worldwide. Oxford is a registered trade mark of Oxford University
Press in the UK and certain other countries.

Published in the United States of America by Oxford University Press
198 Madison Avenue, New York, NY 10016, United States of America.

© Oxford University Press 2024

All rights reserved. No part of this publication may be reproduced, stored in
a retrieval system, or transmitted, in any form or by any means, without the
prior permission in writing of Oxford University Press, or as expressly permitted
by law, by license, or under terms agreed with the appropriate reproduction
rights organization. Inquiries concerning reproduction outside the scope of the
above should be sent to the Rights Department, Oxford University Press, at the
address above.

You must not circulate this work in any other form
and you must impose this same condition on any acquirer.

CIP data is on file at the Library of Congress

ISBN 978–0–19–775751–2 (pbk.)
ISBN 978–0–19–775750–5 (hbk.)

DOI: 10.1093/oso/9780197757505.001.0001

To my family

Contents

List of Illustrations	ix
Acknowledgments	xi
Abbreviations	xv

Introduction: The Dog That Barks	1
1. The (Mis)Alignment Theory	22
2. The Chinese Propaganda System and Media Campaigns	67
3. The Sino-Vietnamese Border War: A Media Campaign to Mobilize	92
4. The Sino-Philippines Arbitration on the South China Sea: A Media Campaign to Pacify	120
5. The Nonbarking Dog: The 2011 Sino-Vietnamese Cable Cutting Incidents and the 2014 Oil Rig Crisis	161
6. Mobilization versus Pacification: A Textual Analysis	186
7. Extending the Argument to Other Autocracies	220
Conclusion	241

Appendix 1: Coding Rules	249
Appendix 2: Case Descriptions	251
Appendix 3: Borderline Media Campaigns	291
Appendix 4: Deviant Cases	295
Appendix 5: Robustness Check Using the ANTUSD Dictionary	301
Appendix 6: Fifty Most Frequent Words for Mobilization Campaigns and Pacification Campaigns	305
Bibliography	307
Index	323

Illustrations

Figures

1.1 State Decision Tree in Making Propaganda Strategy	58
2.1 The Official Hierarchy of Party-State Media	74
3.1 Monthly Count of *People's Daily* Articles on the Sino-Vietnamese Border War during 1978–1991	104
4.1 Baidu.com's Daily Search Index for the Term "South China Sea," May 31, 2015–May 31, 2016	125
4.2 Monthly Count of *People's Daily* Articles on the Sino-Philippines South China Sea Dispute, 2010–2016	132
5.1 Daily Search Volume of "South China Sea" on Baidu.com During One-Year Pre-Crisis Period, May 2, 2013–May 2, 2014	172
6.1 Snapshot of the CMCOR Data Using "Soviet Revisionist" as a Reference Marker in the 1969 Sino-Soviet Border Conflict	196
6.2 Comparison of NTUSD Sentiment Scores with Data Distribution	200
6.3 Predicted NTUSD Sentiment Scores with 95% and 90% Confidence Intervals	200
6.4 Boxplots of NTUSD Sentiment Scores by Campaigns	201
6.5 Predicted NTUSD Sentiment Scores by Campaigns	202
6.6 Predicted NTUSD Sentiment Scores of CMCOR Data with 95% and 90% Confidence Intervals	203
6.7 Boxplots of CMCOR Data NTUSD Sentiment Scores by Campaigns	204
6.8 Top Topics of Mobilization Campaigns	206
6.9 Top Topics of Pacification Campaigns	208
6.10 Comparison of Seven Broad Emotion Categories between Campaign Types	215
6.11 Comparison of Top Six Emotions Among Twenty-One Categories between Campaign Types	216
A2.1 Daily Search Volume of "South China Sea" on Baidu.com During One-Year Pre-Crisis Period, May 2, 2013–May 2, 2014	271
A5.1 Comparison of ANTUSD Sentiment Scores with Data Distribution	302
A5.2 Predicted ANTUSD Sentiment Scores with 95% and 90% Confidence Intervals	302

x   Illustrations

A5.3 Boxplots of ANTUSD Sentiment Scores by Campaigns   303

A5.4 Predicted ANTUSD Sentiment Scores by Campaigns   303

A6.1 Fifty Most Frequent Words for Mobilization Campaigns   305

A6.2 Fifty Most Frequent Words for Pacification Campaigns   306

Tables

1.1 The State–Public (Mis)Alignment Theory   23

1.2 Comparison between a Pacification Campaign and a Mobilization Campaign   37

2.1 Six Disputes, Twenty-One Crises, and Fourteen Media Campaigns   77

2.2 Summary Statistics of Media Coverage on Twenty-One Chinese
      Diplomatic Crises   79

2.3 Predicted and Actual Outcomes on Twenty-One Chinese Diplomatic Crises   83

2.4 Average Monthly Numbers of Front-Page Articles and of All-Relevant
      Articles in the Theoretical Framework   84

2.5 Twenty-One Cases in the Theoretical Framework   85

2.6 Case Selection for Process Tracing   87

4.1 Occasions That Provoked China's Public Relations Responses and
      China's Responses   135

4.2 A Comprehensive but Nonexhaustive List of *People's Daily* Articles
      That Cited Criticism from Non-Chinese Experts   140

6.1 Summary Statistics of the Four Mobilization Campaigns in
      the CMCTD Data   193

6.2 Summary Statistics of the Seven Pacification Campaigns in
      the CMCTD Data   194

6.3 Summary Statistics of the CMCOR Data   195

6.4 Summary of Methods for Testing Each Sets of Hypotheses   197

6.5 CMCTD Data Average NTUSD Sentiment Scores   199

6.6 CMCOR Data Average NTUSD Sentiment Scores   203

6.7 CMCOR Data Average ANTUSD Sentiment Scores   203

A2.1 Chinese Public Thermometer toward Japan, 1999–2015
      (Source: Beijing Area Study)   263

A4.1 Number of *People's Daily* Front-Page and All-Relevant Articles during
      the 1959 Sino-Indian Border Dispute   295

A5.1 CMCTD Data Average ANTUSD Sentiment Scores   301

Acknowledgments

This book came to fruition thanks to the invaluable support of numerous individuals and institutions. Foremost, my gratitude goes to my advisors at the University of Virginia, who were pivotal in nurturing and guiding me throughout my dissertation journey, the cornerstone from which this book emerged. I count myself fortunate to have such an outstanding committee, each member offering their unique expertise and collective collaboration, ensuring the evolution and enhancement of this work.

John Owen was an anchor of encouragement during my initial explorations. His meticulous feedback on countless drafts, coupled with unwavering intellectual and emotional support, has been instrumental throughout my academic journey's peaks and troughs. Brantly Womack has been a guiding light not only for this project but throughout my graduate studies. His insights significantly influenced my perspectives on Vietnamese cases, illuminating the finer details in the evidence. Philip Potter's relentless challenges spurred my progress. His thought-provoking remarks always pushed my boundaries, yet he remained a pillar of moral support and offered invaluable professional counsel. Harry Harding, with his vast experience in Chinese foreign policy, has been a reservoir of wisdom. His accessibility and guidance whenever sought have been nothing short of enlightening. Their continued contributions laid the bedrock for this book.

In addition to my committee members, I owe a tremendous debt of gratitude to numerous mentors whose guidance and support were indispensable in realizing this book. Wang Jisi worked with me closely from the very inception of the idea. My advisors at University of Notre Dame's and George Washington University Mike Desch and Charles Glaser have given me invaluable guidance and encouragement. University of Notre Dame's International Security Center hosted my book workshop, assembling a prestigious panel of International Relations scholars. This panel comprised luminaries such as Ron Krebs, Dan Slater, and Jessica Weiss. Moreover, the university's own international security mavens, including Eugene Gholz, Rose Kelanic, Karrie Koesel, Dan Lindley, and Joe Parent, generously offered their insights, enriching the initial draft of my book with their invaluable feedback.

xii Acknowledgments

The final product was also shaped by the constructive feedback I received from numerous colleagues and friends at multiple conferences and workshops where I presented this work. I am indebted to Tom Christensen, Stacie Goddard, Robert Jervis, Joshua Kertzer, Danielle Lupton, John Mearsheimer, Paul Poast, Maria Repnikova, Elizabeth Saunders, Monica Toft, Chen Wang, and Krista Wiegand. I would like to also thank the participants in the Harvard-Princeton China and the World workshop, the Program on International Security Policy workshop at University of Chicago, Yale Brady-Johnson International Security Studies Research Workshop, workshop at Notre Dame's Liu Institute, and the China and International Relations Graduate Research Workshop at the Center for the Study of Contemporary China at University of Pennsylvania.

I would like to extend special gratitude to two anonymous reviewers for their astute feedback. At Oxford University Press, Dave McBride has consistently championed this project, and I am deeply thankful for his steadfast support. Additionally, my heartfelt thanks go to the dedicated editorial team at OUP for their meticulous work in actualizing this book.

This research has been supported by the United States Institute of Peace, the Thomas Jefferson Memorial Foundation, the Quandt Fund for International Research, the Minerva Research Initiative, the Notre Dame International Security Center, Singapore Management University, and Colgate University Research Council. Furthermore, I extend my heartfelt gratitude to the Beijing University, the East China Normal University, the Chinese University of Hong Kong, and the Vietnam National University for hosting me during my field research.

My fieldwork in China and Vietnam would not have been successful without the immeasurable help from friends and family. I am grateful to all my interviewees, archivists, esteemed historians like Shen Zhihua and Kosal Path for their generous provision of materials, and my research assistants in Vietnam. My friends and classmates from Beijing University were crucial in getting me access to critical interviews. I would also like to thank my colleagues and graduate peers at Colgate, SMU, Notre Dame, GW, and UVA for their enduring friendship and solidarity.

In conclusion, my heart brims with gratitude for my family and their steadfast love and unwavering support. My parents have been instrumental in shaping my character and values; from an early age, they instilled in me the importance of curiosity, dedication to one's passions, and resilience in the face of adversity. My in-laws have consistently shown patience and encouragement throughout this process. My husband and confidant, Steve, is invariably the anchor I turn to, whether for sage advice or emotional uplift. His encouragement and steadfast presence have been my constant through every high and low. And then there is my daughter Skylar, born merely five months prior to my fieldwork and now a lively seven-year-old. Her infectious joy and zest have been a beacon, turning even the most challenging moments of this journey into cherished memories.

Abbreviations

ANOVA	Analysis of Variance
ANTUSD	Augmented National Taiwan University Sentiment Dictionary
APEC	Asia-Pacific Economic Cooperation
ASEAN	The Association of Southeast Asian Nations
BAS	Beijing Area Study
BSI	Baidu Search Index
CATI	Computer-Assisted Telephone Interview
CCP	The Chinese Communist Party
CCTV	China Central Television
CIA	Central Intelligence Agency
CMC	The Chinese Central Military Commission
CMCOR	Chinese Media Campaigns Opponent-Referenced Data
CMCTD	Chinese Media Campaigns on Territorial Disputes
CMS	China Marine Surveillance
CNOOC	China National Offshore Oil Corporation
CPD	The Central Propaganda Department
CPV	Communist Party of Vietnam
DFA	(Philippines) Department of Foreign Affairs
DLUT	Dalian University of Technology Emotion Ontology Dictionary
DOC	Declaration on Conduct of Parties in the South China Sea
EEZ	Exclusive Economic Zone
FBIS	Foreign Broadcast Information Service
FONOP	Freedom of Navigation Operation
ICJ	International Court of Justice
ITLOS	International Tribunal on the Law of the Sea
JYF	Japan Youth Federation
LAC	Line of Actual Control
LDA	Latent Dirichlet Allocation
MC	Media Campaign
MIDs	Militarized Interstate Disputes
MoFA	(Chinese or Vietnamese) Ministry of Foreign Affairs
NTUSD	National Taiwan University Sentiment Dictionary
PLA	People's Liberation Army
PLAN	People's Liberation Army Navy
PRC	People's Republic of China
ROC	Republic of China
SARS	Severe Acute Respiratory Syndrome

xvi Abbreviations

SOE	State-Owned Enterprise
STM	Structural Topic Model
UN	United Nations
UNCLOS	United Nations Convention on the Law of the Sea
WNC	World News Connection

Introduction

The Dog That Barks

Two "Barking Dog" Puzzles

Until the 2010s, the South China Sea dispute was largely unknown to most Chinese citizens. For many, their primary introduction to the "beautiful Spratly Islands" and James Shoal, acclaimed by China as the southernmost point of the country, was through elementary school textbooks—with much of the text likely still memorable for many adults today. They were largely unaware that James Shoal was actually a subject of dispute with Malaysia, not to mention the broader conflict in the Spratlys involving five other claimants.

Nevertheless, by 2011, the South China Sea dispute had transformed into one of China's most prominent foreign policy issues, fueled by an upsurge of nationalist fervor. While international media exposure played a role, the deliberate permission and encouragement of media coverage by the Chinese state also contributed to the sudden spike in public interest. In 2016, when the Sino-Philippines arbitration ruling dismissed most of China's claims, including that of James Shoal, Chinese propagandists launched an intensive campaign, bombarding the country with near-daily tirades in both print and digital platforms.

Similar patterns of heightened public interest and awareness emerged on the Diaoyu/Senkaku Islands dispute between China and Japan. In the backdrop of incidents in 2010 and 2012, Chinese authorities instructed major satellite broadcasters nationwide to feature patriotic or anti-fascist-themed shows. As a result, news coverage of the dispute and anti-Japanese dramas blanketed Chinese television screens.[1] Additionally, Chinese authorities introduced three new public holidays commemorating the Japanese invasion during World War II. However, before the 1980s, the dispute was not nearly as high-profile as it is today. During a comparable dispute in the late 1970s, when a substantial number of Chinese fishing boats surfaced near the contested islands and Japan lodged intense protests, Chinese media coverage

---

The Art of State Persuasion. Frances Yaping Wang, Oxford University Press. © Oxford University Press 2024.
DOI: 10.1093/oso/9780197757505.003.0001

2 Introduction

was virtually nonexistent.[2] The incident went entirely unmentioned in the official media outlets.[3]

These contrasting behaviors in China's use of media in its interstate dispute presents a fascinating puzzle: Why do states consciously engage in efforts to publicize a previously unnoticed dispute? Moreover, when does the state propaganda machine choose to "bark," and when does it opt for silence, and what factors influence these decisions? Particularly intriguing is the deliberate amplification of media coverage by autocrats who wield the power to censor information and downplay disputes—yet at times choose to do the exact opposite. I refer to this variation between highlighting and underplaying disputes as the "barking dog/silent dog" puzzle.

If we dig deeper into what happens following the "barking," we unearth a related second puzzle, which I term the "barking without biting" puzzle. Many instances of seemingly harsh rhetoric remain mere rhetoric; they never turn into actions like some media campaigns do. This raises the question: Why isn't domestic mobilization consistently followed by a hardline policy? To continue our dog metaphor, why does a barking dog sometimes bite while other times does not? What kind of domestic mobilization escalates into a genuine confrontation and what kind does not?

Take the example of the 2016 Sino-Philippines arbitration case. China launched an extensive propaganda campaign and deliberately drew massive domestic attention to a legal case it anticipated losing. Adding to the complexity of this approach, China adopted an unexpectedly moderate foreign policy despite the high-intensity media campaign. Instead of retaliatory measures that could have had significant consequences for the Philippines, China extended olive branches to the Duterte government, making diplomatic gestures and substantive concessions on the dispute. The absence of aggression, and even some conciliatory actions, makes the previous aggressive barking particularly baffling.

Similar patterns were observed in Sino-Japanese disputes in 1990, 1996, and 2005. Despite fierce barking through aggressive media campaigns accompanying a bellicose nationalist public, the foreign policy that followed did not result in aggressive actions in any of these crises. Instead, there were efforts to preempt or suppress anti-Japan protests, and diplomatic dialogues aimed at moving beyond the disputes.

Moreover, the "barking without biting" phenomenon is not unique to China. Prior to the signing of the Iranian nuclear deal, the Iranian media tirelessly promoted a robust anti-West discourse and rejected the idea of seeking talks as a retreat, only to eventually embrace the agreement after two years of negotiation.[4] Similarly, during the 2014 South China Sea oil rig crisis with

China, Vietnam launched an extensive media campaign in the face of an enraged public that had burned down Chinese factories across the country. However, Vietnam subsequently pursued a moderate foreign policy to mend relations with China.[5]

What are states with moderate foreign policies seeking to achieve when they deliberately publicize a dispute? Considering the potential constraints imposed by public sentiment on foreign policy, one might wonder if such publicity inherently limits their options. What, then, explains the barking despite the intention of not biting?

These are the central questions that this book tackles. In particular, it focuses on the "barking," which I call media campaigns. Media campaigns are government-orchestrated, concerted efforts to attract public attention to a dispute by the use of mass media. Two conditions must be satisfied: (1) there is a significant and often rapid increase in media coverage, and (2) this surge in coverage is a result of deliberate action, not merely the media's reflexive reaction to external, provocative events. Hence, the driving force behind the intensified media focus must come from the government.

This book delineates *why* media campaigns occur: the favorable conditions that lead to their adoption, and particularly the subjective motivations driving them. It also describes *how* these campaigns look and work: the appearance and mechanics of these campaigns. Utilizing text analysis, I outline two distinct types of media campaigns: mobilization campaigns, characterized by both "barking" and "biting," and pacification campaigns, involving "barking" without subsequent aggressive measures. In essence, the book focuses on authoritarian states' utilization of propaganda during international crises, exploring the motives and methods of their responses. By scrutinizing the *why* and the *how* behind the "barks" of authoritarian state propaganda machines, this book seeks to clarify the enigmas associated with the conditions that prompt such machines to "bark" or stay silent, as well as the situations where a "barking" state ultimately decides to "bite" or not.

The Argument

I argue that authoritarian states "bark" to align public opinion with their desired foreign policy, for purposes of domestic regime preservation and international security. Two types of misalignment can motivate these "barking" campaigns, and the type of the campaign depends on the nature of the misalignment between the state and the public. When the public opinion is more moderate than the state policy, the state employs a mobilization campaign;

4 Introduction

conversely, when the public opinion is more hawkish than the state policy, the state implements a pacification campaign. Both approaches aim to secure the public's compliance, if not outright support, for the state's preferred policy. In cases where the state and the public are aligned, the state mouthpieces stay quiet.

The pacifying use of propaganda deserves particular attention, as it subverts our traditional understanding of aggressive foreign propaganda. Both the general public and intellectual circles often read bellicose propaganda as cues for aggressive policy intent. However, if these pacification campaigns are indeed prevalent, our intuitive assumptions about aggressive rhetoric can be dangerously misleading.

A pacification campaign calms public opinion by controlling the discourse, echoing public sentiment with ostensibly harsh rhetoric, maintaining the façade of a firm stance, framing the dispute in a positive light, delegitimizing "harmful" emotions, and allowing the public to vent their frustrations on social media. Authoritarian states such as China are well aware of this "open secret" and have repeatedly employed hardline media campaigns for domestic pacification objectives.

In response, when attempting to interpret the foreign policy intentions of these states, it is crucial to recognize that authoritarian states may employ media campaigns not for escalation, but to remove domestic hurdles to de-escalation. Decision-makers need to acknowledge the widespread use of pacifying rhetoric by authoritarian states and understand its rationale and mechanics. Aggressive language should not invariably be read as escalatory. The harsh rhetoric may contain nuances that are not immediately apparent. Only by understanding the intricate domestic dynamics within these nations can foreign leaders start to see beyond the veneer of official nationalist rhetoric and interpret intentions more astutely.

International observers must differentiate between pacification and mobilization rhetoric. While pacification campaigns may adopt seemingly similar aggressive language to mobilization campaigns and increase public awareness and the salience of the dispute, they primarily serve to echo and posture. Therefore, in contrast to the extreme intensity found in mobilization campaigns, pacification rhetoric is typically milder than public sentiment, and more inward-focused than outward-focused: it underscores the government's own diligence and competence in protecting national interests rather than condemning the opponent's aggression. Pacification often accompanies diligent efforts to preempt external escalations and employs threats of punishment that are more rhetoric than substance. On the other hand, states employing mobilization rhetoric do not shy away from escalatory actions or substantial punitive measures.

In terms of content, mobilization and pacification campaigns vary in their valence and narratives, manipulating different emotions with different intensities. Mobilization campaigns typically employ more negative language, while pacification campaigns tend to use more positive words. References to rival nations or their citizens are usually framed more negatively in mobilization campaigns, and conversely, more positively in pacification efforts. Each campaign style is defined by unique frequently used words and themes. Mobilization campaigns are designed to stir stronger, more negative emotions like anger or hatred, while pacification campaigns seek to evoke more positive emotions or less intense negative ones, such as fear or sadness. By recognizing these characteristics, policymakers can differentiate between a mobilization campaign and a pacification one, enabling them to predict the foreign policy intentions of an opposing country based on its domestic media content.

The Significance of Media Campaigns

Unraveling the two "barking dog" puzzles—the selective "barking" of the propaganda machine and the selective "biting" of the state—entails understanding the underlying motivations and strategic calculations behind these media campaigns. By scrutinizing the instances of heightened media attention, we can uncover the rationale behind why states embark on deliberate efforts to bring attention to an otherwise subdued dispute. Furthermore, exploring the specific dynamics surrounding autocrats, who possess censorship capabilities, intentionally boosting media coverage of interstate disputes adds a layer of domestic complexity to a puzzle of foreign policy. By delving into these intricacies, we can gain valuable insights into China's sophisticated management of mass opinion during interstate disputes, shedding light on the underlying strategies and their implications.

Media campaigns are common, particularly among authoritarian states. Historically, security studies have devoted significant attention to exploring factors leading to militarization, often neglecting the critical role of rhetoric. This oversight is particularly problematic given the increasingly frequent "war of words" among nations, where the control and manipulation of state communications and public sentiment emerge as key aspects of modern international relations. Such a shift can be partly credited to the expanding influence of mass media and public opinion in shaping foreign relations, adding

6 Introduction

a theatrical dimension to foreign policy execution. In the nuclear era, the consequences of all-out warfare have become prohibitively high, resulting in a rise of limited conflicts and crises. As a result, nations have shifted toward utilizing state mouthpieces, rather than physical force, to advance their international policy goals.

Fourteen of China's twenty-one diplomatic crises since the establishment of the People's Republic of China (PRC) in 1949 have involved media campaigns. An even larger number of such campaigns have been observed in the 139 countries or territories classified as having unfree or partly free media in 2017. These are countries or regions where "established systems circumscribe news and information for mass audiences and shape the dominant political narrative."[6]

Media campaigns are consequential. Some may dismiss the state rhetoric and publicity in conflict situations as marginal to power politics, the traditional bedrock of security studies.[7] Others disagree. Ronald R. Krebs argues convincingly, "In politics, language is a crucial medium, means, locus, and object of contest. It neither competes with nor complements power politics: it *is* power politics."[8] This book aligns with Krebs's stance, viewing state rhetoric as not only a reflection of power politics, but also as an integral component in its construction.

Numerous official documents in the United States have acknowledged the substantial impact of these media campaigns on international security. Such campaigns offer a cost-effective, relatively low-risk, and covert means to shape perceptions and influence populations.[9] The National Security Strategy of the Trump administration identified China and Russia as "strategic competitors" and "revisionist powers" that "challenge American power, influence, and interests," and warned specifically about these countries' use of "propaganda" "to control information and data to repress their societies and expand their influence."[10] Understanding the function of media and public opinion as tools of statecraft, including their underlying rationale and tactics, thus holds paramount significance for global peace and order.

Media campaigns are also valuable for interpreting policy. Understanding the dynamics of state rhetoric becomes essential in navigating the complexities of contemporary international relations. Media campaigns offer a wealth of data that analysts can use to decipher foreign policy intentions. The lack of transparency in authoritarian states often makes understanding their intentions difficult, increasing the risk of misunderstandings and miscalculations in international relations.

Alexander George's seminal analysis of American interpretations of Nazi German domestic propaganda during World War II revealed an impressive accuracy rate exceeding 80 percent, premised on the assumption of strict top-down political control by the Nazis.[11] However, times have evolved. Despite advancements in control techniques, the rise of media marketization and digitization has rendered total control obsolete in most contemporary authoritarian states. Unfortunately, our comprehension of propaganda has not developed at the same pace. The current research literature struggles to understand the complexities and contradictions presented here. Relevant media studies, which are largely descriptive, seldom view these campaigns from a political standpoint. While an expanding body of political science research on the traits of contemporary authoritarian media adds to this study,[12] the incentives driving media campaigns remain unclear. Moreover, media campaigns with moderate policy intentions—the increasingly common "barking without biting" scenarios—have largely eluded our scrutiny.

The Broader Dialogues

On a broader scheme, this book primarily engages with three ongoing discussions. On authoritarian state–society relations in foreign policymaking, which are at the core of this study, I make assumptions that slightly deviate from some scholarly works regarding the characteristics of the public and the state, as well as their respective roles in formulating foreign policy. Susan Shirk presupposes an informed public and a responsive state—her focus is on the agency of the public, presenting a bottom-up perspective of foreign policy in authoritarian states.[13] James Reilly, on the other hand, assumes a robust society and a strategic state—his focus lies on both state strength and public agency, presenting a cyclical perspective of foreign policy.[14]

This book makes the assumption of a strategic state and a manipulable public—my focus is on the agency of the state, offering a top-down perspective of foreign policy in authoritarian states. The story here is essentially about state autonomy and the ways the state manages public opinion in foreign policymaking. This aligns with the studies of Evgeny Morozov, Daniela Stockmann, and Maria Repnikova on state public opinion manipulation.[15] It is important to note that there is no definitive right or wrong in these theories, as truth often has many faces. When considered collectively, these diverging perspectives offer a more comprehensive and holistic picture of the actual dynamics of authoritarian state–society relations.

Chinese media control has undergone significant evolution over seven decades, marked primarily by the commercialization of Chinese media and the surge of internet use. Commencing in the late 1970s, the shift toward media marketization and privatization led to greater economic incentives influencing news reporting. The advent of the internet led to a rapid increase in users, which coincided with a heightened sense of nationalism. Despite the challenges these changes posed to state control, Chinese propagandists successfully adapted their strategies, leveraging digital technologies and implementing robust censorship systems, new legal frameworks, and a more sophisticated, less forceful approach of guiding public opinion. Although the rise of the internet and heightened nationalist sentiment have increased public engagement in foreign policy and presented potential constraints, the state has utilized these developments to strengthen control over media and public opinion.

Within the domain of domestic theories of international relations, the pacification logic in this book offers a contrast to existing literature on leveraging domestic publics for foreign policy objectives—most notably, the "audience costs" literature and its application to China. The audience costs theory posits that leaders may publicize a foreign dispute—in our context, initiate a media campaign—as a "costly signal" to obtain bargaining advantage with a foreign adversary. Publicly issued threats by leaders in these situations are taken more seriously because involving the domestic public raises the costs of retreat for leaders, a process termed "hands-tying" by James Fearon.[16] Scholars later extend audience costs from democracies to autocracies, and proposes a new mechanism whereby authoritarian states like China could generate audience costs by tolerating anti-foreign street protests.[17]

However, audience costs theories, which rank among the most prominent and contentious in the international relations field, cannot explain the "barking without biting" cases where states publicize to de-escalate. They lack the requisite breadth, thus ignoring pacification as an alternative function of hawkish rhetoric. This book challenges the audience costs theory as it regards pacification campaigns as "hand-freeing" rather than "hands-tying." Moreover, while audience costs theory emphasizes the effect on a foreign audience, my theory underscores the impact on a domestic audience, aiming to achieve state–public alignment for the dual purposes of domestic regime survival and foreign policy execution. Empirical data in this book suggests that the two theories operate under different conditions. The pacifying logic functions under moderate state foreign policy intent, where states seek compromise or status quo; whereas audience costs are most plausible when the state has a hardline intent, in the form of foreign coercions.

Lastly, on a more tactical level, scholars have identified three strategies that authoritarian regimes use in handling public opinion:

1. Exerting coercive, repressive, and prohibitive hard power, predominantly via censorship;[18]
2. Signaling strength or dominance to pre-emptively warn society of the state's might through the act of propaganda itself;[19]
3. Managing public opinion through soft power or persuasion techniques

This book draws upon, and in the process, enriches existing research in the third category. Scholars have explored numerous methods of opinion management, such as astroturfing,[20] emotional demobilization,[21] de-escalation using various media frames,[22] or co-optation of the public through "participatory digital persuasion."[23] In this work, I combine some of these strategies with novel patterns that I have discovered to form a coherent set of behaviors defining a pacification campaign.

Erin Carter and Brett Carter argue in their book that while electorally constrained autocracies must persuade, nonconstrained autocracies like China aim to dominate. "The CCP [Chinese Communist Party]'s propaganda is designed to signal to citizens, not persuade them."[24] I find this contention debatable. While it is plausible that an autocratic state might lean more toward domination in domestic issues pivotal to its survival and less so on foreign policy matters, Carter and Carter's perspective seems to depict authoritarian propaganda as if it still operates in a manner typical during the times of the Soviet Union or Nazi Germany. This perspective overlooks significant recent developments in authoritarian opinion management as described earlier.

According to a leaked internal Chinese Communist Party (CCP) directive circulated by the Party's General Office to local offices, the Party aspires to "improve and innovate our management strategies and methods to achieve our goals in a legal, scientific, and effective way."[25] While Carter and Carter underscore the distinction between persuasion and domination in different types of authoritarian regimes, this book perceives authoritarian propaganda strategies as a blend of both, with the proportion of persuasion and domination dependent on conditions such as the level of public resistance or the extent of state control over the media.

A handful of studies have attempted to broaden the traditional definition of censorship to include opinion management.[26] The Public Opinion Monitoring Office of *People's Daily* online also advocates for "combining hard with soft power."[27] This book aims to showcase the extensive ways in which the CCP uses propaganda as a tool for persuasion, often in tandem with the strategies of coercion and domination.

The Scope of Study: Authoritarian States, China, Diplomatic Crises, and Territorial Disputes

While this book recognizes that democratic nations also manipulate public opinion through media, often more routinely than we acknowledge, the primary focus is on authoritarian states, and particularly China.[28] Authoritarian states, due to their frequently unapologetic control of mass media, exhibit the most conspicuous media tactics.

Authoritarian states were also involved in the majority of territorial disputes in the twentieth century. According to the Huth and Allee Territorial Claims Data, of the 348 territorial disputes spanning seventy-seven years from 1919 to 1995, authoritarian dyads accounted for 43.7 percent of dyad-years, while mixed authoritarian-democratic dyads represented 45.1 percent of dyad-years.[29] This accounts for a substantial 88.8 percent of all disputes in the twentieth century.

While the theory and analysis of empirical implications in this book are designed with broad applicability to similar authoritarian states with direct media control, the principal emphasis is on China. On matters of media control and foreign policy significance, China is the elephant in the room. As the world's most populous nation with the second largest economy and defense budget, the way it manages public opinion of 1.4 billion people concerning its foreign affairs carries vast implications for global security. In this era of escalating geopolitical tensions centered on China, coupled with diminishing formal and informal dialogues with Chinese representatives, particularly since the onset of the COVID-19 pandemic, decoding Beijing's propaganda is gaining crucial importance for both international relations scholars and governments around the globe.

China is also the "pack leader." While its political system possesses unique elements, its media control strategies are emblematic of, and often replicated by, other nondemocracies. The key features of the CCP's Marxist-Leninist state relevant to this analysis—control of mass media and institutionalized manipulation of public opinion—are present in many other states around the world. While the technological prowess in propaganda and censorship may vary across these states, and their individual priorities and methods may diverge, China is far from being the only country striving to utilize media controls to bolster their domestic and foreign policy objectives in the digital age.

Furthermore, given its extensive array of diplomatic crises stemming from territorial disputes, China offers a rare empirical opportunity. As a country with the most borders in the world, China has been involved in eighteen unique territorial disputes with eighteen neighboring countries since its founding. These disputes exhibit wide-ranging characteristics, including differing topographies, populations, natural resources, strategic importance, and historical contexts. This rich array of cases closely mirrors the vast diversity of diplomatic crises that authoritarian nations confront, rendering broader generalizations feasible.

In addition to focusing on authoritarian states, especially China, this book centers its attention on media campaigns during "diplomatic crises" on territorial disputes. I adopt Michael Brecher's definition of a diplomatic crisis, which states that it consists of three perceived elements held by top-level decision-makers: "(a) a threat to basic values, with a simultaneous or subsequent (b) high probability of involvement in military hostilities, and the awareness of (c) finite time for response to the external value threat."[30]

In the realm of international relations, media campaigns predominantly occur during crises. The literature on opinion activation suggests that isolated events are usually "not sufficient to activate public opinion," but incidents posing a direct threat to the "normal conduct of affairs"—consistent with the definition of diplomatic crises—are more likely to stimulate a dormant public.[31] In fact, Philip Powlick and Andrew Katz argue that the "active debate among elites," which they view as a key factor in shaping and awakening public opinion, is often triggered by crisis events.[32]

In order to minimize the impact of confounding factors related to the specific characteristics of different types of disputes, all the cases examined in this book arise from territorial disputes. Many of these territorial disputes tend to spill over into other areas, such as the Senkaku/Diaoyu Island dispute, which also involves the historical issue of Japanese atrocities during World War II. Therefore, the theory outlined in this book can be readily applied to other types of international disputes. However, Chinese territorial disputes provide a sufficiently large sample for testing the theory while also minimizing potential confounding factors associated with the dispute types.[33] Territorial disputes are the contestation over the ownership or control of particular geographical areas, which may include land, rivers, or maritime zones.[34]

Territorial disputes offer an ideal case to explore the dynamics and intricacies of state-led propaganda efforts. The control and manipulation of publicity is particularly salient in territorial disputes. This is because territorial issues are exceptionally inflammatory as "people tend to respond to territorial issues intensely."[35] Territory can be symbolically manipulated for nationalistic purposes, either through ethnic or identity ties or historical claims, usually in the name of "ancestral land." Often imbued with intangible values such as sovereignty, irredentism, religious divinity, or historical glory or humiliation, territorial disputes are particularly "malleable" for states to shape public perceptions. Because of the salience of state manipulation in territorial disputes, they guarantee the largest variation in the focus of the study—the decision to implement or refrain from implementing media campaigns—and as such, they may offer the most transparent insight into the causal logic of the theory. Furthermore, despite arguments that territoriality is decreasing in importance due to globalization and trade, territorial disputes continue to wreak havoc in recent years in the South China Sea, the East China Sea, South Caucasus, and the Arabian Peninsula. While actual military conflicts may be rare, crises related to territorial disputes are abundant and even appear to be increasing.

Conceptual Foundations: Public Opinion and Foreign Policy Intent

Public opinion and a state's foreign policy intent, the two central components of the theory, warrant some elaboration here. The discord between the two motivates the state to employ media campaigns. Public opinion is a "thick" concept with many possible dimensions. Breckler treats public opinion as consisting of beliefs (the *cognitive* component), feelings (the *affective* component), and intentions (the *behavioral* component). All three have an *evaluative* component (positive or negative).[36] The *SAGE Handbook of Public Opinion Research* illustrates each of these four components with examples—"one's belief that Mozart is a great composer" (cognitive), "one's enjoyment in hearing *The Magic Flute*" (affective), "one's intention to attend a Mozart concert next week" (behavioral), and "a positive evaluation of Mozart" (evaluative).[37]

The public's foreign policy preference—that is, whether they support a hardline or moderate foreign policy—primarily pertains to the behavioral or evaluative component. "Behavioral" in terms of the public's intentions as a foreign policy actor, and "evaluative" in terms of whether the public thinks positively of a foreign policy.

The public's preference for a foreign policy encompasses two aspects—whether the public actively endorses a policy and whether it passively condones an opposing policy if the government pursues it. "Condoning" implies tacitly permitting a policy without seeking to penalize the government. In contrast, not "condoning" involves threatening or attempting to punish the government for pursuing a policy that deviates from the public's preferences.

In an authoritarian context, noncondonement typically manifests as public protests, which may escalate to violence or direct action against the government or foreign properties or the lives of foreign nationals. States sometimes seek the public's active support for a policy, while at other times, they aim for mere passive condonement of a policy.

The notion of weak public opinion is akin to the concept of latent public opinion or an unsophisticated public in the opinion activation literature.[38] This body of work presumes that public opinion remains "largely latent or acquiescent as long as policies stay within a range of acceptability."[39] This "acceptability" implies a level of tolerance or acquiescence toward a government policy that diverges from public opinion. The "latency" or "unsophistication" in public opinion is usually a function of lack of factual knowledge or interest.[40] Latent public opinion becomes "activated" or "expressed" when a foreign policy issue "receive(s) major media coverage in terms that are compatible with public frames of reference."[41]

Therefore, the public's foreign policy preference, henceforth simplified as "existing public policy opinion," can be categorized into 1) "hawkish"— supporting or condoning a hardline foreign policy; 2) "dovish"—supporting or condoning a moderate foreign policy; and 3) "weak"—the public has limited knowledge about the issue, or does not have a preference due to a lack of interest in the issue.

"Most opinion change is slow and steady," writes Tom Smith. "Opinions usually do not change rapidly and erratically. They rarely gyrate wildly about, but typically march along at a regular pace in a consistent direction."[42] Changes in public opinion are typically tied to prolonged processes such as generational changes, "structural shifts in important social processes and conditions," and political and economic cycles, and only occasionally with mass events such as wars and crises.[43] In this sense, sometimes but only infrequently does a state really meaningfully change or even reverse public opinion. Most of the time, it merely buys itself some freedom of action by affecting the *expression* of public opinion.

In our complex world where a homogeneous public is uncommon, the public is made up of diverse groups. This perspective moves away from the assumption of a unitary public opinion, aligning more closely with our multifaceted reality. Public opinion then varies among different groups. Opinion formation becomes "the formation of opinion" among groups and "the action of weighted groups."[44] The most prominent groups are the elites (or the "opinion leaders").[45] These groups interact with one another, and the resulting aggregate opinion emerges from these interactions.

The opinions of two groups often carry the most weight in an authoritarian context: the silent majority and a small group of extremists. Shirk contends that "autocracies care more about the vocal extremists who are the most likely to take to the streets and mobilize others to follow them."[46] Similarly, Iain Johnston maintains that "there is considerable evidence that the CCP regime focuses on more extremist attitudes (as found on the internet bulletin boards, for instance), presumably because these views are a barometer of the kinds of emotions that would get protesters into the streets."[47] But there are also compelling reasons for autocracies to pay attention to the views held by the silent majority, as reflected in opinion polls, since state legitimacy comes from the majority. Whereas the few extremists present a larger negative risk, the vast majority offers a larger positive opportunity for the authoritarian regime to consolidate.

A substantial body of work in public opinion studies explores the notion of the "third-person effect," which focuses on perceived public opinion. Perceived public opinion is important because, writes Albert Gunther and his colleagues, "people will do many things—decide to vote, buy a new blouse, stop smoking, argue about politics, trade in that SUV, sell stock, cut down on pasta—at least partially in response to their perceptions of the opinions of others."[48] In this book, the elites' perception of mass opinion is of utmost importance because it informs how the government gauges the public's foreign policy preferences and responds accordingly. Hence, the public's foreign policy preference is essentially the state's assessment of what the public prefers.

In the absence of feedback mechanisms typically provided by democratic institutions, such as free elections and a free press, authoritarian leaders compensate for this information deficit through a variety of unique methods. For instance, they may implement pseudo-democratic institutions;[49] allow small-scale, narrowly economic protests as harbingers of public opinion;[50] and conduct large-scale social surveys and polls.[51] Moreover, they might sponsor public opinion research organizations,[52] enlist professional social media analysis services,[53] maintain loose control over certain social spaces to allow civil groups (within limits) to grow and provide feedback to the government,[54] and tolerate investigative journalism and critical reporting on various domestic issues, thereby allowing these platforms to function as state watchdogs.[55] In addition to maintaining a petitioning system,[56] these leaders might also utilize the internet as a mirror reflecting public opinion.[57] Beyond these measures, governments need to forecast future public responses to governmental policies. In doing so, they often rely on their own political instincts regarding potential public reactions to specific policies.

The other central component of the theory, the state's foreign policy intent, is significantly less complex than public opinion. The definitions of a hardline and moderate policy are drawn from the Militarized Interstate Disputes

(MIDs) dataset,[58] Fearon's seminal work on crisis escalation,[59] and a small body of literature on "inactions" in territorial disputes. A militarized interstate dispute involves states' "threat, display or use of military force short of war,"[60] whereas in international crises, "state leaders choose at each moment whether to attack, back down, or escalate."[61] In addition to these policy options, states could choose to "shelve" a dispute or temporarily set it aside.

In Huth and Allee's Territorial Claims data, which includes all territorial disputes from 1919 to 1995, states "do nothing" in 67 percent of the total 6,542 occurrences in the data set, compared to military actions and negotiations.[62] In Hensel and Mitchell's Issue Correlates of War data (1816–2001), "inaction" years account for approximately 85 percent (8,562) of the total 10,041 claim-years, compared to 13 percent peaceful attempts (1,316) and 3 percent MIDs (305).[63] Fravel defines "inactions" as "maintaining the dispute but doing nothing to compromise or escalate."[64]

Based on these policy choices, a hardline policy is defined as the unprovoked threat, display, or use of force or economic sanctions, or escalated responses when provoked. A moderate policy, on the other hand, is the absence of these, but includes compromises, inaction, or responses of equal or lesser scale when provoked. As a state's foreign policy intent is an intent *ex-ante*, not the actual policy *ex-post*, the challenge with it is more methodological: its measurement and the availability of data (more on this in Chapter 2).

When we relax the assumption of homogeneity in state policy intent, states can alter their policy intent midway through a crisis as circumstances change, or they can adopt a combination of hardline and moderate policies, representing a mixed intent from the very beginning. I address shifts in state policy intent midway in the medium-N study and mixed policy intents in the more detailed case studies.

When we dispense with the unitary actor assumption, various foreign policy actors within the state apparatus can have unique or even conflicting policy intents. The eventual policy that is adopted is a result of competition, bargaining, and compromises among these agencies.[65] I delve into some of these complexities in the case studies.

The Structure of the Book

Chapter 1 provides a detailed overview of the misalignment theory. This includes a comprehensive look at the concepts, scope, theoretical underpinnings of state–society relations, and the logic of misalignment and alignment. It also addresses potential inferential threats to the theory and

16 Introduction

offers alternative explanations derived from existing literature on audience costs and diversionary war.

Chapter 2 contextualizes the misalignment theory in the Chinese propaganda system and media campaigns. The first part of the chapter reviews the evolution and characteristics of the Chinese propaganda system, laying the groundwork for subsequent empirical work. The second part outlines a medium-N congruence test of twenty-one Chinese diplomatic crises to evaluate the overall plausibility of the theory.

Chapters 3, 4, and 5 carry out detailed process-tracing of four cases, each representing one of the four theoretical scenarios. These include the Sino-Vietnamese border war from 1979 to 1990 (Chapter 3), the Sino-Philippine arbitration case in 2016 (Chapter 4), the Sino-Vietnamese cable-cutting incidents in 2011, and the Sino-Vietnamese oil rig crisis in 2014 (Chapter 5). Chapter 6 employs automated text analysis to examine the content of mobilization and pacification campaign media, revealing their subtle differences in valence, narratives, and emotions.

Chapter 7 argues that the media campaigns discussed throughout this book are not exclusive to the Chinese context. This chapter extends the argument by comparing the Chinese propaganda system with other authoritarian systems, and the Chinese context specifically to that of Vietnam. This sets the stage for a case study of Vietnam's media behavior in the 2014 oil rig crisis.

The conclusion reflects on theoretical and policy implications, potential avenues for future research, and anticipates future trends in authoritarian foreign policy propaganda.

Notes

1. Kathy Gao, "Anti-Japanese Dramas to Flood Chinese TV Screens Next Month," *South China Morning Post*, August 28, 2014, http://www.scmp.com/news/china/article/1581474/anti-japanese-dramas-flood-chinese-tv-screens-next-month.
2. Daniel Tretiak, "The Sino-Japanese Treaty of 1978: The Senkaku Incident Prelude," *Asian Survey* 18, no. 12 (December 1, 1978): 1235–49.
3. The incident that occurred on April 12, 1978, remarkably went unnoticed in *People's Daily*. For a period of fifteen days, there was no direct mention of the incident at all. It was only after China's Sino-Japanese Friendship Society President, Liao Chengzhi, met with a delegation from Japan's Socialist Democratic Federation, led by Hideo Den, the day after the incident that some subtle allusion to the event emerged. Liao remarked that "signing the peace treaty between the two countries is historical trend, it cannot be stopped by disruptive forces who conspire to create obstacles." This oblique reference served as the only indication of the incident's acknowledgment.

Introduction   **17**

4. Hossein Bastani, "How Iranian Media Prepared the Public for the Nuclear Deal," *The Guardian*, July 24, 2015, https://www.theguardian.com/world/iran-blog/2015/jul/24/how-iran-media-supreme-leader-prepared-the-public-nuclear-deal.

5. Nhung T. Bui, "Managing Anti-China Nationalism in Vietnam: Evidence from the Media during the 2014 Oil Rig Crisis," *The Pacific Review* 30, no. 2 (2017): 169–87; Frances Yaping Wang and Brantly Womack, "Jawing through Crises: Chinese and Vietnamese Media Strategies in the South China Sea," *Journal of Contemporary China* 28, no. 119 (September 3, 2019): 712–28.

6. Christopher Walker and Robert W. Orttung, "Breaking the News: The Role of State-Run Media," *Journal of Democracy* 25, no. 1 (2014): 71. The total is calculated based on the number of countries or territories whose press is rated by the Freedom House as "not free" (66) or "partly free" (73). See *Freedom of the Press 2017*, Freedom House, April 2017, https://freedomhouse.org/sites/default/files/2020-02/FOTP_2017_booklet_FINAL_April28_1.pdf.

7. Kenneth N. Waltz, *Theory of International Politics* (Long Grove, IL: Waveland Press, 1979); John J. Mearsheimer, *The Tragedy of Great Power Politics* (New York: Norton, 2001); Hans Morgenthau, *Politics Among Nations: The Struggle for Peace and Power* (New York: Knopf, 1948).

8. Ronald R. Krebs, *Narrative and The Making of US National Security*, vol. 138 (Cambridge: Cambridge University Press, 2015), 2.

9. Daniel R. Coats, *Worldwide Threat Assessment of the US Intelligence Community*, Senate Select Committee on Intelligence, March 6, 2018, https://www.dni.gov/files/documents/Newsroom/Testimonies/2018-ATA—-Unclassified-SSCI.pdf.

10. White House, "National Security Strategy of the United States of America" (Washington, DC, December 2017), https://www.whitehouse.gov/wp-content/uploads/2017/12/NSS-Final-12-18-2017-0905-2.pdf.

11. Alexander L. George, *Propaganda Analysis: A Study of Inferences Made from Nazi Propaganda in World War II* (Evanston, IL: Row, Peterson & Co., 1959).

12. Susan L. Shirk, *China: Fragile Superpower* (New York: Oxford University Press, 2007); Andrew Chubb, "Chinese Popular Nationalism and PRC Policy in the South China Sea" (PhD diss., University of Western Australia, 2016); Daniela Stockmann, *Media Commercialization and Authoritarian Rule in China* (New York: Cambridge University Press, 2013); Anne-Marie Brady, *Marketing Dictatorship: Propaganda and Thought Work in Contemporary China* (Lanham, MD: Rowman & Littlefield, 2008); Maria Repnikova, *Media Politics in China: Improvising Power under Authoritarianism* (Cambridge: Cambridge University Press, 2017).

13. Shirk, *China*.

14. James Reilly, *Strong Society, Smart State: The Rise of Public Opinion in China's Japan Policy* (New York: Columbia University Press, 2011).

15. Evgeny Morozov, *The Net Delusion: The Dark Side of Internet Freedom* (New York: PublicAffairs, 2012); Stockmann, *Media Commercialization and Authoritarian Rule in China*; Maria Repnikova and Kecheng Fang, "Authoritarian Participatory Persuasion 2.0: Netizens as Thought Work Collaborators in China," *Journal of Contemporary China* 27, no. 113 (2018): 1–17.

16. James D. Fearon, "Signaling Foreign Policy Interests Tying Hands versus Sinking Costs," *Journal of Conflict Resolution* 41, no. 1 (1997): 68–90; James D. Fearon, "Domestic Political

18   Introduction

Audiences and the Escalation of International Disputes," *American Political Science Review* 88, no. 3 (1994): 577–92.

17. Jessica L. Weeks, "Autocratic Audience Costs: Regime Type and Signaling Resolve," *International Organization* 62, no. 1 (2008): 35–64; Jessica C. Weiss, "Authoritarian Signaling, Mass Audiences, and Nationalist Protest in China," *International Organization* 67, no. 1 (2013): 1–35; Jessica C. Weiss, *Powerful Patriots: Nationalist Protest in China's Foreign Relations* (New York: Oxford University Press, 2014).

18. Gary King, Jennifer Pan, and Margaret E. Roberts, "How Censorship in China Allows Government Criticism but Silences Collective Expression," *American Political Science Review* 107, no. 2 (2013): 326–43; Peter Lorentzen, "China's Strategic Censorship," *American Journal of Political Science* 58, no. 2 (April 1, 2014): 402–14; Christopher Cairns and Allen Carlson, "Real-World Islands in a Social Media Sea: Nationalism and Censorship on Weibo during the 2012 Diaoyu/Senkaku Crisis," *The China Quarterly* 225 (2016): 23–49.

19. Haifeng Huang, "Propaganda as Signaling," *Comparative Politics* 47, no. 4 (2015): 419–44; Erin Baggott Carter and Brett L. Carter, *Propaganda in Autocracies: Institutions, Information, and the Politics of Belief* (Cambridge; New York: Cambridge University Press, 2023).

20. Astroturfing is to distract the public and to flood the internet with pro-government messages, see for example, Rongbin Han, "Defending the Authoritarian Regime Online: China's 'Voluntary Fifty-Cent Army,'" *The China Quarterly* 224 (December 2015): 1006–25; Gary King, Jennifer Pan, and Margaret E. Roberts, "How the Chinese Government Fabricates Social Media Posts for Strategic Distraction, Not Engaged Argument," *American Political Science Review* 111, no. 3 (2017): 484–501.

21. Guobin Yang, "(Un)civil Society in Digital China| Demobilizing the Emotions of Online Activism in China: A Civilizing Process," *International Journal of Communication* 11 (2017): 1945–65.

22. Kai Quek and Alastair Iain Johnston, "Can China Back Down? Crisis De-Escalation in the Shadow of Popular Opposition," *International Security* 42, no. 3 (2018): 7–36.

23. Repnikova and Fang, "Authoritarian Participatory Persuasion 2.0."

24. Carter and Carter, *Propaganda in Autocracies*, 20.

25. "Communiqué on the Current State of the Ideological Sphere: A Notice from the Central Committee of the Communist Party of China's General Office," April 22, 2013, obtained and published by *Mingjing Magazine* and translated by *Chinafile*, https://www.chinafile.com/document-9-chinafile-translation.

26. See, for example, Matthew Bunn, "Reimagining Repression: New Censorship Theory and After," *History and Theory* 54, no. 1 (2015): 25–44.

27. The Public Opinion Monitoring Office, People.com, "2013 Nian Zhongguo Hulianwang Yuqing Fenxi Baogao (Analysis on Internet-Based Public Opinion in China in 2013)," in *Blue Book of China's Society—Analysis and Forecast of Chinese Society 2014*, ed. Peilin Li, Guangjin Chen, and Yi Zhang (Beijing: Shehui Kexue Wenxian Chubanshe (Social Science Academic Press), 2013), 229.

28. For an overview of the relationship between public opinion, mass media and foreign policy in a democratic setting, see Matthew A. Baum and Philip BK Potter, "The Relationships between Mass Media, Public Opinion, and Foreign Policy: Toward a Theoretical Synthesis," *Annual Review of Political Science* 11 (2008): 39–65. For definition of authoritarian regimes, I adopt Geddes's and Weeks's definitions. See Barbara Geddes, "What Do We

Know About Democratization After Twenty Years?" *Annual Review of Political Science* 2, no. 1 (1999): 115–44; Jessica L. Weeks, "Strongmen and Straw Men: Authoritarian Regimes and the Initiation of International Conflict," *American Political Science Review* 106, no. 2 (2012): 326–47; Jessica L. Weeks, *Dictators at War and Peace* (Ithaca, NY: Cornell University Press, 2014).

29. Paul Huth and Todd Allee, "Domestic Political Accountability and the Escalation and Settlement of International Disputes," *Journal of Conflict Resolution* 46, no. 6 (2002): 771–807.

30. Michael Brecher, "State Behavior in International Crisis: A Model," *Journal of Conflict Resolution* 23, no. 3 (1979): 446–80.

31. Philip J. Powlick and Andrew Z. Katz, "Defining the American Public Opinion/Foreign Policy Nexus," *Mershon International Studies Review* 42, no. Supplement_1 (May 1, 1998): 37; Gabriel Abraham Almond, *The American People and Foreign Policy* (Westport, CT: Praeger, 1960).

32. Powlick and Katz, "Defining the American Public Opinion/Foreign Policy Nexus."

33. To avoid any potential confounding factors, I have excluded homeland disputes and intrastate disputes from this study. However, both land border and offshore disputes are included, as the nature of the terrain should not significantly influence a state's propaganda strategies. Homeland disputes are conflicts where two or more governments, each occupying a different part of what was once a unified country, challenge each other's existence and aim to annex each other. Cases such as North Korea and South Korea, or the People's Republic of China (PRC) and the Republic of China (ROC), fall into this category. These disputes are essentially regime disputes rather than territorial ones. They pose fundamental threats to state survival, thereby making them potentially causally different from typical interstate territorial disputes. Intrastate territorial disputes occur within a single state, where internal groups seek to secede from the parent state. Examples of these include Quebec in Canada, or Northern Ireland in the United Kingdom.

34. Paul R. Hensel, Michael E. Allison, and Ahmed Khanani, "Territorial Integrity Treaties and Armed Conflict over Territory," *Conflict Management and Peace Science* 26, no. 2 (2009): 120–43.

35. Jaroslav Tir, "Territorial Diversion: Diversionary Theory of War and Territorial Conflict," *Journal of Politics* 72, no. 2 (April 2010): 413.

36. Steven J. Breckler, "Empirical Validation of Affect, Behavior, and Cognition as Distinct Components of Attitude," *Journal of Personality and Social Psychology* 47, no. 6 (1984): 1191.

37. Roger Tourangeau and Mirta Galešić, "Conceptions of Attitudes and Opinions," in *The SAGE Handbook of Public Opinion Research*, ed. Wolfgang Donsbach and Michael Traugott (London: SAGE Publications, 2008), 142.

38. Powlick and Katz, "Defining the American Public Opinion/Foreign Policy Nexus," 31.

39. Ibid., 33.

40. Ibid., 31.

41. Ibid., 29.

42. Tom W. Smith, "Is There Real Opinion Change?," *International Journal of Public Opinion Research* 6, no. 2 (1994): 187–88.

43. Smith, 188–90.

20   Introduction

44. Francis G. Wilson, "Concepts of Public Opinion," *The American Political Science Review* 27, no. 3 (1933): 373.

45. Paul F. Lazarsfeld, Bernard Berelson, and Hazel Gaudet, *The People's Choice: How the Voter Makes Up His Mind in a Presidential Campaign, Legacy Edition* (New York: Columbia University Press, 1968); Gabriel Weimann, "The Influentials: Back to the Concept of Opinion Leaders?," *The Public Opinion Quarterly* 55, no. 2 (1991): 267–79; Joseph Fewsmith and Stanley Rosen, "The Domestic Context of Chinese Foreign Policy: Does 'Public Opinion' Matter?," in *The Making of Chinese Foreign and Security Policy in the Era of Reform, 1978–2000*, by David M. Lampton (Redwood City, CA: Stanford University Press, 1978), 151–87.

46. Shirk, *China*, 44.

47. Alastair Iain Johnston, "Chinese Middle Class Attitudes Towards International Affairs: Nascent Liberalization?," *The China Quarterly*, no. 179 (2004): 626.

48. Albert C. Gunther, Richard M. Perloff, and Yariv Tsfati, "Public Opinion and the Third-Person Effect," in *The SAGE Handbook of Public Opinion Research*, ed. Wolfgang Donsbach and Michael Traugott (London: SAGE Publications, 2008), 184.

49. Steven Levitsky and Lucan A. Way, *Competitive Authoritarianism: Hybrid Regimes after the Cold War* (New York: Cambridge University Press, 2010); Rory Truex, "Consultative Authoritarianism and Its Limits," *Comparative Political Studies* 50, no. 3 (2017): 329–61.

50. Peter L. Lorentzen, "Regularizing Rioting: Permitting Public Protest in An Authoritarian Regime," *Quarterly Journal of Political Science* 8, no. 2 (2013): 127–58; Kevin J. O'Brien and Lianjiang Li, *Rightful Resistance in Rural China* (Cambridge: Cambridge University Press, 2006); Xi Chen, *Social Protest and Contentious Authoritarianism in China* (Cambridge: Cambridge University Press, 2012).

51. Patricia M. Thornton, "Retrofitting the Steel Frame: From Mobilizing the Masses to Surveying the Public," in *Mao's Invisible Hand: The Political Foundations of Adaptive Governance in China*, ed. E. J. Perry and S. Heilmann (Cambridge, MA: Harvard University Asia Center, 2011), 237–68.

52. "Public Opinion Polls Gain Rising Importance in China," *Hong Kong Hsin Pao* (*Hong Kong Economic Journal*), September 3, 2010, accessed via World New Connection.

53. "Wangluo Yuqing Fenxishi Cheng Guanfang Renke Zhiye, Congyezhe Da 200 Wan (Online Public Opinion Analyst Becomes Officially Recognized Profession, Practitioners Reach 2 Million)," *Xin Jing Bao* (*The Beijing News*), October 3, 2013, http://www.xinhuanet.com//zgjx/2013-10/03/c_132769821.htm.

54. Robert P. Weller, "Responsive Authoritarianism and Blind-Eye Governance in China," ed. Nina Bandelj and Dorothy J. Solinger, *Socialism Vanquished, Socialism Challenged* (New York: Oxford University Press, 2012), 83–100.

55. Shirk, *China*, 10–103; Maria Repnikova, *Media Politics in China* (Cambridge: Cambridge University Press, 2017).

56. Martin K. Dimitrov, "What the Party Wanted to Know: Citizen Complaints as a 'Barometer of Public Opinion' in Communist Bulgaria," *East European Politics and Societies* 28, no. 2 (May 1, 2014): 271–95; Jeremy L. Wallace, "Information Politics in Dictatorships," in *Emerging Trends in the Social and Behavioral Sciences* (New York: John Wiley and Sons, 2015), 1–11.

57. King, Pan, and Roberts, "How Censorship in China Allows Government Criticism but Silences Collective Expression"; Tianguang Meng, Jennifer Pan, and Ping Yang,

"Conditional Receptivity to Citizen Participation: Evidence from A Survey Experiment in China," *Comparative Political Studies* 50, no. 4 (2017): 399–433.

58. Glenn Palmer et al., "Updating the Militarized Interstate Dispute Data: A Response to Gibler, Miller, and Little," *International Studies Quarterly* 64, no. 2 (June 1, 2020): 469–75.

59. James D. Fearon, "Domestic Political Audiences and the Escalation of International Disputes," *American Political Science Review* 88, no. 3 (1994): 577–92.

60. Daniel M. Jones, Stuart A. Bremer, and J. David Singer, "Militarized Interstate Disputes, 1816–1992: Rationale, Coding Rules, and Empirical Patterns," *Conflict Management and Peace Science* 15, no. 2 (1996): 163.

61. Fearon, "Domestic Political Audiences and the Escalation of International Disputes," 577.

62. Paul K. Huth and Todd L. Allee, *The Democratic Peace and Territorial Conflict in the Twentieth Century* (Cambridge: Cambridge University Press, 2002).

63. Paul R. Hensel and Sara M. Mitchell, "The Issue Correlates of War (ICOW) Project Issue Data Set: Territorial Claims Data" (Harvard Dataverse, March 17, 2011), https://doi.org/10.7910/DVN/E6PSGZ.

64. M. Taylor Fravel, *Strong Borders, Secure Nation: Cooperation and Conflict in China's Territorial Disputes* (Princeton, NJ: Princeton University Press, 2008), 16.

65. Graham T. Allison and Morton H. Halperin, "Bureaucratic Politics: A Paradigm and Some Policy Implications," *World Politics: A Quarterly Journal of International Relations* (1972): 40–79.

1

The (Mis)Alignment Theory

In a seminar held in 2011, attended by the heads of the Chinese Communist Party's propaganda departments across various government levels, Liu Yunshan, a senior Chinese propaganda official, underlined the necessity to "strengthen mainstream public opinion and reach ideological consensuses."[1] During the Sino-Philippines arbitration case in 2016, *People's Daily* featured an article proclaiming, "the state's attitude and the public's stand are in unison . . . provid[ing] the public opinion basis and conditions for China to deal with the . . . dispute." Remarks like these, which highlight the significance of establishing a consensus between the public and the state and the aspiration for unity in their actions, inspired the (mis)alignment theory of this book.

This book seeks to elucidate two related questions: what motivates authoritarian domestic media campaigns on foreign policy issues, and how they are carried out. I argue that popular autocrats amplify domestically the rhetoric of a foreign dispute when public opinion and state policy intent are misaligned. Media campaigns are strategic state actions to bring public opinion into alignment with the desired state position. I will describe two types of media campaigns and elaborate how they work to achieve this alignment.

There are two kinds of misalignments that motivate two distinct types of media campaigns: situations where state intent is more aggressive (scenario A, marked by dovish or weak public opinion and hardline state policy preference) or more moderate (scenario B, featuring hawkish public opinion and moderate state policy preference) than public opinion. As shown in Table 1.1, when these combinations occur in Scenarios A and B, autocrats use media campaigns to gain public support for, or at the very least, their acquiescence to, the state's preferred policy. In scenario A, the media campaign mobilizes the public, while in scenario B, it pacifies them.

In the mobilization campaign of scenario A, the state magnifies the dispute to agitate public support and to prepare for the hardline policy that risks

The Art of State Persuasion. Frances Yaping Wang, Oxford University Press. © Oxford University Press 2024.
DOI: 10.1093/oso/9780197757505.003.0002

The (Mis)Alignment Theory 23

Table 1.1 The State–Public (Mis)Alignment Theory

		State Foreign Policy Intent	
		Hardline	Moderate
Existing Public Opinion	Dovish/Weak	Mobilization Campaigns or Diversionary Incentives (scenario A)	No Media Campaigns (scenario D)
	Hawkish	No Media Campaigns or Diversionary/Audience Costs Incentives (scenario C)	Pacification Campaigns (scenario B)

conflict. In scenario B's pacification campaign, the state media on the one hand seeks to control the narrative by responding timely and proactively, to echo public sentiment for the purpose of building the trust necessary for mass persuasion, and to keep up the appearances of a hard stance to deflect nationalistic criticisms, preserve dignity, and maintain social stability. Simultaneously, it seeks to soothe public opinion to pave the way for its preferred moderate foreign policy by positively framing the issue, delegitimizing "overreactive" or "unhelpful" emotions or behaviors on the grounds of rationality and national interests and allowing venting on social media.

Therefore, authoritarian propaganda serves two contrasting functions, to *incite* and to *pacify*, depending on how, specifically, the state and the public are misaligned. In either scenario, the strong rhetoric works as a "bridging" instrument to close the gap between the state and the public before the intended foreign policy is carried out. This bridging instrument is crucial for autocrats who value public support, but simultaneously possess the means—robust propaganda machinery—to influence and mold public opinion to fulfill their objectives. When state and public preferences align (Scenarios C and D), the state media lacks the alignment incentive to launch a media campaign.

The rest of this chapter will outline the theoretical framework of misalignment. First, I clarify why alignment is vital to autocrats by exploring the unique state–society relationship inherent in authoritarian states, a relationship fundamental to the logic of alignment. Next, I elucidate how, under varied combinations of existing public opinion and state foreign policy intent, mobilization and pacification campaigns foster alignment, accompanied by a parallel comparison between these two types of campaigns. I then explicate the assumptions underpinning this theory and address its logical challenges. Lastly, I explore potential alternate motivations that could drive media campaigns and delve into the aftermaths of media campaigns.

Why Is State–Society Alignment Crucial for Autocrats?

State–society alignment is crucial for autocrats, because exercising a foreign policy unsupported by the public is politically risky and potentially costly for authoritarian regimes. If not managed well, public opinion could challenge the state's regime survival and international security.

Regime Survival and International Security

Domestically, public opinion could debilitate authoritarian regimes if public protests turn to social turmoil or if they lead to the regime's gradual atrophy by undermining social trust and strengthening support for opposition forces. The tactic of inciting unrest within a rival country, coupled with supporting regime changes either overtly or covertly, is a time-honored strategy in international competitions. This approach, termed "rollback" by John Mearsheimer, was a tool frequently wielded by the US against the Soviet Union during the Cold War and could be similarly deployed against China.[2] This strategy highlights the enduring reality of such risks for autocratic regimes.

Ted Hopf's work on Soviet Union's social identities confirms this risk. He discusses the tension between elite and popular discourses as an "ongoing struggle between official representations of the Soviet self and its challengers."[3] He recognizes the diverging public discourse as a "constraining" force on elite aspirations.[4] To reconcile this difference, there could be "circumvention of the predominant discourse by daily social practices in society"[5] and possible "rapprochement" between the two.[6] The "predominant discourse" can "win" either "by intimidating challengers, who fear costly punishment, into silence," or "by dint of compelling argumentation."[7]

Internationally, if domestic public opinion, especially anti-foreign nationalism, holds foreign policy hostage, then this could lead to undesirable foreign policies that jeopardize a state's security environment. Violent public reactions can damage economic ties, tarnish a country's international image, and limit a state to suboptimal foreign policy options. Daniela Stockmann referred to a "public opinion crisis" as a "mismatch between the position of the state and public opinion on a particular issue." She argued that the 2005 Sino-Japanese dispute was such a crisis and the Chinese state adopted stricter media control to address it.[8] For these reasons we should not expect states to easily succumb to public opinion pressure, especially if they have alternatives.

One such alternative is alignment through media campaigns, a strategy that allows the state to pursue its foreign policy objectives while maintaining its domestic control.

The Paradox of State–Society Relations in an Authoritarian Setting

These political incentives for alignment are grounded in the authoritarian public opinion literature that describes a paradoxical and reciprocal relationship between the state and public opinion that is common in authoritarian states. On the one hand, authentic, independent public opinion exists and exerts genuine pressure on the state's foreign policy conduct, thereby providing political incentives for leaders to "cater to" or "manage" public opinion. On the other hand, the authoritarian state still enjoys substantial agency because it controls the means to manipulate public opinion toward its preferences and ends.

In fact, this paradoxical relationship between the state and the public originates from democracies. There is a longstanding debate in western democracies about the extent to which public opinion should affect foreign policy. The liberal-democratic tradition, dating back to Kant and Bentham and highlighted by President Wilson after World War I, believes that accountability to the public puts necessary constraints on war-prone elites. Realists, in contrast, hold that the public is often uninterested and ill-informed about foreign affairs that are remote to their daily experiences. Their participation in foreign affairs hinders the secrecy and flexibility required for effective diplomacy and thus jeopardizes foreign policy goals. The Lippmann-Almond consensus proposes that public opinion in the United States is highly volatile, incoherent, and as such provides a shaky foundation for sound foreign policy and has little real impact on policy.[9]

This debate is somewhat reframed by the opinion activation literature, suggesting that a generally poorly informed public "does indeed react to international affairs in an events-driven, rational matter."[10] These studies view the relationship between public opinion and the state as reciprocal. The "reciprocal relationship" describes the public–state dynamic that leaders "try to educate or manipulate public opinion . . . but decision makers also are sensitive to the preferences of the electorate."[11] Public opinion polls are often utilized more as a means of understanding how to educate the public rather than as a policy guide.[12] This perspective aligns closely with the stance of this book.

Autocrats Care About Public Opinion

But do authoritarian regimes care about what the public thinks on foreign issues in the same way that democracies might? A number of studies on authoritarian public opinion, although not necessarily on foreign affairs, engage this very question of state–public relations and the role of public opinion in authoritarian politics. In summary, the agency of the masses and state control are two paradoxical, coexistent components of authoritarian politics. What distinguishes authoritarian manipulation from that in Western democracies is that the former is usually explicit, commonly expected, and sometimes even tacitly accepted, whereas the latter is often condemned and thus usually implicit. Authoritarian public opinion scholars recognize the inherent tension between the importance of public opinion and the agency of the state in authoritarian states. As a result, "the medieval European concept *Vox populi, vox Dei*, and the Chinese concept 'mandate from heaven' . . . exemplify a standard authoritarian resolution" for the tension. The idea that the regime represents the voice of the people, mandated by heaven or God, legitimizes the rule of the few over the many.[13]

Contrary to common beliefs, authoritarian states do demonstrate some concern for public opinion, and are often forced to address public demands. Dating back to the nineteenth century during the First French Empire, Prince von Metternich, the Austrian Empire's ambassador to Napoleonic France, advised his government that public opinion required "peculiar cultivation" because "it penetrates like religion the most hidden recesses where administrative measures have no influence."[14] Even Kim Jong-un, the supreme leader of one of the world's most centralized nations, repeatedly demands that his cabinets "work with popular sentiment in mind."[15] Peter Gries observes that China's extreme popular nationalism, once government-instigated, has since taken on a life of its own and the government must continuously monitor and manage it.[16]

Various studies have provided evidence of authoritarian responsiveness, suggesting both the existence of a genuine, bottom-up public opinion and its independent impact on state policy.[17] For example, studies demonstrate that top-down supervision and bottom-up societal pressures can compel local governments to respond to citizen demands.[18] The research on Chinese and Vietnamese parliamentary bodies provide evidence that authoritarian states do indeed respond to local constituents' needs, albeit within certain limits.[19] In an experiment conducted in China, it was observed that unless provincial- and city-level leaders detect a state–citizen antagonism, they are receptive to citizen suggestions.[20]

The marketization and the advance of the internet and social media have equipped the public with broader access to a diverse pool of information, the ability to express opinions more freely, and the wherewithal to mobilize and thereby pressure or constrain the state. The internet has revolutionized popular expression and activism in China.[21] Scholars have documented various roles of the internet, such as networking and organizing activism,[22] promoting political satire,[23] and facilitating public shaming (for example, through "human flesh searches" or "ren rou sousuo" in Chinese),[24] all of which the public can leverage to pressure the state and instigate societal changes.

Authoritarian rulers recognize the importance of understanding and controlling public opinion. Former Chinese General Secretary Hu Jintao "placed special emphasis on making virtual community management one of the key tasks in current social management," and urged "strengthening" and "perfecting" online opinion management.[25] In one editorial, China's main official newspaper, *People's Daily*, proclaims that "territorial disputes are extremely complex, involving the people's emotions and sometimes becoming bound up with domestic disputes. Unless extra restraint is taken, emotions could get out of control, which would doubtless result in unintended consequences."[26]

The perceived significance of public opinion is also embedded in the Chinese Communist Party's (CCP) "mass line" tradition, initially proposed by Mao and perpetuated as one of the CCP's guiding ideologies ever since. Mao's "mass line" concept describes an interactive consultation process of "from the masses, to the masses." It emphasizes keeping the Party attuned to the wants and needs of the masses, seeking input from them for policy formulation, and then propagating these policies back to the people during policy implementation.[27] Essentially, the "mass line" is a clever way of consulting and co-opting society, engaging the public in policy deliberation, while "reserv[ing] the right to make most decisions and remain unaccountable to society." It is "intended to enhance the Party's authority, not to constrain it."[28] The mass line has persisted as a quintessential element of the Chinese way of governance. The current president Xi Jinping called on officials to "pay more grassroots visits to listen to opinions from the masses . . . think like the masses . . . spare no efforts in eliminating public grievances and safeguarding people's interests."[29]

In fact, authoritarian states care about public opinion largely because they inherently lack regime legitimacy and can leverage public opinion to compensate for this deficiency. As the influence of religion or ideology fades in many theocratic or Communist countries such as China, Cuba, Iran, Russia, and Vietnam, public opinion provides two alternative sources of legitimacy.[30]

One source is anti-foreign nationalism—a rally-around-the-flag sentiment that translate citizens' love of their country into their support for the regime, or deliberately blurs the line between the two. The other is fostering performance-based legitimacy by utilizing public opinion to identify societal issues and grievances, then remedying these problems before they escalate into destabilizing elements, thereby bolstering regime resilience.[31] For instance, one function of the mass line approach, such as petitioning systems, is precisely this—a means of staying in touch with the public's grievances and addressing them before they turn into large-scale mass incidents. An article by Zhu Xinhua, the secretary general of the Public Opinion Monitoring Office of *People's Daily* online, notes that "[The internet] let[s] pursuits at the lowest levels directly reach the government, which saves the government's costs for management and checking corruption. It can also help plug the loopholes and increase the elasticity of the system . . . letting people at the lowest levels restore their confidence in the society."[32] In short, nationalism and performance, as alternative sources of legitimacy, explain why public opinion matters to autocrats.

Autocrats Rarely Bend to Public Opinion

Nevertheless, the influence of public opinion on foreign policy remains substantially curtailed in authoritarian states, which maintain a high degree of autonomy. Public opinion in China "has begun to play a role, albeit one that remains restricted and significant only under certain conditions."[33] When anti-Japan nationalism was high in China, Li Wei, the director of the Chinese Academy of Social Sciences Institute of Japan, warned that diplomatic issues should not "be freely dictated by public opinion and mass sentiments."[34] A study based on five recent maritime disputes demonstrates that popular nationalism has had little to do with China's assertive maritime policy since 2006.[35] Suisheng Zhao finds that Chinese foreign policy before 2008 was not dictated by nationalist sentiment; after 2008, assertive foreign policy and nationalist appeals converged, but that was because the Chinese government was more willing to play to nationalist demands, and not because they were forced to.[36]

Scholars have examined state autonomy in comparison with society in general and have concluded that "the degree of state autonomy vis-a-vis society varies over time and across different states. This variation, in turn, affects whether states respond to international pressures in a timely and efficient fashion."[37] The degree of state autonomy often hinges on the state's monopoly over a plethora of resources and means to affect opinion and meet its foreign policy goals.[38] The role of public opinion in authoritarian states is limited due to the availability of relatively easy and cheap ways for autocratic leaders to change public opinion to suit their preferences. Despite the advance of market forces and information technology, the state has, in turn, revamped its control.[39] These means include information gathering, traditional media and the internet, censorship, selective tolerance of protests, quasi-democratic institutions, and more.[40] There are numerous new "networked" techniques the CCP has mastered to consolidate its control over public opinion.[41] The Chinese state has also modernized mass persuasion in online forms—the digital interface of state media and social media accounts of various government offices, and the government's promotion of patriotic bloggers.[42] In addition to these means, there is also evidence that even the public itself supports state propaganda efforts to guide public opinion.[43] Propaganda in a Communist context is, after all, "devoid of dismissive ('mere propaganda') and negative (propaganda-as-brainwashing) connotations."[44]

In Foreign Policy: Conditions Favoring Pacification Campaigns

We can reasonably apply these state–society dynamics to the domain of foreign policy, considering that public opinion does play a role in foreign policy, albeit a limited one. Foreign policy issues, particularly territorial disputes, offer a unique and vital arena to examine these state–society theories that are predominantly developed in a domestic context. In contrast to domestic policy, foreign policy typically affects a smaller segment of the population. It may present higher stakes for the state, yet carry lower ones for the public, as there is less direct impact on the daily lives of the masses. Moreover, mundane foreign policy issues may not pose as immediate or severe a threat to regime survival as some domestic issues might.

These unique characteristics of foreign policy issues in authoritarian contexts can enhance the effectiveness of pacification campaigns. The public's short attention span toward foreign policy matters can be manipulated by the state, which has the power to change the narrative or shift the focus away from contentious issues before public sentiment becomes too heated or entrenched. Frames such as China's peaceful identity, the economic cost of war, and the availability of alternative tools such as UN mediation and economic sanctions have also proven effective in deescalating public opinion and could be adopted by the state.[45]

Moreover, the nature of foreign policy debates often involves a certain amount of strategic posturing or bluffing. This is more readily accepted by the public in foreign policy contexts, as it is generally understood that the state is engaged in a high-stakes game of diplomacy or even brinkmanship on the world stage. The state can therefore engage in more exaggerated rhetoric or stances without losing credibility or provoking a strong negative reaction from its citizens.

Lastly, the distance of foreign policy from the immediate concerns of the populace, coupled with the controlled media environment of an authoritarian state, helps to minimize the risk of widespread public discontent coalescing into collective action. Online venting, while providing an outlet for individual dissatisfaction, is less likely to catalyze organized, collective resistance due to the scattered focus of discontent and the state's ability to monitor and control online discourse.

In this way, the very nature of foreign policy issues in an authoritarian context becomes fertile ground for the operation of pacification campaigns. The state can effectively utilize these characteristics to manage public sentiment, minimizing domestic pressures and backlash while advancing their international policy objectives.

Because of these state–society dynamics, autocrats cannot just ignore public opinion; they have to do something about it. However, they possess the capability to do so and are, in principle, better equipped to manage public sentiment than most democracies, due to their characteristically efficient control of the media. Media campaigns thus emerge as their responses to state–society misalignments.

How Do Media Campaigns Align? Mobilization

When the state prefers a hardline policy, but the prevailing public opinion is moderate or weak, as in scenario A in Table 1.1, the state launches a mobilization campaign to prepare the public and garner support for the hardline policy. The mobilization use of propaganda is relatively straightforward. A hardline policy would necessarily raise the probability of conflict, and conflict demands material and human resources of the nation. But if the public does not support such a policy, the state will want to mobilize the public before its implementation.

The importance of domestic mobilization on foreign policy has been extensively discussed in various contexts. For instance, Randall Schweller, in an attempt to explain the underaggression and underexpansion of great powers, emphasizes their challenge in rallying domestic public support for such hegemonic bids.[46] Along the same lines, in explaining the delayed American ascendance as a world superpower, Fareed Zakaria cites the lack of mobilization capacities.[47] Both these studies underscore the influence of the domestic public on the state's abilities. This book broadens that argument to include authoritarian states, building upon the state–society dynamics unique to authoritarian regimes, as described earlier.

Thomas Christensen describes a two-level "mobilization" model. He argues that leaders (Truman in 1947–1950 and Mao in 1957–1958) exploit international crises for domestic political purposes. Specifically, they exaggerate external threats through crusading ideological rhetoric to mobilize the public's support for unpopular domestic programs. In Truman's case, he found himself at a crossroads when the need for increased military spending conflicted with the public's desire for tax cuts and the end of conscription. To navigate this, Truman turned to anti-Communist rhetoric. While this approach inadvertently led to confrontations with China, it effectively bolstered domestic political support for his ambitious and previously inconceivable Fair Deal program. The same logic applied to Mao, who used the dispute with the US over Taiwan and anti-imperialist rhetoric to mobilize domestic support for his Great Leap Forward program.[48] Similarly, the "threat inflation" argument, as made by John Mearsheimer and Stephen Walt in various policy publications, uses the Iraq War as a classic example of how an external threat was "inflated" by the state through the control and manipulation of political discourse.[49]

According to this diversionary logic, the state might increase the prominence of an international issue to shift public attention away from a domestic crisis or to endorse a domestic program, essentially using foreign policy to benefit domestic policy. The misalignment theory particularly its mobilization component, bears similarity with these studies on their emphasis on domestic mobilization. However, it is not about using foreign policy for domestic purposes. Rather, it aims to align a state's domestic interests with its international objectives, essentially creating agreement between the two.

A mobilization campaign aims either to change public opinion from a moderate position to a hardline position so that the public will actively support a hardline policy in attitudes or even in action, or increase the public's understanding and tolerance of a hardline policy. Mobilization is akin to the process of "securitization," in which an issue is framed or constructed through a successful speech act to be a matter "posing an existential threat" that "calls for urgent and exceptional measures."[50]

Generally, a mobilization campaign works to raise public awareness of a dispute, elevate the perceived importance of an issue, promote negative evaluation of and arouse intense negative emotions toward a target country or people, cultivate a sense of injustice and unfairness resulting in a consequent

32 The Art of State Persuasion

moral agreement to the use of force, downplay the potential costs of conflicts, and encourage actions against the target country or people.

In a mobilization campaign, the state utilizes the agenda-setting, priming, and framing tactics of mass media.[51] First, people need to know about a dispute if it is not already widely known, especially when a dispute is about some remote and sparsely populated borderlands or uninhabited outlying islands. Media studies calls this first function "agenda-setting," which means the "ability [of media] to influence the salience of topics on the public agenda."[52] This particularly affects the *cognitive* aspects of public opinion: by increasing the volume and frequency of coverage on a particular dispute, the state draws attention to that dispute and provides the public with the basic knowledge about the issue necessary for the "activation" of public opinion.

Moreover, this increased awareness could heighten the perceived importance of the disputed territory. The positive correlation between information availability and perceived importance, known as the "availability heuristic" in social psychology, has been abundantly demonstrated in psychological experiments.[53] The more the public hears about a dispute, the greater importance they are likely to assign to it. Public recognition of an issue's importance lays the groundwork for a shift in opinion toward a more hardline stance, or at least toward a greater understanding of and tolerance for a hardline policy.

Second, the media's priming role works through "stimulat[ing] related thoughts in the minds of audience members."[54] This process involves enhancing the accessibility of certain information (similar to the agenda-setting effect), establishing associations between related ideas, and activating one thought to trigger another.[55] For instance, the Chinese propaganda campaign on the Senkaku/Diaoyu Islands dispute with Japan in 2012 was not necessarily centered on the territorial conflict per se, but rather focused on an anti-fascist theme. The remembrance of the Japanese invasion during World War II was likely to elicit a similar response in the Chinese public to more contemporary events.

This tactic mirrors what Kenneth Arrow referred to as issue dimension manipulation, which involves melding preferences on an old issue with a new issue possessing greater mobilization potential to establish a fresh majority consensus.[56] In such cases, when an issue is characterized in terms of a single dominant dimension detached from the public's everyday experiences, an alternative dimension that the public can more readily connect with is strategically chosen to inflame public opinion. This priming principally impacts the *evaluative* component of public opinion, urging the public to perceive an adversary country's actions as aggressive and unjust, and to harbor negative views about a target country or people. It can also sway the *affective* component of public opinion, amplifying negative emotions toward the target country or people, and thereby influencing the *behavioral* component.

Finally, media framing directly affects people's attitudes toward a dispute. Framing "is based on the assumption that how an issue is characterized in news reports can have an influence on how it is understood by audiences."[57] Social psychologists have demonstrated the significant effects of frames on preferences, and it is well-established that mass media can profoundly influence public opinion.[58] Media framing legitimizes a state's own claim while undermining others. It glosses over the state's own actions, presents itself as the victim, and accuses others of aggression. The campaign seeks to instill a belief that conflicts are necessary, just, and unavoidable; and that fighting is worth the costs. Even if the public remains unsupportive of the use of force, the campaign strives to make them understand that that there is some "legitimate" reason to use force, so that they should not "stand in the way."

Throughout mobilization campaigns, emotions play a significant role in manipulating public opinion. As research on emotions and social movement has shown, emotional underpinning, particularly anger and hatred, is important for all social movements and activism.[59] Mobilization campaigns intensify emotions, particularly those that prompt actions. Psychologists distinguish an "approach-avoidance" dimension of emotions, arguing that certain types of emotions tend to encourage action while others elicit avoidance. Hatred or anger, for example, are potent "approach" emotions. These emotions can "arouse behavior intentions—the tendency to boycott based on anger."[60] Such emotions amplify the public's propensity to blame, to inflict pain or harm on the perceived offender, and to rectify perceived injustices. They also decrease their willingness to consider policy compromises, making these emotions particularly effective in eliciting hazardous and punitive policies.[61]

To summarize, we can identify a mobilization campaign by observing the following features in media coverage. The first two characteristics are common to both mobilization and pacification campaigns, while the last four are unique to mobilization campaigns:

1. There is a significant, deliberate increase in the extent and frequency of media coverage over a short period of time.
2. The media works to elevate the public's perception of the issue's importance.
3. The media focuses on negative framing—criticism and condemnation against the "aggression" of the other, and portraying the extensive harm inflicted upon its own people.

4. The media works to arouse intense negative emotions, mainly a sense of unfairness and sadness toward the situation, and anger and hatred toward the other state or people.
5. The media downplays the costs of conflicts or uses negative framing to diminish the costs and morally justify the use of force.
6. The media encourages actions against the target state or people.

How Do Media Campaigns Align? Pacification

When the state prefers a moderate foreign policy, but public opinion leans toward a hardline stance, as in scenario B in Table 1.1, the state deploys a pacification campaign to mollify public opinion. At first glance, a pacification and a mobilization campaign may appear strikingly similar as they both involve a sharp uptick in media coverage in a short period of time and deploy seemingly similar harsh rhetoric—elements that essentially define a media campaign. However, pacification campaigns differ from mobilization campaigns not only in their end goals but also in the methods and content they employ.

Pacification is comparable to the process of desecuritization, which is essentially the reverse of the securitization process discussed in the mobilization section. Desecuritization refers to the process where an issue is moved out of the realm of "security" and into the realm of normal politics.[62] Essentially, it works to reduce the sense of urgency or existential threat associated with a given issue. While mobilization seeks to elevate an issue to the status of an existential threat requiring extraordinary measures, pacification aims to downgrade the issue back to the realm of normal politics. In this realm, it can be managed through standard diplomatic and political processes. Both processes play crucial roles in the management of public opinion in authoritarian states, helping to align public sentiment with the state's strategic objectives.

Hard and Soft Propaganda

To fully contextualize pacification, we must first discuss the two broad strategies that states can employ to moderate public opinion, as pacification represents only one of them. The first approach involves the coercive, repressive, and prohibitive *hard* power, which may include various forms of censorship—this could range from blocking entire websites, automatic blocking of certain keywords, manually removing posts,[63] encouraging self-censorship, or using censorship as a means to signal strength or domination.[64]

Hard power is marked by repressive measures that are often deemed a "hall-mark" of authoritarian regimes, forming a key part of their strategies for survival.[65] This aligns with "negative measures," which typically involve a direct clampdown on channels of communication. For instance, shutting down internet servers to prevent students from mobilizing during the Diaoyu Islands controversy is a demonstration of hard power. This approach aims to physically restrict the flow of information and limit the avenues for public discourse or collective action.[66]

The second strategy involves the application of *soft* power, a more subtle, persuasive, and possibly manipulative approach to influence public opinion. This soft power approach is often preferred in situations where outright censorship or repression might not be feasible, or could be viewed as too heavy-handed and potentially backfire. They also coincided with surges in nationalism and an increased public role in foreign policy due to the commercialization of media and the expansion of the internet and social media starting in the late twentieth century. While pacification campaigns are typically employed alongside censorship, this subtle form of manipulation is becoming a more favorable choice compared to outright censorship.

In the old dictatorial propaganda system with complete information control, a state could simply snuff out all information on a dispute and enjoy the freedom to pursue a moderate foreign policy with low risk of public backlash. However, such political systems are becoming increasingly rare, if not extinct. With the advent and spread of the internet and social media, foreign sources rush to fill any information vacuum left by domestic state media. Even with a highly sophisticated censorship system in place, such as the one in China, news transmission is usually instantaneous, reaching the public from various platforms and multiple sources. Information leaks, whistleblowers, international media, and the ubiquity of social media make it nearly impossible for a state to keep anything significant completely secret. Moreover, should the public discover that a state has attempted a cover-up, this could provoke backlash, intensifying public anger and resentment, rather than quelling dissent.

As Susan Shirk notes in her work *China: Fragile Superpower*, "Because of its speed and wide reach, the internet sets the agenda, forcing officials, and the print and television media, to react."[67] As a result of this trend, autocrats turn increasingly to soft power. Echoing this sentiment, Bruck Dickson states, "focusing on coercive tools alone misses a crucial fact about politics in China: The Party remains in power not only because it has been able to eliminate or at least suppress all viable alternatives, but also because it enjoys a remarkable degree of popular support."[68]

The soft power approach can be traced back to Herman and Chomsky's "manufacturing consent" propaganda model, which was originally developed within democratic societies. In their model, Herman and Chomsky outline five filters that can distort mass media reporting, enabling states to manufacture public consent.[69] There is also an extensive range of other soft power techniques.[70] These techniques offer a more nuanced and potentially less overtly contentious way of influencing public opinion, as compared to hard power tactics like censorship. By leveraging the power of digital media and insights from social psychology, these techniques empower states to mold and guide public sentiment in ways that align with their foreign policy objectives. Pacification campaigns represent such soft power strategies.

How Pacification Campaigns Pacify

For a pacification campaign to sway public opinion toward active support of a moderate foreign policy, it needs to persuade the public that a moderate stance is superior to a hardline one. To shift opinion toward passive cooperation, the campaign can merely placate hardline public opinion while soothing emotions and encouraging implicit cooperation. Reversing public opinion is a more challenging task, but it is not necessary for the success of the campaign. The campaign is deemed successful as long as the public remains disengaged when the state implements a moderate policy. Thus, a successful pacification campaign requires some degree of alignment or unspoken understanding, but not necessarily absolute agreement.

At first glance, the concept and execution of pacification campaigns may appear counterintuitive. It seems odd to launch a media campaign when a state harbors moderate foreign policy intentions. After all, such a campaign could inadvertently heighten public awareness and agitate public opinion when the state seeks to do the exact opposite—to free itself from public constraints.

Nevertheless, given the high level of public awareness already attached to these issues, as evidenced by the existing hawkish public sentiment, further awareness is unlikely to significantly impede the pacification goal. As the data in the upcoming chapter illustrates, out of twelve territory-related diplomatic crises that have transpired since 1990, China has executed seven media campaigns with the intention of pacification.

But how precisely do pacification campaigns pacify? I propose six tactics—dictating the discourse, echoing public sentiment, hardline posturing, positive framing, delegitimizing unhelpful emotions, and allowing the public to vent.

Table 1.2 Comparison between a Pacification Campaign and a Mobilization Campaign

	Tactics	Pacification	Mobilization
I. Setting the Stage for Pacification	1. Dictating the Discourse	Yes	Yes
	2. Echoing	Moderately harsh rhetoric in restrained manner, with painstaking efforts to preempt escalations and avoid inflaming the opponent	Strongly harsh rhetoric without reservations, accompanied by actions with intended escalatory effects
	3. Posturing	No threats or hollow threats; amplify proactive measures taken by authorities	Threatens substantive punishment
II. The Actual Pacification	4. Positive Framing	Abundant	Little to nonexistent
	5. Emotions	Delegitimize approach-oriented emotions such as anger or hatred and substitute with avoidance-oriented emotions such as sadness or fear; promotes positive emotions or less emotion	Provokes intense negative emotions such as anger or hatred
	6. Venting (w/ Actions?)	Allows or even encourages venting, but bars or prevents actions	Calls for actions

The first three tactics set the stage for mass persuasion—by seizing control of the narrative and establishing a connection with the audience. The remaining three execute the actual persuasion process. These tactics are summarized in Table 1.2, with each of them compared in parallel to the strategies used in mobilization campaigns. Except for the first pacification mechanism, dictating the discourse, which is common to both mobilization and pacification campaigns, the remaining five mechanisms set pacification campaigns apart from mobilization campaigns.

First, pacification campaigns help the state gain control of the narrative by disseminating large volumes of authoritative information expeditiously and frequently, and by responding to developments proactively and even preemptively, as opposed to delayed, passive responses. This tactic is the only one that pacification and mobilization campaigns share.

One unique challenge to information control in the internet era is the public's new capacity for accessing and sharing information and expressing political opinions. If the government remains silent, it empowers information from alternative sources and rumors. States are wary that their silence may give way to biased foreign media, tabloids, or rumors, all of which could sow confusion, erode public trust, or even incite outrage. Moreover, due to easier access to information, the public might uncover what the government tries to conceal. This could further backfire and infuriate the public.

Pacification campaigns help avoid these potential pitfalls and grant the state the advantage of the "primacy effect." This psychological effect refers to the cognitive bias where people prioritize the first piece of information they encounter.[71] Being the first to voice narratives about new events during crises is therefore crucial to shaping public opinion. A media campaign provides a convenient and concentrated platform for achieving this. While new media can "easily be used by the hostile forces of the West and lawless elements to carry out their 'Westernization,' 'division,' infiltration, and sabotage against us," it can also "serve as an important window for propagandizing the positions of the party, fostering healthy trends in society, understanding the situation in society and the will of the people, guiding hot-spot [issues] in society, and channeling public sentiment." Therefore, Zhang Jianhua, a Beijing University professor, stresses the necessity to "face up to [it] actively, taking the initiative and responding effectively."[72] In a speech at the CCP's News and Public Opinion Work Conference in February 2016, Chinese top leader Xi Jinping also emphasized the importance of "increasing the first move advantage, grasping the initiative, and striking the first blow."[73]

The second tactic, echoing, involves the state media mimicking what the public feels, which shows that the government is "connected" to the public. The "echo effect" in psychology demonstrates that verbal mimicry increases affinity and cohesion.[74] This tactic presents a unified front of "us" versus "them," as opposed to setting the state against the public. It fosters an illusion of shared positions and emotions, bolstering the social trust necessary for shifting opinions.

This approach aligns with the concept of resonance in communication studies. Here, the propagandist acts as the audience's alter ego, expressing their concerns, tensions, aspirations, and hopes, thereby shortening the distance between the state and the audience.[75] The social judgment theory argues that persuasion is more effective when the message is close to the audience's accepted view.[76] Media slants conforming to the audience's prior beliefs can help the media source acquire a reputation for credibility.[77] All of these explain the efficacy of echoing. Chinese officials' remarks show that they understand this function well. Vice director of the Information Office of the Chengdu municipal government Xie Wen says that "If the government only releases 'dogmatic' information and ignores negative public opinions, it will result in a communication imbalance and impair the credibility of government microblogs."[78] Echoing can also serve to soothe an angry public by providing them with a voice and expressing their outrage on their behalf, thereby indirectly aiding in the venting of their anger.

However, the state must delicately balance remaining relatable by echoing the public sentiment while avoiding jeopardizing its ultimate moderate foreign policy objective. As a result, the echoing approach does not mean the state blindly parrots public sentiment. To avoid further agitation of the public, the echoing is usually down a notch from the public sentiment. Shirk mentions China's "toning down the message" during US-China security crises. In the aftermath of the 1999 Belgrade embassy bombing, besides "ban[ning] all press criticism of the American president," the CCP also "directed the media to report on the United States in a less hostile manner." "Journalists were frustrated by their instructions to keep their reporting subdued . . . A university expert who appeared on a CCTV talk show a few days after the collision to discuss it found that all the panel participants were handed the themes they were supposed to address. When he asked who had prepared the points, he was told 'the Party center.' "[79] Being moderately harsh but not too harsh enables the media content to still relate to the public, while minimizing the risk of further enraging it.

States also take painstaking efforts to pre-empt escalations and avoid aggravating opponents. For instance, the state can condemn opponents by using third-party perspectives or by assigning the echoing task to the commercial media while loosely overseeing the process. Daniela Stockmann's study of the 2005 Chinese anti-Japan protests showcases how media's commercial liberalization bolsters its credibility with the public and enables it to guide public opinion positively.[80] In contrast, during mobilization campaigns, states readily employ inflammatory rhetoric or actions with intended escalatory effects. This nuanced difference in ostensibly similar harsh coverage reflects the distinct policy objectives of these campaigns.

The third tactic involves maintaining a façade of a hardline stance through bellicose media content. This posturing serves domestic purposes: it safeguards the government from nationalist criticisms, preserves its dignity, and fosters social stability. Considering that nationalists frequently perceive a moderate foreign policy as an indication of weakness or failure, maintaining a potent hardline rhetoric becomes a vital measure for the regime's self-preservation.

Typically, the state's threats against a foreign adversary in this context are hollow and do not imply substantial punishment, demonstrating that the harsh rhetoric is primarily a domestic rhetorical subterfuge. This approach stands in contrast to mobilization campaigns, where the state's threats usually signify tangible punitive action.

40   The Art of State Persuasion

Hardline posturing not only involves condemning the foreign adversary, but sometimes also emphasizes the state's proactive measures. By indicating its full capability to manage the situation and safeguard national interests, the government aims to boost public trust in its competence to handle the crisis. This tactic can also deflect criticisms directed toward the government as it seeks to implement a moderate policy. Essentially, pacification campaigns are orchestrated performances, intended to placate an agitated public and subtly conceal a restrained policy intention.

Contrary to the basic premise of audience costs theory, which asserts that the public will penalize a leader who retreats from a previously publicized threat, posturing does not necessarily impede a state's capacity to pursue a moderate foreign policy.[81] Critics of the audience costs theory argue that domestic punishment is rarely observed. Besides, the public may not always follow up on actual policies, and when they do, their focus is more on the overall substantive outcomes of a leader's policy than on the consistency between the leader's words and deeds. They are primarily concerned with their nation's reputation for resolve and honor, largely regardless of whether a leader has issued an explicit threat.[82] The public is often quick to "forgive" a state's failure to match tough talk with tough action. Weiss and Dafoe even suggest that citizens approve of government "blustering"—tough but vague talk that does not lead to action.[83] The state also has many means to deescalate and retrench public opinion to maintain policy flexibility.[84]

Furthermore, the public may "forget" about a foreign dispute that has little impact on their day-to-day lives. This allows the government to buy some freedom of action. The public's short attention span has been well studied in media studies.[85] The "issue attention cycle" hypothesis describes the public attention cycle during which a problem "suddenly leaps into prominence, remains there for a short time, and then—though still largely unresolved—gradually fades from the center of public attention."[86] Issues that only affect a minority of people on a day-to-day basis, that are caused by social arrangements beneficial to a powerful few, and that are not intrinsically exciting in a sustained way, are likely to progress through the cycle quickly.[87] Foreign policy issues, usually described as "high politics," meet these criteria. The public's forgiveness and forgetfulness allow the state to employ hardline posturing to shield itself from nationalist criticisms without repercussion, while still pursuing a moderate foreign policy.

While the above three mechanisms all *prepare* the way for mass persuasion, the actual persuasion takes place through three other mechanisms—positive-framing, delegitimizing "unhelpful" emotions, and allowing the public to vent. These means of mass persuasion help win the much-needed public acquiescence, if not outright support, for a moderate foreign policy.

First, a pacification campaign balances the hardline echoing and posturing through positive framing, a method that effectively steers public opinion and encourages more cooperative public behaviors. As its name suggests, positive framing selects positive stories, uses positive language, cultivates positive emotions, and promotes pro-government, pro-status quo, anti-violence, and anti-unrest messages. The ultimate goal is to subtly adjust the message to promote cooperation and deter dissent from the public, preventing any violence or collective action that could threaten social stability and regime security. These efforts, however, are largely absent in mobilization campaigns.

Positive framing is conceptually akin to the practice of "astroturfing," a term borrowed from the marketing literature. Astroturfing, named after the artificial grass used on sports fields, refers to the practice of crafting the illusion of grassroots support or opposition to a particular cause or issue. Within the realm of digital media, this can entail the deployment of automated bots or paid individuals to inundate the internet with pro-government and anti-violence messages. Additionally, states might promote patriotic bloggers or writers to foster positive public responses that align with the state's preferences.[88]

A *People's Daily* commentary points out that Chinese authorities are striving to create a more balanced internet environment amidst escalating online discord. "Although negative opinions are inevitable, the role of 'warm' information should not be ignored."[89] A study finds that the *People's Daily* "mentions of the polemical anti-American terms 'hegemonism' (referring to American dominance in the world) and 'multipolarity' (referring to the goal of reducing American power) peaked in 1999, and then declined thereafter except for a minor upturn after the 2001 aircraft collision incident. Mentions of the cooperative term 'win-win' increased over the same period," and "the censors directed the media to report on the United States in a less hostile manner."[90]

Since crisis coverage in the media tends to lean toward the negative, with a strong emphasis on attributing responsibility,[91] positive framing in diplomatic crises is particularly necessary to overcome potentially damaging conversations and redirect public opinion away from violent and defiant attitudes. A study reveals that media showed significantly less negativity under state propaganda directives and this contributed to cooling public hostility toward Japan.[92] A 2013 survey of 1,413 Chinese adults about the South China Sea maritime dispute also found that respondents who sourced their information from traditional mass media—which were more regulated by the state—tended to be less supportive of hardline policies. The study concludes that state media coverage of the issue was "more of a dampener than a driver of nationalistic policy preferences."[93]

Second, the delegitimization of "unhelpful" emotions works in tandem with positive framing. While mobilization campaigns tend to promote approach-oriented emotions, such as anger or hatred, due to their capacity to fuel social movements and activism, pacification campaigns aim to delegitimize these same emotions due to their potential to cause destabilization. To counter these "unhelpful" emotions, pacification campaigns cultivate a distaste for social unrest and violence, whilst asserting the moral superiority of reason, rationality, and patriotism.[94] This emotional manipulation often employs a utilitarian argument: order and citizens' obedience are beneficial, whereas social upheaval and violence are detrimental to the collective good— the well-being of the country. The media plays a pivotal role in underscoring the merits of a moderate foreign policy and the harms of a hardline approach. The underlying logic is that true love for one's country should lead to support or at least understanding of a moderate foreign policy, even if it diverges from their original policy preference.

Such utilitarian and moral arguments can sometimes be internalized by elites and the public, becoming an enduring feature of the political culture. In their book, Nathan and Scobell discuss how Chinese leaders propagate traditional Asian values such as "obedience, thrift, industriousness, respect for elders, and authority." This enables them to "prioritize economic and social rights over civil and political ones," emphasize "the community over the individual," and favor "social order and stability over democracy and individual freedom."[95]

Pacification campaigns not only work to delegitimize "unhelpful" emotions but also substitute them with avoidance-oriented emotions such as sadness or fear. In this context, anger commonly features in mobilization campaigns, while fear is a prominent emotion in pacification campaigns. Fear, as an avoidance-oriented emotion, increases people's awareness of the critical need for precautionary measures, erodes their confidence and support for dangerous programs, and strengthens their preference for withdrawal or conciliatory policies.[96]

Contrasting with mobilization campaigns, which aim to intensify emotions, pacification campaigns also work to dull emotions. Not only do they aim to reduce emotional intensity, but they also strive to encourage positive emotions like gratitude and satisfaction to offset negative ones, aligning with the strategy of positive framing. In this context, Huysmans's proposal of "objectivist strategy," "constructivist strategy," and "deconstructivist strategy" for desecuritization come into play, highlighting the importance of teaching objective facts, enhancing understanding of the securitization process, and transforming social identities.[97] Encouraging rationality and reducing emotional responses are key strategies in pacification. To facilitate this, tools such as investigative journalism providing detailed information, cost-benefit analysis reasoning, and reference to expert opinions are often used. It is argued that the ability to "legitimately claim authoritative knowledge" makes it easier to "convince a skeptical public audience."[98]

Lastly, the government usually allows the public to vent their anger on social media, as long as the online discussions do not directly attack the leadership. While mobilization campaigns call for action, pacification campaigns discourage action by allowing or even encouraging venting while only censoring action-oriented content. Condemnation of the foreign opponent is allowed or even encouraged, so long as it remains rhetorical. Even outright criticism of the government is tolerated sometimes, to the extent that it remains isolated and does not gain momentum.

This liberal approach toward online expressions of sentiment serves three key purposes. First, it helped dissipate some of the public ire by providing a platform for collective catharsis. It allowed people to air their feelings and frustrations, reducing the likelihood of these sentiments spilling over into real-world, potentially violent, actions. Fewsmith and Rosen put the need to release public anger in an example: "When the government provided buses for student demonstrators in the wake of the Chinese embassy bombing in Belgrade, understanding full well that students were going to take to the streets in any event and that if they did not throw stones at the American embassy they would throw them at Zhongnanhai (the leadership compound)."[99]

Chinese politicians and propagandists have long understood the utility of venting. As early as the late nineteenth century, Chinese scholar and reformist Liang Qichao advised "using newspaper to communicate political affairs . . . to unclog the blocked channels and ensure the free flow of information." Echoing this sentiment, a 2010 article in *China Youth Daily* highlighted how "microblogs used fragmented postings to release social pressure . . . let the people express their views," and prevented social pressure from accumulating into a "rupture."[100]

Recent research on social media confirms the effectiveness of venting in releasing public anger. Cairns and Carlson find that the Chinese government used social media as a safety valve for the public to let off steam during the 2012 Sino-Japanese dispute.[101] Similarly, Hassid argues that blogs can alleviate public pressure, provided that the mainstream media continues to dictate the agenda.[102] These findings are consistent with empirical observations that the Chinese state practices selective censorship of action-oriented online content, while generally allowing venting.[103]

Second, in addition to diffusing anger, allowing citizens to express their views within a controlled setting can serve to undermine the public's capacity to organize and mobilize. This strategy can be particularly effective when public opinion is fragmented on policy matters. When there are divergent views in the public domain, the state can strategically permit public expression of these varying opinions. This can lead to a heightened sense of confusion and discord among the public, causing them to become disorganized. This state-induced discord effectively weakens collective action, curbing the ability of the public to successfully rally against policies or actions of the state.[104]

Third, the state could monitor these online platforms to gauge public sentiment and adjust their strategies accordingly. By analyzing the tone, content, and volume of online discussions, the government could get a sense of how well their strategies were working, what the public's concerns were, and what additional steps, if any, they needed to take.

In effect, by allowing such online discourse, the government strikes a balance between maintaining control and letting the public express their grievances. It also demonstrates a sophisticated understanding of the role of social media in shaping public sentiment and the necessity to manage it appropriately in the context of an international dispute.

In short, a pacification campaign steers nationalist sentiment toward a moderate foreign policy by proactively controlling the narrative, echoing nationalist sentiments while posturing hardline stances, employing positive framing, delegitimizing "unhelpful" emotions, and providing outlets for the public to vent their frustrations. By utilizing these strategies, the state can placate nationalist fervor, ultimately obtaining the public's tacit acceptance or even active endorsement of a moderate foreign policy.

Observable Implications of Mobilization and Pacification Campaigns

The observable implications for a mobilization campaign and a pacification campaign are listed below. Each of these is a critical "hoop test" that falsifies the explanation in question if the observation is not present. However, a passed test will not constitute strong verification. We can further verify the explanation by examining how closely the contours of the media campaign align with the characteristics described in Table 1.2. To enhance the robustness of our findings, we can also employ text analysis, as detailed in Chapter 6, providing an additional layer of empirical evidence to support or challenge our theoretical explanations.

Mobilization

1. *Evidence of concerns of dovish/weak public opinion*: If the state is aiming to mobilize public sentiment, this is often in response to perceptions that public opinion is too passive, apathetic, or pacifist (dovish) concerning a particular issue. This could be observed through internal communications or policy documents that express concerns about the state of public opinion, or through public statements that criticize or lament the lack of public support or enthusiasm.
2. *Instructions from central propaganda authorities convey intent to mobilize, or available strategic estimates stress importance of public support on issue at hand*: If the state is pursuing a mobilization strategy, this should be reflected in directives from propaganda authorities or strategic communications from the government. Such instructions may explicitly call for a mobilization effort, or they may emphasize the importance of public support for a given policy or action.
3. *Media content deploys inflammatory and emotive language, with themes of victimization, accusations of aggression and injustice.*

Pacification

1. *Evidence of concerns of overheated public opinion threatening social stability, regime security, or foreign policy flexibility preceding campaign*: If the state is pursuing a pacification strategy, this is often in response to fears that public opinion is becoming too heated or volatile, threatening social stability, the security of the regime, or the flexibility of foreign policy. This can be manifested in a variety of ways, such as government statements expressing concern about social unrest, policy documents highlighting the risks of public opinion, or actions taken to suppress dissent or calm public anger.
2. *Instructions from central propaganda authorities convey intent to pacify*: If the state is aiming to pacify public opinion, this intent should be evident in directives from propaganda authorities or strategic communications from the government. These instructions may explicitly call for a

pacification campaign or highlight the need to cool public sentiment or to guide it in a more manageable direction.

3. *State media adopt soft manipulation techniques such as echoing, posturing, positive framing, delegitimizing unhelpful emotions, or allowing venting on social media.*

Theoretical Assumptions and Time Associations of Media Campaigns

Our discussion so far has suggested three key assumptions that underpin the misalignment theory. The theory only applies to the extent that a situation meets these assumptions. The first assumption applies to both mobilization and pacification.

1. The existence of a domestic cost by the public associated with executing an unsupported foreign policy. Nevertheless, this cost is surmountable, meaning that the state has the capacity to avert it by manipulating public opinion. This is what I call an "existing but surmountable domestic cost by the public."

   The domestic cost is crucial because it gives the state a reason to work toward alignment. Without it, there would be no incentive to pursue such a strategy. The surmountability of this cost is equally important because it enables the state to take active steps to achieve alignment.

   This assumption has been confirmed by our discussion of the paradoxical and reciprocal state–society relationship in authoritarian contexts. To assess whether the misalignment theory applies to a particular country or setting, our primary consideration is whether the state–society relationship in that country or setting fulfills this condition.

   The second and third assumptions are as follows. These two relate specifically to pacification:

2. The absence of hard power alternatives—such as complete, blackout-style censorship. This assumption suggests that more forceful or direct means of controlling public opinion, like extreme censorship, are either infeasible or ineffective.

3. The rising need for pacification, particularly in response to the growth of nationalism. This indicates that as nationalism increases, likely due to the state's own strategies for legitimizing its power by stoking nationalism, so too does the state's need to pacify or manage this nationalistic sentiment.

These latter two conditions are increasingly observed in China and many contemporary authoritarian countries. As we previously discussed, the archaic propaganda systems of dictatorial regimes, which were based on complete information control, are becoming progressively obsolete. In today's digitally connected world, achieving a total cover-up of information is not only close to impossible, but can also be counterproductive. Furthermore, we are witnessing surges in nationalism and a growing influence of public opinion on foreign policy. With the commercialization and digitization of media over the past few decades, public opinion is playing a larger role in shaping foreign policy than it did in the past. This shift has led to an environment where states must not only manage international relations, but also carefully navigate domestic sentiment.

These shifts suggest that pacification campaigns are likely a more prominent feature of contemporary settings than in the past. As these trends continue to intensify and become more widespread, we can reasonably expect to see an upswing in the frequency of pacification campaigns in the future.

There may also be a time association with mobilization campaigns. Because of the prohibitively high cost of conflict since the advent of nuclear weapons, the world has seen a significant decrease in the frequency and severity of large-scale wars, especially among the great powers.[105] Accordingly, truly aggressive foreign policies that were once associated with these conflicts have also dwindled. As a result, mobilization campaigns, which prepare societies for conflict, are likely more characteristic of the past than of the contemporary era or future.

The upcoming empirical testing in the next chapter will provide more substantial evidence to support these time-related correlations. The analysis will reveal trends over time, demonstrating how the nature of state–society relationships and state responses in the form of mobilization or pacification campaigns have evolved.

With regards to mobilization campaigns, the empirical analysis will likely show a decline over time, in line with the global reduction in large-scale conflicts. This could provide strong evidence that mobilization campaigns are indeed more characteristic of the past. On the other hand, the analysis should demonstrate an increase in pacification campaigns in line with the changing dynamics of censorship, the rise of nationalism, the democratization of information due to digital technologies, and the increasing influence of public opinion on foreign policy.

By confirming these temporal correlations, the empirical testing will not only support the validity of the misalignment theory's assumptions, but it will also shed light on the changing tactics of states as they navigate the complex

Logical Challenges

Two significant theoretical challenges confront the misalignment theory. First, there is the challenge of the endogeneity of diplomatic crises to media campaigns. Diplomatic crises may not always be independent events that happen due to purely external factors, but can also be a result of media campaigns. If diplomatic crises are created by media campaigns in the first place, this makes it hard to assess the true nature of these crises and attribute cause and effect.

In the introduction, I have outlined, justified, and defined the scope of the study with regards to "diplomatic crises." I have argued that media campaigns predominantly occur during crises, as crises hold potent influence over public opinion. This argument suggests two possible scenarios. The first scenario is one where diplomatic crises, arising from exogenous factors independent of state policy, offer leaders opportunities to shape public opinion. In these cases, the decision to initiate a media campaign, and the type of campaign to be used, becomes part of the state's response to the externally provoked crisis.

The second scenario is one where a state strategically manufactures a crisis in order to shape public opinion. In these instances, the crisis is endogenous, born from the state's recognition of the potential propaganda value in certain crisis-material events—situations or developments that, with the right framing or narrative, could be escalated into a crisis. The state then leverages these events, consciously shaping them into a diplomatic crisis to serve its interests, which could range from boosting nationalistic sentiments, diverting attention from domestic issues, to influencing international relations and negotiations.

The distinction between exogenous and endogenous crises, however, does not impact the functionality or relevance of the misalignment theory. Pacification campaigns, by their nature, are a response to exogenous factors— they are strategies employed by the state to address an existing hawkish public opinion and to manage crises that are currently underway and need addressing. These crises are externally driven, brought about by forces beyond the state's immediate control.

On the other hand, mobilization campaigns can be either exogenous or endogenous. Even in situations where they are endogenous—where the state orchestrates a crisis through a mobilization campaign—it does not contradict the state's objective to use the campaign as a tool to rally support and align public opinion with its aggressive policy stance. This allows for the state to effectively manage any potential misalignment between public sentiment and its desired policy direction.

A second challenge lies in the possible interdependence of state and societal preferences. On the one hand, a hardline state policy is likely to induce and sustain hawkish public opinion, while a moderate state policy fosters dovish public opinion. States "inherit" public opinion from numerous historical factors, including past policies of their own. There is also a path dependence in public opinion where public opinion from previous crises on the same dispute provides a baseline public opinion for subsequent crises.

While I recognize the endogenous nature of public opinion, the primary issue we face is methodological. We must isolate the "pre-existing" public opinion, making it exogenous to the state policy during *this* crisis. I will tackle this challenge from a methodological standpoint in the next chapter. To briefly address our theoretical concern here, I will measure public opinion separately from any government media coverage of the issue during a given crisis. This way, we can separate the exogenous part of an inherently endogenous variable.

On the other hand, an aggressive policy can be significantly influenced by prior hawkish public opinion. However, in the context of China and the majority of authoritarian states, this assertion may not hold true. When discussing the significance of aligning state and society on foreign policy for autocrats, I highlighted the international repercussions if the state were to allow public opinion to run rampant and dictate its foreign policy. I posited that we should not anticipate states readily capitulating to public pressure, particularly if they possess alternatives, such as media campaigns, to shift public sentiment. Rather than permitting public opinion to shape foreign policy, the state can skillfully manipulate public opinion to align with its foreign policy objectives.

Echoing the arguments of Downs and Saunders, states seldom compromise their foreign policy priorities to placate domestic public opinion.[106] More often, they opt to harness the energy of nationalism without surrendering control over it. This confidence stems partly from the public's propensity for forgiveness and forgetfulness, as previously discussed, and partly from the state's proven ability to move opinions to meet their needs.

While the Chinese state may not be omnipotent, it has demonstrated the willingness and capability to effectively sway and even reverse public opinion. For instance, Elizabeth Perry provides an illustrative example of

50   The Art of State Persuasion

how China managed to revamp the tarnished image of the People's Liberation Army (PLA) after the brutal suppression of the 1989 student movement. By launching a propaganda campaign following the PLA's battle against the catastrophic floods of 1998, the state was able to replace public impressions of the PLA's brutality with bravery, loyalty, discipline, and selflessness.[107]

Moreover, the evolution of public opinion surrounding the Diaoyu/ Senkaku Islands serves as a strong testament to the state's capacity to strategically escalate or deescalate public opinion. The Chinese public opinion toward Japan during the 1970s largely mirrored the official Chinese rhetoric. Protests erupted overseas, particularly among students, in May 1972, following the signing of the US-Japan Okinawa Reversion Treaty. *People's Daily* published numerous articles condemning the treaty and expressing support for the protestors. However, in 1972, China experienced a significant shift in its policy toward Japan. When a large-scale fishing boat incident occurred six years later, official media outlets remained entirely silent to avoid disrupting the signing of the Peace Treaty. The official rhetoric shifted from condemning Japan's "imperialism" and denouncing the treaty as a "dirty deal and shameless scam" before 1972, to adopting a more conciliatory tone, describing the two countries as "close neighbors separated by only a strip of water" post-1972.[108] Under this influence, public opinion tacitly went along with the moderate state policy, ensuring the smooth signing of the Peace Treaty.

Chinese public opinion shifted again in the 1990s, remaining in lockstep with the official narrative. In the 1980s, China gave free rein to anti-Japan nationalist sentiment, even stoking it with a massive state-led "patriotic education" campaign. As a result, territorial and historical issues became so brittle that they could snap at the slightest pressure. The state then managed to lower the nationalist temperature during the Diaoyu/Senkaku Islands disputes in 1990 and 1996. Downs and Saunders assert that "the Chinese government proved willing to incur significant damage to its nationalist credentials by following restrained policies and cooperating with the Japanese government to prevent the territorial disputes from harming bilateral relations."[109]

Four additional challenges specifically pertain to the logic of pacification. The first involves a potential "ratchet effect," whereby public opinion, once incited, may be unable to revert to its pre-mobilization state. Authoritarian states fostering nationalism to bolster their regimes may struggle to attenuate it back to pre-mobilization levels. As Downs and Saunders articulate, "elites can become trapped in their own rhetoric and choose to pursue risky security strategies rather than jeopardize their rule by not fulfilling popular nationalist demands."[110] This sentiment is reflected in a conversation with a Chinese think-tank expert, as reported by Susan Shirk. The expert lamented, "China

The (Mis)Alignment Theory **51**

couldn't ignore the many small slights against the People's Republic made by Taiwanese figures . . . [because] we are the hostages to our own propaganda. Our propaganda makes it hard for us not to react when Taiwan or the U.S. do things."[111]

Nonetheless, we should not underestimate the public's amnesia of past feuds or the state's determination and capability to shift opinions. We have previously discussed the public's propensity for forgiveness and forgetfulness, particularly on foreign policy issues, as well as the Chinese state's demonstrated willingness and ability to alter public opinion. The Chinese public's ability to set aside their resentment against the US following the 1999 Belgrade bombing and support—or at least tacitly permit—the restoration of a broadly normal bilateral relationship serves as a clear example. Admittedly, toning down public opinion may be more challenging than ramping it up, requiring additional energy, resources, and skill. However, Chinese autocrats have exhibited their competence in both tasks. The basic reality is that mobilization today does not foreclose the possibility of pacification tomorrow.

Another challenge specific to pacification is managing the unintended external consequences of such campaigns and their pre-emptive effects. On the one hand, a pacification campaign could inadvertently provoke escalations if it is misinterpreted as hostile by an international audience, thereby undermining its very purpose of pacification. As Downs and Saunders note, "other states may misinterpret them [nationalist myths] as a serious threat and respond in kind, giving rise to a security dilemma."[112] On the other hand, the apprehension of these risks might deter a state from initiating a pacification campaign to begin with.

This risk and its preemptive effect certainly exist, but they can be overcome in various ways.

First, there are natural barriers, such as language and choice of media, that separate a domestic media campaign from an international audience. Even if some content is translated, not all of it will be. Thus, only a small portion of domestic media content penetrates these barriers to reach an international audience.

Second, the literature on secret diplomacy demonstrates that states have private channels through which they can credibly signal their intentions to a foreign rival, thereby pre-empting unintended escalations.[113]

Third, a state has a multitude of conflict reduction measures at its disposal. Some low-cost, dramatic yet routinized confrontations are tacitly understood by foreign rivals to be merely symbolic or domestically oriented.[114]

Finally, and most importantly, there are numerous ways that state media can echo strong public sentiment without exacerbating the crisis. For instance, during the 2014 Sino-Vietnamese oil rig crisis, the Vietnamese media mirrored the anti-China public sentiment primarily through indirect condemnation, such as reporting on foreign observers' assessments, rather than issuing direct criticism.[115]

A third challenge to pacification concerns the "nonbarking" cases in the hawkish-hardline scenario (scenario C in Table 1.1). Considering that several pacification strategies work effectively with a hawkish public opinion and can help strengthen regime survival—such as using echoing and posturing to shorten the state–society psychological distance, satisfying nationalism, and preventing public fervor from turning against the government—one might wonder why the state would not adopt a media campaign in scenario C.

First, since the foreign policy objective here is hardline, the media campaign would not include any pacifying strategies such as positive framing, or delegitimizing "unhelpful" emotions. As such, the media campaign then primarily serves to legitimize the regime, rather than pacify the public.

Second, media campaigns carry inherent risks and costs. The "ratchet effect" we discussed earlier is real. States generally have the ability to tone down public sentiment, but their efforts may not always succeed; or given time constraints, it may not even be possible. Moreover, more effort is required to lower public sentiment than to stoke it. The next section will discuss some alternative explanations that might motivate media campaigns in this scenario.

The final challenge pertains to the combined effect of hard power and soft power. We have discussed the coercive, repressive, and prohibitive measures of censorship, as well as the contemporary limitations of censorship, and the necessity to adopt soft power strategies as a complement to hard power tactics in the theory of pacification. In cases where hard and soft power are used concurrently, it becomes difficult to discern which measure plays the pivotal role in shaping public opinion. However, one thing remains unequivocal: the state would not have been successful in shifting public opinion without employing soft power strategies like pacification campaigns. Censorship alone would not have sufficed. In a sense, soft power strategies such as pacification campaigns are not only necessary but are also gaining predominance in modern diplomacy and opinion management. Hard power strategies such as censorship, with their inherent constraints, have been relegated to a supplementary role.

Alternative Explanations

The diversionary theory and the audience costs theory offer alternative explanations for why states launch media campaigns. It is important to understand that these theories are not mutually exclusive, implying a situation of "equifinality," where multiple causal paths can lead to the same outcome. I have argued elsewhere that these theories, often framed as "alternative explanations," are logically compatible, allowing them to operate concurrently and reinforce one another. These theories communicate a variety of messages to diverse audiences.[116]

The diversionary theory, fundamentally inward-focused, proposes that the state may escalate an international dispute to deflect public attention from a domestic crisis or bolster a domestic agenda, thus leveraging foreign policy to advance domestic policy.[117] The diversionary theory operates on a typical assumption that the state's intent in foreign policy is hardline, which means that the state intends to act in a more assertive, aggressive, or unyielding manner in international matters. This intent could manifest as a determination to assert territorial claims, maintain a firm stance, or confront an international rival with force. Doing these could help the state to amplify the importance of the international dispute, thereby diverting public scrutiny away from domestic problems. The state could also use the heightened nationalist sentiment to bolster its own legitimacy and popularity.

On the other hand, the theory also assumes that public opinion on the foreign dispute is weak, hence necessitating its elevation to effectively divert public attention. Given its typical assumption of a hardline state foreign policy intent, this theory would most likely manifest in scenario A or C in Table 1.1. If it were to offer an alternative explanation, it would primarily contest the mobilization component of the misalignment theory.

Based on the diversionary logic, a media campaign driven by diversionary motives should exhibit the following observable implications:

1) There must be *an ongoing domestic crisis or a pressing domestic policy issue* (that offers incentives for the state to create a diversion).
2) The domestic crisis or policy priority should be *significantly threatening or important* (to justify the inherent risks and costs associated with the diversion).
3) The diplomatic crisis should have the potential to *rally people "around the flag,"* not incite them to rebel against the government.
4) There should be *minimal or no coverage of the domestic crisis*, (as such exposure could counteract the intended diversion).

The audience costs theory offers another alternative explanation for media campaigns. To recall from the introduction, audience costs are the potential penalties leaders might incur if they retract publicly made threats to a target state. The audience costs theory posits that by publicizing their threats, states intentionally restrict their own flexibility to signal a commitment to stand firm.[118] Traditional versions of the audience costs theory argue that only democracies can generate and leverage audience costs to enhance the credibility of their threats.[119] Jessica Weeks expands this capability from democracies to most autocracies.[120] Jessica Weiss's study on authoritarian states' management of anti-foreign protests corroborates this finding and introduces a mechanism through which authoritarian regimes generate audience costs: their management of anti-foreign protests.[121] Weiss contends that because protests in authoritarian states are costly to repress and risk becoming uncontrollable, these states can generate audience costs to signal resolve by tolerating popular mobilization, or signal their willingness to cooperate by suppressing popular mobilization.

At its heart, the audience costs logic reveals a trade-off for leaders—a trade-off between enhancing the credibility of their threats and increasing scrutiny of their foreign policy decisions. While the former could lead a state to prevail in a crisis without a fight, the latter can result in more constraints in foreign policy and greater risks of domestic punishment if outcomes are not good.

Audience costs hinge on public awareness of the issue: the domestic audience can only punish leaders for retracting a publicly made threat if they are informed and care about the matter at hand. Thus, the audience costs theory suggests that propaganda is utilized to generate these costs to gain an advantage in foreign coercion situations. In other words, if it is a state's intention to prevail in coercions in a dispute through exploiting audience costs, then that should motivate the state to amplify the dispute. Because coercion is largely a hardline policy, and an existing hawkish public opinion is the most convenient to exploit, we should most likely see audience costs in action in the hawkish public opinion—hardline state policy intent scenario (scenario C in Table 1.1).[122] This suggests that pacification and audience costs should operate under different conditions. The pacifying logic functions under moderate state foreign policy intent, where states seek compromise or status quo; whereas audience costs are most plausible when the state has a hardline intent, in the form of foreign coercions.

The pacification mechanism diverges from the audience costs theory in its interpretation of the role of public constraint. While audience costs theory views public constraint as advantageous, pacification perceives it as a disadvantage. Audience costs theory sees media campaigns as hands-tying and coercion-enhancing, but pacification sees these campaigns as hands-freeing. Pacification stresses the effect on a domestic audience by seeking to align domestic public opinion on foreign policy. Unlike the audience costs theory, it assumes that the public may not necessarily seek to punish the government if the government backs down from a previously announced threat. Additionally, pacification acknowledges that the state has a multitude of means to deescalate and retrench public opinion to maintain policy flexibility. These perspectives align with several criticisms of the audience costs theory.[123]

Based on our discussion above, we can identify the following observable implications of the audience costs theory regarding media campaigns:

1) *Ongoing foreign coercion*: There should be a situation of foreign coercion, where the state puts forward demands to a foreign rival with the expectation that they will concede without resorting to conflict.
2) *Public disclosure of demands or threats*: The demands or threats put forth by the government should be made public to engage the wider public.
3) *Specific, executable demands or threats*: The demands or threats put forth should have specific terms and deadlines, indicating their feasibility and the state's commitment. This distinguishes them from vague and hollow threats commonly seen in pacification campaigns, which are mainly for domestic posturing or echoing purposes.
4) *Negative view of backing down*: The domestic public should view backing down negatively, and they can and will coordinate to punish the leader for backing down.[124] In other words, the government should be held accountable to execute the threats and would be punished if it fails to do so.
5) *Perception of constrained action*: The foreign rival must perceive that the state's actions are constrained by its domestic public opinion, as audience costs can only act as leverage if it is perceived to be credible.[125]

We will evaluate these observable implications in the subsequent empirical chapters.

Effects of Media Campaigns

Similar to other motivational theories that focus on the origins of state behavior or strategies, our discussion so far has not covered the *outcomes* of these media campaigns. These outcomes are not the focus of this book, as our primary interest lies in the causes rather than the effects of these campaigns. Nevertheless, outcomes still warrant a brief discussion here, as they are an integral and inescapable part of the equation. They affect how states learn to handle the media from one case to another, and past attempts to foment or suppress nationalist sentiment affect the baseline public opinion in the next case. Given how authoritarian governance has evolved in the last few decades, especially amidst international upheaval, technological advancements, and the reinvention of mass communication, it becomes crucial to examine the complete causal processes from start to finish, and then to the start of the next cycle.

After all, propaganda is a delicate art of winning hearts and minds, which can indeed falter. Occasionally, the crisis window might be too brief for a campaign to make an impact, or a campaign might backfire due to public pushback and unforeseen external consequences (despite preventive efforts). Alternatively, an exogenous shock might interrupt a campaign and distract the public. However, the continuous adoption of these campaigns by states attests that such risks are conquerable, indicating the potential effectiveness of these campaigns.

Current research presents contrasting viewpoints on the efficacy of authoritarian propaganda. On one side, critics of propaganda argue that it is generally ineffective and can often backfire. For instance, a survey conducted in China during 1993–1994 reveals that the Chinese media failed to foster public trust in the government in the post-Tiananmen era.[126] Scholars have found that the CCP's propaganda was least successful in instilling trust in authorities.[127] Some attribute this failure to the declining government control of information flow, while others associate it with the dissonance and tension between propaganda and reality created by the message bombardment. Certain studies point out the countervailing effects of hard propaganda—while it may effectively deter dissent and help in maintaining regime stability in the short term, it decreases regime legitimacy in the long run.[128] The public often ignores, resists or ridicules these propaganda efforts in other authoritarian states as well.[129]

Conversely, proponents of propaganda assert that authoritarian propaganda has been predominantly successful. Geddes and Zaller argue that factors such as education and media exposure account for substantial public support for authoritarian regimes, a conclusion bolstered by survey data from Brazil.[130] This viewpoint is further validated by John Kennedy's analysis of Chinese survey data.[131] Other research attributes the high level of public trust in China to a concept they term as "government-controlled politicization."[132] This concept refers to the process in which a government or ruling body controls and shapes political discourse and public engagement in politics. Through the use of state-run media, censorship, education systems, and public messaging, governments can guide public political opinions and attitudes, which can be used to consolidate power and maintain social stability.

The apparent contradiction between these different views may be explained by the elements that arguably condition propaganda's effectiveness. Kennedy has found that education level has a nonlinear relationship with public support for the regime—while well-educated people often exhibit high support, this effect diminishes and even turns negative at the highest education levels.[133] The temporal perspective also matters—the short-term efficacy of propaganda in deterring dissent and upholding regime stability can eventually yield long-term negative effects.[134]

The effectiveness of propaganda also hinges on its objectives. Although CCP propaganda may fall short in fostering public trust, research suggests that it was "most effective" and "somewhat effective" in repressing dissent and promoting government policies.[135] The nature of the propaganda—namely, how it is carried out—also has implications for its success. Huang's research suggests that the crude, heavy-handed, "hard" propaganda is less effective than the more subtle and sophisticated "soft" propaganda.[136]

The pacification campaigns discussed in this book represent instances of soft propaganda aimed at aligning public policy opinions with those of the state. Based on the findings suggesting that propaganda promoting government policies is "somewhat effective" and Huang's contention that soft propaganda can be more persuasive, it follows that pacification campaigns are more likely to succeed than other forms of propaganda.

Conclusion

This chapter has outlined a theoretical framework to elucidate why and how media campaigns are implemented, centering on their underlying motivations and methods. Authoritarian states employ these media campaigns to adjust public opinion so that it actively endorses or passively tolerates the foreign policy preferences of the state. This need for alignment essentially originates from the paradoxical and cyclical interplay between public opinion and foreign policy in authoritarian states, wherein public opinion is significant to the extent that the state allows and shapes it to be. Within this larger theoretical framework, I have also distinguished two types of propaganda campaigns that work to shift public opinion in opposite directions.

The decision tree in Figure 1.1 encapsulates the theoretical argument of the book from the state's perspective. It delineates how states decide whether to initiate a media campaign and, if they choose to do so, what type to launch.

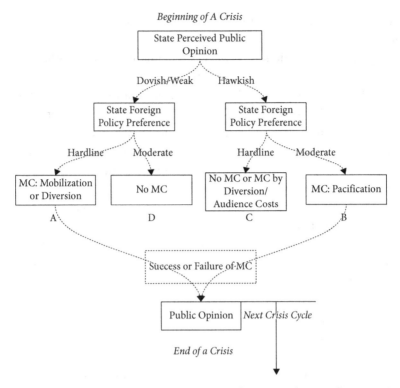

Figure 1.1 State Decision Tree in Making Propaganda Strategy (MC: Media Campaign)

Additionally, it integrates potential scenarios proposed by alternative theories and the effects of media campaigns.

Once a crisis unfolds, a state makes both foreign policy and propaganda decisions. The strategy they opt for depends on the state's evaluation of the prevailing public opinion and its alignment with the state's preferred foreign policy. When there is a misalignment between the state policy intent and existing public opinion (scenarios A and B in Figure 1.1), leaders launch aggressive media campaigns. This misalignment can occur in two ways: when state intent is more hawkish than public opinion (scenario A), and when state intent is more dovish than public opinion (scenario B). In scenario A, the media campaign aims to mobilize the public, while in scenario B, it seeks to pacify the public.

When state policy intent and existing public opinion align (scenarios C and D), states typically refrain from engaging in media campaigns, or they may sporadically launch campaigns driven by diversionary or audience costs incentives. The success or failure of the media campaigns in Scenarios A and B can further influence the baseline public opinion in the next crisis cycle.

Notes

1. "Summary: Liu Yunshan Urges Public Opinions Control at Propaganda Seminar 22 Sep," Xinhua Domestic Service (New China News Agency), September 22, 2011, accessed through World News Connection (WNC).
2. John J. Mearsheimer, "Can China Rise Peacefully?" *The National Interest*, October 25, 2014, https://nationalinterest.org/commentary/can-china-rise-peacefully-10204.
3. Ted Hopf, *Reconstructing the Cold War: The Early Years, 1945–1958* (New York: Oxford University Press, 2012), 27.
4. Ted Hopf, "Common-Sense Constructivism and Hegemony in World Politics," *International Organization* 67, no. 2 (April 2013): 349.
5. Hopf, *Reconstructing the Cold War*, 27.
6. Hopf, "Common-Sense Constructivism and Hegemony in World Politics," 342.
7. Hopf, *Reconstructing the Cold War*, 26.
8. Daniela Stockmann, "Who Believes Propaganda? Media Effects during the Anti-Japanese Protests in Beijing," *The China Quarterly* 202 (2010): 270–71.
9. Walter Lippmann, *Public Opinion* (New York: Macmillian, 1922).
10. Ole R. Holsti, "Public Opinion and Foreign Policy: Challenges to the Almond-Lippmann Consensus," *International Studies Quarterly* 36, no. 4 (1992): 447.
11. Philip J. Powlick and Andrew Z. Katz, "Defining the American Public Opinion/Foreign Policy Nexus," *Mershon International Studies Review* 42, no. Supplement_1 (May 1, 1998): 30.
12. Andrew Z. Katz, "Public Opinion and Foreign Policy: The Nixon Administration and the Pursuit of Peace with Honor in Vietnam," *Presidential Studies Quarterly* 27, no. 3 (1997): 496–513.
13. Irving Crespi, *The Public Opinion Process: How the People Speak* (London: Routledge, 2013), 100.
14. Hans Speier, "Morale and Propaganda," in *Propaganda in War and Crisis: Materials for American Policy*, ed. Daniel Lerner (New York: G. W. Stewart, 1951), 4–5.
15. Hiroshi Minegishi, "On Kim Jong Un's List of Worries, Public Opinion Outranks a Coup," *Nikkei Asian Review*, September 17, 2018, https://asia.nikkei.com/Spotlight/N-Korea-at-crossroads/On-Kim-Jong-Un-s-list-of-worries-public-opinion-outranks-a-coup.
16. Peter Hays Gries, *China's New Nationalism: Pride, Politics, and Diplomacy* (Berkeley: University of California Press, 2004).
17. Jidong Chen, Jennifer Pan, and Yiqing Xu, "Sources of Authoritarian Responsiveness: A Field Experiment in China," *American Journal of Political Science* 60, no. 2 (2016): 383–400; Edmund Malesky and Paul Schuler, "Nodding or Needling: Analyzing Delegate Responsiveness in an Authoritarian Parliament," *American Political Science Review* 104, no. 3 (2010): 482–502; Melanie Manion, "Authoritarian Parochialism: Local Congressional Representation in China," *The China Quarterly* 218 (2014): 311–38; Tianguang Meng, Jennifer Pan, and Ping Yang, "Conditional Receptivity to Citizen Participation: Evidence from A Survey Experiment in China," *Comparative Political Studies* 50, no. 4 (2017): 399–433; Rory Truex, "Consultative Authoritarianism and Its Limits," *Comparative Political Studies* 50, no. 3 (2017): 329–61; Gries, *China's New Nationalism*; Jonathan Sullivan and Lei Xie, "Environmental Activism, Social Networks and the Internet," *The China Quarterly*

60 The Art of State Persuasion

198 (June 2009): 422–32; Guobin Yang, *The Power of the Internet in China: Citizen Activism Online* (New York: Columbia University Press, 2009).

18. Chen, Pan, and Xu, "Sources of Authoritarian Responsiveness."

19. Truex, "Consultative Authoritarianism and Its Limits"; Manion, "Authoritarian Parochialism"; Malesky and Schuler, "Nodding or Needling."

20. Meng, Pan, and Yang, "Conditional Receptivity to Citizen Participation."

21. Yang, *The Power of the Internet in China.*

22. Sullivan and Xie, "Environmental Activism, Social Networks and the Internet."

23. Guobin Yang and Min Jiang, "The Networked Practice of Online Political Satire in China: Between Ritual and Resistance," *International Communication Gazette* 77, no. 3 (April 1, 2015): 215–31.

24. "Human flesh search" refers to "the activity of tracking down and publishing on the Internet the personal information of those whom according to Chinese Internet users have engaged in corrupt practices and immoral behaviour." See Patrick Gorman, "Red Guard 2.0: Nationalist Flesh Search in China," *Journal of Contemporary China* 26, no. 104 (March 4, 2017): 183–98; Rebecca Ong, "Online Vigilante Justice Chinese Style and Privacy in China," *Information & Communications Technology Law* 21, no. 2 (June 1, 2012): 130.

25. "PRC Article Urges Enhancing Management of Virtual Society, Online Public Opinion," *Zhongguo Qingnian Bao (China Youth Daily)*, April 18, 2011, accessed via WNC.

26. Zhong Sheng, "Bie rang Nanhai wenti ganrao hezuo daju (Don't Let the South China Sea Problems Interfere with the General Situation of Cooperation)," *People's Daily*, August 20, 2011, 3.

27. Zedong Mao, "Some Questions Concerning Methods of Leadership," in *Selected Works of Mao Zedong (Mao Zedong Wenji)*, vol. 3 (Beijing: Foreign Languages Press, 1967), 119.

28. Bruce J. Dickson, *The Dictator's Dilemma: The Chinese Communist Party's Strategy for Survival* (New York: Oxford University Press, 2016), 103.

29. "Xinhua: Chinese Vice President Urges Officials To Listen To Opinions From Masses," Xinhua News, January 5, 2011, accessed through WNC.

30. For examples of religion and nationalism in the Middle East, see G. Hossein Razi, "Legitimacy, Religion, and Nationalism in the Middle East," *American Political Science Review* 84, no. 1 (1990): 69–91; Mohammad Ayatollahi Tabaar, "As Islamism Fades, Iran Goes Nationalist," *New York Times*, April 3, 2019, https://www.nytimes.com/2019/04/03/opinion/iran-trump-sanctions.html. For examples of nationalism in post-communist countries, see Jack Snyder, *Myths of Empire: Domestic Politics and International Ambition* (Ithaca, NY: Cornell University Press, 1991); and Erica S. Downs and Phillip C. Saunders, "Legitimacy and the limits of nationalism: China and the Diaoyu Islands," *International Security* 23, no. 3 (1999): 114–46.

31. Xi Chen, *Social Protest and Contentious Authoritarianism in China* (Cambridge: Cambridge University Press, 2012); Peter L. Lorentzen, "Regularizing Rioting: Permitting Public Protest in an Authoritarian Regime," *Quarterly Journal of Political Science* 8, no. 2 (2013): 127–58; Martin K. Dimitrov, "What The Party Wanted To Know: Citizen Complaints as a 'Barometer of Public Opinion' in Communist Bulgaria," *East European Politics and Societies* 28, no. 2 (2014): 271–95.

32. Zhu Xinhua, "How Microblogs Alleviate Social Pressure in 2010," *Zhongguo Qingnian Bao (China Youth Daily)*, December 28, 2010, accessed via WNC.

33. Joseph Fewsmith and Stanley Rosen, "The Domestic Context of Chinese Foreign Policy: Does 'Public Opinion' Matter?," in *The Making of Chinese Foreign and Security Policy in the Era of Reform, 1978–2000*, by David M. Lampton (Redwood City, CA: Stanford University Press, 1978), 152.

34. "Public Opinion Should Not Dictate Diplomatic Affairs: CASS Scholar," Wen Wei Po Online, April 11, 2011, accessed via WNC.

35. Andrew Chubb, "Chinese Popular Nationalism and PRC Policy in the South China Sea" (PhD diss., University of Western Australia, 2016).

36. Suisheng Zhao, "Foreign Policy Implications of Chinese Nationalism Revisited: The Strident Turn," *Journal of Contemporary China* 22, no. 82 (2013): 535–53.

37. Steven E. Lobell, Norrin M. Ripsman, and Jeffrey W. Taliaferro, eds., *Neoclassical Realism, the State, and Foreign Policy* (Cambridge: Cambridge University Press, 2009), 27.

38. James Reilly, *Strong Society, Smart State: The Rise of Public Opinion in China's Japan Policy* (New York: Columbia University Press, 2011); Kai Quek and Alastair Iain Johnston, "Can China Back Down? Crisis De-Escalation in the Shadow of Popular Opposition," *International Security* 42, no. 3 (2018): 7–36.

39. Espen Geelmuyden Rød and Nils B. Weidmann, "Empowering Activists or Autocrats? The Internet in Authoritarian Regimes," *Journal of Peace Research* 52, no. 3 (May 1, 2015): 338–51.

40. See, for example, Quek and Johnston, "Can China Back Down?"; Susan L. Shirk, *China: Fragile Superpower* (New York: Oxford University Press, 2007); Gary King, Jennifer Pan, and Margaret E. Roberts, "How Censorship in China Allows Government Criticism but Silences Collective Expression," *American Political Science Review* 107, no. 2 (2013): 326–43; Steven Levitsky and Lucan A. Way, *Competitive Authoritarianism: Hybrid Regimes After the Cold War* (New York: Cambridge University Press, 2010); Lorentzen, "Regularizing Rioting."

41. Wen-Hsuan Tsai, "How 'Networked Authoritarianism' Was Operationalized in China: Methods and Procedures of Public Opinion Control," *Journal of Contemporary China* 25, no. 101 (September 2, 2016): 731–44.

42. Maria Repnikova and Kecheng Fang, "Authoritarian Participatory Persuasion 2.0: Netizens as Thought Work Collaborators in China," *Journal of Contemporary China* 27, no. 113 (2018): 1–17; Jesper Schlæger and Min Jiang, "Official Microblogging and Social Management by Local Governments in China," *China Information* 28, no. 2 (July 1, 2014): 189–213.

43. Ashley Esarey, Daniela Stockmann, and Jie Zhang, "Support for Propaganda: Chinese Perceptions of Public Service Advertising," *Journal of Contemporary China* 26, no. 103 (January 2, 2017): 101–17.

44. Kristin Roth-Ey and Larissa Zakharova, "Communications and Media in the USSR and Eastern Europe," *Cahiers Du Monde Russe. Russie—Empire Russe—Union Soviétique et États Indépendants* 56, no. 56/2–3 (April 17, 2015): 1.

45. Quek and Johnston, "Can China Back Down?"

46. Randall L. Schweller, "Neoclassical Realism and State Mobilization: Expansionist Ideology in the Age of Mass Politics," in *Neoclassical Realism, the State, and Foreign Policy*, ed. Steven E. Lobell, Norrin M. Ripsman, and Jeffrey W. Taliaferro (Cambridge: Cambridge University Press, 2009), 227–50.

62 The Art of State Persuasion

47. Fareed Zakaria, *From Wealth to Power: The Unusual Origins of America's World Role* (Princeton, NJ: Princeton University Press, 1999).

48. Thomas J. Christensen, *Useful Adversaries: Grand Strategy, Domestic Mobilization, and Sino-American Conflict, 1947–1958* (Princeton, NJ: Princeton University Press, 1996).

49. John J. Mearsheimer, "Imperial by Design," *The National Interest*, no. 111 (2011): 16–34; Stephen M. Walt, "The Threat Monger's Handbook," *Foreign Policy*, May 4, 2009, https://foreignpolicy.com/2009/05/04/the-threatmongers-handbook/; Stephen M. Walt, "Threat Inflation 6.0: Does al-Shabab Really Threaten the US," *Foreign Policy*, September 26, 2013, https://foreignpolicy.com/2013/09/26/threat-inflation-6-0-does-al-shabab-really-threa ten-the-u-s.

50. Barry Buzan, Ole Waever, and Jaap de Wilde, *Security: A New Framework for Analysis* (Boulder, CO: Lynne Rienner Publishers, 1998), 21; Barry Buzan and Ole Wæver, *Regions and Powers: The Structure of International Security*, Cambridge Studies in International Relations (Cambridge: Cambridge University Press, 2003), 491.

51. Leonard Berkowitz, "Some Effects of Thoughts on Anti-and Prosocial Influences of Media Events: A Cognitive-Neoassociation Analysis," *Psychological Bulletin* 95, no. 3 (1984): 410; Noel Brown and Craig Deegan, "The Public Disclosure of Environmental Performance Information—A Dual Test of Media Agenda Setting Theory and Legitimacy Theory," *Accounting and Business Research* 29, no. 1 (1998): 21–41; Maxwell E. McCombs and Donald L. Shaw, "The Agenda-Setting Function of Mass Media," *Public Opinion Quarterly* 36, no. 2 (1972): 176–87; M. E. McCombs and A. Reynolds, "News Influence on Our Pictures of the World," in *Media Effects. Advances in Theory and Research*, ed. J. Bryant and D. Zillmann (Mahwah, NJ: Lawrence Erlbaum Associates, 2002), 1–18; Dietram A. Scheufele and David Tewksbury, "Framing, Agenda Setting, and Priming: The Evolution of Three Media Effects Models," *Journal of Communication* 57, no. 1 (2007): 9–20; David H. Weaver, *Media Agenda-Setting in a Presidential Election: Issues, Images, and Interest* (Westport, CT: Praeger, 1981).

52. McCombs and Reynolds, "News Influence on Our Pictures of the World," 1.

53. Amos Tversky and Daniel Kahneman, "Availability: A Heuristic for Judging Frequency and Probability," *Cognitive Psychology* 5, no. 2 (1973): 207–32; Amos Tversky and Daniel Kahneman, "Judgment under Uncertainty: Heuristics and Biases," *Science* 185, no. 4157 (September 27, 1974): 1124–31.

54. Joseph Straubhaar, Robert LaRose, and Lucinda Davenport, *Media Now: Understanding Media, Culture, and Technology* (Boston: Cengage Learning, 2013), 421.

55. David Domke, Dhavan V. Shah, and Daniel B. Wackman, "Media Priming Effects: Accessibility, Association, and Activation," *International Journal of Public Opinion Research* 10, no. 1 (March 20, 1998): 51–74.

56. Kenneth J. Arrow, *Social Choice and Individual Values*, vol. 12 (New Haven, CT: Yale University Press, 2012).

57. Scheufele and Tewksbury, "Framing, Agenda Setting, and Priming," 11.

58. Thomas E. Nelson, Zoe M. Oxley, and Rosalee A. Clawson, "Toward a Psychology of Framing Effects," *Political Behavior* 19, no. 3 (September 1, 1997): 221–46; A. Tversky and D. Kahneman, "The Framing of Decisions and the Psychology of Choice," *Science* 211, no. 4481 (January 30, 1981): 453–58.

59. Helena Flam and Debra King, *Emotions and Social Movements* (London: Routledge, 2007); Jeff Goodwin, James M. Jasper, and Francesca Polletta, *Passionate Politics: Emotions and Social Movements* (Chicago: University of Chicago Press, 2009); James M. Jasper, "The

The (Mis)Alignment Theory **63**

Emotions of Protest: Affective and Reactive Emotions in and around Social Movements," in *Sociological Forum* 13 (1998): 397–424.

60. Hans Mathias Kepplinger, "Effects of the News Media on Public Opinion," in *The SAGE Handbook of Public Opinion Research*, by Wolfgang Donsbach and Michael Traugott (London: SAGE Publications, 2008), 8.

61. James N. Druckman and Rose McDermott, "Emotion and the Framing of Risky Choice," *Political Behavior* 30, no. 3 (2008): 297–321; Michael MacKuen et al., "Civic Engagements: Resolute Partisanship or Reflective Deliberation," *American Journal of Political Science* 54, no. 2 (2010): 440–58; Deborah A. Small, Jennifer S. Lerner, and Baruch Fischhoff, "Emotion Priming and Attributions for Terrorism: Americans' Reactions in a National Field Experiment," *Political Psychology* 27, no. 2 (2006): 289–98.

62. Paul Roe, "Securitization and Minority Rights: Conditions of Desecuritization," *Security Dialogue* 35, no. 3 (2004): 279–94; Ole Wæver, "3. Securitization and Desecuritization," in *On Security*, ed. Ronnie D. Lipschutz (New York: Columbia University Press, 1995), 46–86.

63. King, Pan, and Roberts, "How Censorship in China Allows Government Criticism but Silences Collective Expression."

64. Haifeng Huang, "Propaganda as Signaling," *Comparative Politics* 47, no. 4 (2015): 419–44.

65. Dickson, *The Dictator's Dilemma*, 7.

66. Fewsmith and Rosen, "The Domestic Context of Chinese Foreign Policy," 172.

67. Shirk, *China*, 82.

68. Dickson, *The Dictator's Dilemma*, 8.

69. Edward S. Herman and Noam Chomsky, *Manufacturing Consent: The Political Economy of the Mass Media* (New York: Pantheon, 2002).

70. See for example, Rongbin Han, "Defending the Authoritarian Regime Online: China's 'Voluntary Fifty-Cent Army,'" *The China Quarterly* 224 (December 2015): 1006–25; Gary King, Jennifer Pan, and Margaret E. Roberts, "How the Chinese Government Fabricates Social Media Posts for Strategic Distraction, Not Engaged Argument," *American Political Science Review* 111, no. 3 (2017): 484–501; Guobin Yang, "(Un) Civil Society in Digital China| Demobilizing the Emotions of Online Activism in China: A Civilizing Process," *International Journal of Communication* 11 (2017): 1945–65; Repnikova and Fang, "Authoritarian Participatory Persuasion 2.0."

71. James Deese and Roger A. Kaufman, "Serial Effects in Recall of Unorganized and Sequentially Organized Verbal Material," *Journal of Experimental Psychology* 54, no. 3 (1957): 180; Bennet B. Murdock, "The Serial Position Effect of Free Recall," *Journal of Experimental Psychology* 64, no. 5 (1962): 482.

72. Jianhua Zhang, "China: Impact of 'New Media' on Public Opinion During 'Non-War Military Actions,'" *PLA Daily* (*Jiefangjun Bao*), October 11, 2011, acccssed via WNC.

73. "Cong Quanju Chufa Bawo Xinwen Yulun Gongzuo (Approach News and Public Opinion Work from A Holistic Viewpoint)," *People's Daily*, February 21, 2016, 1.

74. William W. Maddux, Elizabeth Mullen, and Adam D. Galinsky, "Chameleons Bake Bigger Pies and Take Bigger Pieces: Strategic Behavioral Mimicry Facilitates Negotiation Outcomes," *Journal of Experimental Social Psychology* 44, no. 2 (2008): 461–68.

75. Paul Kecskemeti, "Propaganda," in *Handbook of Communication*, ed. Ithiel D. Pool et al. (Chicago: Rand McNally, 1973), 864.

76. Garth S. Jowett and Victoria O'Donnell, *Propaganda & Persuasion* (Thousand Oaks, CA: SAGE Publications, 2014), 180.

64 The Art of State Persuasion

77. Matthew Gentzkow and Jesse M. Shapiro, "Media Bias and Reputation," *Journal of Political Economy* 114, no. 2 (April 1, 2006): 280–316, https://doi.org/10.1086/499414.

78. "Positive Voices Necessary To Balance Online Public Opinion: People's Daily," *Xinhua News*, July 24, 2012, accessed via WNC.

79. Shirk, *China*, 98–99.

80. Stockmann, "Who Believes Propaganda?"

81. James D. Fearon, "Domestic Political Audiences and the Escalation of International Disputes," *American Political Science Review* 88, no. 3 (1994): 577–92; Kenneth A. Schultz, *Democracy and Coercive Diplomacy*, vol. 76 (Cambridge: Cambridge University Press, 2001).

82. Jack Snyder and Erica D. Borghard, "The Cost of Empty Threats: A Penny, Not a Pound," *American Political Science Review* 105, no. 3 (2011): 437.

83. Snyder and Borghard, "The Cost of Empty Threats"; Jessica C. Weiss and Allan Dafoe, "Authoritarian Audiences, Rhetoric, and Propaganda in International Crises: Evidence from China," *International Studies Quarterly* 63, no. 4 (December 1, 2019): 963–73.

84. Marc Trachtenberg, "Audience Costs: An Historical Analysis," *Security Studies* 21, no. 1 (January 1, 2012): 3–42.

85. Frank R. Baumgartner and Bryan D. Jones, *Agendas and Instability in American Politics* (Chicago: University of Chicago Press, 2010); Carol A. Bodensteiner, "Predicting Public and Media Attention Span for Social Issues," *Public Relations Quarterly* 40, no. 2 (1995): 14; Anthony Downs, "Up and Down with Ecology: The 'Issue-Attention Cycle'," *The Public Interest* 28, no. 28 (1972): 38–50.

86. Downs, "Up and Down with Ecology."

87. Ibid.

88. Han, "Defending the Authoritarian Regime Online"; King, Pan, and Roberts, "How the Chinese Government Fabricates Social Media Posts for Strategic Distraction, Not Engaged Argument."

89. "Positive Voices Necessary to Balance Online Public Opinion: People's Daily," *Xinhua News*, July 24, 2012, accessed via WNC.

90. Shirk, *China*, 98.

91. Seon-Kyoung An and Karla K. Gower, "How Do the News Media Frame Crises? A Content Analysis of Crisis News Coverage," *Public Relations Review* 35, no. 2 (2009): 107–12.

92. Daniela Stockmann, "Who Believes Propaganda? Media Effects during the Anti-Japanese Protests in Beijing," *The China Quarterly* 202 (2010): 269–89.

93. Andrew Chubb, "Chinese Popular Nationalism and PRC Policy in the South China Sea" (PhD diss., University of Western Australia, 2016), 193–94.

94. Yang, "Demobilizing the Emotions of Online Activism in China."

95. Andrew J. Nathan and Andrew Scobell, *China's Search for Security* (New York: Columbia University Press, 2012), 331.

96. Charles S. Carver and Eddie Harmon-Jones, "Anger Is an Approach-Related Affect: Evidence and Implications," *Psychological Bulletin* 135, no. 2 (2009): 183; Druckman and McDermott, "Emotion and the Framing of Risky Choice"; Andrew J. Elliot, Andreas B. Eder, and Eddie Harmon-Jones, "Approach–Avoidance Motivation and Emotion: Convergence and Divergence," *Emotion Review* 5, no. 3 (2013): 308–11; Jennifer S. Lerner et al., "Effects of Fear and Anger on Perceived Risks of Terrorism: A National Field Experiment," *Psychological Science* 14, no. 2 (March 2003): 144–50; MacKuen et al., "Civic Engagements."

97. Jef Huysmans, "Migrants as a Security Problem: Dangers of 'Securitizing' Societal Issues," in *Migration and European Integration: The Dynamics of Inclusion and Exclusion*, ed. Robert Miles and Dietrich Thränhardt (London: Pinter Publishers, 1995), 65–67; Roe, "Securitization and Minority Rights," 287.

98. Thomas Risse, "'Let's Argue!': Communicative Action in World Politics," *International Organization* 54, no. 1 (2000): 22.

99. Fewsmith and Rosen, "The Domestic Context of Chinese Foreign Policy."

100. Zhu Xinhua, "How Microblogs Alleviate Social Pressure in 2010," *Zhongguo Qingnian Bao (China Youth Daily)*, December 28, 2010, accessed via WNC.

101. Christopher Cairns and Allen Carlson, "Real-World Islands in a Social Media Sea: Nationalism and Censorship on Weibo during the 2012 Diaoyu/Senkaku Crisis," *The China Quarterly* 225 (2016): 23–49.

102. Jonathan Hassid, "Safety Valve or Pressure Cooker? Blogs in Chinese Political Life," *Journal of Communication* 62, no. 2 (2012): 212–30.

103. King, Pan, and Roberts, "How Censorship in China Allows Government Criticism but Silences Collective Expression."

104. Jidong Chen and Yiqing Xu, "Why Do Authoritarian Regimes Allow Citizens to Voice Opinions Publicly?" *Journal of Politics* 79, no. 3 (2017): 792–803.

105. Steven Pinker, *The Better Angels of Our Nature: Why Violence Has Declined* (New York: Viking, 2011); Joshua S. Goldstein, *Winning the War on War: The Decline of Armed Conflict Worldwide* (New York: Penguin, 2011).

106. Erica Strecker Downs and Phillip C. Saunders, "Legitimacy and the Limits of Nationalism: China and the Diaoyu Islands," *International Security* 23, no. 3 (1999): 114–46.

107. Elizabeth Perry, "Moving The Masses: Emotion Work In The Chinese Revolution," *Mobilization: An International Quarterly* 7, no. 2 (June 1, 2002): 123.

108. "Angzang de Jiaoyi, Wuchi de Pianju (Dirty Deal, Shameless Scam)," *People's Daily*, June 20, 1971, p.4.

109. Downs and Saunders, "Legitimacy and the Limits of Nationalism," 117.

110. Ibid., 115.

111. Shirk, *China*, 98.

112. Downs and Saunders, "Legitimacy and the Limits of Nationalism," 115.

113. Keren Yarhi-Milo, "Tying Hands Behind Closed Doors: The Logic and Practice of Secret Reassurance," *Security Studies* 22, no. 3 (2013): 405–35.

114. Paul D. Senese and John A. Vasquez, "Assessing the Steps to War," *British Journal of Political Science* 35, no. 4 (2005): 607–33.

115. Wang and Womack, "Jawing through Crises."

116. Andrew Chubb and Frances Yaping Wang, "Authoritarian Propaganda Campaigns on Foreign Affairs: Four Birds with One Stone," *International Studies Quarterly* 67, no. 3 (2023): https://doi.org/10.1093/isq/sqad047.

117. Bruce M. Russett, *Controlling the Sword: The Democratic Governance of National Security* (Cambridge, MA: Harvard University Press, 1990); Alastair Smith, "Diversionary Foreign Policy in Democratic Systems," *International Studies Quarterly* 40, no. 1 (1996): 133–53; Richard J. Stoll, "The Guns of November: Presidential Reelections and the Use of Force, 1947–82," *Journal of Conflict Resolution* 28 (1984): 231–46.

118. Fearon, "Domestic Political Audiences and the Escalation of International Disputes."

66   The Art of State Persuasion

119. Fearon; Schultz, *Democracy and Coercive Diplomacy*.
120. Jessica L. Weeks, "Autocratic Audience Costs: Regime Type and Signaling Resolve," *International Organization* 62, no. 1 (2008): 35–64; Jessica L. Weeks, "Strongmen and Straw Men: Authoritarian Regimes and the Initiation of International Conflict," *American Political Science Review* 106, no. 2 (2012): 326–47.
121. Jessica C. Weiss, "Authoritarian Signaling, Mass Audiences, and Nationalist Protest in China," *International Organization* 67, no. 1 (2013): 1–35; Jessica C. Weiss, *Powerful Patriots: Nationalist Protest in China's Foreign Relations* (New York: Oxford University Press, 2014).
122. Scenarios with dovish/weak public opinion, although also possible, is harder for an audience costs logic to operate, because the necessary process to stoke up public opinion would be exposed to the target country and render audience costs ingenuine and unconvincing.
123. Snyder and Borghard, "The Cost of Empty Threats"; Weiss and Dafoe, "Authoritarian Audiences, Rhetoric, and Propaganda in International Crises"; Trachtenberg, "Audience Costs."
124. Weeks, "Autocratic Audience Costs."
125. This is similar to the "visibility" condition of audience costs in Weeks.
126. Xueyi Chen and Tianjian Shi, "Media Effects on Political Confidence and Trust in the PRC in the Post Tiananmen Period," *East Asia* 19 (September 1, 2001): 84–118.
127. Jian-Hua Zhu, "Information Availability, Source Credibility, and Audience Sophistication: Factors Conditioning the Effects of Communist Propaganda in China" (PhD diss., Indiana University, 1990).
128. Haifeng Huang, "The Pathology of Hard Propaganda," *Journal of Politics* 80, no. 3 (2018): 1034–38.
129. Vaclav Havel and Václav Havel, *The Power of the Powerless: Citizens Against the State in Central-Eastern Europe* (Armonk, NY: M. E. Sharpe, 1985); Lisa Wedeen, *Ambiguities of Domination: Politics, Rhetoric, and Symbols in Contemporary Syria* (Chicago: University of Chicago Press, 1999); Sarah Sunn Bush et al., "The Effects of Authoritarian Iconography: An Experimental Test," *Comparative Political Studies* 49, no. 13 (2016): 1704–38.
130. Barbara Geddes and John Zaller, "Sources of Popular Support for Authoritarian Regimes," *American Journal of Political Science* 33, no. 2 (1989): 319–47.
131. John James Kennedy, "Maintaining Popular Support for the Chinese Communist Party: The Influence of Education and the State-Controlled Media," *Political Studies* 57, no. 3 (2009): 517–36.
132. Qing Yang and Wenfang Tang, "Exploring the Sources of Institutional Trust in China: Culture, Mobilization, or Performance?" *Asian Politics & Policy* 2, no. 3 (2010): 415–36.
133. Kennedy, "Maintaining Popular Support for the Chinese Communist Party."
134. Huang, "The Pathology of Hard Propaganda."
135. Zhu, "Information Availability, Source Credibility, and Audience Sophistication."
136. Huang, "The Pathology of Hard Propaganda."

2

The Chinese Propaganda System and Media Campaigns

In 2017 the Dalai Lama, the spiritual leader of Tibetan Buddhism residing in exile in India, made a visit to Arunachal Pradesh, a region that has long been disputed between India and China. Given that the Dalai Lama is regarded by Beijing as a separatist figure, his visit to this contested territory was viewed as highly sensitive and politically charged. As a result, it sparked a significant flare-up and drew substantial media attention in China and India.

Interestingly, the media behaviors in these two countries were starkly different. The Chinese state-run media published strong editorials condemning the visit as a direct challenge to China's territorial claims and sovereignty. Through their control over the media the Chinese government was able to present a unified narrative, leaving little room for public contradiction. Meanwhile, Indian media also covered the visit extensively, but the coverage encompassed a broad spectrum of opinions, including both supporters of the visit and critical voices expressing concerns about potential diplomatic repercussions with China.

This intriguing contrast between the portrayal of the same dispute by Chinese and Indian media underscores the importance of understanding the Chinese propaganda system before delving into the details of such disputes. India boasts a vibrant and independent media landscape with press freedom as a cornerstone. On the other hand, the Chinese media system exhibits not only the common traits of authoritarian systems, but also unique features specific to China. To contextualize the misalignment theory effectively, it is crucial to examine the Chinese propaganda system—its historical development, present characteristics, and operational mechanisms. This exploration will not only provide valuable background for subsequent empirical tests, but also enable an assessment of the theory's potential applicability beyond the Chinese context.

This chapter contextualizes the misalignment theory and its competing theories in the Chinese propaganda system and media campaigns. The first section provides an overview of the Chinese propaganda system and typical

The Art of State Persuasion. Frances Yaping Wang, Oxford University Press. © Oxford University Press 2024.
DOI: 10.1093/oso/9780197757505.003.0003

Chinese media coverage of territorial crises, establishing the background for the empirical tests to follow. The second section conducts a medium-N test of the theory in twenty-one Chinese diplomatic crises. The medium-N test of twenty-one cases serves a dual purpose: on the one hand, it operates as a plausibility probe for the misalignment theory; on the other hand, it offers a summary of Chinese media campaigns concerning territorial disputes, thereby laying the groundwork for more thorough case studies in the ensuing chapters.

Development of the Chinese Propaganda System

Over the course of the seven decades covered in this book, Chinese media control has undergone significant evolution. Notably, the commercialization of Chinese media and the widespread adoption of the internet have brought about profound changes. As a result, state control over media has become more nuanced and intricate. Furthermore, the Chinese government contends with a stronger wave of popular nationalism today, partly of its own making. All these new developments enrich the temporal variation among the cases examined in this book. However, amidst these transformations, certain elements have remained constant. The fundamental imperative of regime survival and national security has persisted throughout time, underscoring the enduring importance of propaganda in fulfilling these needs.

In the Mao Zedong era, propaganda was the hallmark of central political control. As early as the revolutionary era Mao himself recognized the importance of propaganda, considering it the "first most important task of the Red Army."[1] Mao learned much of the organizational structure and control techniques of propaganda from the Soviet and the Nazi governments.[2] The main pillar of Maoist "thought work" (*sixiang gongzuo*) was indoctrination and mass persuasion. The media, under the tight control of the central government, was regarded as the Party's "throat and tongue."

Despite the limited reach of traditional media due to the technological constraints at the time, the Chinese government had a variety of "thought control" channels and techniques that reached far and penetrated deep into the Chinese public. These channels and techniques included community- and village-based ideological study groups, the widely used loudspeaker systems in almost every village, the distribution of pamphlets, the deployment of traveling propaganda teams (*xuanchuan dui*), "thought reform" (*sixiang gaizao*) or brainwashing in prisons, the creation and promotion of template "models" or exemplars, and the dissemination of documents and slogans to be memorized.[3] Through this comprehensive approach to propaganda, the Chinese government sought to shape public opinion, instill ideological conformity, and maintain a tight grip on the flow of information and thought within society.

By the end of the twentieth century, the Chinese propaganda system had transitioned from a totalitarian system characterized by stringent "thought control" to a new form of authoritarian control that employed softer methods of "guiding" and "channeling" public opinion. Maria Repnikova summarizes that Maoist media control has the features of "more uniformity of political discourse, deployment of violence and explicit top-down directives," whereas the new authoritarian media control is "somewhat flexible."[4] Although these two systems differ in style and specific means, they share similarities in terms of their aim to control public opinion. The extent to which control has strengthened or weakened in the current, more diffuse media landscape is still a subject of debate. The evolving nature of the Chinese propaganda system and its impact on public opinion continue to be topics of analysis and discussion.

This transition began in the late 1970s as China embarked on a path of reform and openness under Deng Xiaoping's leadership. During this era, the Chinese media underwent marketization and privatization, leading to varying degrees of privatization among media outlets. While the state retained a strong hold on official media and maintained majority ownership, many other media organizations had to adapt their mindset regarding funding and profitability.[5]

Beyond political considerations, economic incentives started to play a significant role in shaping reporting decisions. Newspapers, for instance, had to write stories not only to ensure their political survival, but also to secure their economic viability. The changing media landscape reflected a shift toward a more market-oriented approach, where considerations of financial sustainability became increasingly important alongside political factors.

The advancement of information technology brought about a second significant change—the emergence of the internet and the widespread use of social media platforms, including micro-blogging. China first connected to the internet in 1995, and since then, the number of internet users has skyrocketed. From 111 million users (8.5 percent of the population) in 2005, the figure surged to 731 million users (53.2 percent of the population) by 2016. Today, Chinese internet users constitute approximately 20 percent of internet users worldwide.[6]

Simultaneously in the 1990s, strong popular nationalism began to surface. The publication of the bestselling book *China Can Say No* in 1995 became a benchmark for nationalist sentiments. Nationalist online forums such as "qiangguo luntan" (Strong China Forum) managed by *People's Daily* and

70 The Art of State Persuasion

"Tiexue" (Iron Blood) proliferated. Hawkish PLA generals, whose remarks were often championed by nationalists, became more outspoken.[7] Anti-foreign protests became more frequent, particularly during diplomatic crises.[8]

These developments highlight the intersection between the rise of information technology and the surge in popular nationalism during the 1990s. The internet and social media platforms have played a significant role in amplifying nationalist sentiments, enabling broader public participation in nationalistic discussions and providing platforms for the expression of nationalist viewpoints.

These changes posed both challenges and opportunities for the Chinese propaganda system. On the one hand, some scholars argue that these transformations have had a corrosive effect on state control over the media and society. Daniel Lynch suggests that administrative fragmentation, property rights reform, and technological advancements have diminished the Party's control over traditional "thought work."[9] Geoffry Taubman highlights the challenges posed by "the scope and ease of obtaining information on the Web," "the communication capabilities available to users," and "the decentralized nature of the Internet," all of which present hurdles to nondemocratic rule.[10] Guobin Yang's research delineates the strong activism and innovative forms of protest nurtured by the Chinese cyberspace.[11] However, these scholars also acknowledge that the Chinese state still retains ultimate control over the media and public opinion.

On the other hand, Chinese propagandists have quickly adapted to the new environment and upgraded their game. The emergence of new challenges, described by Min Jiang as the "coevolution of the internet, (un)civil society, and authoritarianism," has prompted adaptations within the Chinese propaganda system.[12] In response to the spread of the internet, the Chinese government established a highly sophisticated censorship system. This system, often jokingly known as the "Great Firewall," effectively blocks access to entire websites.

Under the Xi Jinping government, the institutional framework governing the internet has also been significantly overhauled, placing digital technologies at the core of propaganda work. This has resulted in a more centralized and streamlined control process within the Chinese propaganda system, enhancing its ability to harness the power of digital platforms for propaganda purposes.[13]

On the one hand, a greater emphasis has been placed on the strategic utilization of digital platforms to disseminate state-approved narratives. In the era of social media and online news, propaganda delivery has evolved from static, one-way broadcasts to more interactive and dynamic forms. Government messages are crafted not only to inform but also to engage, using digital techniques such as hashtags, memes, and shareable content to increase their reach and influence.

On the other hand, the government has tightened its control over digital platforms, imposing stricter regulations and enforcement measures. Examples of these measures include the implementation of the real name registration policy in 2015 as part of the Cybersecurity Law, requiring internet users to register with their real names, and data localization laws that require that Chinese user data be stored within the country. Additionally, institutions such as the Cyberspace Administration of China (*guojia hulianwang xinxi bangongshi*) and the Central Leading Group for Internet Security and Informatization (*zhongyang wangluo anquan he xinxihua lingdao xiaozu*) were established to provide oversight and support in online opinion control. The internet has also led to the recruitment of an army of state-funded nationalist trolls, the so-called 50 cent army, so named because these commentators are paid RMB ¥0.50 per post.[14] During diplomatic crises, these internet workers inundate the online space with pro-government messages or white noise—irrelevant content, effectively drowning out negative or destructive messages.

This reconfiguration has equipped the Chinese propaganda system with a more effective way to manage the online information landscape. State messages can be propagated more extensively and with greater speed, while dissenting voices can be rapidly identified and suppressed. Moreover, the increased use of data analytics enables the government to gauge public sentiment and adjust its strategies accordingly.

The state strategy has also evolved to become more sophisticated over time. Following the Tiananmen crackdown, Chinese President Jiang Zemin introduced the concept of guiding public opinion (*yulun daoxiang*), favoring a softer approach to directing public sentiment as opposed to the traditional, forceful approach of indoctrination.[15] President Hu Jintao further refined this soft approach, introducing the concept of channeling public opinion (*yulun yindao*). On January 23, 2007, Hu first used the term "channeling" in an address to CCP Politburo members, stating, "[we should] grasp the online discourse power, enhance our ability to channel online discussions, emphasize the art of 'channeling,' actively leverage new technologies, increase positive coverage, and promote a positive mainstream discourse."[16] Then, at a 2008 National Propaganda Thought Work Meeting (*quanguo xuanchuan sixiang gongzuo huiyi*), Hu articulated the need to "enhance our ability to channel public opinion."[17] During a visit to the Strong China Forum at *People's Daily*

72　The Art of State Persuasion

in June 2008, he fully elaborated on this idea, stating, "[We should] strengthen our traditional media and new media and form a new setting for channeling public opinion."[18]

Drawing from the wisdom of the legendary leader Yu the Great, who tamed the floods through effective "channeling" rather than mere obstruction, Hu clarified that "channeling public opinion" underscores the importance of using market forces and the internet to "guide public sentiments in useful directions," instead of relying solely on straightforward censorship and repression.[19] He suggested that "channeling is less focused on suppressing negative news coverage and more concerned with spinning news in a direction favorable to the leadership."[20] The deployment of the gargantuan 50 cent army is just one part of this broader strategy to create a "new setting for channeling public opinion." By flooding the internet with state-sanctioned, pro-government messages, this strategy seeks to shape public discourse in a way that supports state objectives.

With an eye to these changes, some scholars argue that state control over media has actually been fortified. This perspective stands in contrast to the first group of scholars who maintain that market forces and the internet have eroded the state's monopoly over media and public opinion.

Anne-Marie Brady contends that the Chinese propaganda machine has reinvented itself and strengthened its hold on Chinese society not despite but because of marketization and globalization.[21] Daniela Stockmann contends that the impact of marketization is contingent upon institutional traits. In the case of China and many other authoritarian states, marketization sustains, rather than destabilizes, authoritarianism.[22]

Stockmann and Gallagher delineate how the marketized Chinese media, complete with reinvented propaganda outlets, has boosted citizens' trust in the authoritarian legal system to resolve grievances, thereby reducing the need for protests.[23] In the case of the Severe Acute Respiratory Syndrome (SARS) outbreak in 2003, the state utilized commercial incentives to encourage media to produce content that was both politically acceptable and popular with the public.[24] By tracing the physical network infrastructure control, the content control, and foreign influence on the network in China, Harwit and Clark demonstrate that the state is the unmistakable, powerful invisible hand that shapes the internet in China.[25] Morozov further confirms the repressive nature of the internet in China and Iran, effectively debunking the illusion that the internet is inherently liberating.[26]

The evolution of the Chinese propaganda system has had mixed effects in the domain of foreign policy. The diversification of information sources has made it more challenging, even unfeasible, for the government to hide a dispute entirely, but the state has a legion of resources and means to either downplay such events or steer public opinion in beneficial directions. The emergence of the internet has also led to broader and deeper public engagement in foreign policy. This shift, paired with an intensification of nationalist sentiment among the public, has introduced additional constraints on foreign policymaking. However, with the advent of new technologies, the state has also acquired newfound power to circumvent these potential limitations. Ultimately, what has not changed is the effective state control over media and public opinion, as well as the fundamental state logic that underpins the decision to either launch or refrain from launching a media campaign on a foreign dispute—a dynamic that this study aims to elucidate.

The Nuts and Bolts of the Chinese Propaganda System

The Central Propaganda Department (CPD), the heart of CCP propaganda, commands an extensive network of media outlets and government branches in the bureaucratic system. This amounted to over 3,442 television stations, 1,906 newspapers, and 10,014 in 2015, as well as a dozen corresponding institutional organs in the State Council and the People's Liberation Amy (PLA).[27] Figure 2.1 illustrates the hierarchy of state media outlets according to their level of authority, with specific examples for each tier.

In a rare and high-profile tour of the country's top state media outlets in 2016, Chinese President Xi Jinping asserted the need for unwavering loyalty from the state media, demanding that they "must have the Party as their family name." He emphasized that all media work "must reflect the party's will, safeguard the party's authority, and safeguard the party's unity." He urged the media to "love the party, protect the party, and closely align themselves with the party leadership in thought, politics and action."[28]

The reach of CCP propaganda also extends deeply into society. In the Mao era, this was epitomized by study sessions and loudspeakers in every village. Nowadays, it is epitomized in the 98.77 percent TV coverage and a 53.2 percent internet penetration rate across the entire country.[29]

At the pinnacle of the system, media policy on foreign affairs issues falls under the purview of the Central Leading Group on Propaganda and Ideological Work (*zhongyang xuanchuan sixiang gongzuo lingdao xiaozu*), with the consultation of the Foreign Affairs Leading Group (*waishi lingdao xiaozu*). Long-term and medium-term policies are delivered at the National Propaganda Thought Work Meetings (*quanguo xuanchuan sixiang gongzuo*

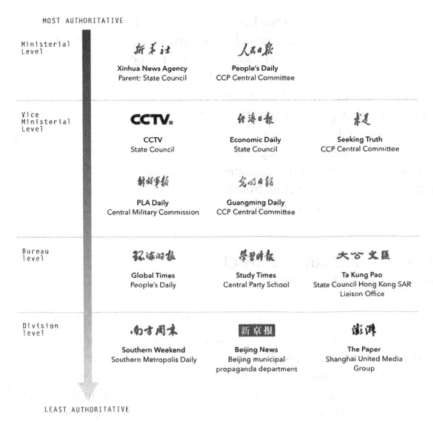

Figure 2.1 The Official Hierarchy of Party-State Media
Source: The Initium Media
Xixi Pi, "Whoever controls the present, controls the future—The 'psychological strategy' of the Chinese Communist Party's propaganda system (shui kongzhi xianzai, jiu kongzhi weilai—zhonggong xuanchuan xitong de 'gongxinji,'" Initium Media, September 23, 2017, https://theinitium.com/article/20170924-CCP-Propaganda-System/.

huiyi) and the annual National Conferences of Propaganda Department Directors (*quanguo xuanchuan buzhang huiyi*). Speeches and other crucial guidelines are subsequently disseminated either verbally at lower-level propaganda department meetings or through internal publications.[30] A working group within the CPD then sets short-term guidelines, specifying the themes and issues to be emphasized. These are delivered to senior editors during their regular meetings with CPD officials.[31]

During diplomatic crises, depending on the severity of the situation, the two corresponding Leading Small Groups might become involved. Daily guidelines outlining what to cover and how, and what to avoid, are disseminated through the CPD to senior editors at key official media outlets, and subsequently passed down to the on-duty editors.

Some of these event-based, article- or topic-specific daily directives have been leaked to the *China Digital Times*, which maintains an online archive of these documents.[32] These directives, referred to as the *"zhenlibu zhiling* (The Truth Department directives)," are valuable, but their origins are unclear, necessitating further validation. In this regard, interviews with senior editors who have firsthand experience of the relevant diplomatic crises can be particularly enlightening, as editors may disclose the policy directives they received during these crises.

The CCP exercises control over news reporting through a variety of mechanisms.[33] The first is financial, either via direct ownership or through incentives such as fiscal rewards to media outlets and bonuses to journalists who comply with the guidelines of state propaganda.[34] The second mechanism is personnel-based, where the Party appoints the senior management of all official media outlets. The third mechanism is legal and structural, encompassing aspects like licensing, mandatory organizational sponsorship, and so forth.[35] The fourth is the application of brute force, which can involve censorship, closure of media outlets, and imprisonment of journalists.

The fifth mechanism is administrative, referring to the editor responsibility system: the chain of approval for an article assigns responsibility not only to the author but also to a series of editors, extending up to the top management of a news outlet. As a result, the editors usually err on the side of caution for articles that touch upon sensitive topics. The last mechanism is coercive; through a mix of rewards and threats of punishment, the state sets examples to encourage self-censorship. To further promote self-censorship among journalists and internet users, the state purposely obscures the limits of state tolerance and performs random inspections.[36]

Typical Chinese Media Coverage of Territorial Crises

When a crisis unfolds, the Chinese propaganda apparatus springs into action, typically under the explicit directive of the top leadership and the Central Propaganda Department (CPD). This goes beyond merely devising a foreign policy response; it involves the strategic planning of media communication. The top leadership takes into account domestic public opinion and constructs a media strategy based on this crucial evaluation. It deliberates which messages should be censored and which should be promulgated.

With an attention to detail, the CPD releases a series of instructions to major state-owned media outlets. These directives can occur daily or even hourly, depending on the gravity of the situation. The CPD vigilantly monitors the compliance of these media outlets, ensuring their alignment with the state's objectives. If there are discrepancies or errors, the CPD exercises disciplinary actions. Not only does this rectification correct the error at hand, but it also serves as a deterrent and a teaching moment for other media outlets, encouraging them to adhere to the state's mandates. In the process, these media entities gain a deeper understanding of the state's policies and preferences.

The narrative themes that are typically reinforced encompass a variety of key points. One significant theme is to draw upon historical and legal evidence that underpins China's claim to the disputed territory and weakens the stance of the adversary. Another commonly pursued narrative thread exposes the unreasonable demands, greed, or even aggressive tendencies of the opposing state. In parallel, Chinese media frequently lauds the bravery and steadfastness of related personnel such as soldiers or international legal experts, showcasing them as exemplars for the wider public.

Furthermore, the media's coverage tends to concentrate on those events that align with and amplify China's position in the dispute, while actively downplaying or completely ignoring events that might potentially undermine its stance. There is a conscious and selective presentation of facts that serves to vindicate China's claims, often portraying it as the righteous actor. This narrative manipulation extends to the promotion of what the state perceives as the appropriate course of action, shaping the public perception and rallying support for the government's actions.

Testing the Theory in Twenty-One Chinese Diplomatic Crises

To determine causality, association is a prerequisite, so I begin by assessing the theory's plausibility through a medium-N congruence test using twenty-one Chinese diplomatic crises. This method requires identifying the theoretical predictors in each case and formulating expected results based on the theory. Next, I examine how well the theory's predicted results conform to the actual outcomes. While a high degree of conformity is essential to support the theory, it does not conclusively prove causality, as confounding factors could also impact the outcomes. Yet if the theory regularly fails to accurately forecast results, it is effectively falsified.[37]

Table 2.1 comprehensively categorizes all diplomatic crises pertaining to China's interstate territorial disputes since the establishment of the People's Republic of China (PRC) in 1949. A total of twenty-one crises are delineated across six unique territorial disputes. These disputes encompass borders with

Chinese Propaganda System and Media Campaigns   77

Table 2.1 Six Disputes, Twenty-One Crises, and Fourteen Media Campaigns

Dispute	Year of Crises
India, Border	<u>1959</u>, <u>1962</u>, 1967, 1986, 2013, 2014, <u>2017</u>
Soviet, Border	<u>1969</u>
Vietnam, Border	<u>1979</u>
Japan, Senkaku/Diaoyu Islands	1978, <u>1990</u>, <u>1996</u>, <u>2005</u>, <u>2010</u>, <u>2012</u>
Vietnam, South China Sea	<u>1974</u>, <u>1988</u>, 2011, 2014
Philippines, South China Sea	<u>2012</u>, <u>2016</u>

MC: Media Campaign. Crises w/ MCs are underlined.

India, the Soviet Union, and Vietnam, as well as the South China Sea disputes with Vietnam and the Philippines, and the Senkaku/Diaoyu Islands dispute with Japan. The years of the crises range from 1959 to 2017, providing a significant temporal scope for analysis.

Out of these twenty-one crises, China embarked on media campaigns in fourteen instances. The instances of media campaigns are underlined, indicating active engagement of the Chinese state in shaping the narrative and public opinion surrounding these crises. They highlight China's active and strategic use of media as part of their diplomatic approach during territorial disputes.

Interestingly, the disputes involving India and Japan have the most number of crises, and also see several instances of media campaigns. This pattern might hint toward the strategic importance of these disputes for China and the level of complexity and tension involved. In contrast, the Soviet border crisis in 1969 had only one instance, but was significant enough to prompt a media campaign.

I measure the outcome variable of the study, whether media campaigns are adopted or not, by treating Chinese official media as a proxy and tallying the number of relevant articles in *People's Daily*. As indicated in Figure 2.1, this newspaper is China's most authoritative state media outlet. It represents the mainstream official line. Historically edited by Mao Zedong, it is a standard resource for government offices, and it is essential reading for officials and Party members seeking to understand the Party's perspective on current issues. Even though the average citizen rarely reads it, other official media regularly reprint from it and rarely stray from it. As one of the most long-standing state media outlets—in existence since 1946—it offers a relatively time-consistent measurement of state media behavior in China.[38] Based on interviews with retired editors with extensive experience in China's state media system, *People's Daily* is one of the few official media that have largely retained their style and influence over time.[39]

China Central Television (CCTV) News transcripts serve as an additional metric. Unlike *People's Daily*, which primarily caters to party cadres, CCTV has a wider reach amongst the general populace. However, given that CCTV News has only been operational since 2003, it cannot provide data for almost half of the cases covered in this book, and it rarely covers China's foreign disputes. When it does cover these disputes, it typically copies the Ministry of Foreign Affairs statements or the *People's Daily* editorials. Therefore, I resort to CCTV news transcripts only as a supplementary measure for the more recent cases.

For this purpose, I collected all *People's Daily* articles spanning from 1949 to 2017. This covered all twenty-one diplomatic crises that occurred over six of China's territorial disputes. For an article to be included in the dataset, it must have a dispute as the first main subject; it would be excluded if it only mentioned the dispute in passing.[40] The final dataset comprised 7,198 articles on the border dispute with Vietnam, 446 articles on the border dispute with the Soviet Union, 1,146 articles on the border dispute with India, 58 articles on the maritime dispute with Vietnam, 272 articles on the maritime dispute with the Philippines, and 479 articles on the maritime dispute with Japan.

I then counted the number of front-page articles and all related articles for each case. Both these counts serve as crucial indicators of the scale of media coverage. This is because when a state initiates a media campaign, it attracts public attention by both the salience and the volume of the coverage. Table 2.2 presents the summary statistics of media coverage for all twenty-one cases. I have cataloged the duration of each campaign,[41] the number of front-page articles, and that of all relevant articles, along with their monthly averages.

A media campaign is identified only when the monthly number of front-page articles surpasses two, and the monthly number of all relevant articles exceeds ten. The campaign is considered ongoing until these figures fall below these thresholds for at least two consecutive months. This criterion accounts for distractions from random external events, such as holidays or natural disasters.

These seemingly arbitrary benchmarks were suggested by experienced Chinese editors and journalists, who deemed them compatible with the operations at *People's Daily*. *People's Daily* adheres to a stringent set of internal criteria concerning the number, placement, and nature of articles to be published. While these guidelines are primarily unwritten, they are deeply ingrained within the organization and are learned through practical experience

Table 2.2 Summary Statistics of Media Coverage on Twenty-One Chinese Diplomatic Crises

#	Case	MC Start	MC End	Case	MC Start	MC End	Duration (Days)	Front-Page Articles
1	Sino-India 1959	9/10/1959	11/27/1959	77	17	91	6.6	35.5
2	Sino-India 1962	6/1/1962	12/31/1963	570	346	1034	18.2	54.4
3	Sino-India 1967	9/13/1967	9/26/1967	13	0	7	0.0	16
4	Sino-Soviet 1969	3/3/1969	9/21/1969	198	56	445	2.8	67.4
5	Sino-Vietnam 1974	1/12/1974	2/18/1974	36	7	12	5.8	10
6	Sino-Japanese 1978	4/12/1978	5/11/1978	29	NG	NG	NG	NG
7	Sino-Vietnam 1979	11/5/1978	3/31/1990	4164	579	7195	4.2	51.8
8	Sino-India 1986	5/1986	8/1987	457	NG	NG	NG	NG
9	Sino-Vietnam 1988	2/23/1988	4/28/1988	65	7	10	3.2	4.6
10	Sino-Japan 1990	9/29/1990	10/30/1990	31	7	18	7	18
11	Sino-Japan 1996	7/25/1996	10/30/1996	97	12	108	3.7	33.4
12	Sino-Japan 2005	4/1/2005	6/1/2005	61	13	163	6.4	80.2
13	Sino-Japan 2010*	9/9/2010	11/6/2010	57	2	31	1.1	16.3
14	Sino-Vietnam 2011	5/26/2011	6/26/2011	31	NG	NG	NG	NG
15	Sino-Philippines 2012*	4/12/2012	6/4/2012	53	1	64	0.6	36.2
16	Sino-Japan 2012	9/3/2012	10/31/2012	58	25	137	12.9	70.9
17	Sino-India 2013	4/15/2013	5/5/2013	20	NG	NG	NG	NG
18	Sino-Vietnam 2014	5/2/2014	7/17/2014	74	0	36	0.0	14.6
19	Sino-India 2014	8/18/2014	10/1/2014	44	NG	NG	NG	NG
20	Sino-Philippines 2016	6/1/2016	8/1/2016	61	13	208	6.4	102.3
21	Sino-India 2017	6/27/2017	8/4/2017	38	2	17	1.6	13.4

MC: Media Campaign. NG: Negligible. Borderline MCs are marked with asterisks [*].

80 The Art of State Persuasion

and professional practice. As a robustness check, I adjusted these benchmarks slightly up and down, but found that the rigidity of these criteria does not impact the identification of media campaigns significantly.

Table 2.2 identifies fourteen media campaigns that meet these benchmarks (highlighted in bold). Many media campaigns are so prominent that they are hard to overlook by any standard. Examples of these include the Sino-Indian border war in 1962, the Sino-Vietnamese border war from 1979 to 1990, the Senkaku/Diaoyu Islands dispute in 2012, and the Sino-Philippines arbitration case in 2016. Most media campaigns easily meet the quantitative qualifiers and are indisputable.

However, there are four cases that come close to these benchmarks (#9, #13, #15, and #18). A more thorough examination of these four cases in Appendix 3 shows that there was indeed a media campaign during the 1988 Sino-Vietnamese clash in the Spratlys (case #9), but not in the 2014 Sino-Vietnamese Oil Rig Standoff (case #18). The 1988 campaign was a component of a larger media campaign. The specific campaign had a lower volume because the state deemed additional articles about this particular dispute unnecessary within the broader context of the war. The 2014 standoff did not result in deliberate state efforts to publicize the dispute. The state permitted a moderate level of commercial media coverage, but even without state interference, the provocative events garnered substantial media attention.

Meanwhile, the media coverage in the 2010 Sino-Japanese Boat Incident near Senkaku/Diaoyu Islands (case #13) and the 2012 Sino-Philippines Scarborough Shoal Standoff (case #15) represent true borderline media campaigns that blend media amplification with censorship. These two borderline cases are marked with asterisks in Table 2.2.

Based on the definitions of existing public opinion and state foreign policy intent laid out in the introduction, I measure the first theoretical predictor—a state's foreign policy intent—by the type of policies deliberated, motivated, or enacted. Foreign policy intent is coded as hardline if one of the following policies is deliberated, motivated, or enacted: (1) the unprovoked threat, display, or use of force; (2) the unprovoked threat or use of economic sanctions; or (3) if provoked, responses of a larger scale or higher severity. Conversely, it is coded as moderate if none of the hardline policies are deliberated, motivated, or enacted, but one or more of the following is/are: (1) compromises, (2) inaction, or (3) if provoked, responses of equal or lesser scale or severity. I measure the second predictor variable—existing public opinion—by determining whether public opinion is perceived, directly measured, or inferred to be hawkish or dovish/weak. Hawkish public opinion corresponds to a preference for a hardline policy, whereas dovish public opinion a preference for a moderate foreign policy, following the same operational definitions of hardline/moderate policy preference of the state as elaborated above.

To boost the reliability of the measurements and mitigate any subjectivity or bias from having only one person code the data, all cases were independently coded by three people (including myself) following established coding rules and qualitative case descriptions (Appendices 1 and 2). These descriptions, verified by a dozen area specialists, provided the factual foundation for the coding.

The coders came from varied disciplinary backgrounds, and aside from me, they had limited prior knowledge about the cases. Following the "fully crossed design," they were each given identical sets of coding rules and case descriptions and asked to code the cases independently during the same timeframe.[42] The level of agreement among the coders, or intercoder reliability, was then evaluated.

Fleiss's kappa, a statistical measure used for assessing intercoder reliability for more than two coders working on categorical variables, was calculated as 1 for "public opinion" and 0.84 for "state foreign policy intent," denoting perfect or near-perfect agreement among coders beyond chance. This underscores the high replicability and reliability of the results.

The inherently endogenous nature of public opinion presents challenges in its measurement. We must separate public opinion from any government-influenced media coverage related to a specific crisis, allowing us to isolate the exogenous part of an inherently endogenous variable. I try to capture the unadulterated public opinion by timing data collection to either precede or coincide with the start of a crisis, thus occurring before any orchestrated government media strategies. Additionally, I incorporate personal testimonies collected online and through direct interactions. Public opinion that diverges from or directly contests the government's advocated stance is also more likely to be independent from state influence.

As detailed in Appendix 1, I employ a triangulation strategy by identifying multiple measures and diverse data sources. Public opinion is gathered from various sources including archives, interviews, secondary resources, polls, internet search indices, protests, and social media. While such data is not always available, its reliability is heightened when multiple sources validate one another—a process referred to as "evidence piling up." Furthermore, each judgment is made independently by different coders, demonstrating near-perfect intercoder reliability. This robust process is especially reliable in certain historical events such as the 1979 Sino-Vietnamese border war, where the verdict is largely unambiguous. It is worth noting that the opaqueness of

82   The Art of State Persuasion

some territorial disputes to the general public suggests the absence of a strong public opinion or distinct policy preferences regarding the dispute.

Determining policy intent presents another challenge due to its elusive nature. Because "state foreign policy intent" pertains to *ex-ante* intentions rather than *ex-post* actions, the actual policies implemented serve only as one of the three measures. This has to be further validated by examining policy deliberation processes and motivating factors. This should resolve concerns about "revealed preferences," in which the state action does not reveal the state's true preferences, but rather reflects a concession to other pressures, including those from nationalist domestic forces. Adding to the challenge, consistent or comparable data sources are not always readily available for all measures across cases. I adopt a similar triangulation strategy detailed in Appendix 1, which involves the use of archives, interviews, historical accounts, and news reports. In the absence of access to party-state materials that include records of high-level decision-making processes or direct speech evidence from involved individuals, the task of confirming evidence relies heavily on composite analysis. This involves carefully considering a series of "straws in the wind" derived from the available information. By examining these indicators collectively, a more comprehensive understanding can be achieved. Involving multiple coders in analyzing the same set of cases further enhances the reliability of the measurements and mitigates subjectivity and bias.

Table 2.3 presents the results of the congruence test. It enumerates the predictor values, the expected outcomes derived from these predictor values—specifically, whether or not a media campaign should be anticipated—and the actual observed outcomes—whether or not a media campaign actually took place. By comparing the anticipated outcomes with the actual ones, I reach a summary judgment regarding the accuracy of the misalignment theory's predictions for each case.

Except for three cases (cases #1, #9, and #15, highlighted in bold and marked as "false" under the "theory" column), the test has demonstrated an overall consistency (18 out of 21 cases) between the predicted and actual outcomes, suggesting a consistent historical pattern. All three deviant cases, as per the misalignment theory, were predicted to have no media campaigns due to alignment between the state and the society. However, media campaigns were observed in all these instances. Appendix 4 provides a detailed examination of the three deviant cases.

Upon further scrutiny, only two of these cases truly diverge from the expected outcomes.

During the Sino-India border dispute in 1959 (case #1), the Chinese government initiated a propaganda campaign despite public alignment with its

Chinese Propaganda System and Media Campaigns   83

Table 2.3 Predicted and Actual Outcomes on Twenty-One Chinese Diplomatic Crises

No.	Case	State Foreign Policy Intent	Existing Public Opinion	Predicted Outcome	Actual Outcome	Theory
1	Sino-India 1959	Moderate	Dovish/Weak	No MC	MC	False
2	Sino-India 1962	Hardline	Dovish/Weak	MC	MC	True
3	Sino-India 1967	Moderate	Dovish/Weak	No MC	No MC	True
4	Sino-Soviet 1969	Hardline →Moderate#	Dovish/Weak	MC	MC	True
5	Sino-Vietnam 1974	Hardline	Dovish/Weak	MC	MC	True
6	Sino-Japanese 1978	Moderate	Dovish/Weak	No MC	No MC	True
7	Sino-Vietnam 1979	Hardline	Dovish/Weak	MC	MC	True
8	Sino-India 1986	Moderate	Dovish/Weak	No MC	No MC	True
9	**Sino-Vietnam 1988**	**Hardline**	**Hawkish**	**No MC**	**MC**	**False**
10	Sino-Japan 1990	Moderate	Hawkish	MC	MC	True
11	Sino-Japan 1996	Moderate	Hawkish	MC	MC	True
12	Sino-Japan 2005	Moderate	Hawkish	MC	MC	True
13	Sino-Japan 2010*	Moderate →Hardline	Hawkish	MC	MC*	True
14	Sino-Vietnam 2011	Hardline	Hawkish	No MC	No MC	True
15	**Sino-Philippines 2012***	**Hardline**	**Hawkish**	**No MC**	**MC***	**False**
16	Sino-Japan 2012	Moderate →Hardline	Hawkish	MC	MC	True
17	Sino-India 2013	Moderate	Dovish/Weak	No MC	No MC	True
18	Sino-Vietnam 2014	Moderate	Dovish/Weak	No MC	No MC	True
19	Sino-India 2014	Moderate	Dovish/Weak	No MC	No MC	True
20	Sino-Philippines 2016	Moderate	Hawkish	MC	MC	True
21	Sino-India 2017	Moderate	Hawkish	MC	MC	True

MC: Media Campaign. Deviant cases are marked in **bold**. Borderline MCs are marked with asterisks [*].

In the majority of cases, the state maintained a consistent policy intent throughout each crisis. However, three instances (cases #4, #13, and #16) saw noticeable policy shifts. These shifts were significant enough for all three coders to acknowledge and account for in their coding. Importantly, these policy adjustments were not a response to public opinion pressures but were driven by changes in the state's security circumstances. In the Sino-Soviet case of 1969, the policy shift was brought on by the Chinese government's apprehension of total annihilation under potential Soviet nuclear assault. During the China-Japan dispute in 2010, the shift was prompted by Japan's unyielding stance. Initially, Japan refused to release the detained captain, denied the existence of a dispute, made statements deviating from the long-standing shelving policy, and threatened to invoke protection under the US-Japan Security Alliance. China's stance hardened only after the anniversary of the Mukden Incident, by which time nationalist sentiment had slightly cooled and was somewhat under control. In the Sino-Japan dispute of 2012, the public outbursts, marked by numerous and widespread anti-Japanese demonstrations in China, were more of a result of the shift in governmental foreign policy rather than the cause. This is evidenced by the sequence of the public sentiment peak and the policy shift. Prior to Japan's announcement of the purchase on September 10, public sentiment was fervent but still under control. However, it escalated to full-scale violence only after Beijing responded aggressively to Tokyo's announcement. The peak of public sentiment occurred around September 18, the anniversary of the Mukden Incident, subsequent to Beijing declaring the baselines around the Islands, conducting navy and air force drills near the disputed area, and sending more surveillance ships to the region. This chronological order implies that the government policy shift stimulated and thus accounted for the rise in nationalist sentiment, rather than being propelled by it.

84 The Art of State Persuasion

policy due to India's aggressive media campaign, necessitating China's clarification of its stance. The worsening geopolitical context, including the Sino-Soviet split and Soviet's support for India, also prompted China to prepare the public for a more hostile environment. Although the implementation of a media campaign in this case appeared to contradict the (mis)alignment theory at first glance, the campaign's delayed, restrained nature and the preparation for a hostile environment, still upheld the fundamental logic of the theory.

The other two deviant cases are indeed outliers, but it is important to note that the media campaigns associated with both cases hover near the quantitative benchmarks, indicating state reservations in escalating the disputes. Further analysis provided in Appendix 4 reveals that case #9, the 1988 Sino-Vietnamese offshore clash, aligns more closely with the diversionary theory, while case #15, the Sino-Philippines Scarborough standoff in 2012, may be better explained by the audience costs theory.

Table 2.4 offers an important consolidation of the test results by summarizing the average monthly numbers of articles corresponding to the scenarios under consideration. In each quadrant of the table, two numbers are presented. The first represents the average monthly number of articles appearing on the front page of *People's Daily*, thus reflecting the prominence of the related topic. The second number signifies the average of all articles relevant to each scenario, indicative of the overall volume of media coverage.

The upper left quadrant of the table shows a situation where a hardline state policy intent coincides with dovish or weak public opinion. In this scenario, we see a high level of media coverage with an average of eight front-page articles and 37.7 relevant articles per month. The lower-right quadrant depicts a scenario where a moderate state policy intent coincides with hawkish public opinion, resulting in a similarly elevated level of media coverage with an average of six front-page articles and 52.9 relevant articles per month.

Table 2.4 Average Monthly Numbers of Front-Page Articles and of All-Relevant Articles in the Theoretical Framework

		State Policy Intent	
		Hardline	Moderate
Existing Public Opinion	Dovish/Weak	*8.0, 37.7*	*1.0, 9.7*
	Hawkish	*0.5, 18*	*6, 52.9*

The other two quadrants, where state policy intent and public opinion align, demonstrate significantly lower media coverage. In the scenario of moderate state policy intent and dovish/weak public opinion (upper right quadrant), the averages drop to one front-page article and 9.7 relevant articles per month. Likewise, when there is a hardline state policy intent and hawkish public opinion (lower-left quadrant), the averages are only 0.5 front-page articles and 18 relevant articles per month.

These comparisons clearly illustrate that scenarios of misalignment between state policy intent and existing public opinion are accompanied by significantly greater media exposure in terms of both prominence and volume. This observation strengthens the connection between misalignment and the extent of media coverage, suggesting that the state may leverage media campaigns to bring public opinion in line with policy intent, particularly in cases of misalignment.

Table 2.5 situates all twenty-one cases within the theoretical framework established by the state policy intent and the existing public opinion, from which I assess the congruence of the theoretical expectations with the actual data for each scenario.

In the lower right quadrant, where the state policy intent is moderate and public opinion is hawkish, there are seven pacification cases. Notably, all seven cases occurred in the twenty-first century and are predicted correctly. This temporal correlation suggests a stronger association between such scenarios

Table 2.5 Twenty-One Cases in the Theoretical Framework

		State Policy Intent	
		Hardline	Moderate
Existing Public Opinion	Dovish /Weak	Sino-Indian Border 1962 Sino-Soviet Border 1969 Sino-Vietnamese Paracels 1974 Sino-Vietnamese Border 1979–1991	**Sino-Indian Border 1959** Sino-Indian Border 1967 Sino-Japanese Diaoyu/Senkaku 1978 Sino-Indian Border 1986 Sino-Indian Border 2013 Sino-Vietnamese Oil Rig Crisis 2014 Sino-Indian Border 2014
	Hawkish	**Sino-Vietnamese Spratlys 1988** Sino-Vietnamese Cable-Cuttings 2011 **Sino-Philippines Scarborough Shoal 2012***	Sino-Japanese Diaoyu/Senkaku 1990 Sino-Japanese Diaoyu/Senkaku 1996 Sino-Japanese Various Dispute 2005 Sino-Japanese Diaoyu/Senkaku 2010* Sino-Japanese Diaoyu/Senkaku 2012 Sino-Philippines Arbitration 2016 Sino-Indian Border 2017

MC: Media Campaign. Deviant cases are marked in **bold**. Borderline MCs are marked with asterisks [*].

86 The Art of State Persuasion

and pacification media campaigns in recent times, confirming the time associations for pacification outlined in Chapter 1.

The upper left quadrant, where the state policy intent is hardline and public opinion is dovish or weak, houses four mobilization cases. Again, the predictions align correctly with the outcomes, and all these cases occurred before the 1990s. This supports the idea that the state was more likely to employ mobilization campaigns in the past, particularly when the public opinion was not in alignment with a hardline policy intent.

The upper right quadrant, where the state policy intent is moderate and public opinion is dovish or weak, includes seven cases with only one deviant case. This shows a high rate of accuracy for the theoretical predictions in this scenario.

However, the lower left quadrant, where the state policy intent is hardline and public opinion is hawkish, includes three cases but two are incorrectly predicted. This pattern resonates with the presumption that audience costs may have influence in this scenario, suggesting that the misalignment conditions proposed are sufficient, but not necessary—signifying a case of "equifinality" where multiple causal pathways can lead to the same outcome.[43] Meanwhile, the observed state reservations in one borderline media campaign within the hawkish—hardline scenario also underscore the existing challenges to the audience costs theory and introduce subtleties to the behavior of authoritarian states in relation to binding their own hands.

Overall, this analysis not only tests the predictive power of the theoretical framework but also highlights temporal trends and offers insights into the intricate dynamics of state policy, public opinion, and media campaigns.

The Selection of Typical Cases

While the medium-N test and its corresponding mini-case studies of the extreme cases convincingly demonstrate an association between misalignment and media campaigns, they are not adequate to confirm a causal relationship. To discover the causal paths of how misalignment motivates media campaigns and to answer the question of how these campaigns align public opinion with state policy intent, we must study in detail the typical cases.

My strategy of case selection for the detailed process-tracing in the next chapters involved selecting the most similar, corroborating cases that represent all four scenarios postulated by my theory. Specifically, I selected one case from each quadrant of Table 2.5. This approach ensures a diverse representation of the theoretical predictors. It is important to note that only conforming

Chinese Propaganda System and Media Campaigns 87

Table 2.6 Case Selection for Process Tracing

		State Policy Intent	
		Hardline	Moderate
Existing Public Opinion	Dovish /Weak	Sino-Indian Border 1962 Sino-Soviet Border 1969 Sino-Vietnamese Paracels 1974 **Sino-Vietnamese Border 1979–1991**	Sino-Indian Border 1959 Sino-Indian Border 1967 Sino-Japanese Diaoyu/Senkaku 1978 Sino-Indian Border 1986 Sino-Indian Border 2013 **Sino-Vietnamese Oil Rig Crisis 2014** Sino-Indian Border 2014
	Hawkish	Sino-Vietnamese Spratlys 1988 **Sino-Vietnamese Cable-Cuttings 2011** Sino-Philippines Scarborough Shoal 2012	Sino-Japanese Diaoyu/Senkaku 1990 Sino-Japanese Diaoyu/Senkaku 1996 Sino-Japanese Various Dispute 2005 Sino-Japanese Diaoyu/Senkaku 2010 Sino-Japanese Diaoyu/Senkaku 2012 **Sino-Philippines Arbitration 2016** Sino-Indian Border 2017

Cases selected for process-tracing are in **bold**.

cases, not outliers, are likely to clearly depict the causal logic.[44] The choice of similar cases also provides an opportunity for cross-case comparison.

Taking into account both similar dyads and similar timeframes led to the selection of the four bolded cases in Table 2.6: the Sino-Vietnamese border war in 1979–1990, the Sino-Philippine arbitration case on the South China Sea in 2016, the Sino-Vietnamese cable-cutting incidents in the South China Sea in 2011, and the Sino-Vietnamese oil rig crisis in 2014.

The four selected cases, three involving China and Vietnam and one involving China and the Philippines, might not be perfectly parallel due to different historical contexts, as three of them occurred in the 2010s and one in the 1980s, with three tied to the South China Sea dispute. However, these cases offer the most similarities available for an effective comparative study.

Countries such as India, Japan, and the Soviet Union each have unique historical relationships with China, which make their interactions and disputes quite different in nature and less comparable. The historical and geopolitical contexts in which these countries interact with China are shaped by different factors and considerations that diverge significantly from the dynamics between China and its South China Sea neighbors.

In contrast, Vietnam and the Philippines are the most comparable nations available for the purpose of this analysis. Despite the distinct historical and geopolitical circumstances of each case, they offer instructive insights into the different ways that China manages its territorial disputes and how it uses media campaigns to shape domestic and international opinion. Moreover,

88 The Art of State Persuasion

these cases occupy all four quadrants of the analysis table, offering a well-rounded perspective across different variables and outcomes. This allows for a nuanced understanding of the interplay between domestic opinion, media campaigns, and territorial disputes in the context of China's foreign policy. It also provides a foundation to evaluate and compare China's strategic approach across different temporal and situational contexts.

Notes

1. Zhonggong Zhongyang Wenxian Yanjiushi (Party Documents Research Office of the CPC Central Committee), "Zhongguo Gongchandang Hongjun Disijun Dijiuci Daibiao Dahui Jueyian (Resolution of the Chinese Communist Party the Fourth Red Army Nineth Plenary Meeting)," in *Selected Works of Mao Zedong (Mao Zedong Wenji)* (Beijing: Renmin Chubanshe (People's Publishing House), 1993), 96.
2. For comprehensive studies of the propaganda systems and techniques of the Third Reich, see David Welch, *The Third Reich: Politics and Propaganda* (New York: Routledge, 2008). For studies of the Soviet propaganda, see Martin Ebon, *The Soviet Propaganda Machine* (New York: McGraw-Hill, 1987); Alex Inkeles, *Public Opinion in Soviet Russia: A Study in Mass Persuasion* (Cambridge, MA: Harvard University Press, 2013); Peter Kenez, *The Birth of the Propaganda State: Soviet Methods of Mass Mobilization, 1917–1929* (New York: Cambridge University Press, 1985).
3. For studies of the Maoist propaganda techniques, see, for example, Julian Chang, "The Mechanics of State Propaganda: The People's Republic of China and the Soviet Union in the 1950s," ed. Timothy Cheek and Tony Saich, *New Perspectives on State Socialism in China* (Armonk, NY: M. E. Sharpe, 1997), 76–124; Franklin W. Houn, *To Change a Nation* (Charleston, SC: BiblioLife, 1961); Robert Jay Lifton, *Thought Reform and the Psychology of Totalism: A Study of "Brainwashing" in China* (Chapel Hill: University of North Carolina Press, 1961); Alan P. L. Liu, *Communications and National Integration in Communist China* (Berkeley: University of California Press, 1975); Michael Schoenhals, *Doing Things with Words in Chinese Politics: Five Studies* (Berkeley: Center for Chinese Studies, Institute of East Asian Studies, University of California, 1992); Franz Schurmann, *Ideology and Organization in Communist China* (Berkeley: University of California Press, 1971); Martin King Whyte, *Small Groups and Political Rituals in China* (Berkeley: University of California Press, 1983); Frederick T. C. Yu, *Mass Persuasion in Communist China* (Westport, CT: Praeger, 1964).
4. Maria Repnikova and Kecheng Fang, "Authoritarian Participatory Persuasion 2.0: Netizens as Thought Work Collaborators in China," *Journal of Contemporary China* 27, no. 113 (2018): 2.
5. Daniela Stockmann, *Media Commercialization and Authoritarian Rule in China* (New York: Cambridge University Press, 2013).
6. Calculated on data from the China Internet Network Information Center (CNNIC).
7. Andrew Chubb, "Propaganda, Not Policy: Explaining the PLA's 'Hawkish Faction,'" *China Brief* 13, no. 15 (2013): 6–10.

Chinese Propaganda System and Media Campaigns   89

8. Jessica C. Weiss, "Powerful Patriots: Nationalism, Diplomacy, and the Strategic Logic of Anti-Foreign Protest" (PhD diss., University of California, San Diego, 2008); Jessica C. Weiss, "Authoritarian Signaling, Mass Audiences, and Nationalist Protest in China," *International Organization* 67, no. 1 (2013): 1–35; Jessica C. Weiss, *Powerful Patriots: Nationalist Protest in China's Foreign Relations* (New York: Oxford University Press, 2014).

9. Daniel C. Lynch, *After the Propaganda State: Media, Politics, and "Thought Work" in Reformed China* (Redwood City, CA: Stanford University Press, 1999).

10. Geoffry Taubman, "A Not-So World Wide Web: The Internet, China, and the Challenges to Nondemocratic Rule," *Political Communication* 15, no. 2 (April 1, 1998): 255–72.

11. Guobin Yang, *The Power of the Internet in China: Citizen Activism Online* (New York: Columbia University Press, 2009).

12. Min Jiang, "The Co-Evolution of the Internet, (Un)Civil Society & Authoritarianism in China," in *The Internet, Social Media, and a Changing China*, ed. Jacques deLisle, Avery Goldstein, and Guobin Yang (Philadelphia: University of Pennsylvania Press, 2016), 28–48.

13. Rogier Creemers, "Cyber China: Upgrading Propaganda, Public Opinion Work and Social Management for the Twenty-First Century," *Journal of Contemporary China* 26, no. 103 (January 2, 2017): 85–100.

14. Rongbin Han, "Defending the Authoritarian Regime Online: China's 'Voluntary Fifty-Cent Army,'" *The China Quarterly* 224 (December 2015): 1006–25; Gary King, Jennifer Pan, and Margaret E. Roberts, "How the Chinese Government Fabricates Social Media Posts for Strategic Distraction, Not Engaged Argument," *American Political Science Review* 111, no. 3 (2017): 484–501; Blake Andrew Phillip Miller, "Automatic Detection of Comment Propaganda in Chinese Media," April 21, 2016, available at https://ssrn.com/abstract=2738 325 or http://dx.doi.org/10.2139/ssrn.2738325.

15. Guangchun Xu, "Jiang Zemin Xinwen Sixiang de Hexin Neirong (The Core Ideas of Jiang Zemin's Thoughts on Media)," *Xinwen Zhanxian (News Frontline)*, no. 2 (2004): 4–6. Xu was then Vice Minister of the Central Propaganda Department and head of the State Administration of Radio, Film, and Television (SARFT).

16. "Hu Jintao: Yi Chuangxin de Jingshen Jiaqiang Wangluo Wenhua Jianshe he Guanli (Hu Jintao: Strengthen Internet Culture Construction and Management with An Innovative Spirit)," Xinhua Net, January 24, 2007, https://web.archive.org/web/20100830035521/http://news.xinhuanet.com/politics/2007-01/24/content_5648188.htm.

17. "Hu Jintao: Tigao Guojia Ruanshili (Hu Jintao: Enhance the National Soft Power)," Xinhua Net, January 22, 2008, https://web.archive.org/web/20150924025229/http://www.hbnu.edu.cn/sqjlz/hjt2.htm.

18. "Hu Jintao Zongshuji Kaocha Renminribaoshe, Jiu Tigao Yulun Yindao Nengli Tichu Wudian Yijian (General Secretary Hu Jintao Visits *People's Daily* Office and Proposed 5 Points on Improving the Ability to Channel Public Opinion)," *People's Daily*, June 27, 2008, https://web.archive.org/web/20161112210338/http://media.people.com.cn/GB/40699/7433316.html.

19. David Bandurski, "Taming the Flood: How China's Leaders 'Guide' Public Opinion," *ChinaFile*, July 20, 2015, http://www.chinafile.com/reporting-opinion/media/taming-flood; Andrew Chubb, "Chinese Popular Nationalism and PRC Policy in the South China Sea" (PhD diss., University of Western Australia, 2016), 269.

90 The Art of State Persuasion

20. David Bandurski, "How Officials Can Spin the Media," China Media Project, June 19, 2010, http://chinamediaproject.org/2010/06/19/how-officials-can-spin-the-media/.

21. Anne-Marie Brady, *Marketing Dictatorship: Propaganda and Thought Work in Contemporary China* (Lanham, MD: Rowman & Littlefield, 2008). A similar argument is made in Anne-Marie Brady and Juntao Wang, "China's Strengthened New Order and the Role of Propaganda," *Journal of Contemporary China* 18, no. 62 (November 1, 2009): 767–88.

22. Stockmann, *Media Commercialization and Authoritarian Rule in China.*

23. Daniela Stockmann and Mary E. Gallagher, "Remote Control: How the Media Sustain Authoritarian Rule in China," *Comparative Political Studies* 44, no. 4 (April 1, 2011): 436–67.

24. Ashley Esarey, "Cornering the Market: State Strategies for Controlling China's Commercial Media," *Asian Perspective* 29, no. 4 (2005): 37–83.

25. Eric Harwit and Duncan Clark, "Shaping the Internet in China: Evolution of Political Control over Network Infrastructure and Content," *Asian Survey* 41, no. 3 (2001): 377–408.

26. Evgeny Morozov, *The Net Delusion: The Dark Side of Internet Freedom* (New York: PublicAffairs, 2012).

27. National Bureau of Statistics of China, *China Statistical Yearbook 2016* (Beijing: China Statistics Press, 2016). For comprehensive studies on the organizational structure of the Chinese propaganda system, see Brady, *Marketing Dictatorship*; David Shambaugh, "China's Propaganda System: Institutions, Processes and Efficacy," *The China Journal*, no. 57 (2007): 25–58.

28. "Xi Jinping Asks for 'Absolute Loyalty' from Chinese State Media," Associated Press, February 19, 2016, https://www.theguardian.com/world/2016/feb/19/xi-jinping-tours-chinas-top-state-media-outlets-to-boost-loyalty.

29. TV coverage data is from National Bureau of Statistics of China, *China Statistical Yearbook 2016*. Internet penetration rate is from CNNIC 2016.

30. Shambaugh, "China's Propaganda System," 54.

31. Brady, *Marketing Dictatorship*, 19.

32. These directives are available at https://goo.gl/6edxde, accessed February 22, 2018.

33. Some of these categories are borrowed from and explained in more detail in Jonathan Henry Hassid, "Pressing Back: The Struggle for Control over China's Journalists" (PhD diss., University of California, Berkeley, 2010), 8–10.

34. Brady, *Marketing Dictatorship*, 110; Esarey, "Cornering the Market."

35. Brady has a section examining the legal regulations as a means of control in China. See Brady, *Marketing Dictatorship*, 104–8.

36. Rachel E. Stern and Jonathan Hassid, "Amplifying Silence: Uncertainty and Control Parables in Contemporary China," *Comparative Political Studies* 45, no. 10 (October 1, 2012): 1230–54.

37. Alexander L. George and Andrew Bennett, *Case Studies and Theory Development in the Social Sciences* (Cambridge, MA: MIT Press, 2005), 181.

38. Michel Oksenberg and Gail Henderson, *Research Guide to People's Daily Editorials, 1949–1975* (Ann Arbor: University of Michigan Press, 2020).

39. Author interviews, May 2017, Beijing.

40. Based on this criterion, I conducted a search using the key words of the six disputes and manually filtered out articles in which a dispute was mentioned but not as the main subject.

41. Or the duration of the crisis if a campaign is not observed.
42. Kevin A. Hallgren, "Computing Inter-Rater Reliability for Observational Data: An Overview and Tutorial," *Tutorials in Quantitative Methods for Psychology* 8, no. 1 (2012): 23–34.
43. Alexander L. George and Andrew Bennett, *Case Studies and Theory Development in the Social Sciences* (Cambridge, MA: MIT Press, 2005), 157.
44. The 2011 Sino-Vietnamese cable-cutting incidents is the only conforming case in the hawkish public opinion—hardline state foreign policy quadrant, so it is imperative look into this case and why it conforms to the (mis)alignment theory. If established, although it does not necessarily "defeat" the alternative theories, it can show that the alignment logic is still possible under these conditions.

3

The Sino-Vietnamese Border War

A Media Campaign to Mobilize

> If there is something big to happen, there must first be propaganda. Public opinion must be made before opening fire. This is the importance of propaganda—it mobilizes people's hearts and wins their support.
>
> **—author's interview to a retired journalist who reported on the Sino-Vietnamese border war[1]**

> Why have we delayed the attack? . . . We want to create public opinion . . . Our repeated toleration will enable everyone to know the aggressiveness of the Cuba in the East. Only through such exposure can we . . . educate the people . . . and strengthen the morale of the broad masses of our officers and men. At a suitable time, we may launch fierce attacks and win a sweeping victory over our enemies.
>
> **—in a leaked report by Geng Biao, a Chinese Politburo member and the then Secretary General of the Central Military Commission (CMC), addressing to an enlarged Politburo meeting on January 16, 1979, one month before the outbreak of the war[2]**

The Sino-Vietnamese border war in 1979–1990 is the last war China has fought to date. It was catalyzed by specific problems along the Sino-Vietnamese border, but these local tensions were inextricably tied to global Cold War dynamics and the Sino-Soviet split. The conflict subsided following the end of the Cold War and the collapse of the Soviet Union, yet its reverberations carried significant implications for the balance of power worldwide. This case is intertwined with several historical events of note: the exodus of Chinese Vietnamese in 1978–1979, the establishment of a security alliance between Vietnam and the Soviet Union, the normalization of Sino-US relations, and

The Art of State Persuasion. Frances Yaping Wang, Oxford University Press. © Oxford University Press 2024.
DOI: 10.1093/oso/9780197757505.003.0004

Vietnam's invasion of Cambodia. Also prominent was the extensive propaganda campaign orchestrated by the Chinese government.

This chapter reviews this campaign in depth, utilizing historical facts to test one scenario of the (mis)alignment theory and its competing theories.[3] This case study focuses on the period from the deterioration of the Sino-Vietnamese relationship, beginning in 1975, up to the outbreak of the war on February 17, 1979. While the war encompassed issues beyond the border dispute, this study will concentrate on the territorial conflict, integrating additional aspects of the war as required within this context.

The Break of the Relationship and the Break of the War

The Sino-Vietnamese relationship began to sour in the mid-1970s, even before the Vietnam War ended on April 30, 1975. A multitude of issues contributed to the escalating tension: Vietnam's choice of sides in the Sino-Soviet split; regional competition between China and Vietnam; Vietnam's invasion of Cambodia; Vietnam's maltreatment of ethnic Chinese residents; and border conflicts. These issues culminated in China's attack of Vietnam in February 1979, sparking a conflict that dragged on for the next ten years.

The conflict was partially triggered by territorial disputes, but it was also steeped in other sources of disagreement. Historians often point to the Sino-Soviet split as a key, geopolitical catalyst. The Soviets could exploit Vietnam to widen their influence in Southeast Asia and counter China from the south, an eventuality that stirred fears of encirclement in China. For a long time, Vietnam sought to maintain a policy of neutrality to avoid upsetting either party, but this approach did not sit well with the Chinese. Internally, the Vietnamese leadership was also divided. As the pro-Soviet faction led by Le Duan gained momentum, and with other external developments such as China's secret rapprochement with the US, maintaining a balancing act became increasingly challenging for Hanoi. Hanoi considered China's rapprochement with the US a betrayal, suspecting that Beijing had negotiated a US troop withdrawal from Taiwan at the price of "press[ing] Hanoi to accept a compromise solution with the United States."[4] Vietnam Prime Minister Pham Van Dong asked Mao to cancel the planned Nixon trip in November 1971, but was refused.[5] As evidenced by a classified Vietnamese document obtained by China in 1979, Hanoi had already come to regard China as an enemy following Nixon's visit in 1972.[6]

As a result, Hanoi increasingly leaned toward the Soviets. Vietnamese archives indicate that, from late 1975 onward, Vietnam secretly began to foster military alignment with the Soviet Union. "On 30 December 1975, with an urgent request from the Ministry of Defense, Pham Van Dong agreed to send a military delegation to bring 'secret documents' of the Ministry of Defense to Moscow and to maintain total secrecy as they traveled through China." The secret documents were lists of military supplies Hanoi requested from Moscow.[7]

On June 28, 1978, Vietnam joined the Council for Mutual Economic Assistance, an economic alliance system led by the Soviet Union to counter the Western Bloc's Marshall Plan. The value of Soviet military aid to Vietnam increased tenfold, from $75–$125 million US dollars in 1977 to $600–$800 million US dollars in 1978.[8] On November 3, 1978, Hanoi signed a military treaty with Moscow, thereby eliminating any lingering doubts in Beijing regarding the formal military alliance between Vietnam and the Soviet Union.

The regional competition between China and Vietnam in Southeast Asia, particularly Vietnam's rapid expansion of influence into Laos and Cambodia, was a significant factor that catalyzed the Chinese attack in 1979. The inclusion of Laos into Vietnam's sphere of influence was confirmed in February 1976, shortly after the establishment of the Lao People's Democratic Republic. In July 1977, the two countries signed a twenty-five-year Treaty of Friendship and Cooperation, which explicitly defined their relationship a "special relationship."[9] The Treaty allowed for the continued presence of Vietnamese troops in Laos, preferential trade terms for Vietnam, and gave Vietnam permission to participate in the Laotian propaganda machinery—essentially transforming Laos into a satellite state of Vietnam.

On its southern borders, Vietnam saw Cambodia's anti-Vietnamese Khmer Rouge regime as its most imminent threat, while China sustained and even increased its support to the Khmer Rouge. From Hanoi's perspective, Vietnam also feared an encirclement by China and Cambodia, and complained about Beijing's "big-nation expansionist and great-power hegemonistic ambitions toward our country and other countries in the region."[10] With Soviet backing, Vietnam launched a full-scale invasion of Cambodia on Christmas Day in 1978. In January 1979, Vietnam occupied Cambodia and replaced the Khmer Rouge government with a puppet government.

Another source of tension was the treatment of ethnic Chinese residents by the Vietnamese authorities. In February 1976, Vietnamese officials initiated citizen registration programs in the South.[11] These programs forced ethnic Chinese to adopt Vietnamese citizenship or leave the country, despite many having resided in Vietnam for decades, or even generations. In early 1977, Vietnam implemented a "purification" policy in the border areas and ostracized border residents to the Chinese side.[12] In March 1978, Hanoi released a "socialization" decree, which triggered the mass exodus of "large and unmanageable numbers" of Chinese people to Southern China.[13] From August 8 to September 26 of 1978, Beijing and Hanoi conducted negotiations over the issue, but failed to make any progress due to deeply rooted disagreements. By early 1979, the total number of Chinese people expelled from Vietnam had swelled to as many as 280,000.[14]

The Sino-Vietnamese land border spans 1,347 kilometers, adjoining two Chinese provinces—Guangxi and Yunnan—and seven Vietnamese provinces, specifically, Dien Bien, Lai Chau, Lao Cai, Ha Giang, Cao Bang, Lang Son, and Quang Ninh. One hundred and sixty-four locations along this border were disputed, representing a total contested area of 227 square kilometers.[15] Due to the absence of clear demarcation, local Vietnamese and Chinese authorities resorted to retaliatory land grabbing and violence.[16] The number of border skirmishes escalated year after year, from 125 incidents in 1974, to 423 in 1975, 926 in 1976, 1,940 in 1977, and 2,175 in 1978.[17] Initially, Beijing and Hanoi sought peaceful negotiations to address the dispute. However, these negotiations broke down and became platforms for accusations. The second round of negotiations in August 1978 coincided with one of the most severe border conflicts—the Youyi (Friendship) Pass incident, which essentially doomed the negotiations. In this incident, the Vietnamese army and police forcibly expelled 2,500 refugees across the border, beat and stabbed many refugees and "nine Chinese civilian border workers" whom the Vietnamese claimed to be "Chinese soldiers 'in civilian clothing.'"[18] The Vietnamese subsequently occupied the Pu Nian Ling area, a territory claimed by China.[19]

By the summer of 1978, the Sino-Vietnamese relationship had visibly deteriorated across all aspects—rhetoric, diplomacy, economic assistance, and military strategy. The leadership of both countries not only publicly aired their disagreements but did so with vitriolic language. In a speech delivered on Vietnamese National Day in September 1978, Pham Van Dong denounced China's "dark and perfidious scheme" of "enticing, coercing and organizing tens of thousands of Hoa [Chinese] people in Viet Nam to leave for China," so that China could accuse Vietnam of "ostracizing, persecuting and expelling" these people. Regarding the border dispute, he stated, "They organized all kinds of people to cross the border illegally, they used armed forces to encroach upon our border, used military aircraft to violate our air space, and naval crafts to encroach upon Viet Nam's territorial waters, and built fortifications and concentrated their armed forces directed against Viet Nam."[20] Equally, Chinese leader Deng Xiaoping made no effort to conceal his hostility toward Vietnam. As remembered by a Thai diplomat at a diplomatic event in July 1978, "the moment the topic of Vietnam came up, one could see

96   The Art of State Persuasion

something change in Deng Xiaoping. His hatred [for the Vietnamese] was just visceral." "He spat forcefully into this spittoon and called the Vietnamese 'dogs.'"[21]

Diplomatic relations were significantly downgraded. In June 1978, Beijing rescinded the appointment of a consul-general to Ho Chi Minh City and instructed Hanoi to close down three of its consulates-general in China.[22] The economic relationship also took a major hit. By the end of July, China had suspended all aid programs to Vietnam and recalled all its experts.[23] The General Political Bureau of the Vietnamese People's Army released orders on July 8 to adopt an "offensive strategy" against China and to "attack and counterattack within and beyond the border." Two weeks later, the Vietnamese Communist Party's Fourth Plenary Session labeled China as Vietnam's "most direct and dangerous enemy" and a "new combat target," calling for "doing everything to defeat China."[24] The session "passed a resolution alleging China's hegemonic ambition to annex Vietnam." It also reached a decision to send people abroad to carry out anti-China activities in other Southeast Asian countries.[25] From September 28 to 30, the Vietnamese army conducted a military exercise with China as an imaginary opposing force.[26]

On December 8, 1978, the Chinese Central Military Commission (CMC) ordered the Guangzhou and Kunming Military Regions to ready themselves for military action against Vietnam by January 10, 1979.[27] On December 25, the Guangxi–Vietnamese border was closed as troops arrived nearby.[28] On December 30, "the Vietnam Army chief of staff held an emergency meeting . . . [predicted] there will be major conflicts at the border . . . [they] put the Northern Regional Force on an emergency war alert."[29] At a February 11 CCP Politburo expanded session that further discussed the military campaign, Beijing issued orders to Guangxi and Yunnan military commands to launch the attack on February 17.[30] On February 14, 1979, the CCP Central Committee issued a notice to party organizations of the provinces, military regions, and government ministries, announcing and justifying the attack. The committee requested that the information be disseminated to party cadres at all levels and, essentially, to all Chinese citizens.[31] It amounted to a war announcement. A military campaign was launched three days later.

An Existing Dovish/Weak Public Opinion

Before 1978, the Chinese public had little knowledge about the border dispute, let alone strong feelings about it. The Sino-Vietnamese relationship used to be one intimately characterized by Mao Zedong and Ho Chi Minh as "comrade plus brother." In 1963, Chinese vice chairman Liu Shaoqi described the relationship as follows: "Our friendship has a long history. It is a militant friendship, forged in the storm of revolution, a great class friendship that is proletarian internationalist in character, a friendship that is indestructible."[32]

During the 1970s, a time predating the digital age, the only sources of news for the Chinese people were the official media outlets firmly in the government's grip. Prior to the emergence of the border dispute in 1973, the official media consistently propagated the notion of a fraternal relationship between China and Vietnam, emphasizing the unwavering support of the Chinese people for Vietnam's struggle for independence. Even as border skirmishes increased to 926 in 1976, *People's Daily* made no mention of them, and the Chinese people were kept in the dark.[33]

The Chinese domestic political and economic context even fueled some resistance to the war. The year 1978 marks the beginning of economic reform and opening up. After a decade of political turmoil in the Cultural Revolution, the public sentiment was ripe for economic development and rehabilitation. "The newly adopted economic reform and opening-up policy brought great hope for a return to normalcy and increasing prosperity."[34] People feared that a war might disrupt it. Xiaoming Zhang's work draws observations on the public opinion specifically in the border provinces of Guangxi and Yunnan leading up to the war:

> Public opinion in these two provinces was pessimistic about Beijing's war decision. The local communities had undergone much hardship in the Cultural Revolution and had made considerable sacrifices for the Vietnamese war effort . . . these areas remained socially and economically backward. Nevertheless, citizens there hoped that economic reform—now the highest national priority—would bring peace, development, and better standards of living. The people and local governments in these two provinces seemed unenthusiastic about the Chinese attack on Vietnam and feared that the military action would conflict with the economic development agenda.[35]

The refugee issue burdened the border provinces the most. According to the *History of Yunnan Province*, a total of 35,342 Chinese refugees from Vietnam were displaced and resettled in Yunnan by late 1980.[36] With the outbreak of a war on the border, these provinces would have to allocate more resources to handle the situation, potentially resulting in an even larger influx of refugees.

Lack of enthusiasm for the war, or even resistance to it, was especially prevalent among soldiers. Even after mobilization and deployment orders were issued in December 1978, many soldiers were not sure "whether the military campaign was righteous or not, active or passive, invasion or counterattack."[37] They did not understand why "we support Vietnam in the past but punish it today."[38] A retired government official attests in an interview that "voicing opposition against the war, some offspring of government officials even used their personal connections to flee the military."[39]

Historical works generally confirm this lack of enthusiasm toward the war in the People's Liberation Army (PLA) and the public.[40] Andrew Scobell notes the "mixed views of the public" and the "varying opinions" of the intellectuals. Foreign correspondents picked up on the lack of enthusiasm for the war and intellectuals freely voiced this sentiment.[41] During a visit to Kunming in August 1979, even after the war had broken out, Nayan Chanda noted a remarkable sense of apathy among the population toward an exhibition showcasing China's proclaimed "counterattack in self-defense" victory.[42]

A Hardline State Policy Intent

Despite the dovish/weak public opinion, the Chinese government became increasingly determined to "teach Vietnam a lesson." To be clear, China acted with restraint at the start of the refugee issue and the border dispute, as was evident not only in its internal deliberations but also in its efforts to negotiate. The meeting between Pham Van Dong and Li Xiannian in June 1977 was probably the last honest exchange between the top leaderships, who sought to overhaul and shore up the deteriorating relationship. However, that meeting also signaled a change in the relationship: the two sides started to shed the pretense of cordiality and talked candidly, even acrimoniously, about their problems. In the meeting, Li Xiannian handed a written memorandum to Dong with a litany of complaints about Vietnam's anti-China policy.

In the memo, Li cited Vietnam's anti-China rhetoric; increased tension at the border; its obstruction of a railroad maintenance on the Chinese side of the border; the maritime dispute over the Paracels, the Spratlys and the Gulf of Tonkin; and its mistreatment of ethnic Chinese in Vietnam.[43] In the Vietnamese archives that record Dong and Li's subsequent unscripted discussion, Pham discredited his earlier recognition of China's sovereignty over the Paracels and explained that the 1958 recognition was made only under the pressure of the war against the US.[44]

The conversation yielded no progress. In fact, during Le Duan's last Beijing visit in November 1977, just a few months after the Li-Dong talk, Duan acted as though the conversation had never happened. Duan sought additional

Chinese aid, praised the brotherly Sino-Vietnamese relationship as usual, and completely ignored the problems Li had raised to Dong.[45]

Following the failure of the second round of border negotiations, Deputy Premier Li Xiannian conveyed to personnel on October 1 that "the dispute had gone beyond possible conciliation and that the situation would not be helped even if China were 'to cede' its two border provinces to Vietnam."[46] As the situation continued to deteriorate, China adopted a more aggressive stance in the summer of 1978. In May of that year, China conducted provocative overflights of the border area and the Gulf of Tonkin, sometimes penetrating into Vietnamese airspace. This escalated response was a direct reaction to the border clashes, indicating Beijing's readiness to heighten tensions as early as May. In contrast, Hanoi attempted to contain the dispute at the ground level, refraining from issuing a protest until July 10, and the Vietnamese air force did not respond with their own fighters until September 14.[47]

Additionally, according to a Central Intelligence Agency (CIA) analysis, "as a result of the killing of Chinese and signs of an imminent invasion of Kampuchea," China started an "open fire" policy on the border between December 13 and 23 1978, which permitted border personnel to "open fire, not only in retaliation, but on sight of Vietnamese personnel," as well as to "initiate aggressive, forward patrolling up to and beyond Vietnamese border defense posts." China also began deploying People's Liberation Army (PLA) units, transforming the clashes from minor skirmishes to more significant military engagements along the border.[48]

In September, the General Staff of the PLA convened for the first time to contrive a war plan against Vietnam.[49] The meeting was convened under the theme of "how to counter Vietnam's encroachment on Chinese territory." At the meeting, the key PLA personnel involved in the decision-making were informed of the atrocities the Vietnamese authorities had committed against the ethnic Chinese, and of Vietnam's continuous military deployment on the border. They reached a consensus about launching a military campaign against Vietnam but could not agree on the scale of the attack. The goal of the military campaign was determined to be punitive, but also coercive; namely, to force Vietnam's retreat from Cambodia, to stop the border encroachment, and to check Vietnam's and hence the Soviet Union's regional ambition in Southeast Asia. Chanda estimates that the Chinese decision was made even earlier: "A Peking official revealed to me that during one of its regular weekly meetings in early July 1978, the Chinese Politburo decided to 'teach Vietnam a lesson' for its 'ungrateful and arrogant' behavior."[50]

China's intention to undertake a significant military action against Vietnam, with potential international repercussions, can be inferred from Deng

Xiaoping's diplomatic maneuvers between September and February, just prior to the launch of the attack. Deng engaged in a series of foreign visits, commencing with North Korea from September 8 to 13, followed by Japan from October 22 to 29, and Thailand, Malaysia, and Singapore from November 5 to 14. He then embarked on a historic visit to the United States from January 29 to February 5 before returning to Japan shortly before the attack. These visits served, at least in part, to gauge world opinion on the Vietnam issue, and test the waters to gain support for the planned Chinese attack.

The international landscape provided a conducive backdrop for China's decision to launch an attack on Vietnam. Vietnam's growing alignment with the Soviet Union, which was China's principal external threat at the time, culminated in the formal Vietnam-Soviet alliance in November 1978. Additionally, Vietnam's occupation of Cambodia in December 1978 further heightened the geopolitical threat to China from the south.

In an effort to break the encirclement by the Soviet Union, China pursued the normalization of its relationships with the United States and Japan. During Deng Xiaoping's visit to the United States prior to the attack, President Jimmy Carter did not explicitly endorse the idea of an attack but also did not strongly object to it. Later documents suggest that the United States shared intelligence with China, with the then CIA Deputy Director Robert Gates recalling in his memoir that Carter and Deng had reached an agreement for technical intelligence cooperation against the Soviet Union.[51] Furthermore, according to accounts in the book *About Face*, Zbigniew Brzezinski, then National Security Advisor, met with Chinese ambassador Chai Zemin daily during the Chinese attack, turning over American intelligence on Soviet military deployments at the Sino-Soviet border.[52]

While the United States attempted to avoid being seen as a collaborator in the Chinese attack, it did seek to deter potential Soviet intervention through private channels. In a special coordination meeting attended by high-level US officials, the meeting suggested the need to consider the option of informing Moscow, "if the Soviets appear to be moving toward acquiring Cam Ranh Bay for a naval base," that "their action could lead to our reconsideration of our position that we would not enter into a security relationship with the People's Republic of China."[53]

China's eventual hardline policy was hardly debated. The 1979 campaign was a massive military operation, involving 17 Chinese armies comprising a total of 220,000 troops.[54] According to Vietnamese sources, "Beijing fielded almost 600,000 regular troops including 11 army corps and many unattached divisions, about 700 aircraft of various kinds, almost 600 tanks and armored vehicles, and thousands of artillery pieces."[55] The battle extended deeply into the northern part of Vietnam. Despite the eventual withdrawal, it was an operation on a foreign country's soil. Despite the claimed Vietnamese provocations, the scale of the Chinese so-called counterattack was viewed as disproportionate.

A Massive Mobilization Campaign

Once China embarked on the path of war, it became essential to mobilize public support due to the prevalent lack of enthusiasm among the population. Beijing had three key reasons for mobilizing public support during the war. First, for a large-scale conflict like the 1979 attack, which occurred as the country was emerging from the tumultuous Cultural Revolution and grappling with a struggling economy, China required human and material resources from its citizens, particularly those residing in the bordering provinces. The local communities in Guangxi and Yunnan played a crucial role in providing the PLA with personnel in the form of militiamen and women, as well as logistical support such as food and housing. For instance, Longzhou County in Guangxi organized 10,700 militiamen and women to support the PLA, while Maguan County in Yunnan mobilized 25,000 individuals for the same purpose.[56] These militia members carried out a range of vital tasks, including transportation of food and supplies, construction of roads, bridges, and trenches, and tending to the wounded, among other responsibilities. Their contributions were integral to the war effort.

Second, Beijing required public support to maintain regime legitimacy. The previous failures of the ultraleft Cultural Revolution, Mao Zedong's passing, and the introduction of a market-based economic system had all contributed to ideological confusion and a decline in regime legitimacy based on Communist ideology. Therefore, Beijing needed the people's backing for a significant foreign policy decision like never before. By rallying public support for the war, the Chinese government aimed to strengthen its legitimacy and bolster its standing among the population amidst the ideological and economic transitions taking place in the country.

Finally, Beijing sought the people's support for the war to counter opposition pressure from within the Party. The conflict had the potential to significantly disrupt the ongoing reform agenda and China's economic development, which were top national priorities at the time. Without popular support, the potential costs and consequences of the war could be exploited by opposition forces within the Party. This could pose a threat to regime security and hinder the progress of the reform initiatives. Therefore, garnering public support for the war was crucial for Beijing to fend off internal opposition and ensure the continuity of its reform and development agenda.

Chinese leaders were deeply concerned about the lack of public enthusiasm and dovish sentiment regarding the war. This apprehension is highlighted in an interview with a retired government official, who revealed that the Chinese leadership was particularly worried that the public might not fully comprehend the drastic shift in policy.[57]

These concerns were also evident in the internal political guidelines circulated within Party organs and the PLA. There were worries about public opinion, especially regarding soldiers' morale, and the potential lack of certainty among the public about the justifiability of the war. The target of the attack had previously been seen as a "comrade plus brother," adding to the challenges of swift public opinion transition. Moreover, the fact that the conflict took place on foreign territory raised concerns that the public, including soldiers, might struggle to justify such military action.[58]

Furthermore, some soldiers, even those already deployed to the border, might have viewed the Chinese government's threats of punishment and military deployment as mere bluffing. "The focus of our work has changed to the four modernizations, [so we] don't want to fight a war; our American and Japanese friends do not support a war either because they want to do business with us."[59]

Lastly, concerns were raised about the lack of confidence among the public, as well as the soldiers, regarding the prospects of victory. Vietnamese forces had been engaged in warfare for nearly three decades, and their officers possessed significant battlefield experience. In contrast, Chinese troops had not participated in a war for over twenty years, and commanders at battalion level and below lacked any battlefield experience at all. These factors contributed to the overall concerns about public perception, soldiers' morale, and the potential challenges associated with the war.[60]

In fact, the concern over dovish/weak public opinion was so significant that it played a crucial role in the Chinese leaders' decision to postpone the attack until February. This can be seen in a leaked report addressing an expanded Politburo meeting in January 1979, where Central Military Commission (CMC) General Secretary Geng Biao emphasized the importance of preparing public opinion for the war. While Geng Biao acknowledged the significance of world opinion, he specifically highlighted the need to "strengthen the morale of the board masses of our officers and men." He stated, "we want to create public opinion. Our repeated toleration will enable everyone to know the aggressiveness of the Cuba in the East. Only through such exposure can we . . . educate the people."[61]

As a result, Beijing launched an aggressive mobilization campaign aimed at shifting the dovish/weak public opinion to align with its hardline foreign policy intentions. The rhetoric employed by the Chinese government took a noticeably negative turn against Vietnam starting from late May 1978. At first, coverage primarily addressed the Chinese refugee issue. The first refugee article in *People's Daily* appeared on May 27, 1978 on the front page, with the title "The Chinese Government to Send Ships to Pick up the Overseas Chinese Persecuted by the Vietnamese Authorities."[62] This seemingly ordinary article marked a significant departure from the previous consistently positive portrayals of Vietnam in Chinese state media. It brought the China–Vietnam rift into the open, indicating a fundamental shift in the media's approach toward Vietnam.

In a September 1978 speech on the occasion of the National Day of the Socialist Republic of Vietnam, Pham Van Dong accused Beijing of deliberately stoking an "anti-Vietnam psychosis" among the Chinese people. He claimed that Beijing had fabricated absurd stories of Vietnam ostracizing the Chinese diaspora and opposing China.[63] This indicates the increasing hostility and propaganda war between the two countries as Beijing sought to shape public opinion against Vietnam and build support for its aggressive stance.

As the refugee issue, particularly the expulsion of Chinese residents at the border, became intertwined with the border dispute, the media rhetoric began to address the border dispute more explicitly. The first article specifically focusing on the border dispute was published on August 15, 1978, with the headline "Director of the Department of Asian Affairs at Chinese Ministry of Foreign Affairs Summoned Vietnamese Representative in Beijing and Strongly Protested against the Invasion of Yunnan Border by Armed Vietnamese Police."[64] This article marked a significant shift in the media's coverage, highlighting the Chinese government's official protest against the incursion of armed Vietnamese police into the Yunnan border region. It further signaled the escalation of tension and the explicit framing of the conflict in the media discourse.

Starting in November 1978, the Chinese government initiated an extensive media campaign against Vietnam. The structure of this campaign closely aligns with the observable implications of a mobilization campaign, as outlined in Chapter 1.

This campaign lasted for over a decade and totaled 7,195 *People's Daily* articles, including 579 front-page articles, averaging at 51.8 articles and 4.2 front-page articles a month. Figure 3.1 illustrates the monthly numbers of relevant

104 The Art of State Persuasion

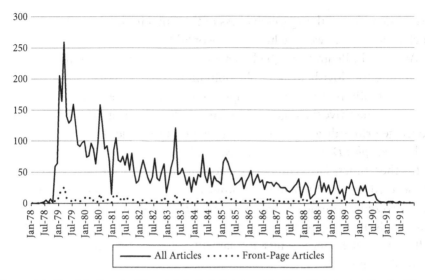

Figure 3.1 Monthly Count of *People's Daily* Articles on the Sino-Vietnamese Border War during 1978–1991

articles in *People's Daily* on the dispute. The solid line follows the count of all relevant articles and the dotted line the count of front-page articles. As the graph demonstrates, media reports picked up dramatically in November 1978 and peaked in March 1979. The campaign, despite ups and downs that likely track the occurrence of other major events, was sustained over a decade and gradually tapered off by 1990.

These numbers are remarkable considering the public's short attention span on matters that affect only a minority of people on a daily basis. The sustained and extensive media coverage observed in this case, spanning over a decade, strongly suggests a concerted effort by the state. It indicates that the Chinese government actively prioritized shaping public opinion and maintaining a consistent narrative throughout the Sino-Vietnamese border war. Such a focused and persistent media campaign would require substantial resources and coordination, highlighting the significance the government placed on influencing public perception and garnering support for its actions.

During the war preparation, the Department of Propaganda, *People's Daily* top editorial staff, and the General Political Department of the PLA were all closely involved, and they issued guidelines to their subordinates for political mobilization. A retired propaganda official confirms that the CCP Central Committee issued propaganda guidelines as soon as the refugee issue emerged in the summer of 1978. They continued to monitor the situation and issued more directives throughout the war.[65] These policy directives included general guidelines on "exposing the Vietnamese crimes against Chinese citizens and border residents, on educating the people about the swollen regional ambitions of Vietnam and its brazen invasion of Cambodia, as well as the socialist-imperialist 'anti-China' scheme of the Soviets behind the Sino-Vietnamese problems." The various propaganda organs at the Central Propaganda Department (CPD), the PLA, and state media outlets also had specific guidelines on weekly themes to follow, how much each issue should be reported, where they should appear, and what arguments the articles should make.[66] As the war went on, the propaganda efforts continued. "In 1985, the CCP's propaganda department and the PLA's political department intensified the campaign by sending war heroes and model soldiers selected from the entire armed forces to lecture around the country."[67]

Besides influencing the general public, the political apparatus also ran full steam to mobilize local communities and soldiers. The propaganda departments of the CCP in Guangxi and Yunnan provinces compiled extensive lists of alleged crimes committed by Vietnam against the Chinese people. These lists were then distributed to city, district, county, and subdistrict party organizations, with instructions to use the information to educate and galvanize the local population, fostering a sense of patriotism in support of the war effort. Guangxi Autonomous Region, for instance, organized over 530 mass meetings with a combined attendance of 263,400 individuals.[68] Meanwhile, the CCP committee of Yunnan Province issued a mobilization order that called upon local communities to "do all for the front and do all for victory."[69] These actions reflect the comprehensive nature of the mobilization campaign, as the political apparatus sought to rally support for the war among local communities and soldiers.

Within the PLA, mobilization efforts took various forms, including denunciation meetings, the establishment of role models and hero figures, and exhibits and lectures featuring soldiers, villagers from border areas, and Chinese refugees from Vietnam. These activities aimed to inspire and rally the troops, instilling a sense of purpose and commitment to the war. One PLA political work guideline disclosed that due to time constraints, mobilization efforts were conducted on the move during the deployment itself.[70] This indicates the urgency and significance attached to garnering support and maintaining morale among the soldiers. Additionally, the publication of several volumes by the PLA's Political Department, detailing their experiences in mobilizing the soldiers, serves as further evidence of the extensive mobilization process.[71]

These orders provided a clear outline of the three primary objectives for war preparation education during the Sino-Vietnamese border war:

1. *Clarifying the fundamental changes in the Sino-Vietnamese relationship*: The political work aimed to educate the people about the shift in the nature of the Sino-Vietnamese relationship. It emphasized portraying Vietnam as a puppet of Soviet revisionists, a "Cuba in the East," an Asian "hooligan," and a sinister enemy of China. The objective was to explain why China had previously supported Vietnam's independence cause but now needed to punish it. The political work aimed to convey that China's counterattack was an act of self-defense and that the war was just.

2. *Highlighting the relationship between punishing Vietnam and the four modernizations*: The political work was intended to clarify the connection between punishing Vietnam and China's goals of achieving the four modernizations. It aimed to emphasize that the war would not hinder the progress of China's modernization efforts. On the contrary, the aggression by Vietnam posed a significant threat to China's socialist modernization. Therefore, a severe punishment of Vietnam was deemed necessary to safeguard and advance China's modernization goals.

3. *Strengthening the troops' confidence in victory*: The political work focused on bolstering the soldiers' confidence in their ability to win the war. It aimed to educate them about China's advantages and strengths in the conflict. By emphasizing these advantages, the goal was to instill a sense of determination, resilience, and belief among the troops that victory could be achieved.[72]

The media content focused on arousing public animosity toward Vietnam. The themes ranged from accusing Vietnam of brutal treatment of the ethnic Chinese, recalling the sacrifice the Chinese people made for Vietnam and condemning the "ingratitude" of the Vietnamese by "returning good with evil," reminding the public of their frequent "infringement" on Chinese territory and their expansionist ambitions and invasion of Cambodia, and accusing them of "colluding" with Soviet revisionists and "slandering" China. All of these inflammatory themes aimed to rally public support for a hardline policy.

On the first theme, China openly condemned Vietnam's policy of "purifying the border areas" in the provinces adjacent to China and its "discrimination against, and ostracism, persecution and expulsion of, Chinese residents."[73] In a protest lodged by the Chinese Vice Foreign Minister on August 25, 1978 and a statement issued by the Overseas Chinese Affairs Office of the PRC State

Council on September 4, China strongly denounced the "bloody oppression" and "outrageous massacre" of Chinese nationals by Vietnamese authorities.[74] When reporting on the refugee issue, *People's Daily* articles used strong words such as "extremely cruel," "inhuman," "dehumanizing," "barbaric," and "blood sucking." An article called Vietnam's massive expulsion of Chinese nationals a "beggar-thy-neighbor" policy that even surpassed in scale and brutality the Jewish persecution in the Holocaust.[75] They spared no details when describing the living conditions of the refugees:

> Inhumane and appalling. The Vietnamese authorities ... forc[ed] large numbers of people to be displaced. Many people were unable to survive after being deprived of their production and living materials. Some committed suicide, and some were forced to flee Vietnam and became 'refugees.' After causing this kind of human tragedy, the Vietnamese authorities used the 'refugees' as money cows, not only extorting gold from them, but also driving them to wooden ships and dilapidated cargo ships that could not sail safely, leaving them hungry and cold in the stormy sea. Resigned to fate, many people were buried under the sea.[76]

The second theme recalled the sacrifice the Chinese people had made for Vietnam and condemned Vietnam's "ingratitude." *People's Daily* articles such as "Treachery and Biting the Hand That Feeds Him," "Prince Sihanouk Condemned Vietnam for Ungratefulness in Cairo," "A Snake in Our Bosom?" elaborated the hard work, frugality, and great sacrifices the Chinese people had made in order to aid the Vietnamese people in the past three decades.[77] A front-page article on February 17, 1979 told stories of how a hospital on the Sino-Vietnamese border, which had saved many Vietnamese soldiers and civilians in the past, now became the target of the Vietnamese army, trying to rescue the many Chinese who were injured by their fire; a Chinese Vietnamese elderly recalling how her neighbors saved up rice by eating yuca to aid the Vietnamese people and the irony that the very Vietnamese young soldiers who grew up on this rice aid were now expelling Chinese people, using weapons donated also by the Chinese. A war hero who had aided the Vietnamese in their independence fight against the French and Americans had a son who was now an amputee because of Vietnamese fire.[78] These descriptions and narratives were undoubtedly intended to evoke strong emotions and provoke a sense of outrage among ordinary Chinese citizens.

A third theme focused on Vietnam's frequent "infringement" on Chinese soil. At least 8 percent of all relevant articles were predominantly focused on the border conflict. Out of the total of 7,195 articles, 598 titles contained the key word "invade" or "border."[79] As is typical in mobilization campaigns, the media reports on border conflicts elevated the public awareness of the dispute, invoked emotions of injustice, victimhood, and hatred toward Vietnam, and justified the use of aggressive force. Media highlighted the lost territory and atrocities committed by the Vietnamese invaders, painted the Vietnamese invasion, which occurred after repeatedly ignoring Chinese warnings, as a provocative and reckless disturbance to economic development and regional peace. Thus, the Chinese use of force was self-defensive and just.

A fourth theme revealed Vietnam's regional ambition and closely tracked Vietnam's invasion of Cambodia and Thailand. This was often combined with a fifth theme—the Soviet Union's backing of Vietnam's expansion in Southeast Asia and its use of Vietnam as an outpost in the region. Articles portrayed Vietnam as a Soviet minion, often in mocking tones. On November 10, 1978, *People's Daily* published a front-page editorial titled "What Are the Vietnamese Authorities Up To?" In this article, Beijing pointed out that Vietnam's escalating provocations on the refugee and the border issue with China was consistent with the Soviet Union's global expansion policy. The article accused Vietnam of practicing regional hegemonism as the Soviet Union's "lapdog" and revealed its ambition to occupy Cambodia and extend its influence deeper into Southeast Asia. "When Vietnam invaded Cambodia, the Soviet Union offered advice, created public opinion, and provided it with a large number of weapons and consultants."[80] In another article Beijing warned that Vietnam's creation of the puppet organization "Kampuchean United Front for National Salvation" was "a signal for a larger-scale armed aggression against Cambodia that was yet to come" and "a new step toward regional hegemony."[81] After Vietnam's launch of a full-scale invasion of Cambodia on December 25, 1978 and the fall of Phnom Penh on January 7, 1979, Beijing published another article titled "Who Is the Next?," further extending its argument that Cambodia was only the beginning and characterizing "Vietnam's regional hegemonists" as "extremely vicious, lunatic, and opportunist."[82] When condemning the Vietnam-Soviet collusion, Deng Xiaoping warned that the military alliance "threatens world peace and security."[83]

The last theme aimed to expose Vietnam's "lies" and "slandering" of China. This was a countereffort against Vietnam's media campaign. China's propaganda machine chastised Vietnam for standing facts on their head. In articles such as "Who Were the Invaders and Who Opened Fire?" "A Thief Calling 'Stop Thief,'" "A Lie Performance," "Bizarre Rumors," and "Let's See Who Sabotaged the China-Vietnam Railway," Beijing tried to refute Vietnamese accusations on a number of confrontations and put all the blame on Vietnam. In an editorial "Our Forbearance Is Limited," Beijing pointed out that Hanoi used its small size to win sympathy from the world—"the Vietnamese authorities bullied China in such a way"—but still pretended to be the one getting bullied. "The Vietnamese propaganda machine keeps saying that Vietnam is a small country and cannot afford to provoke China; it suffered much tormenting when accepting China's aid; even occupying China's South China Sea islands was 'submitting to humiliation.'"[84]

This media campaign confirms the observable implications of a mobilization campaign listed in Chapter 1. First, the media concentrated on negative framing—they criticized, condemned, highlighted damages, and issued warnings. All of the above six themes involved strident accusations, although from different angles. Some positive framing focused on the heroic acts of soldiers and patriotism of civilians. After the war began, articles glorified the war efforts by providing stories of heroic soldiers, militiamen and women, and Vietnamese people who had had positive experiences with Chinese troops; nevertheless, negative rhetoric still dominated the pages.

Second, the media aimed at intensifying emotions of anger, hatred, injustice, and betrayal. As we saw with the refugee theme, the ingratitude theme, and the border dispute theme, the media were good at using personal experiences, graphic language, and bloody images to vividly describe the cruel crimes committed by Vietnamese authorities. In exposing Vietnam's expansionist ambitions, the articles often cited arrogant remarks of the Vietnamese soldiers, such as "Phnom Penh has fallen. Aren't you afraid?" or "We will soon advance to Dongxing (a town in Guangxi) to have breakfast there."[85] In an order issued on February 12, 1979, the CMC and the PLA General Political Department stipulated that the main task of political work was to "incite hatred towards the Vietnamese revisionists, and continuously encourage the troop's fighting mood." "The focus of the war preparation education is to expose and condemn the crimes of the Vietnamese revisionists . . . [arouse] hatred, despise and disdain towards the Vietnamese revisionists."[86]

Aside from newspaper articles the Chinese propaganda resorted to other forms of media to arouse the public's emotions. Literature works such as Li Cunbao's *Gaoshan xia de huahuan* (*Wreaths of Flowers at the Foot of the Mountains*, 1982), later adapted into a movie, extolled the heroic acts of the soldiers and incited patriotism among the public. Other movies did the same, such as *Leichang xiangsishu* (*The Lives They Left Behind*, 1988), and *Changpaishan zhi zhan* (*The Battle of Changpaishan*, 1981), as well as songs, such as *Shiwu de yueliang* (The Moon on the Fifteenth, 1984), and *Xueran de fengcai* (The Blood-Stained Valor, 1987). Some of these became popular favorites. *The Moon on the Fifteenth*, for example, is about a soldier's warm thoughts of his wife and family at home, which sets a positive tone for the defense of family at the border. The song "The Blood-Stained Valor" commemorates soldiers who lost their lives in the war, and to whom the country will always owe a debt. These works personalized and humanized patriotic themes. A retired journalist recalls, "when a college-student-turned solider Xu Liang, who lost a leg in the war, was invited to the CCTV annual Chinese New Year gala to sing the song 'The Blood-Stained Valor,' it brought many people to tears."[87]

Third, China threatened substantive punishment. Chinese threats escalated gradually, from modest statements that Hanoi should not mistake Beijing's restraint as "weakness and submissiveness,"[88] to "sternly" worded warnings that Hanoi should retreat from Chinese territory and not "turn a deaf ear to China's warnings,"[89] to "China's forbearance has limits,"[90] to China will "certainly counterattack if attacked" and Vietnam will "meet the punishment it deserves,"[91] to "we mean what we say" and Hanoi must be taught "some necessary lessons,"[92] and, finally, to China has been "driven beyond forbearance" and "forced to counterattack."[93]

Fourth, the Chinese rhetoric encouraged action. In a front-page article, "Lawless aggression must be stopped," Beijing called on the Chinese people "not to be indifferent to the brutal invasion of brotherly Cambodia." China should "continue to provide various forms of assistance to the Cambodian people," and "this is an unshirkable proletarian internationalist duty of the Chinese people."[94] In a front-page article on the day of the Chinese attack, Beijing demanded that "the people of the whole country must unite more closely around the Party Central Committee . . . increase production, work hard, heighten vigilance, strengthen combat readiness, maintain social order."[95]

Fifth, although the state did not try to ignore the cost of the war, the media emphasized that the counterattack was "just." It stressed the "disruption to the normal life and production" at the border as a result of the Vietnamese incursions and argued that the Chinese counterattack was "necessary."[96]

An Alternative Explanation of Diversion?

Building on the theoretical discussion in Chapter 1, the diversionary theory presents an alternative explanation for the dovish/weak public opinion— hardline state foreign policy intent scenario. Can the media campaign in this case be justified through a diversionary explanation?

Recalling the observable implications of a diversionary explanation discussed in Chapter 1, the only conceivable crisis concerned Deng's reemergence in the Party and his power struggle with the then CCP chairman

Hua Guofeng. After the fall of the Gang of Four, Hua upheld many of Mao's ideologies and policies. On February 7, 1977, in a joint editorial published by *People's Daily*, the *Journal of Red Flag*, and the *PLA Daily*, Hua articulated the slogan of the "Two Whatevers": "We will resolutely uphold whatever policy decisions Chairman Mao made, and unswervingly follow whatever instructions Chairman Mao gave."[97] Deng Xiaoping denounced the "Two Whatevers" as being contrary to the essence of Marxism, even before his complete rehabilitation.[98] Deng was reinstated in July 1977 at the Third Plenum of the Tenth Party Congress, where he regained his positions as the vice chairman of the CCP, vice premier, vice chairman of the CMC, and the PLA general chief of staff. His views on ideology and China's future development diverged significantly from those of Hua. Deng pushed for the reinstatement of party officials who had been victimized in the Cultural Revolution, including Chen Yun, Deng Yingchao, Hu Yaobang, Wang Zhen, and posthumously, Liu Shaoqi. On May 11, 1978, *Guangming Daily* published a front-page editorial titled "Practice Is the Sole Criterion of Testing Truth."[99] This article implicitly criticized Hua's "Two Whatevers," and Deng explicitly endorsed it at the All-Army Political Work Conference the next month. Deng emphasized that Marxist theory should not be regarded as "lifeless dogma," and quoted Mao's own method of "seeking truth from facts," insisting that "only through practice can the correctness of one's ideas be proved, and there is no other way of testing truth."[100] Consistent with his ideological stance, Deng advocated for employing western capitalist elements to the four modernizations, and the reform and open policy as the focus of future work.

Due to the coincidence of the decision to attack Vietnam and the Deng-Hua power struggle, some might argue that Deng Xiaoping utilized the propaganda and the war as a diversion from the power struggle and as a means to garner support for a domestic economic program. However, the timing and nature of the Deng-Hua power struggle contradict the logic of a diversionary war explanation. A diversionary argument in this context is flawed in at least three ways. First, the power struggle was not a public crisis that required distraction—it was more of a private contest for power. The ideological debate that peaked in the summer of 1978 was more public, but it did not threaten the regime, and hence, did not necessitate diversion of public attention.

Second, by November 1978, three months before the war, Deng had already gained the upper hand in the power struggle. Scholars regard Hua's toast at the National Day reception on September 30 as a clear indication of his decision to withdraw. In his toast, Hua reiterated Deng's stance by stating that "we must emancipate our minds," which echoed Deng's position on the "emancipation of the minds."[101] The Central Work Conference in November 1978 endorsed not only Deng's dominant role in the leadership and the policy of reform and openness, but also the decision to attack Vietnam. The Third Plenum of the Eleventh Party Congress validated these three decisions the following month. Therefore, Deng did not need a war to divert public attention from a struggle he had already won, and crucial war preparations continued even after Deng's consolidation of power.

Third, regarding the rallying support for a domestic economic program argument, economic reform detracted from, rather than prompted, a war decision. As mentioned earlier, many people were concerned that a war might distract from China's reform efforts, and hence were opposed to it. Even Deng himself was worried that the war might hinder and delay China's process of economic modernization.[102] He specifically consulted with Chen Yun, a member of the Politburo and vice chairman of the CCP, who later played a pivotal role in promoting economic reform, to weigh the advantages and disadvantages of the attack.[103]

Conclusion

The 1979–1990 Sino-Vietnamese border war and its accompanying propaganda campaign has proven to be an archetypical mobilization case. The misalignment between apathetic public opinion before the war and hardline state policy intent called for the state to launch the most aggressive and long-lasting propaganda campaign in modern Chinese history. The propaganda campaign was pivotal in agitating the general public, local communities in the border provinces, and soldiers toward support for the war, dedicating labor, resources, and even lives. A wealth of historical evidence substantiates the observable implications related to the leaders' concerns about weak public opinion. Clear and authoritative propaganda directives and mobilizing orders, and broadly inflammatory media content aimed at inciting public sentiment, border residents, and soldiers against Vietnam.

Notes

1. Author interview, June 8, 2017, Beijing.
2. Biao Geng, "Geng Blao's Report on the Situation of the Indochinese Peninsula," *Journal of Contemporary Asia* 11, no. 3 (January 1, 1981): 390. "Cuba in the East" is a name Chinese leaders had given Vietnam since the relationship soured.
3. The case has received limited attention from a handful of Cold War historians and has not been extensively explored within the field of political science. In the 2000s and 2010s,

a number of historical studies emerged due to newly available Russian, Chinese, and Vietnamese archives following the collapse of the Soviet Union. However, these scholars have not reached a consensus on the causes of the war. Several other aspects of the case, such as the involvement of the United States and the precise timing of China's decision to engage in the war, remain subjects of debate or unresolved due to insufficient evidence. For historical studies of the case, see Nayan Chanda, *Brother Enemy: The War after the War* (New York: Collier Books, 1986); King C. Chen, *China's War with Vietnam, 1979: Issues, Decisions, and Implications* (Stanford, CA: Hoover Institution Press, 1987); William J. Duiker, *China and Vietnam: The Roots of Conflict*, vol. 1 (Berkeley: Institute of East Asian Studies, 1986); Steven J. Hood, *Dragons Entangled: Indochina and the China-Vietnam War* (Armonk, NY: M. E. Sharpe, 1993); Robert S. Ross, *The Indochina Tangle: China's Vietnam Policy, 1975–1979* (New York: Columbia University Press, 1988).

4. Christopher Goscha, *Vietnam: A New History* (New York: Basic Books, 2016); Nicholas Khoo, *Collateral Damage: Sino-Soviet Rivalry and the Termination of the Sino-Vietnamese Alliance* (New York: Columbia University Press, 2011).

5. Qiang Zhai, *China and the Vietnam Wars, 1950–1975* (Chapel Hill: University of North Carolina Press, 2000), 114. Quoting Seymour Hersh, *The Price of Power: Kissinger in the Nixon White House* (New York: Simon & Schuster, 2013), 442. "Hersh's account was based on his interview with North Vietnamese deputy foreign minister Nguyen Co Thach in Hanoi in August 1979. Thach had been present with Pham Van Dong in Beijing in November 1971."

6. "Tiezheng Rushan, Qirong Dilai: Bei Wo Jiaohuo de Liangfen Yuejun Wenjian Baolu Yuenan Dangju Qinjian Fanhua Zhenxiang (Ironclad Evidence—Two Seized Vietnamese Documents Exposed the Truth about Vietnam's Invasion of Cambodia and Anti-China Scheme)," *People's Daily*, March 31, 1979, 5.

7. Kosal Path, "Sino-Vietnamese Relations, 1950–1978: From Cooperation to Conflict" (PhD diss., University of Southern California, 2008), 299. Quoting Vice Minister of Defense Tran Sam's letter (Number 551/QP) to the Prime Minister's Office on 26 December 1975, titled "Send Officials to Work in the Soviet Union," in the Ministry of Defense, "Document on Defense Cooperation with China for 1976," National Archives No. 3, Collection of the Prime Minister's Office, Folder 10090, 1.

8. Khoo, *Collateral Damage*, 113.

9. Alexander Woodside, "Nationalism and Poverty in the Breakdown of Sino-Vietnamese Relations," *Pacific Affairs* 52, no. 3 (1979): 7.

10. "Speech made by Pham Van Dong," September 5, 1978, History and Public Policy Program Digital Archive, S-0442-0365-03, United Nations Archives and Records Management Section. Obtained for CWIHP by Charles Kraus, http://digitalarchive.wilsoncenter.org/document/118418, accessed July 11, 2023.

11. Jiaxuan Tang, *Zhongguo Waijiao Cidian (The Chinese Dictionary of Diplomacy)* (Beijing: Shijie Zhishi Chubanshe (World Affairs Press), 2000), 421.

12. Ibid.

13. "Research Paper Prepared in the National Foreign Assessment Center, Central Intelligence Agency: The Sino-Vietnamese Border Dispute," Carter Library, National Security Affairs, Staff Material, Far East, Oksenberg Subject File, Box 49, Mondale 8/79 China trip: Briefing Material: 3/78–8/79, Top Secret; also see Ming Guo, ed., *ZhongYue Guanxi Yanbian*

114   The Art of State Persuasion

Sishinian (Forty-Year Evolution of the Sino-Vietnamese Relations) (Nanning: Guangxi Renmin Chubanshe (Guangxi People's Publishing House), 1992), 117.

14. Tang, *Zhongguo Waijiao Cidian (The Chinese Dictionary of Diplomacy)*, 117.

15. Jiazhong Li, "ZhongYue Bianjie Tanpan Pianduan Huiyi (Recollection of the Sino-Vietnamese Border Negotiation)," *Zhonggong Dangshi Ziliao (CCP History Material)*, no. 1 (2005): 58.

16. Path, "Sino-Vietnamese Relations, 1950–1978," 304–5.

17. Li Min, *ZhongYue Zhanzheng Shinian (Ten Years of the Sino-Vietnamese War)* (Chengdu: Sichuan Daxue Chubanshe (Sichuan University Press), 1993), 2; Brantly Womack, *China and Vietnam: The Politics of Asymmetry* (New York: Cambridge University Press, 2006), 199. According to Womack, the 1978 number of 2,175 was reported by Vietnam; the number report by China that year was 1,108.

18. Deli Zhou, *Yige Gaoji Canmouzhang de Zishu (Personal Recollections of a High-Ranking Chief of Staff)* (Nanjing: Nanjing Chubanshe (Nanjing Publishing House), 1992), 240–42. Also see "Research Paper Prepared in the National Foreign Assessment Center, Central Intelligence Agency."

19. Zhou, *Yige Gaoji Canmouzhang de Zishu (Personal Recollections of a High-Ranking Chief of Staff)*, 240–42.

20. "Speech made by Pham Van Dong."

21. Chanda, *Brother Enemy*, 261.

22. "Notes of the Ministry of Foreign Affairs of the People's Republic of China to the Ministry of Foreign Affairs of the Socialist Republic of Viet Nam," July 24, 1978, History and Public Policy Program Digital Archive, S-0442-0365-03, United Nations Archives and Records Management Section. Obtained for CWIHP by Charles Kraus, http://digitalarchive.wilsoncenter.org/document/118417, accessed July 11, 2023.

23. "Zhongguo Zhengfu Zhaohui Yuenan Zhengfu, Wo Beipo Tingzhi dui Yue Jingji Jishu Yuanzhu Diaohui Gongcheng Jishu Renyuan (The Chinese Government Delivered a Diplomatic Note to the Vietnamese Government; We Are Forced to Stop Our Economic and Technology Aid to Vietnam and to Recall Our Engineers and Technicians)," *People's Daily*, July 4, 1978, 1; Path, "Sino-Vietnamese Relations, 1950–1978," 355.

24. Nianlong Han, ed., *Dangdai Zhongguo Waijiao (Contemporary China's Diplomacy)* (Beijing: Shehui Kexue Chubanshe (China Social Sciences Press), 1987), 285–86. Also see Deli Zhou, *Xu Shiyou de Zuihou Yizhan (The Last Battle of Xu Shiyou)* (Nanjing: Jiangsu Renmin Chubanshe (Jiangsu People's Publishing House), 1990), 30; Van Hoan Hoang, "YueZhong Zhandou de Youyi Shishi Burong Waiqu (The Reality of the Sino-Vietnamese Friendship in Fighting Ought Not to Be Distorted)," in *Selected Works of Hoang Van Hoan* (Beijing: Renmin Chubanshe (People's Publishing House), 1988), 11.

25. Hoang, "YueZhong Zhandou de Youyi Shishi Burong Waiqu (The Reality of the Sino-Vietnamese Friendship in Fighting Ought Not to Be Distorted)," 11.

26. Chengdu Military Region Intelligence Department, *YueNan Junshi Dashi Ji (Vietnam Military Affairs Timeline)* (Beijing: Junshi Yiwen Chubanshe (Military Translation Work Press)), 1990, 123, For Internal Use. Obtained from a historian, who wishes to stay anonymous.

27. Zhou, *Yige Gaoji Canmouzhang de Zishu (Personal Recollections of a High-Ranking Chief of Staff)*, 246; also see Min, *ZhongYue Zhanzheng Shinian (Ten Years of the Sino-Vietnamese War)*, 18.

The Sino-Vietnamese Border War   115

28. Zhou, *Yige Gaoji Canmouzhang de Zishu (Personal Recollections of a High-Ranking Chief of Staff)*, 269–71.
29. Chengdu Military Region Intelligence Department, *YueNan Junshi Da Shi Ji (Vietnam Military Affairs Timeline)*, 125.
30. Junlun Zhou, ed., *Nie Rongzhen Nianpu (Chronicles of Nie Rongzhen)* (Beijing: Renmin Chubanshe (People's Publishing House), 1999), 1147; Feng Jiang, Xiaochun Ma, and Yishan Dou, *Yangyong Jiangjun Zhuan (Biography of General Yang Yong)* (Beijing: Jiefangjun Chubanshe (People's Liberation Army Publishing House), 1991), 496–97.
31. For content of the notice, see Min, *ZhongYue Zhanzheng Shinian (Ten Years of the Sino-Vietnamese War)*, 34.
32. Cited in Khoo, *Collateral Damage*, 201.
33. Min, *ZhongYue Zhanzheng Shinian (Ten Years of the Sino-Vietnamese War)*, 2.
34. Xiaoming Zhang, *Deng Xiaoping's Long War: The Military Conflict Between China and Vietnam, 1979–1991* (Chapel Hill: University of North Carolina Press, 2015), 40.
35. Ibid., 85.
36. Yunnan Province Foreign Affairs Office, *Yunnan Province History: Foreign Affairs History*, 53 vols. (Kunming: Yunnan Renmin Chubanshe (Yunnan People's Publishing House), 1996), 149.
37. Political Teaching Office of PLA Nanjing Advanced Infantry School, *ZhongYue Bianjing Ziwei Huanji Zuozhan Zhengzhi Gongzuo Jingyan Xuanbian (Selected Experiences of Political Work during the Counterattack in Self-Defense on the Sino-Vietnamese Border)* (Nanjing: Nanjing Junqu Gaoji Bubing Xuexiao (Guangzhou Military Region Advanced Infantry School), 1979), 7.
38. General Office of the General Political Department, *ZhongYue Bianjing Ziwei Huanji Zuozhan Zhengzhi Gongzuo Jingyan Xuanbian (Compilation of Experiences of Political Work during the Counterattack in Self-Defense on the Sino-Vietnamese Border)*, vol. 1 (Beijing: Zhongguo Renmin Jiefangjun Zongzhengzhibu Bangongting (Chinese Liberation Army General Political Department, 1980), 7.
39. Author interview, June 2017, Beijing.
40. Zhang, *Deng Xiaoping's Long War*, 67; Chanda, *Brother Enemy*; Andrew Scobell, *China's Use of Military Force: Beyond the Great Wall and the Long March* (New York: Cambridge University Press, 2003), 140.
41. Scobell, *China's Use of Military Force*, 140.
42. Chanda, *Brother Enemy*, 361.
43. "1977 Nian 6 Yue 10 Ri Li Xiannian Fu Zongli tong Pham Van Dong Zongli Tanhua Beiwanglu (Memorandum of the Meeting between Vice Premier Li Xiannian and Prime Minister Pham Van Dong on June 10, 1977)," *People's Daily*, March 23, 1979, 1. This Chinese version, published in *People's Daily* after the break of the war, is a written memo Li Xiannian read to Pham Van Dong at the beginning of their meeting. The Vietnamese version, kept in No. 3 Archives in Hanoi, has rich detail on the conversation between the two that ensued. See "Minutes of the meeting between Prime Minister Pham Van Dong and Vice Premier Li Xiannian in Beijing on 10 June 1977," National Archives No. 3, Collection of the Prime Minister's Office, Folder 10460.
44. "Minutes of the meeting between Prime Minister Pham Van Dong and Vice Premier Li Xiannian in Beijing on 10 June 1977."
45. Zhang, *Deng Xiaoping's Long War*, 37.

116 The Art of State Persuasion

46. Zhou, *Yige Gaoji Canmouzhang de Zishu (Personal Recollections of a High-Ranking Chief of Staff)*, 240–42.

47. "Research Paper Prepared in the National Foreign Assessment Center, Central Intelligence Agency."

48. Ibid.

49. For details of the meeting, see Zhou, *Yige Gaoji Canmouzhang de Zishu (Personal Recollections of a High-Ranking Chief of Staff)*, 239–43.

50. Chanda, *Brother Enemy*, 261.

51. Robert M. Gates, *Duty: Memoirs of a Secretary at War* (New York: Vintage, 2015), 413.

52. James Mann, *About Face: A History of America's Curious Relationship with China, from Nixon to Clinton* (Washington, DC: National Geographic Books, 2000), 100.

53. "Summary of Conclusions of a Special Coordination Committee Meeting," Washington, DC, February 19, 1979, Carter Library, National Security Affairs, Staff Material, Office, Meetings File, Box 14, Folder 20, SCC Meeting #141 Held 2/19/79, 2/79, Secret.

54. Min, *ZhongYue Zhanzheng Shinian (Ten Years of the Sino-Vietnamese War)*, 19.

55. Truong-Chinh, "The Vietnamese People Are Determined to Defeat Any Aggressive Schemes of Chinese Expansionism and Hegemonism," *Nhan Dan*, February 17, 1982. Truong-Chinh was a member of the Communist Party of Vietnam (CPV) Politburo and president of the Council of State. The piece was published on the third anniversary of the attack.

56. General Office of the General Political Department, *ZhongYue Bianjing Ziwei Huanji Zuozhan Zhengzhi Gongzuo Jingyan Xuanbian (Compilation of Experiences of Political Work during the Counterattack in Self-Defense on the Sino-Vietnamese Border)*, 249, 257.

57. Author interview, June 2017, Beijing.

58. Political Teaching Office of PLA Guangzhou Military Region Infantry School, *ZhongYue Bianjing Ziwei Fanji Zuozhan Zhengzhi Gongzuo Ziliao (Selected Materials on Political Work during the Counterattack in Self-Defense on the Sino-Vietnamese Border)* (Guangzhou: Guangzhou Junqu Gaoji Bubing Xuexiao (Guangzhou Military Region Advanced Infantry School), 1979), 6.

59. Ibid., 5.

60. Ibid., 7.

61. Geng, "Geng Biao's Report on the Situation of the Indochinese Peninsula," 390.

62. "Wo Guo Zhengfu Jueding Pai Chuan Qianwang Yuenan, Jieyun bei Yue Dangju Pohai de Huaqiao Huiguo (The Chinese government has decided to dispatch ships to Vietnam to evacuate overseas Chinese who have been harmed by the Vietnamese authorities)," *People's Daily*, May 27, 1978, 1.

63. "Speech made by Pham Van Dong."

64. "Wo Waijiaobu Yazhousi Fuzeren Yuejian Yue Zhuhua Shiguan Daibiao, Qianglie Kangyi Yuenan Wuzhuang Gong'an Ruqin Wo Yunnan Bianjing (The head of the Asian Affairs Department of our Ministry of Foreign Affairs met with representatives of the Vietnamese Embassy in China, strongly protesting against the intrusion of Vietnamese armed police into our Yunnan border)," *People's Daily*, August 15, 1978, 5.

65. Author interview, June 2017, Beijing.

66. Ibid.

67. Zhang, *Deng Xiaoping's Long War*, 174.

68. Ibid., 86. Citing from Local History Compilation Committee of Guangxi Zhuang Autonomous Region, ed., *Guangxi Tongzhi Junshi Zhi (General History of Guangxi: Military History)* (Nanning: Guangxi Renmin Chubanshe (Guangxi People's Publishing House), 1994), 322.

69. Zhang, *Deng Xiaoping's Long War*, 86. Citing from War Preparation and Aid-the-Front Leading Group of Yunnan Province, and Propaganda Department of the Chinese Communist Party Committee of Yunnan Province, eds., *Yingxiong de Fengbei: Yunnan Renmin Shinian Zhiqian Jishi (Heroic Monument: True Record of the Ten-Year Aid-the-Front Work by the Yunnan People)* (Kunming: Yunnan Renmin Chubanshe (Yunnan People's Publishing House), 1991), 531.

70. General Office of the General Political Department, *ZhongYue Bianjing Ziwei Huanji Zuozhan Zhengzhi Gongzuo Jingyan Xuanbian (Compilation of Experiences of Political Work during the Counterattack in Self-Defense on the Sino-Vietnamese Border)*, 1:6.

71. Ibid.

72. Ibid., 7.

73. "Statement of the Ministry of Foreign Affairs of the People's Republic of China on the Expulsion of Chinese Residents by Viet Nam," June 12, 1978, History and Public Policy Program Digital Archive, S-0442-0365-01, United Nations Archives and Records Management Section. Obtained for CWIHP by Charles Kraus. http://digitalarchive.wilsoncenter.org/document/118404, accessed July 11, 2023. The statement was sent to the United Nations on June 19, 1978 and circulated as an official document of the United Nations at the request of China.

74. "Chinese Protests against Vietnam," September 7, 1978, History and Public Policy Program Digital Archive, S-0442-0365-03, United Nations Archives and Records Management Section. Obtained for CWIHP by Charles Kraus. https://digitalarchive.wilsoncenter.org/document/118419, accessed July 11, 2023.

75. "Zhizhi Yuenan Dangju Yilinweihe de Fandong Zhengce (Stop the Vietnamese Authorities' Reactionary 'Beggar-Thy-Neighbor' Policy)," *People's Daily*, January 20, 1979, 5.

76. "Miejue Renxing de Yeman Zuixing (Barbaric Crimes Devoid of Humanity)," *People's Daily*, November 28, 1978, 5.

77. "Beixinqiyi, Enjiangchoubao (Treachery and Biting the Hand That Feeds Him)," *People's Daily*, January 10, 1979, 5; "Xihanuke Qinwang zai Kailuo Qianze Yuenan Wang'enfuyi (Prince Sihanouk Condemned Vietnam for Ungratefulness in Cairo)," *People's Daily*, July 29, 1984, 6; "Enjiangchoubao hu? (A Snake in Our Bosom?)," *People's Daily*, December 25, 1985, 6.

78. "Shi Ke Ren, Shu Bu Ke Ren (If This Can Be Tolerated, What Cannot?)," *People's Daily*, February 17, 1979, 1.

79. Titles that contain "Cambodia" or "Thailand" were excluded because Vietnam's invasion into Cambodia and later into Thailand were also relevant events to the 1979 war. This estimate, although conservative, provides a glimpse into the extent of media coverage on the border dispute. However, it is important to note that there were likely numerous additional articles that addressed the subject in their content but did not explicitly include the key words in their titles.

80. "Yuenan Dangju Xiang Gan Shenme? (What Are the Vietnamese Authorities Up To?)" *People's Daily*, November 10, 1978, 1.

118 The Art of State Persuasion

81. "Jingti Yuenan Tuixing Quyu Baquanzhuyi de Xin Buzhou (Be Vigilant About Vietnam's New Step in Promoting Regional Hegemony)," *People's Daily*, December 8, 1978, 5.

82. "Xia Yige Lundao Shui (Who Is the Next Next?)," *People's Daily*, January 17, 1979, 6.

83. "Deng Fuzongli zai Jizhe Zhaodaihui shang Zhichu, Su Yue Tiaoyue Weixie Shijie Heping yu Anquan (Vice Premier Deng Pointed Out at a Press Conference That the Vietnam-Soviet Treaty Threatens World Peace and Order)," *People's Daily*, November 9, 1978, 1.

84. "Women de Rennai Shi You Xiandu de (Our Forbearance Is Limited)," *People's Daily*, December 25, 1978, 3.

85. "Shi Ke Ren, Shu Bu Ke Ren (If This Can Be Tolerated, What Cannot?)"

86. Ibid.

87. Author interview, June 2017, Beijing.

88. "Wo Waijiaobu Zhaohui Yuenan Zhuhua Dashiguan, Qianglie Kangyi Yue Dangju Zhizao Yanzhong Liuxue Shijian (The PRC MoFA Sends a Note the Vietnamese Embassy in China and Strongly Protest the Extremely Serious Bloodshed Incident Caused by the Vietnamese Authorities)," *People's Daily*, November 8, 1978, 1.

89. "Yuenan Dangju Xiang Gan Shenme? (What Are the Vietnamese Authorities Up To?)"

90. This wording first appeared in Chinese Vice Premier Li Xiannian's remarks when he was meeting Thai delegates on December 13, 1978. See "Li Xiannian Fu Zongli Huijian Taiguo Qian Waizhang Chacuo Shi Zhichu, Women dui Yuenan Dangju Tiaoxin de Rennai Shi You Xiandu de (Vice Premier Li Xiannian Met with Former Thai Foreign Minister Chatichai Choonhavan and Pointed Out That Our Forbearance to the Vietnamese Provocations Is Limited)," *People's Daily*, December 14, 1978, 4. It was adopted by an official MoFA statement on the same day and later used as article title in the *People's Daily* editorial "Our Forbearance Is Limited."

91. "Women de Rennai Shi You Xiandu de (Our Forbearance Is Limited)."

92. "Oral Message from Chinese Vice Premier Deng Xiaoping to President Carter," Washington, DC, undated. Carter Library, National Security Affairs, Staff Material, Office, Outside the System File, Box 47, China: Sino-Vietnamese Conflict, Heads of State Exchanges: 2/79, Secret.

93. "Shi Ke Ren, Shu Bu Ke Ren (If This Can Be Tolerated, What Cannot?)" These escalation of warnings are also elaborated in Paul H. Godwin and Alice L. Miller, "China's Forbearance Has Limits: Chinese Threat and Retaliation Signaling and Its Implications for a Sino-American Military Confrontation," China Strategic Perspectives (Center for the Study of Chinese Military Affairs, Institute for National Strategic Studies, 2013).

94. "Bixu Zhizhi Wufawutian de Qinlue (Lawless Aggression Must Be Stopped)," *People's Daily*, January 7, 1979, 1.

95. "Fenqi Huanji, Baowei Bianjiang (Stand Up and Fight Back to Defend the Frontier)," *People's Daily*, February 18, 1979, 1.

96. "Jinggao Yuenan Dangju (A Warning to the Vietnamese Authorities)," *People's Daily*, April 17, 1983, 1.

97. Hua Guofeng, "Xue Hao Wenjian, Zhua Zhu Gang (Study the Documents Well and Grasp the Key Link)," *People's Daily*, February 7, 1977, 1.

98. CCP Central Documentary Editorial Committee, ed. 1993. *Deng Xiaoping Wenxuan (Selected Works of Deng Xiaoping)*, Vol. 2 (Beijing: Renmin Chubanshe (People's Publishing House)), 38.

The Sino-Vietnamese Border War   119

99. "Shijian Shi Jianyan Zhenli de Weiyi Biaozhun (Practice Is the Sole Criterion of Testing Truth)," *Guangming Daily*, May 11, 1978, 1.

100. CCP Central Documentary Editorial Committee, *Deng Xiaoping Wenxuan (Selected Works of Deng Xiaoping)*, 116–17.

101. Chen, *China's War with Vietnam, 1979*, 74–75.

102. Zhang, *Deng Xiaoping's Long War*, 58.

103. Jiamu Zhu, *Chen Yun Nianpu (Chronicles of Chen Yun)* (Beijing: Zhongyang Wenxian Chubanshe (Central Party Literature Press), 2000), 235–36.

4

The Sino-Philippines Arbitration on the South China Sea

A Media Campaign to Pacify

> Sometimes the politically correct stuff [in the media] is just not enough for the people. Only the language we often find in *Global Times* [*Huanqiu Shibao*, a well-known hawkish newspaper under *People's Daily*] help the public vent their spleen. They help the people let off steam by resonating their feelings.
>
> **—author's interview with a government official[1]**

> When the tides are too high, the method of barrier blocking gives way to the drainage systems.
>
> **—author's interview with an editor of an official media's online forum[2]**

Among the six pacification cases identified in the medium-N study, the 2016 Sino-Philippines arbitration crisis stands out as a recent, highly relevant, and extensively documented case, with a remarkable modern-day media campaign that demands attention.[3] The case was, in short, a legal and diplomatic disaster for Beijing, with a predominantly adverse ruling against China that was largely expected. The question that arises is why Beijing launched a full-scale campaign to draw additional public attention toward a case it presumably anticipated losing, rather than merely denouncing and disregarding it?

This chapter examines this case to determine the motivations behind the media spectacle and explains why it was a public–state misalignment, rather than other factors, that drove the state's media masterplan. It also minutely describes the campaign to illustrate how a pacification campaign looks, how it works to align public opinion with state policy, and how it differs characteristically from a mobilization campaign.

The Art of State Persuasion. Frances Yaping Wang, Oxford University Press. © Oxford University Press 2024.
DOI: 10.1093/oso/9780197757505.003.0005

This chapter first presents the historical background and a brief timeline of the case, followed by an in-depth analysis of the causes of the campaign. I then provide a detailed description of the campaign itself and discuss how it managed to calm public sentiment. After considering potential alternative explanations, the chapter concludes with an assessment of the campaign's effectiveness.

The Arbitration and the Crisis

The South China Sea is a half-closed sea of the Pacific Ocean surrounded by mainland China and Taiwan in the north, Vietnam in the west, the Philippines in the east, and Malaysia, Brunei, and Indonesia in the south. It consists of over two hundred land features including small islands, shoals, atolls, banks, cays and other low-tide elevations, covering an entire sea area of 3.5 million square kilometers.[4] China and the Philippines are two of the six adjacent states that have conflictual claims toward the land features in the South China Sea, and the maritime rights these land features generate under the United Nations Convention on the Law of the Sea (UNCLOS) clauses.

The South China Sea, a vital economic and strategic hub, hosts abundant fishing stocks and potential energy reserves. About one-third of global trade ($3.4 trillion as of 2016) traverses through its critical shipping routes.[5] It is also significant in the power dynamics between China and the US due to its importance in naval power projection. As the Philippine Foreign Secretary Albert del Rosario put it, "They [China] want to be a maritime power but to be that, you need your own lake. We think they have selected the South China Sea as their lake."[6]

Manila's initiation of the arbitration case against China did not come out of thin air. Two related issues galvanized Manila's decision to go to court: fishing disputes and China's land reclamations. The former provoked the initial decision and the latter reinforced Manila's determination to see it through, and also dragged the US into the conflict.

The 2012 Scarborough Shoal fishing dispute (detailed in Appendices 2, 3, and 4 as a deviant case with a borderline media campaign), which resulted in China seizing control of the Shoal after a two-month standoff, precipitated the arbitration.[7] China had reportedly "strung a barrier across the mouth of the Shoal to block Philippine access" and "kept surveillance ships nearby."[8] China's aggressive response in the Scarborough Shoal incident provoked Manila's sense of vulnerability and injustice.[9]

In October 2012, Chinese Vice Foreign Minister Fu Ying visited Manila, attempting to discourage the Philippines from internationalizing the dispute or coordinating with the US. However, Manila responded by initiating arbitration, an action that later led to criticism of China's earlier bullheaded approach and contributed to a more conciliatory stance in the 2016 crisis.[10]

Manila fortified its ties with the US as another response to China's actions in the South China Sea, further heightening tensions. The US, while publicly neutral, supported the arbitration due to China's increased naval power projection.[11] The maritime contest between the US and China formed a crucial backdrop to the arbitration. China, initially left with only sparse land features in the Spratlys, embarked on an aggressive land reclamation campaign, amassing 3,200 acres of new land since 2013.[12] This generated significant concerns and unease among neighboring countries in the region. The US reacted by publicly exposing China's activities, offering diplomatic and military aid to Southeast Asian claimants, and conducting high-profile freedom of navigation operations (FONOPs) near China-occupied land features.

On January 22, 2013, the Philippine government initiated an international arbitration case against China regarding maritime rights in the South China Sea. In response, China swiftly rejected the arbitration, blaming the territorial disputes on the Philippines' "illegal occupation" of some of its islands and reefs, and announced that it would neither accept nor participate in the arbitration.[13]

Over the next few months, China elaborated its nonacceptance and nonparticipation position with three points. First, it claimed that Manila violated their mutual agreement for bilateral negotiations by unilaterally initiating the arbitration process. Second, it contended that the Tribunal had no jurisdiction over the sovereignty issues disguised in the Philippines' claims. Lastly, Beijing posited that the arbitration undermined regional stability and the international legal system, accusing Manila of manipulating international law to damage China's territorial claim.

Despite Beijing's rejection and refusal to participate, a tribunal was formed in The Hague on June 21, 2013. The Philippines officially presented its petition to the Tribunal on March 30, 2014. The petition primarily disputed the validity of China's nine-dash line claim, the nature of specific land features, the legality of Chinese harassment of Filipino vessels, and China's harmful environmental activities. Additional objections regarding China's escalated land reclamation efforts were added in 2015. The Chinese Ministry of Foreign Affairs (MoFA) spokesperson Hong Lei reacted by reiterating China's "nonparticipation" and "nonacceptance" position, invoking a 2006

UNCLOS exclusion clause that China signed which removes issues of sovereignty and maritime boundary delimitation from arbitration procedures.[14]

In December 2014, the Chinese MoFA released a position paper "On the Matter of Jurisdiction in the South China Sea Arbitration Initiated by the Republic of the Philippines," which further elaborated the legal basis of China's position.[15] Following this, the Tribunal agreed to hold separate hearings on jurisdiction and admissibility. During a hearing in July 2015, the Tribunal ruled it was "properly constituted" and would continue with the case, which China denounced as "null and void."[16] Hearings on the actual case proceeded in November 2015 without China's attendance. Tensions escalated as China accused the Philippines of "political provocation," while the Philippine Foreign Secretary urged China to respect the forthcoming ruling.[17]

With an impending ruling expected to be negative for China, the situation escalated into a full-blown diplomatic crisis as Beijing scrambled to devise a strategy and brace for impact. However, the situation appeared to take a significant turn when Rodrigo Duterte assumed office as the new president of the Philippines on June 30. Duterte adopted a more conciliatory approach than his predecessor. He met with the Chinese Ambassador to the Philippines on July 9 and agreed "not to make any provocative statements following the release of the ruling." The Duterte administration also expressed willingness to resume bilateral talks on sharing the South China Sea resources, even if it won the lawsuit.[18]

On July 12, the Tribunal announced its decision, favoring the Philippines on most counts. The verdict invalidated China's nine-dash line claim, ruled the disputed land features as rocks, not islands—thereby restricting their maritime rights. It highlighted China's transgressions of Philippine sovereignty and environmental damage and declared China's construction of artificial islands as unlawful, dismissing any consequent maritime rights.[19]

This was an overwhelming victory for the Philippines, yet Manila chose not to flaunt it. The Philippine Foreign Secretary Yasay welcomed the result and called for "restraint and sobriety."[20] His speech on TV was notably measured in contrast to the public fervor on the streets of Manila.[21]

Riding a Tiger

To determine if the 2016 arbitration case was a pacification story caused by misalignment, we need to complete two logical steps. First, it is important to identify whether a misalignment existed between public opinion and state foreign policy intent, and if such misalignment prompted state actions. We need to understand public opinion and state policy intent during the crisis, whether there was a discrepancy, and if other factors, like audience costs or diversion, could have motivated the state. Additionally, we should consider whether methods other than a media campaign, such as censorship, could have been used to address the misalignment.

Second, it is crucial to verify if a media campaign was implemented and if it successfully aligned public opinion. We need to explore how this state act functioned and whether it pacified public sentiment, thereby illuminating the characteristics and workings of a pacification campaign, and how it contrasts from a mobilization campaign.

Starting with the misalignment criterion, public opinion in China had already hardened prior to the 2016 crisis, largely due to the 2012 Scarborough Shoal incident. A *Global Times* survey conducted during the 2012 crisis among 1,482 randomly selected respondents in seven Chinese cities found that 78.5 percent of respondents supported a military response.[22] Further, in May 2013, the shooting of a Taiwanese fisherman by the Philippine Coast Guard in the overlapping exclusive economic zones (EEZs) of Taiwan and the Philippines led to a follow-up *Global Times* survey, which revealed 92.5 percent of 1,047 respondents from mainland China supported forming an alliance with Taiwan to exert pressure on the Philippines.[23]

In response to a multi-option question, 61.4 percent of respondents preferred strong diplomatic pressure, 57.6 percent opted for economic sanctions, and 44.3 percent favored military responses. Although fewer respondents opted for military action compared to diplomatic pressure, the hardline stance was prevalent, despite the incident involving a Taiwanese, not a mainland Chinese, fisherman.

Although the *Global Times*, typically seen as a hardline Chinese tabloid, may potentially skew these results, they should be interpreted with caution, but not dismissed outright. These surveys were conducted by the Global Times Research Center, a subsidiary of *Global Times* that focuses on gauging public opinion rather than shaping it. As explained by an employee involved in these surveys, the study adopted a robust, conventional sampling methodology. It used a representative sample based on the national census and leveraged a computer-assisted telephone interviewing (CATI) system for random selection.[24] Moreover, when integrated with other evidence presented later, this data presents a plausible representation of public sentiment at the time.

Throughout 2015 and the first half of 2016, China's land reclamation activities and US freedom of navigation operations (FONOPs) heightened the South China Sea dispute's prominence among the Chinese public, edging toward a crisis. These events, including the US's monthly FONOPs near China-claimed islands since January 2016 and high-level officials' acrimonious public debates, grabbed media and public attention both globally and within China. Key moments included US Secretary of Defense Ashton Carter's assertion at the 2015 IISS Shangri-La Dialogue that the US would "fly, sail and operate wherever international law allows" and President Obama's singling out China at the 2015 APEC meeting to cease reclamation activities.[25] These events spurred awareness and heightened emotions in China, setting the stage for the Sino-Philippines arbitration.

Prior to the diplomatic crisis ignited by the upcoming arbitration ruling, the Beijing Area Study (BAS) survey conducted from April 10 to June 30, 2015, used a "country thermometer" to evaluate Chinese public sentiment toward various nations. The Philippines scored a poor 36 out of 100, ranking second lowest, only marginally better than Japan with its score of 30 out of 100, a country with a contentious relationship with China marred by brutal invasions in the past and unresolved territorial and historical disputes.[26]

Although the BAS survey was not directly related to the South China Sea dispute, it did express a general resentment or even strong hostility toward the Philippines among the Chinese public. While low scores on such a scale do not necessarily suggest a preference for conflict escalation, it does imply that Chinese public opinion could be inclined toward a more aggressive policy against the Philippines.

Figure 4.1 displays a one-year average of approximately 4,000 in the Baidu Search Index (BSI) for the term "South China Sea," preceding the onset of the crisis.[27] This data reveals several peaks of heightened interest throughout this period. For context, the all-time average for such searches stands at 2,773.

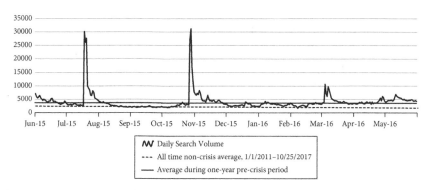

Figure 4.1 Baidu.com's Daily Search Index for the Term "South China Sea," May 31, 2015–May 31, 2016

It is important to note that the BSI is primarily a measure of public attention, and an increase in attention does not exclusively signify hardline policy preference; it can also indicate moderate policy preference. However, in the escalating context of the Sino-US tensions over land reclamation and FONOPs, alongside the existing antipathy toward the Philippines among the Chinese public, an amplified level of public attention to the South China Sea dispute suggests a likely escalation in animosity and a shift toward a more hardline policy preference among Chinese citizens.

This inference is further bolstered by other concurrent developments, including the hawkish tone of social media posts pertaining to the dispute and the government's measures to stifle spontaneous public protests. This complex interplay of factors creates a backdrop against which the heightened public attention captured by the BSI can be interpreted as an indicator of growing hardline sentiments among the Chinese public. The subsequent sections will provide a more detailed exploration of these additional indicators.

Following the Tribunal's decision, there was an immediate and massive public response that shook the digital landscape in China, as evidenced by the surge of over five million microblog posts from July 1 to 20 that directly addressed the ruling.[28] The public's frustration and anger were palpable and spontaneously erupted across the internet, making this issue one of the most discussed topics online during this period.

In physical spaces, authorities anticipated significant protests and quickly stepped up security measures, particularly around the Philippine Embassy in Beijing, to manage potential unrest. Despite these precautions, demonstrations still occurred in various cities across China. A notable manifestation of public dissent was seen outside Kentucky Fried Chicken (KFC) restaurants, a symbol of American presence in China. Protestors congregated outside these establishments, vehemently denouncing the perceived meddling of the United States in the territorial dispute and urging fellow Chinese citizens to boycott the fast-food chain.[29]

According to observations made by Zhao, public sentiment was so charged that many were ready for a war if the ruling was unfavorable to China. There was a prevalent belief among the populace that street protests were almost inevitable and that the Philippine and American Embassies might even become targets of public outrage.[30] The entire nation was on edge, awaiting the unfolding of events.

Contrastingly, despite Beijing's stern rhetoric, substantial evidence supports its inclination toward a more moderate policy. Discussions with scholars privy to relevant policymaking circles indicate that Beijing initially wished for the issue to "fade away."[31] Following Manila's initiation of the case, fiery internal debates ensued over whether China should participate in the arbitration or not.

Beijing found itself in a dilemma. Participation in the high-profile case and suffering a loss could lead to grave domestic and regional implications, particularly affecting China's other offshore disputes. The likelihood of China losing the case was substantial. Its nine-dash line claim, which predates the UNCLOS, was largely incompatible with international law, due to its lack of defined coordinates and clear implications. Beijing had purposefully kept this ambiguity in hopes of preserving the status quo, so that it can continue to develop relations peacefully with its neighboring countries without appearing to relinquish an inch of its "ancestral land."

China also harbored concerns that the arbitration process would not be fair, given that the president of the International Tribunal on the Law of the Sea (ITLOS), Shunji Yanai, was Japanese.[32] There had also been no precedent of resolving any of China's territorial disputes through international arbitration, which naturally raised their suspicion toward this approach. Hence, when China declared its position on UNCLOS Article 298 on August 28, 2006, it consciously exempted itself from the jurisdiction of international arbitration of maritime disputes.[33]

However, by not participating, China would lose the opportunity to influence the ruling in its favor. For example, after the Philippines initiated the case, if China had chosen to participate, it would have the right to appoint an arbitrator, potentially a Chinese national. Instead, the Tribunal based the hearing on China's 2014 position paper and letters sent to the Tribunal by the Chinese ambassador to the Netherlands. These were far less effective than direct and proactive representation. Nonparticipation would also damage China's soft power and taint China's international image. Professor Jerome Cohen of the New York University School of Law remarked that China's nonparticipation and nonacceptance makes it appear "like a bully that rejects its legal obligation to settle a dispute under UNCLOS."[34] This view was shared by others. For instance, Gregory Poling stated that "being branded an international outlaw will involve significant reputational costs for Beijing. It will undermine China's narrative that it is a responsible rising power that deserves a greater hand in global governance. It will make other countries wary of Chinese commitments and will drive regional states even closer to Tokyo and Washington."[35]

After a thorough consultation with international legal experts and the creation of a comprehensive internal legal document, Beijing decided not to participate in the arbitration nor accept the results.[36] Interestingly, throughout this process, there was little consideration toward punishing or threatening to punish Manila for challenging China.[37] Subsequent events confirmed Beijing's restraint from imposing penalties on Manila. Instead, China engaged in diplomatic endeavors to make the Philippines to drop the case. But apparently such endeavors failed—Manila was determined to pursue the case. As the case continued to unfold and tensions escalated, China's behavior became largely "reactive" and "remedial."[38] The domestic and international propaganda campaign, the diplomatic efforts to forestall an Association of Southeast Asian Nations (ASEAN) statement mentioning the ruling, and the international campaign to rally support are all components of this reactive and remedial policy.[39]

Beijing's actual policy approach further underscores its moderate intent. When initial polling results on May 10 indicated Rodrigo Duterte's electoral win, Beijing did not hesitate to express its hope that the new Philippine government would "work towards the same direction with China."[40] Notably, even amidst the height of the crisis in late June, Beijing made a point to congratulate Duterte, who had just been sworn in as the new president. This marked a clear sign that Beijing was actively seeking new diplomatic avenues to address the issue rather than escalating tensions or pursuing retaliation. Chinese President Xi Jinping expressed his "willing[ness] to work with Duterte to push for improvement of relations," a statement which notably left out any mention of the ongoing arbitration, indicating a preference for diplomacy over confrontation.[41]

The military largely refrained from making statements, with the exception of the day the award was announced. On this day, the Ministry of Defense spokesperson proclaimed that irrespective of the ruling, the People's Liberation Army (PLA) would unflinchingly defend China's national sovereignty, security, and maritime rights. Even in this statement, the spokesperson took care to point out that the ongoing naval exercise in the South China Sea was merely an annual routine exercise. This clarification was evidently intended to dispel any suggestions that China was signaling a possibility of using force in response to the arbitration outcome.[42]

Following the announcement of the ruling, Chinese Vice Foreign Minister Liu Zhenmin addressed a press conference on July 13, where he stated that China had "taken note of the positive attitude of the new Philippine government under President Duterte toward resuming dialogue with China and progressing bilateral relationships from various aspects. We welcome this initiative with open arms."[43] Evidently, Beijing was prepared to move forward.

Beijing's position in ignoring the award while simultaneously seeking negotiation with the Philippines was unequivocal. This standpoint is evident in two significant documents released by the Chinese government immediately after the ruling: a statement concerning China's territorial sovereignty and maritime rights in the South China Sea, and a white paper on resolving disputes with the Philippines through negotiation. Interestingly, both documents only mention the controversial nine-dash line map in passing. The key focus, rather, is on China's willingness to establish practical temporary arrangements with the Philippines to ease tension and promote cooperation.[44]

On August 8, less than a month after the ruling, the Philippines dispatched its former president, Fidel V. Ramos, to Hong Kong to "break the ice." Ramos met with Fu Ying, chairperson of China's Foreign Affairs Committee of the National People's Congress, and Wu Shicun, president of the National Institute for South China Sea Studies. They issued a statement in their personal capacities, emphasizing cooperation and dialogue, which notably omitted any reference to the ruling.[45] Ramos also conveyed his government's willingness to engage in formal discussions to mitigate tensions with China.[46]

Alongside its verbal overtures to the Duterte administration, Beijing undertook a series of cooperative and conciliatory actions. None of these maneuvers would have made sense if China were bent on a hardline policy. At the July 24 China-ASEAN Foreign Ministers' summit, which immediately followed the ruling, Beijing made a significant concession by assuring ASEAN that it would not conduct land reclamation on the Scarborough Shoal. The summit also culminated in the issuance of a Joint Statement emphasizing the full and effective implementation of the Declaration on the Conduct of Parties in the South China Sea.[47] The Statement urged parties to refrain from inhabiting presently uninhabited islands, reefs, shoals, cays, and other features, restricting the actions of both the Philippines and China.

On August 15–16, 2016, the thirteenth Senior Officials' Meeting and the eighteenth Joint Working Group Meeting on the implementation of the Declaration took place in Manzhouli, China. This gathering laid the groundwork for a hotline to handle maritime emergencies, adopted a Joint Statement on the Application of the Code for Unplanned Encounters at Sea in the South China Sea, and made a commitment to finalize a draft code of conduct by mid-2017.[48]

On October 20, Philippine President Duterte visited China, during which he and President Xi agreed to resume direct talks on the dispute. Post-visit, China announced that "China-Philippine relations have been turned around and put on a track of all-around improvement."[49] In a gesture of substantial cooperation, China allowed Filipino fishermen to return to the vicinity of the Scarborough Shoal.[50]

The Misalignment

This review indicates a stark discrepancy between the hawkish public sentiment and the more measured state foreign policy approach. The case prominently displays the paradoxical relationship between public opinion and foreign policy that is typical in authoritarian regimes. On the one hand, divergent public opinion was not potent enough to influence foreign policy decisions, whether it was the choice to abstain from participating in the arbitration or adopting a reconciliatory stance toward Manila following the ruling. The nebulous role of public opinion in foreign policy, as displayed in this case, was apparent in all my conversations with government officials and policy analysts. Public opinion was a concern to be addressed and a problem to be resolved, but it was far from a decisive factor influencing foreign policy decisions.

The Chinese government saw the benefits and feasibility of a moderate policy toward Manila, and also understood the cost of alternate policy options. According to a senior Chinese scholar, the Chinese government had become aware of the drawbacks of its previous unyielding approach, particularly in the Scarborough Shoal standoff and disputes with the US over artificial islands. Beijing was wary that its actions might further estrange regional states.[51] Moreover, the legal character of the arbitration differentiated the case from other civilian (e.g., fishing), commercial (e.g., oil exploration), paramilitary (e.g., coast guards), and military confrontations at sea. Thus, a military escalation would not only be inappropriate but unwise as it could tarnish China's international reputation and reinforce its alleged image as an international "outlaw." Therefore, in the best interest of its foreign policy, the Chinese government was unwilling and unlikely to yield to public opinion. Based on past experiences, the government knew it had the ability to shape public sentiment to meet its objectives.

On the other hand, the divergence of public opinion was sufficiently concerning to impel the government to take corrective measures. While the Chinese authorities did not necessarily need active public endorsement for the conciliatory stance they adopted—unlike the material and manpower support required during the 1979 Sino-Vietnamese border war—they did require a degree of passive approval from the public. This implicit consent was necessary to prevent hindrances to the implementation of their foreign policy and to maintain public confidence in the Chinese government's ability to defend national interests.

There were two layers to the goal of tacit consent. First, public opinion should be calm enough to avoid turmoil that might threaten domestic stability or raise international concern. There had been instances globally in which public activism had backed governments into a corner, sparking apprehension about regime security. The implementation of foreign policy could also be obstructed if foreign assets or the safety of foreign nationals within the country were jeopardized. Tacit consent implied that despite holding strong opinions, the public would refrain from taking any detrimental actions. An official admitted in an interview that there was a "dire need to prepare the public to accept and understand the ruling."[52]

The second layer of tacit consent was to ensure that public trust in the government's ability to protect national interests was not undermined. As many authoritarian states turned toward their performance record as a source of regime legitimacy, formulating an optimal foreign policy that serves state interests without compromising regime legitimacy in the public's eyes has become a significant political goal. At the beginning of the crisis, Chinese leaders faced the formidable task of defending their performance record. As a veteran diplomat and China scholar disclosed, many within China— including political elites—viewed the arbitration as a diplomatic debacle and privately blamed the government.[53] A senior scholar involved in the decision process revealed, "The government did not want the public to know that it actually made a mistake . . . The result turned out to be the most unfavorable [to China]. Then the government had to adopt a damage control approach."[54] The government needed to do something to blunt criticism, while freeing its hands to pursue a remedy—in this case, a moderate policy—to pull itself out of the predicament. For these reasons, the government strived to close the gap between public sentiment and state policy to a point where the public would at least tolerate a moderate foreign policy without taking actions that might jeopardize social stability, hinder foreign policy implementation, or damage regime legitimacy.

To narrow the state–public gap, an autocratic state could presumably erase all information on the arbitration if the state had complete information control. If the state could do that, or even just a fraction of that, the public would not have as strong an opinion about what to do, or even an opinion at all, and the state would have the freedom to pursue a moderate policy with low risk of social turmoil. However, even with China's mighty and sophisticated censorship apparatus, complete cover-ups had become a modern-day fantasy. The internet was the most porous space imaginable. The diverse sources of information, foreign and private, as well as the instant mode of transmission, made a black-out infeasible. Accompanying the freer flow of information was a more expressive and active public that could easily be inflamed by nationalist sentiments. The CPD did pursue a censorship order on the KFC demonstrations, but only used this tactic sparsely. More importantly, the Chinese government resorted to another tool, more potent than censorship, to calm public opinion.

The Dog That Barked but Did Not Bite

To reconcile the state–public dissonance and to secure the public's tacit consent needed for the safe implementation of a moderate policy, China initiated a media campaign in June and July 2016. In a brief period of sixty-one days, *People's Daily* published a total of 208 articles, with thirteen making the front pages. This coverage included an eight-part series of commentaries by the *People's Daily* editorial staff. Similarly, Xinhua News released a ten-part editorial series, publishing one article per day in the ten days leading up to the ruling's announcement. The timeline plot of *People's Daily* coverage between 2010 and 2016, depicted in Figure 4.2, demonstrates a massive spike in June and July of 2016.

Not only was there a big increase in the media coverage, but internal notes circulated at major state media outlets showed that top leadership deliberated this increase. An internal note, dated July 11, called editors to "continue to follow the Party Central Committee's directives ... and fight well this public opinion battle." Another note dated July 13 instructed "the editorial departments and relevant branches to follow the leadership's command and

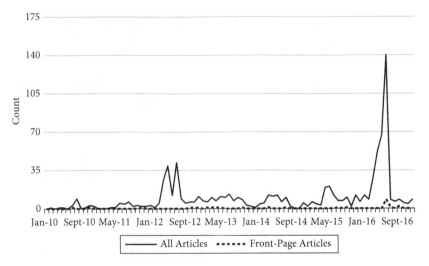

Figure 4.2 Monthly Count of *People's Daily* Articles on the Sino-Philippines South China Sea Dispute, 2010–2016

the reporting plan previously prepared."[55] The note outlined several reporting strategies for editors, such as "releasing news, commentaries and interviews in bundled format on various platforms, reporting leaders' speeches and MoFA statements in a timely manner; providing comprehensive and accurate elaboration of our (government's) policy, rejecting the illegal Tribunal ruling."[56] An interview with a government official confirmed that these media trends were indeed "authorized."[57]

This media campaign was remarkable, considering China's traditional position of keeping a low profile about the South China Sea dispute. Domestically, Beijing had always been mindful about not elevating the rhetoric. Even during the 2012 Scarborough Shoal crisis, despite a spike in media coverage, Beijing deliberately kept the news off of front pages and prime time.[58] Internationally, Beijing consistently strived to avoid the issue's internationalization and to keep it off the agenda of multilateral forums. However, this campaign marked a departure from China's longstanding low-key approach. Despite this, the campaign was deemed necessary as it worked to move hardline public opinion to support or acquiesce to a moderate foreign policy.

The pacification campaign achieved this feat by dictating the discourse, echoing public sentiment, hardline posturing, positive framing, delegitimizing "unhelpful" emotions, and allowing for emotional venting. The campaign helped the state gain control of the narrative by circulating authoritative information swiftly and frequently, and by proactively addressing developments, rather than dodging and reacting passively.

Information voids, or even delays, can breed suspicion and rumors, and empower information from alternative sources such as foreign media. If Beijing had stayed silent or passive instead of engaging in an active media campaign, the arbitration would have been widely perceived as a diplomatic failure. Foreign media had generally applauded Manila's resort to international law and had painted Beijing's response as yet another example of a recalcitrant rising power that bullied its smaller neighbors. If Beijing had stayed silent, the international media would have filled the information void and stoked confusion, anguish, and stronger public hostility toward the government. A government official confirmed the state's concern about the hawkish public opinion during my interview: "The government was worried that the public might hear about the arbitration from foreign media anyways."[59] Under these circumstances, narrative control seemed absolutely vital. The state took charge of its propaganda machinery to effectively mold public opinion to align with its foreign policy objectives.

The government made sure its voice was the first one heard. A media campaign provided a convenient platform for that. A media campaign provided an ideal platform for this. For each unfavorable argument that surfaced, the Chinese MoFA spokesperson responded quickly, and *People's Daily* consistently published these remarks the following day. For instance, on May 6, *People's Daily* published MoFA spokesperson Hong Lei's rebuttal of accusations that China's nonparticipation showed a disregard for international law. Hong Lei defended China's stance by referring to the UNCLOS exclusion clause that China had signed, arguing that the arbitration was essentially a political provocation from Manila disguised as a legal maneuver. Manila defended its decision to initiate the arbitration as a desperate final recourse because it had "exhausted all political and diplomatic avenues for a peaceful negotiated settlement of its maritime dispute with China," and bilateral talks had led nowhere.[60] Hong Lei dismissed this, countering that none of Manila's submissions to the Tribunal had ever been discussed in bilateral talks.[61] On the same day, the Director-General of the MoFA Department of Boundary and Ocean Affairs, Ouyang Yujing, unprecedently gave a lengthy interview to Chinese and foreign media and detailed China's position.[62]

A few days later, an argument emerged that justified Manila's legal pursuit on the grounds of its vulnerability as a much smaller and weaker state than China, and its inability to negotiate as a true equal in bilateral talks with China. Chinese MoFA spokesperson Lu Kang responded that China "would never bully its smaller neighbors" and "such argument distorts the truth." He warned that China "would not tolerate blackmails either." These remarks were published in *People's Daily* the following day.[63] On May 12, Director-General of the MoFA Department of Treaty and Law Xu Hong also gave a briefing and fielded questions from journalists.[64] This was again reported in *People's Daily* the next day.

Subsequently, at almost every juncture, a response from the Chinese MoFA would accompany nearly every piece of international news that portrayed China negatively. This response would appear in the next day's *People's Daily* and be reposted by other Chinese media outlets. The occasions that provoked a Chinese public relations response during this period are listed in Table 4.1. While the list is extensive, it does not capture every single instance. However, it clearly demonstrates the pattern of Chinese media behavior: the strategy was to dominate the discourse by reacting quickly to unfavorable arguments before they could gain traction among the Chinese public.

This media campaign utilized an echoing effect as well. The state echoed the hardline public sentiment with strongly worded statements, and, according to an internal note circulated among all state media outlets, required that these statements be featured in salient places and reposted extensively.[65] For example, Vice Foreign Minister Zhang Yesui stated, "China opposes and

Sino-Philippines Arbitration on the South China Sea   135

Table 4.1 Occasions That Provoked China's Public Relations Responses and China's Responses

Occasions That Provoked Chinese Response	China's Public Relations Responses
US Publication of its China military report mentioning China's "use of low-intensity coercion in maritime disputes" in April[1]	*People's Daily* published on May 18 a special commentary by "Zhong Sheng," which criticized the report for "fanning the theory of 'China threat' on no grounds and twisting China's defense policies in the South China Sea." It accused Washington of "provoking conflicts in the South China Sea and defaming China's national defense."[2]
Former President Obama's remarks during his visit to Vietnam on May 24 commenting that "big nations should not bully smaller ones," insinuating at China[3]	Chinese MoFA spokesperson Hua Chunying reacted by saying "a country should not be judged right or wrong merely based on its size." "Countries outside the region should respect regional countries' efforts to safeguard peace and stability . . . should not . . . threaten littoral countries' sovereignty and security in any form and under any excuse, jeopardize regional rules and order and undermine regional peace and stability."[4] *People's Daily* published the remarks the following day. Sohu, Sina, *Global Times* online edition and several local and private news outlets reposted the statement.
The mentioning of the dispute in the concluding communiqué of the G7 Summit held on May 26–27 in Japan[5]	China expressed strong dissatisfaction. Chinese MoFA spokesperson Hua Chunying protested that the G7 countries should not "hype up this issue for selfish gains."[6] Xinhua News published an editorial asking the G7 countries to refrain from "meddling." *People's Daily* published Hua Chunying's statement the next day and a commentary by Zhong Sheng entitled "What did they get by hyping an issue like this?"[7]
The discussion of the dispute at the Shangri-La Dialogue on June 3–5 in Singapore[8]	Chinese MoFA spokesperson Hua Chunying responded that the "freedom of navigation and over-flight in the South China Sea is a false statement." "We . . . hope that relevant countries will stop disturbing peace and stability of the region under the pretext of safeguarding or exercising freedom of navigation."[9] *People's Daily* published the remarks the following day.
The Tribunal Court's June 29 announcement of its plan to release the award on July 12	Chinese MoFA spokesperson Hong Lei responded that "the Arbitral Tribunal has no jurisdiction over the case and the relevant subject-matter, and that it should not have heard the case or rendered the award . . . China does not accept any means of third party dispute settlement or any solution imposed on China."[10] *People's Daily* published the remarks the next day and a commentary by Zhong Sheng entitled "Illegal Arbitration is a Political Farce."[11]

Notes:

1. Office of the Secretary of Defense, "Annual Report to Congress: Military and Security Developments Involving the People's Republic of China 2016," April 26, 2016, https://dod.defense.gov/Portals/1/Docume nts/pubs/2016%20China%20Military%20Power%20Report.pdf.

2. "Duplicity of US in Relations with China Hurts Bilateral Ties," *People's Daily*, May 18, 2016, 3.

(continued)

136 The Art of State Persuasion

Table 4.1 Continued

3. "Remarks by President Obama in Address to the People of Vietnam," The White House, Hanoi, Vietnam, May 24, 2016, https://obamawhitehouse.archives.gov/the-press-office/2016/05/24/remarks-president-obama-address-people-vietnam.

4. "Foreign Ministry Spokesperson Hua Chunying's Regular Press Conference on May 24, 2016," Ministry of Foreign Affairs of the People's Republic of China, May 24, 2016, https://www.fmprc.gov.cn/mfa_eng/xwfw_665399/s2510_665401/t1366103.shtml.

5. "China says extremely dissatisfied with G7 statement on South China Sea," *Reuters*, May 27, 2016, https://www.reuters.com/article/us-g7-summit-china-idUSKCN0YI0RV.

6. "Foreign Ministry Spokesperson Hua Chunying's Regular Press Conference on May 26, 2016," Foreign Affairs of the People's Republic of China, May 26, 2016, https://www.fmprc.gov.cn/mfa_eng/xwfw_665399/s2510_665401/2535_665405/t1367062.shtml.

7. *People's Daily*, May 28, 2016, 3.

8. "Special Session 5: Managing South China Sea Tensions," 15th Asia Security Summit the IISS Shangri-La Dialogue, June 4, 2016, transcript available at https://www.iiss.org/events/shangri-la-dialogue/shangri-la-dialogue-2016.

9. "Foreign Ministry Spokesperson Hua Chunying's Remarks on Freedom of Navigation and Over-flight in the South China Sea Discussed at the Shangri-La Dialogue," Foreign Affairs of the People's Republic of China, June 6, 2016, https://www.fmprc.gov.cn/nanhai/eng/fyrbt_1/t1369692.htm.

10. "Foreign Ministry Spokesperson Hong Lei's Regular Press Conference on June 30, 2016," Foreign Affairs of the People's Republic of China, June 30, 2016, http://is.china-embassy.org/eng/fyrth/t1376587.htm.

11. *People's Daily*, June 30, 2016, 3, 10.

---

will not accept any proposition and action based on the award and will never negotiate with any other country over the South China Sea based on the illegal award."[66] The Foreign Ministry Spokesperson Lu Kang criticized the US for not remaining impartial as it had claimed, as well as its hypocrisy in supporting the ruling short of ratifying UNCLOS.[67] Cui Tiankai, Chinese ambassador to the US, impugned the impartiality of the Tribunal by pointing out that Shunji Yanai, the jurist who appointed most of the arbitrators, was "a right-wing Japanese intent on ridding Japan of post-war arrangement."[68] Former Chinese State Councilor Dai Bingguo dismissed the ruling as "nothing but a piece of waste paper."[69] In an interview to state media on July 14, the then–State Councilor Yang Jiechi stated that "history brooks no distortion and law no abuse." He belittled the arbitration as being a "political farce all along, staged under the cover of law and driven by a hidden agenda." He accused "certain countries outside the region"—alluding to the US—for attempting to "deny China's sovereign rights and interests in the South China Sea" and bringing "other countries into the scheme to isolate and discredit China in the international community with a view to holding back China's peaceful development."[70] The strong rhetoric, as it turned out, greatly satisfied the public. For example, commenting on MoFA spokesperson Lu Kang's statements regarding the arbitration, Weibo (China's most popular Twitter-like social media platform) posts praised the spokesperson as "confident" and "cool."[71]

Echoing builds the social trust needed for mass persuasion by demonstrating that the government is attuned to its citizens, reinforcing an "us" versus "them" dynamic, where the common "enemy" is foreign, not internal. This strategy aims to prevent a scenario where the public feels at odds with the state. Echoing placates an angry public by voicing public outrage on their behalf. As a government official in one of my interviews put it:

> Sometimes the politically correct stuff [in the media] is just not enough for the people. Only the language we often find in *Global Times* [a newspaper under *People's Daily* knows for its hawkish content] helps the public vent their spleen. It helps the people let off steam by resonating with their feelings.[72]

People's Daily commentaries abandoned the banal style and empty slogans in traditional Soviet-style propaganda and used colorful and lively rhetoric that caught the public's attention and resonated with its sentiments. For example, a July 8 commentary had the title "It Is Time to End the Political Farce Under the Cover of International Law." The author "Zhong Sheng" mocked that "if international law works in its favor, the US would hold up the banner high; but if it proves inconvenient, the US would trample on it."[73] Another commentary by Zhong Sheng on July 10 titled "Flying the Flag of International Law can Hardly Conceal Its Absurd Nature" writes that "Such a gaffe is frivolous and self-exposing. The so-called Arbitral Tribunal is nothing but a toy in its hands, and the award brandished under the banner of international law is nothing more than a lie."[74]

Among other themes, the state media's echoing efforts primarily targeted the Philippine government. It dismissed the Philippines' territorial claim as baseless and condemned the arbitration as "politicizing" and "abusing" international law.[75] It argued that the Philippines' actions violated international law,[76] contradicted the country's previous attempts to resolve the issue through negotiations,[77] and opportunistically fragmented the broader territorial dispute into smaller, entitlement-based disputes to fit within the Tribunal's jurisdiction.[78]

The Chinese state media also capitalized on political opponents of the Aquino government within the Philippines. For instance, *People's Daily* first reprinted an article from *Manila Standard* by Philippine columnist Rod Kapunan, and then published an interview they conducted with him.[79] Kapunan wrote that "after six years of hypocrisy and deceit, this shameless stooge (referring to Aquino III) has brought us right into the doorstep of possible armed conflict with China all because it has chosen to pursue the US-designed policy of inciting hostility with our neighbor." He warned that "the lives of the Filipinos would be sacrificed to enforce a decision that if examined closely is a US proxy war which the Philippines would serve as cannon fodder in securing its interest in this part of the globe."[80]

Furthermore, Xinhua News interviewed Alberto Encomienda, former Secretary-General of the Maritime and Oceans Affairs Center at the Philippines Department of Foreign Affairs (DFA). Encomienda, who oversaw negotiations with China on the maritime dispute prior to the arbitration, accused the Aquino government of lying when they claimed to have exhausted bilateral means before resorting to arbitration. He divulged that "Manila never responded" to China's repeated efforts to bring the Philippines back to the negotiation table. Encomienda blamed Manila, not Beijing, for escalating tensions in the South China Sea. China Central Television (CCTV) News also aired this interview.[81]

The echoing also cast doubt on the neutrality and authority of the Tribunal, from the appointment of its judges, its finances, and its operations. *People's Daily* ran a series of articles on the Tribunal's background, calling it "makeshift," "lack[ing] legitimacy," a "troupe," "a political tool," a collection of "judicial hooligans," and even "the cancer cell of the international rule of law."[82] These articles pointed out that the Tribunal had nothing to do with the International Court of Justice (ICJ), the principle judicial organ of the United Nations;[83] that it had financial transactions with the Philippines;[84] that most of the arbitrators were appointed by a right-wing Japanese;[85] and that the Tribunal overstepped its authority in taking on the case, despite widespread criticism.[86]

A third echoing theme accused the US of being the "invisible hand" behind the case. A *People's Daily* article on May 15 quoted Philippine columnist Rod Kapunan in saying that the Aquino government was "pulling chestnuts out of the fire for the US."[87] In the same vein, articles criticized the US for "meddling" in and "militarizing" the South China Sea issue, destabilizing regional security, absurdly and ignorantly judging right or wrong based on countries' sizes and wealth. They dismissed as irrelevant the freedom of navigation issue to the South China Sea dispute and condemned the US's hypocrisy with regard to international law, its intention to contain China, and the western media's smear campaign against China.[88] Articles also bashed Japan and Australia for their interference on the issue.[89]

A fourth echoing theme argued for the negative regional and international ramifications of the arbitration; for example, that the arbitration "harmed" the regionalization process by "dividing" ASEAN, "damaged" international law, "disrupted" international order, and made the South China Sea issue even more intractable.[90] The ruling did a "disservice" to regional peace, "threatened regional stability," and "ruined justice and rule of law."[91]

An important feature of echoing in a pacification campaign is that the harsh tone is usually down a notch from public sentiment. In other words, it is still harsh language for the purpose of echoing, yet not as harsh as the strong, antagonistic public sentiment. As a result, the media content still appeared relatable on the one hand, but on the other hand it minimized the risk of further inflaming the public. The "moderately harsh" attribute of pacification propaganda, evident in this media campaign, was the frequent citation of foreign experts or reprinting their articles from international media.

Citing foreign experts for the purposes of harsh echoing could have two benefits: it implied the impartiality of a noninvolved party and it attenuated the risk of escalation by sending the wrong signals to the foreign opponent. In other words, foreign-bashing rhetoric from non-Chinese experts is safer, because the foreign opponent is less likely to mistake third-party harshness for hardline intentions from China and thus would be less likely to react aggressively. An internal note circulated among state media outlets on July 13 tasked editors and journalists specifically to "search for and take advantage of news and information that work in our favor."[92] For example, *People's Daily* reprinted an interview from the Czech Republic's largest political commentary website, Prvnizpravy.cz (PZ), with Oskar Krejčí, a political science professor and former adviser to the Czech Prime Minister. Krejčí vehemently criticized the arbitration: "Forced arbitration is a deliberate provocation, the purpose of which is purely propaganda, and it only increases tensions. Feigned good office on the dispute in the South China Sea, while warming up selfish geopolitical ambitions, is dangerously playing with fire."[93]

Table 4.2 presents a comprehensive but not exhaustive list of articles included in this media campaign, that echoed the assertive public opinion by citing foreign experts or republishing articles from international media.

The harsh rhetoric also functioned as a "posturing" device to keep up the "tough" appearances demanded by the public, so as to fend off nationalistic criticisms, save face, and maintain social stability. As a scholar describes the posturing logic in this case:

> Although publicizing the American, the Philippine or the Japanese military activities in the South China Sea might fan too much popular nationalism, the government does not want to suppress coverage too bluntly as too little noise might make the government appear weak and easily cowed.[94]

140   The Art of State Persuasion

Table 4.2 A Comprehensive but Nonexhaustive List of *People's Daily* Articles That Cited Criticism from Non-Chinese Experts

Date	Page	Article Title
5/13/2016	3	《菲律宾舆论抨击阿基诺政府将南海问题提交仲裁》 "Philippine media criticizes the Aquino government for submitting the South China Sea issue for arbitration" (Article quoted Philippine columnist Rod Kapunan at *Manila Standard*)
5/21/2016	3	《南非资深国际问题评论员刊文--全面介绍南海问题历史经纬，深刻揭露美国插手南海问题实质》 "South African senior commentator on international issues publishes article that comprehensively introduces the South China Sea issue and uncovers the US' meddling)
6/5/2016	3	《美国的航行自由行动：是公理还是强权?》 "America's Freedom of Navigation Operations: right or might?" (Author is former senior executive vice president of Singapore Press Holdings Group and former editor-in-chief of *The Strait Times*. The original text was published in *The Straits Times* on May 29.)
6/6/2016	3	《加拿大学者批西方媒体给南海问题乱贴标签》 "Canadian scholar criticizes Western media for labeling the South China Sea issue indiscriminately"
6/11/2016	3	《菲律宾外交部海事中心前秘书长--加剧南海局势紧张的正是菲律宾》 "Former Secretary-General of the Maritime & Oceans Affairs Center at the Philippines Department of Foreign Affairs (DFA)—The Philippines is the One Heightening the South China Sea Tensions"
6/12/2016	3	《俄外交部称第三方势力介入南海问题只会加剧局势紧张 》 "Russia Ministry of Foreign Affairs says that interference by third parties into the South China Sea issue will only heighten the tensions"
6/16/2016	21	《美国作家及外交政策分析人士--《纽约时报》在南海问题上错了》 "American writer and foreign policy analyst Ben Reynolds—The *New York Times* Is Wrong About the South China Sea"
7/4/2016	3	《捷克众议院副议长--菲律宾提起南海仲裁的行为自相矛盾》 "Deputy Speaker of the Czech Republic Parliament—the Philippines' submission of the arbitration is self-contradictory)"
7/11/2016	3	《非洲媒体批评美国干涉南海问题》 "African media criticizes the US for interfering in the South China Sea issue"
7/11/2016	21	《柬埔寨政府--不支持国际仲裁庭就南海问题做出裁决》 "Cambodian government does not support the South China Sea ruling made by the Arbitral Tribunal"
7/12/21	21	《南海仲裁有百害而无一利--访美国国务院前法律顾问亚伯拉罕·索费尔》 "South China Sea arbitration has much harm but no benefit—Interview with former legal adviser of the U.S. State Department Abraham Sofaer"
7/13/2016	3	《台湾当局--南海仲裁结果无拘束力，绝不接受》 "Taiwan authorities—the South China Sea arbitration ruling is nonbinding and they will never accept it"

Sino-Philippines Arbitration on the South China Sea 141

Table 4.2 Continued

Date	Page	Article Title
7/24/2016	3	《国际法不能沦为政治工具--德国专家塔尔蒙谈南海仲裁案》 "International law cannot be reduced to a political tool—German expert Talmon on the South China Sea arbitration case"
7/29/2016	3	《"域外国家在南海问题上没有发言权"--访印度尼赫鲁大学教授狄伯杰》 "'Outside countries have no say in the South China Sea issue'—Interview with Jawaharlal Nehru University Professor Deepak"
7/29/2016	21	《"谈判才是解决南海问题的最佳方式"--澳大利亚专家质疑南海仲裁合法性》 "'Negotiation is the best way to resolve the South China Sea issue'—Australian experts question the legality of South China Sea arbitration"

A government official confirmed that the arbitration had a "significant impact on China's national image," hence Beijing had to engage in a bit of "theatrics."[95] The posturing rhetoric, while sounding assertive, never truly threatened substantive consequences. For instance, in two commentaries by Zhong Sheng in *People's Daily*, Beijing cautioned that "Washington should recognize that there is a bottom line with every issue and a price will be paid if that line is crossed."[96] But where that bottom line lies was never clearly defined.

On the day the ruling was released, Chinese President Xi Jinping, the PRC government, the Foreign Ministry, and the National People's Congress all issued statements, declaring the ruling to be "null and void with no binding force."[97] The State Council Information Office released a white paper detailing the history and the legal basis of China's claim, and calling for bilateral negotiations for dispute settlement.[98] During the press release of the white paper, China's Vice Foreign Minister Liu Zhenmin warned that the decision to establish an air defense identification zone (ADIZ) in the South China Sea—a potential retaliation—would depend on "a comprehensive judgement" about "our threat perception."[99] The bellicose Chinese stand, however, subsided dramatically within the week. The dispute faded from people's sight as soon as Beijing and Manila took steps to repair the relationship.

A variation on the theme of hardline posturing in this media campaign was the reportage on the government's proactive actions. This coverage emphasized the authorities' ability to handle the situation and safeguard China's sovereignty and interests. In doing so, it also aimed to deflect nationalist criticisms, maintain face, and preserve social stability. Among the proactive government measures amplified by *People's Daily* were, for example, the Twelfth Senior Officials Meeting to implement the "Declaration on the Conduct of Parties in the South China Sea," a second-track discussion between former

142 The Art of State Persuasion

State Councilor Dai Bingguo and former Deputy Secretary of State John D. Negroponte, as well as Chinese and American scholars. Other activities featured were Foreign Minister Wang Yi's telephone talk with US Secretary of State John Kerry, the meeting between the head of the People's Liberation Army Navy (PLAN) Admiral Wu Shengli and his US counterpart Chief of Naval Operations Admiral John Richardson, and the Joint Communiqué of The 49th ASEAN Foreign Ministers' Meeting.[100] Furthermore, a "Think Tank Seminar on South China Sea and Regional Cooperation and Development," attended by former Chinese State Council Information Office Minister Zhao Qizheng and held in Singapore, was reported on in *People's Daily* for three consecutive days.[101]

As a crucial complement to the hardline rhetoric that echoes and postures, a pacification campaign also uses "positive framing" to balance the harsh rhetoric and guide public opinion toward acquiescence and obedience. Positive framing tweaks the message carefully to encourage cooperation and discourage dissent from the public. It focuses on and selects the positive aspects of a dispute, uses positive language, promotes positive emotions, and advocates for pro-government, anti-violence public responses.

In this media campaign, a central theme of positive framing aimed to validate China's territorial claims, clarify China's stance on the arbitration, and explicate its legal reasoning. An article by Zhong Sheng on June 27, for instance, posited that "the Spratly Islands have been a part of China since ancient times." Starting from the 1970s, numerous coastal nations began to claim and occupy islands and reefs "that had always belonged to China." China's lack of immediate action was "not due to incapacity to halt these unlawful occupations," but rather it chose to adopt a highly restrained approach. "The genes of peace are deeply ingrained in the Chinese people's DNA . . . China will persist in its role as a participant, a builder, and a contributor to the international order."[102]

This theme partly elucidated and championed China's preference for bilateral negotiations to address the dispute. State media repeatedly underscored China's preference for bilateral talks over third-party arbitration, evidenced by publishing remarks of a MoFA spokesperson in an official statement titled "Adhering to Resolving Disputes between China and the Philippines in the South China Sea through Bilateral Negotiations," as well as multiple commentaries by Zhong Sheng bearing similar titles like "Building Trust through Institutionalized Dialogues," "Negotiation is the Sole Method to Resolve the Dispute," and "Negotiation Is the Exclusive Solution to the Problem."[103]

Positive framing also entailed citation of favorable remarks from international legal experts and enumerated countries and organizations that supported China's position. Articles with this theme totaled 46 and accounted for more than a quarter of the 206 total articles published on the issue during the crisis. On June 14, Chinese MoFA spokesperson Lu Kang cited at a regular press conference "nearly 60 countries ha[d] publicly endorsed China's stance."[104] That number rose to 70 on July 15.[105]

A third positive framing theme focused on technological or infrastructure achievements related to the islands to invoke a sense of pride among average citizens. Examples in this cluster included a briefing on the construction progress of five lighthouses on the China-occupied features, which stressed how they facilitated "navigation safety and search and rescue;" an announcement of a China Maritime Day to promote maritime awareness; a front-page picture news story on China's 10,000-meter-class manned submersible, arriving in the target waters of the South China Sea for scientific research; and a travel essay from a writers group that visited the Robert Island of the Paracels.[106]

Other positive framing underscored China's cooperation with multilateral organizations such as ASEAN, an organization with strategic significance given that the Philippines is a member state and the organization is deeply involved in the dispute. For instance, on May 25, a report covering Chinese Defense Minister Chang Wanquan's participation in the 6th China-ASEAN Defense Ministers Informal Meeting in Vientiane, Laos quoted Chang's reiteration that "China's peaceful development path will not change . . . its sincerity for settling disputes through peaceful negotiations will not waver, and China will not shirk its responsibility to maintain regional peace and stability."[107] *People's Daily* published the full text of the Joint Statement from the July 24 China-ASEAN Foreign Ministers' summit following the release of the ruling,[108] and devoted almost its entire page 21 to the summit, including a detailed summary, a commentary by Zhong Sheng with the title, "Eliminate Disturbances, Promote China-ASEAN Cooperation," and a news report on meetings between the Chinese Foreign Minister and his Japanese, Russian, and US counterparts during the summit.[109]

The media also positive-framed the issue simply by using more positive language (more on this in Chapter 6). Studies find that articles with positive attitudes dominated the media during this time, which is unusual given media's natural tendency to "attribute responsibility" in a crisis. In June 2016, articles with positive attitudes exceeded those with negative attitudes by 25.5 percent, and this number rose even higher to 40 percent in July.[110] State media articles with titles such as "Nothing Can Shake the Power of Peace and Justice," "China is the real keeper of peace and stability in the South China Sea," and "Adhere to win-win cooperation and promote mutual development" exemplify the government's efforts to spin a positive story out of a difficult situation.[111]

144   The Art of State Persuasion

Fifth, working in tandem with positive framing, the promotion of positive emotions such as national pride and the delegitimization of negative and "unhelpful" emotions prevents violence and dissent that would put the state in a precarious position. In this crisis, given the concern that hardline public opinion might turn on the state, the campaign worked to delegitimize "unhelpful" emotions by claiming the high moral ground of reason and rationality. As an editor attested in an interview:

> Because the ruling was expected to be unfavorable [to China], we need to help the public to understand it "objectively" and "rationally." Thus, after the release [of the award], the public would know how to refute the ruling with reason, but not to vent their anger recklessly.[112]

Toward this end, the state media dedicated considerable effort to investigative reporting. Instead of promulgating negative emotions, as is common in a mobilization campaign, these articles provided reasoned arguments, citing evidence from history and law. For instance, several *People's Daily* commentaries by Zhong Sheng defended China's claims to the South China Sea by referencing historical documents and artifacts as proof of China's early discovery, naming, and development of the islands.[113] Regarding legal matters, they widely sought out expert opinions. *People's Daily* interviewed or published articles authored directly by various Chinese and international law professors and maritime law experts, including former ICJ judge Abdul Gadire Koroma.[114] During the arbitration, Chinese scholars were summoned by the state and published a total of 2,880 academic papers on the subject.[115] All these measures indicate the adoption of an evidence- and reasoning-based approach, acting as a counterbalance to negative emotions that could threaten social and political stability.

The state media was unequivocal about its distaste for the kind of "patriotism" that took it to the street. A *People's Daily* article called it "confused love" that fell to the whims of "blind impulse and extreme action," "bringing harm to our society and country." Instead, it advocated for the kind of "patriotism" infused with "rationality, pragmatism, and tolerance." The "correct" form of patriotism should aslo incorporate a "great power mentality" that featured "tolerance, inclusiveness, calm and confidence." All of these aimed at inducing a more dovish or tolerant public opinion. The article highlighted the significance of achieving state–public alignment, providing direct confirmation of the alignment logic at play: "In the realm of public opinion, the state's attitude and the public's stand are in unison . . . [This] provides the public opinion basis and conditions for China to deal with the South China Sea dispute, and demonstrates a new level of patriotism."[116]

Lastly, in this media campaign, social media platforms served as a convenient space for the public to express their anger within the "safe boundaries" established by the state. Discussions on all major online platforms were largely allowed. One editor from an official media's online forum likened her job to flood control, stating, "When the tides are too high, the method of barrier blocking gives way to the drainage systems."[117]

The outpouring of public emotion in online forums and social media was phenomenal. During July 1–20, over five million online comments were posted on Sina Weibo.[118] In the 31 hours following the release of the award, 3,941,730 Weibo comments and 25,130 WeChat articles were published.[119] The Weibo accounts of *People's Daily*, *Global Times*, and CCTV were all very active. *People's Daily*'s threaded comment "the Philippines-initiated Arbitral Tribunal on the South China Sea released an illegal and null ruling. China declared non-acceptance and non-recognition." was retweeted 444,587 times and attracted 53,149 comments.[120]

At the release of the award, *People's Daily*'s official Weibo account launched a special topic discussion, which featured the hashtag "China: not even a bit can be left behind (*Zhongguo, yidian dou bu neng shao*)." The phrase, which is a play on words suggesting China's nine-dash line (as the Chinese word for "bit" is the same as that for "dash"), was retweeted over 1.5 million times by the same evening.[121] Numerous Chinese celebrities also voiced their support for China's position on Weibo, inspiring an even broader public response.

Research on social media behavior during the crisis characterized the posts as being filled with anger, mockery, and censure. Xie and Zhu found the public comments to be "overly entertaining," replete with jokes and parodies.[122] Examples included slogans such as "boycotting dried mango"; parodies involving the Goddess of Mercy, who, according to legend, resides in the South China Sea; a cartoon of a girl clutching a fish in her hand, stating "I'd rather throw it away than give it to you"; and using the word "Philippines" as an adjective in phrases such as "Don't be too Philippine (*zuo ren bu yao tai Feilvbin*)."

The light-hearted approach, filled with jokes, spoofs, and parodies, made these posts more of a social commentary rather than a call to action. These posts, characterized by their playful nature, served as an effective outlet for the public to express their frustrations regarding the crisis. By voicing their sentiments openly in a nonthreatening and casual manner, citizens were able to vent their feelings about the issue, thus reducing potential societal tension. In comparison, posts that are advocating for serious actions or decisions are generally more straightforward, dire, and urgent in tone. Such posts would not typically employ humor or satire but would present arguments, appeal to logic or emotions, and propose specific steps to be taken. The government's allowance of this kind of expression suggests an understanding of the need for the public to have a means to vent frustrations, as long as it does not cross the line into promoting unrest or disorder.

As part of the Chinese government's effort to maintain social stability, the state limited public venting to verbal or written expressions, while discouraging physical manifestations such as public protests. In this instance, the Central Propaganda Department (CPD) clearly instructed the media to avoid promoting or disseminating information about "recent illegal gatherings and protests."[123] This directive reflects a broader policy of suppressing any form of potential civil unrest, especially when it pertains to sensitive international issues.

Despite the heated national sentiment around the South China Sea arbitration, large-scale public protests were noticeably absent in the aftermath of the Tribunal's decision. Instead, what was observed were only a few isolated, small-scale protests, predominantly in Beijing. This can be attributed to the state's careful management of public sentiment and its stringent control over potential collective action. This approach allowed the state to manage the narrative around the dispute and avoid escalations that could lead to widespread public demonstrations.

Alternative Explanations of Diversion or Audience Cost?

Audience costs and a diversionary narrative are important factors to assess in this scenario. One might speculate whether the Chinese state orchestrated the media campaign to sway public sentiment, compelling the Philippines to withdraw its case or reinforcing its claim over the South China Sea. However, the case does not meet the expectations of the audience costs theory.

If China were operating under this theory, it would have publicly declared its threats while engaging in coercion. Indeed, Beijing did employ coercive tactics before Manila initiated the case and during the initial stages of the arbitration. Following the 2012 Scarborough Shoal standoff but prior to the Philippines officially announcing the initiation of the case, Beijing attempted to force Manila to acknowledge the fait accompli in the Scarborough Shoal and to dissuade Manila from taking the issue to an international forum. To recall, during Fu Ying's visit to Manila in October 2012, Fu advised Manila "not to appeal to the UN to resolve the dispute . . . not to 'internationalize' the issue in forums such as the Association of Southeast Asian Nations (ASEAN), not to collaborate with any other country such as the US, and even not to issue press releases."

However, this coercion took place quietly behind closed doors. Fu's comments were not reported until January of the following year, and then only by the *Wall Street Journal*, not by any Chinese media outlet. Beijing did not issue any official public threats aimed at deterring Manila from any actions. This indicates that the media campaign's purpose was unlikely about generating audience costs by making public threats.

The coercion timeline in this case also fails to support an audience costs hypothesis. After Manila announced its intentions to proceed with the arbitration case against Beijing in January 2013—following the failure of Beijing's initial deterrence efforts—Beijing attempted to coerce Manila into dropping the case and reverting to a bilateral approach. In August 2013, China insisted that Philippine President Benigno Aquino III abandon the arbitration case as a precondition for his participation at the annual China-ASEAN Expo. Aquino declined the demand and cancelled the trip, marking a second failed coercive attempt by Beijing.[124]

As Philippine Secretary of Foreign Affairs Albert del Rosario recalled in an interview with *Foreign Policy*, Beijing had repeatedly asserted that the dispute "should not be resolved through arbitration, but through bilateral consultations." This effort also proved unsuccessful. Despite Beijing's objections and refusal to participate, the court proceeded with the case. The Philippines officially submitted its petition to the Tribunal on March 30, 2014. However, a propaganda campaign was not initiated until June 2016, long after coercion had failed multiple times, and it was too late to instigate any change. This timeline suggests that the media campaign was not designed to create audience costs.

The audience costs theory traditionally applies when a state proactively leverages a situation to make threats that it then must follow through to avoid losing credibility. This requires the state to publicly commit to a course of action, creating a cost if it later must back down. It is a strategic move that is usually premeditated, aiming to gain an advantage in international relations by creating a situation where backing down would be costly.

However, the Chinese propaganda campaign, as described here, was predominantly "reactive" and "remedial." The campaign was reactive—launched only after the Philippines had committed to the arbitration and Beijing's attempts at coercion had failed. Furthermore, it was remedial—it sought to remedy or mitigate the fallout from the failed coercion and the move to arbitration. This suggests that the campaign was a response to the failed attempts at coercion rather than a premeditated strategy to generate audience costs. Therefore, while the audience costs theory may be applicable to some aspects of China's South China Sea policy, it is not an accurate frame to understand this specific propaganda campaign.

The substance of the media campaign also does not align with an audience costs scenario—a situation where a leader makes a public commitment to a course of action, effectively tying their hands and creating costs for backing down. The bulk of this campaign relied on presenting evidence, reasoning, and expert opinions. It focused on reflecting public sentiment while refraining from inciting anger, and consistently underscored positive aspects in most publications. These characteristics are hard to reconcile with a conventional antagonistic media campaign designed to stir up hostilities or generate audience costs.

Furthermore, Beijing's efforts to preempt public protests contradict the logic of audience costs. Rather than mobilizing public sentiment to pressure the Philippines, the actions taken by Beijing appear more oriented toward maintaining internal stability and managing the narrative around the arbitration case. This approach diverges from the expected behavior under the audience costs theory, further supporting the notion that the media campaign was not intended to generate audience costs.

The diversionary theory, which posits that leaders may instigate international conflicts to divert public attention away from domestic problems, also seems difficult to substantiate in this case. There was no significant domestic crisis concurrent with these events that would necessitate a diversion of public attention. The only potential candidate could be the stock market turbulence that started in the summer of 2015 and fueled early 2016 speculations about a possible economic collapse with global ramifications.[125]

However, the stock market turbulence was far from becoming a real crisis. Speculations about a potential economic collapse did not gain substantial traction and soon lost steam. Therefore, it is difficult to consider it as a driver for a diversionary strategy.

Moreover, the timing of the media campaign was evidently influenced by the progression of the territorial dispute, particularly the impending announcement of the Tribunal ruling. There is little to suggest that it was initiated in response to any domestic crisis. If any other crisis did exist, there is no clear evidence linking it to the launch of this media campaign. In this context, it seems more plausible to interpret the campaign as a response to the external, not internal, developments that were unfolding at the time.

After the Campaign

Substantial evidence in this case bolsters the logic of the (mis)alignment theory and a pacification campaign. By controlling the discourse, echoing public sentiment, posturing through stern remarks, framing the situation positively, delegitimizing counterproductive emotions, and allowing the public to express their views online (but not in action), the Chinese state managed to calm public opinion to a level that aligned with the more moderate policy China adopted.

A senior editor at an official media outlet noted that the state and public opinions were "highly aligned" when the Tribunal ruling was issued, signifying the state's success in achieving its media campaign goals.[126] Another editor mentioned that after the ruling, the public seemed less invested in the arbitration. He said, "Before the result came out, the general public stance was that the Philippines was manipulating international law to bully China. However, the public didn't necessarily follow up with the actual policy the state implemented afterward."[127]

As predicted by the (mis)alignment theory and confirmed by studies of popular sentiment, public emotion cooled a few days following the announcement of the award and remained relatively subdued thereafter. This suggests the effectiveness of China's media campaign in realigning public sentiment with the state's subsequent moderate policy approach.

Notes

1. Author interview, June 9, 2017, Beijing.
2. Author interview, June 5, 2017, Beijing.
3. The case is very well-documented thanks to its legal nature and the documentations collected and published by Permanent Court of Arbitration (PCA). For all PCA documentations on the case, see https://pca-cpa.org/en/cases/7/, accessed June 4, 2020.
4. The Permanent Court of Arbitration (PCA), "Award in the Matter of the South China Sea Arbitration between The Republic of the Philippines and the People's Republic of China," July 12, 2016, https://www.pcacases.com/web/sendAttach/2086, accessed April 12, 2018, 1.
5. "How Much Trade Transits the South China Sea?," Center for Strategic and International Studies China Power Project. https://chinapower.csis.org/much-trade-transits-south-china-sea/, accessed April 16, 2018.
6. "Interview with Albert del Rosario: You Will Have Chaos and Anarchy," *Foreign Policy*, October 5, 2015, https://foreignpolicy.com/2015/10/05/you-will-have-chaos-and-anarchy-albert-del-rosario-philippines-south-china-sea/.
7. Sourabh Gupta, "Philippines v. China Arbitration: Be Careful What You Wish For," *PacNet*, no. 28 (March 17, 2016), https://csis-website-prod.s3.amazonaws.com/s3fs-public/legacy_files/files/publication/160317_PacNet_1628.pdf.

150 The Art of State Persuasion

8. "Manila Takes a Stand," *Wall Street Journal Asia*, January 25, 2013, https://www.wsj.com/articles/SB10001424127887323539804578261140985134254.

9. "Interview with Albert del Rosario: You Will Have Chaos and Anarchy," *Foreign Policy*, October 5, 2015, https://foreignpolicy.com/2015/10/05/you-will-have-chaos-and-anarchy-albert-del-rosario-philippines-south-china-sea/.

10. "Manila Takes a Stand"; author interview, May 29, 2017, Beijing.

11. In a press appearance with the visiting then-Philippine President Benigno Aquino on April 28, 2014, President Obama said: "The United States supports his [Aquino's] decision to pursue international arbitration concerning territorial disputes in the South China Sea." See The White House, "Remarks by President Obama and President Benigno Aquino III of the Philippines in Joint Press Conference," April 28, 2014, http://www.whitehouse.gov/the-press-office/2014/04/28/remarks-president-obama-and-president-benigno-aquino-iii-philippines-joi; Daniel Russel, US Assistant Secretary of State also talked positively about the arbitration at the Fifth Annual South China Sea Conference held by the Center for Strategic and International Studies (CSIS) on July 21, 2015. See Daniel Russel, "Remarks at the Fifth Annual South China Sea Conference," US Department of State, https://2009-2017.state.gov/p/eap/rls/rm/2015/07/245142.htm, accessed June 5, 2020; in his testimony before the House Committee on Foreign Affairs on April 28, 2016, the US Deputy Secretary of State Antony J. Blinken confirmed that "we have worked very hard to establish across the region an understanding that this [the arbitration] is an appropriate mechanism." See US Congress, House Committee on Foreign Affairs, "America as a Pacific Power: Challenges and Opportunities in Asia," 114th Congress, 2nd session, April 28, 2016, https://foreignaffairs.house.gov/hearing/hearing-america-as-a-pacific-power-challenges-and-opportunities-in-asia/.

12. CSIS, "China Island Tracker," Asia Maritime Transparency Initiative, https://amti.csis.org/island-tracker/china/, accessed April 17, 2018.

13. "Statement by Secretary of Foreign Affairs Albert del Rosario on the UNCLOS Arbitral Proceedings against China to Achieve a Peaceful and Durable Solution to the Dispute in the WPS," January 22, 2013, http://www.philippineembassy-usa.org/news/3071/300/Statement-by-Secretary-of-Foreign-Affairs-Albert-del-Rosario-on-the-UNCLOS-Arbitral-Proceedings-against-China-to-Achieve-a-Peaceful-and-Durable-Solution-to-the-Dispute-in-the-WPS/d,phildet/. For full text of the Notification and Statement of Claim, see http://www.philippineembassy-usa.org/uploads/pdfs/embassy/2013/2013-0122-Notification%20and%20Statement%20of%20Claim%20on%20West%20Philippine%20Sea.pdf, accessed April 12, 2018; "Note Verbale from the Embassy of the People's Republic of China in Manila to the Department of Foreign Affairs, Republic of the Philippines, No. (13) PG-039," 19 February 2013, Memorial of the Philippines—Volume III, Annex 3, https://www.pcacases.com/web/view/7, accessed April 12, 2018.

14. PRC MoFA, "Remarks by Foreign Ministry Spokesperson Hong Lei on the Philippines' Submission of a Memorial to the Arbitral Tribunal in Relation to Disputes with China in the South China Sea," March 30, 2014, http://www.fmprc.gov.cn/nanhai/eng/fyrbt_1/t1142356.htm.

15. PRC MoFA, "Position Paper of the Government of the People's Republic of China on the Matter of Jurisdiction in the South China Sea Arbitration Initiated by the Republic of the Philippines," December 7, 2014, http://www.fmprc.gov.cn/nanhai/eng/snhwtlcwj_1/t1368895.htm.

16. PRC MoFA, "Statement of the Ministry of Foreign Affairs of the People's Republic of China on the Award on Jurisdiction and Admissibility of the South China Sea Arbitration by the Arbitral Tribunal Established at the Request of the Republic of the Philippines," October 30, 2015, http://www.fmprc.gov.cn/mfa_eng/zxxx_662805/t1310474.shtml.

17. "China Says Philippines Guilty of 'Political Provocation,'" Associated Press, February 25, 2016, https://www.philstar.com/headlines/2016/02/25/1557009/china-says-philippines-guilty-political-provocation; "Philippines Asks China to Respect Sea Dispute Arbitration," *Reuters*, February 29, 2016, https://uk.reuters.com/article/uk-southchinasea-philippines/philippines-asks-china-to-respect-sea-dispute-arbitration-idUKKCN0W20RG.

18. "Philippines 'Willing to Share' South China Sea Resources," *Global Times*, July 9, 2016, http://www.globaltimes.cn/content/993126.shtml.

19. PCA, "Award in the Matter of the South China Sea Arbitration."

20. "Philippines Urges 'Restraint and Sobriety' After South China Sea Ruling," *Reuters*, July 12, 2016, https://www.reuters.com/article/us-southchinasea-ruling-philippines/philippines-urges-restraint-and-sobriety-after-south-china-sea-ruling-idUSKCN0ZS0W0.

21. "After Victory at Sea, Reality Sets In for Philippines," *New York Times*, July 15, 2016, A3.

22. "Bacheng Minzhong Zhichi Junshi Huiji Nanhai Tiaoxin—Zhongguo Zhoubian Anquan Gongzhong Taidu Diaocha Baogao (80 Percent Citizens Support Military Response to South China Sea Provocations—Survey Report on Public Attitudes on China's Peripheral Security)," *Global Times*, May 2, 2012, 3.

23. "Huanqiu Yuqing Diaocha Zhongxin he Taiwan Zhongshi Mindiao Zhongxin Lianhe Diaocha Xianshi Liang'an Minzhong Zhichi Lianshou Shiya Feilvbin (Huanqiu Public Opinion Survey Center and Taiwan Zhongshi Public Opinion Poll Center Joint Survey Shows Citizens Across the Strait Support Joint Pressure Against the Philippines)," *Global Times*, May 13, 2013, 3.

24. Author interview, July 18, 2023, Beijing.

25. Ashton Carter, "A Regional Security Architecture Where Everyone Rises," speech delivered at IISS, Shanri-La Dialogue, Singapore, May 30, 2015, https://www.defense.gov/News/Speeches/Speech-View/Article/606676/; "Obama Calls on Beijing to Stop Construction in South China Sea," *New York Times*, November 18, 2015, https://www.nytimes.com/2015/11/19/world/asia/obama-apec-summit-south-china-sea-philippines.html.

26. Mingming Shen; Ming Yang; Jie Yan; Liying Ren, 2018, "Beijing Area Study-2015," https://doi.org/10.18170/DVN/I2KVEU, Peking University Open Research Data Platform, V2

27. The Baidu Search Index (BSI) data spans from January 1, 2011, to October 15, 2017. It is important to clarify that these indices do not represent the exact count of daily searches. Instead, they offer a relative measure of search activity. While the specific calculations remain undisclosed, the BSI takes into account the growing population of internet users in China. Consequently, these data allow for reliable comparisons over time and across different search keywords.

28. Jiang Yesha and Luo Jiaojiang, "Hulianwang Meijie Zhiyu Guojia Rentong de Goujian: Yi Nanhai Zhongcaian Yuqing Chuanbo Wei Li (The Internet Media and the Construction of National Identity—Using the South China Sea Arbitration Case as An Example)," *Xinwenjie* (*The News World*) 24 (2016), 57–72.

29. Austin Ramzy, "KFC Targeted in Protests over South China Sea," *New York Times*, July 19, 2016, https://www.nytimes.com/2016/07/20/world/asia/south-china-sea-protests-kfc.html.

152 The Art of State Persuasion

30. Zhao Jinsong, "Ying Jiajin Yulun Yingdui 'Feilvbin Nanhai Zhongcaian' (China Must Strengthen Media Counter-Measures Against the Philippines' South China Sea Arbitration Case)," *Gonggong Waijiao Jikan* (Public Diplomacy Quarterly), no. 2 (2016).

31. Author interview, May 29, 2017, Beijing.

32. Irene Chan and Mingjiang Li, "New Chinese Leadership, New Policy in the South China Sea Dispute?," *Journal of Chinese Political Science* 20, no. 1 (March 1, 2015): 38–39.

33. For China's declaration under Article 298, see United Nations Division for Ocean Affairs and the Law of the Sea, "Declarations and Statements," http://www.un.org/depts/los/convention_agreements/convention_declarations.htm#China%20after%20ratification; for content of Article 298, see http://www.un.org/depts/los/convention_agreements/convention_declarations.htm, accessed April 19, 2018.

34. "Beijing Looks Like a 'Bully' By Rejecting Arbitration on South China Sea Issue," *South China Morning Post*, May 25, 2013, http://www.scmp.com/news/china/article/1245471/beijing-looks-bully-rejecting-arbitration-south-china-sea-issue, April 19, 2018.

35. Gregory B. Poling, "A Tumultuous 2016 in the South China Sea," CSIS Commentary, February 18, 2016, https://www.csis.org/analysis/tumultuous-2016-south-china-sea.

36. Author interview, June 9, 2017, Beijing.

37. Author interviews, May 26, 2017, Beijing; May 29, 2017, Beijing.

38. Author interviews, May 22, 2017, Beijing; May 29, 2017, Beijing.

39. Chinese diplomats expected that the ASEAN Foreign Ministers' summit would be held right after the release of the ruling, so they also worked to forestall the issuance of an ASEAN statement that mentioned the ruling. On April 23, 2016, Chinese Foreign Minister Wang Yi took a whirlwind tour of Brunei, Cambodia, and Laos that resulted in a four-point consensus among the countries. The consensus stated that the South China Sea dispute was not an ASEAN-China issue; the dispute should be resolved through dialogues and consultations by parties directly concerned; no unilateral will should be imposed on them; and countries outside the region should play a constructive role. This consensus implicitly supported China's position that the dispute should be resolved through bilateral negotiations, opposed the Philippines' approach of seeking third-party arbitration, and criticized outside powers such as the US and Japan for their involvement.

40. "Xiwang Feilvbin Xinyijie Zhengfu Tong Zhongfang Xiangxiang'erxing (Hope the New Philippine Governnment Will Work toward the Same Direction with China)," *People's Daily*, May 10, 21.

41. "China Congratulates Philippines' New President Duterte," *The Diplomat*, 1 July 2016, https://thediplomat.com/2016/07/china-congratulates-philippines-new-president-duterte/.

42. "Guofangbu Xinwen Fayanren: Zhongguo Jundui Jiang Jianding Buyi Hanwei Guojia Zhuquan, Qnquan he Haiyang Quanyi (Department of Defense Spokesperson: Chinese Military Will Unswervingly Defend National Sovereignty, Security, and Maritime Rights)," *People's Daily*, July 13, 2016, 3.

43. PRC MoFA, "Foreign Ministry Spokesperson Lu Kang's Regular Press Conference on July 14, 2016," July 14, 2016, http://www.chinaconsulatechicago.org/eng/fyrth/t1381622.htm.

44. Feng Zhang et al, "China's Claims in the South China Sea Rejected," *ChinaFile*, July 13, 2016, http://www.chinafile.com/conversation/chinas-claims-south-china-sea-rejected.

45. "Ramos the Icebreaker: Former Philippine President Heads to Hong Kong to Test China Waters," *South China Morning Post*, August 8, 2016, http://www.scmp.com/news/china/diplomacy-defence/article/2000842/former-philippines-presid

ent-fidel-ramos-heads-beijing; for content of the joint statement, see https://www.china usfocus.com/news/2016/0812/3714.html.

46. "Philippines Wants Formal Talks to Ease Tensions with China, Says Ex-President Ramos," *South China Morning Post*, August 12, 2016, http://www.scmp.com/news/china/diplom acy-defence/article/2002784/philippines-wants-formal-talks-ease-tensions-china-says.

47. PRC MoFA, "Joint Statement of the Foreign Ministers of ASEAN Member States and China on the Full and Effective Implementation of the Declaration on the Conduct of Parties in the South China Sea," July 25, 2016, http://www.fmprc.gov.cn/nanhai/eng/zcfg_1/t1384 245.htm.

48. "The 13th Senior Officials' Meeting on the Implementation of the DOC Held in Manzhouli, Inner Mongolia," August 16, 2016, http://www.fmprc.gov.cn/nanhai/eng/wjbxw_1/t1389 619.htm; "Can Manzhouli Work Its Magic on the South China Sea Disputes?," *South China Morning Post*, August 21, 2016, http://www.scmp.com/week-asia/politics/article/2006260/ can-manzhouli-work-its-magic-south-china-sea-disputes.

49. PRC MoFA, "Foreign Ministry Spokesperson Hua Chunying's Regular Press Conference on May 19," May 19, 2017, http://www.fmprc.gov.cn/mfa_eng/xwfw_665399/s2510_665 401/t1463588.shtml.

50. "Filipino Fisherman Back in Disputed South China Sea Shoal After Duterte's Beijing Pivot," *South China Morning Post*, October 30, 2016, http://www.scmp.com/news/asia/southeast-asia/article/2041371/filipino-fisherman-back-disputed-south-china-sea-shoal.

51. Author interview, May 29, 2017, Beijing.

52. Author interview, June 9, 2017, Beijing.

53. Author interview, May 22, 2017, Beijing.

54. Author interview, May 29, 2017, Beijing.

55. These notes were quoted in several author interviews with Chinese journalists and editors working in official media outlets, Beijing, China, May 2017.

56. Ibid.

57. Author interview, May 26, 2017, Beijing.

58. See more detailed discussion in Appendix 3.

59. Author interview, May 26, 2017, Beijing.

60. The Philippines Department of Foreign Affairs, "SFA Statement on the UNCLOS Arbitral Proceedings against China," January 22, 2013, https://www.dfa.gov.ph/127-newsroom/unc los/216-sfa-statement-on-the-unclos-arbitral-proceedings-against-china.

61. "Feilvbin Zhongcai'an Shi Pizhe Falv Waiyi Dui Zhongguo Jinxing Zhengzhi Tiaoxin (The Philippine Arbitration Is A Political Provocation Under A Legal Cloak)," *People's Daily*, May 6, 2016, 21.

62. PRC MoFA, "Director-General of the Department of Boundary and Ocean Affairs of the Ministry of Foreign Affairs Ouyang Yujing Gives Interview to Chinese and Foreign Media on South China Sea Issue," May 6, 2016, http://www.fmprc.gov.cn/nanhai/eng/wjbxw_1/ t1365689.htm.

63. "Zhongguo Buhui Zongrong Gebie Guojia Zai Nanhai Wenti shang 'Yixiao'eda' (China Will Not Condone Individual Countries' Blackmails in the Name of Being Small)," *People's Daily*, May 10, 2016, 21.

64. PRC MoFA, "Briefing by Xu Hong, Director-General of the Department of Treaty and Law on the South China Sea Arbitration Initiated by the Philippines," May 12, 2016, http:// www.fmprc.gov.cn/mfa_eng/wjdt_665385/zyjh_665391/t1364804.shtml.

154 The Art of State Persuasion

65. Author interview, May 28, 2017, Beijing.

66. PRC MoFA, "China's Sovereignty and Maritime Rights and Interests in the South China Sea Shall Not Be Affected by Arbitration Award" (Beijing: PRC MoFA, July 16, 2016), http://www.fmprc.gov.cn/nanhai/eng/wjbxw_1/t1382766.htm.

67. PRC MoFA, "Foreign Ministry Spokesperson Lu Kang's Remarks on Statement by Spokesperson of US State Department on South China Sea Arbitration Ruling" (Beijing: PRC MoFA, July 13, 2016), http://www.fmprc.gov.cn/mfa_eng/xwfw_665399/s2510_665401/t1380409.shtml.

68. PRC MoFA, "Yang Jiechi Gives Interview to State Media on the So-called Award by the Arbitral Tribunal for the South China Sea Arbitration" (Beijing: PRC MoFA, July 15, 2016), https://www.fmprc.gov.cn/eng/wjdt_665385/zyjh_665391/201607/t20160715_678561.html.

69. "Veteran Chinese Diplomat Warns on South China Sea Ruling," *Wall Street Journal*, July 6, 2016, https://blogs.wsj.com/chinarealtime/2016/07/06/veteran-chinese-diplomat-warns-on-south-china-sea-ruling/.

70. "Lishi Bu Rong Cuangai, Falv Bu Rong Lanyong—Yang Jiechi jiu Nanhai Zhongcai'an Zhongcaiting Zuochu Suowei Caijue Jieshou Renmin Ribao deng Zhongyang Meiti Caifang (History Brooks No Distortion and Law No Abuse—Yang Jiechi Gives Interview to State Media on the So-called Award by the Arbitral Tribunal for the South China Sea Arbitration)," *People's Daily*, July 15, 2016, 3.

71. PRC Ministry of Foreign Affairs, "Foreign Ministry Spokesperson Lu Kang's Remarks on Statement by Spokesperson of US State Department on South China Sea Arbitration Ruling," July 13, 2016, http://www.fmprc.gov.cn/mfa_eng/xwfw_665399/s2510_665401/t1380409.shtml; Jiang and Luo 2016, 60.

72. Author interview, June 9, 2017, Beijing, China.

73. "Na Guojifa Zhexiu de Zhengzhi Naoju Gai Jieshu le (It Is Time to End the Political Farce Under the Cover of International Law)," *People's Daily*, July 8, 2016, 3.

74. "Guojifa Qihao Nanyan Nanhai Zhongcai'an Huangmiu Dise (Flying the Flag of International Law can Hardly Conceal Its Absurd Nature)," *People's Daily*, July 10, 2016, 3.

75. "Zai Helan Xuexi Guojifa de Zhongguo Liuxuesheng Fabiao Lianming Gongkaixin—Guojifa Buneng Chengwei Zhengzhi Gongju (Chinese Students Studying International Law in the Netherlands Issue a Joint Open Letter—International Law Cannot Be a Political Tool)," *People's Daily*, July 14, 2016, 12.

76. "Nanhai Wenti Zhongcai Weifan Guojifa (South China Sea Arbtration Violates International Law)," *People's Daily*, July 20, 2016, 3.

77. "Jieke Zhongyiyuan Fuyizhang—Feilvbin Tiqi Nanhai Zhongcai de Xingwei Zixiangmaodun (Deputy Speaker of the Czech Republic Parliament—the Philippines' Submission of the Arbitration Is Self-Contradictory)," *People's Daily*, July 4, 2016, 3.

78. "'Qiege' Shoufa Tiaozhan Xiguan Guojifa ('Slicing' Technique Challenges Customary International Law)," *People's Daily*, July 21, 3.

79. For the interview with Rod Kapunan, see "Miscalculation—Interview with Philippine Political Commentator Kapunan," *People's Daily*, June 18, 2016, 11.

80. "Feilvbin Yulun Pengji Ajinuo Zhengfu Jiang Nanhai Wenti Tijiao Zhongcai (Philippine Media Criticizes the Aquino Government for Submitting the South China Sea Issue for Arbitration)," *People's Daily*, May 15, 2016, 3.

81. "Feilvbin Cai Shi Nanhai Zhengduan de Shizuoyongzhe—Fang Feilvbin Waijiaobu Haishizhongxin Qian Mishuzhang A'erweituo Ai'enkemi'enda (The Philippines Should Be the One Responsible for the South China Sea Tensions—Interview with Former Secretary-General of the Philippines Department of Foreign Affairs Maritime & Oceans Affairs Center Alberto Encomienda)," *Xinhua News*, June 9, 2016, http://www.xinhuanet.com/world/2016-06/09/c_1119016590.htm?from=timeline&isappinstalled=0; for the CCTV video clip, see http://tv.cctv.com/2016/06/09/VIDEyOOwU7t6bjO8vjpSaGro160609.shtml, accessed July 17, 2020.

82. Zhong Sheng, " 'Zhongcaiting' Jing Shi Waibu Shili Dailiren (How the Tribunal Is an Agent for External Forces)" *People's Daily*, July 13, 2016, 2; "Sikai Linshi Zhongcaiting 'Fali Quanwei' de Xujia Baozhuang (Tearing the False Packaging of 'Legal Authority' of the Temporary Tribunal)," *People's Daily*, July 15, 2016, 3; "Zhaiqu Caotai Banzi de Guanghuan (qidi linshi zhongcaiting) (Taking Off the Halo of the 'Troupe' (the Temporary Tribunal revealed))," *People's Daily*, July 17, 2016, 3; "Jiajie Falv Mingyi Yushe Zhongcai Jieguo (Qidi Linshi Zhongcaiting) (Presume the Result of the Arbitration Under the Guise of Law (the Temporary Tribunal Revealed))," *People's Daily*, July 21, 2016, 21; "Guoji Fazhi de Aixibao (Qidi Linshi Zhongcaiting) (The Cancer Cell of the International Rule of Law (the Temporary Tribunal Revealed))," *People's Daily*, July 22, 2016, 21.

83. "Qishidaoming de 'Guaitai'—Jielu Feilvbin Nanhai Zhongcai'an Zhongcaiting de Zhen Mianmu (The 'Freak' Who Deceived the World—Revealing the True Face of the Philippine South China Sea Arbitral Tribunal)," *People's Daily*, July 19, 2016, 21.

84. "Gei Zhongcaiting Suan bi Zhang (Qidi Linshi Zhongcaiting) (Balancing the Books of the Arbitral Tribunal (the Temporary Tribunal Revealed))," *People's Daily*, July 20, 2016, 21; "Nanhai Zhongcai Zhangmu Ying Xiang Shijie Gongkai (The Balance Sheet of the South China Sea Arbitration Should Be Made Public to the World)," *People's Daily*, August 1, 2016, 3.

85. "Liujing yu Linshi Zhongcaiting de Naxie Goudang (Qidi Linshi Zhongcaiting) (Yanai's Activities with the Makeshift Arbitral Tribunal (the Temporary Tribunal Revealed))," *People's Daily*, July 18, 2016, 3.

86. "Nanhai Zhongcai'an Shi Pizhe Falv Waiyi de Zhengzhi Naoju—Linshi Zhongcaiting Wanggu Falv he Shishi Zao Guoji Shehui Piping (South China Sea Arbitration Is a Political Farce Under the Cloak of Law—the Arbitral Tribunal Is Criticized By the International Society for Ignoring Law and Fact)," *People's Daily*, July 13, 2016, 3; "Nanhai Zhongcai'an Linshi Zhongcaiting Wushi 'Lianheguo Haiyang Gongyue' Zhengwen Guiding, Lanyong Fujian Yuequan Guanxia (The Makeshift Arbitral Tribunal on the South China Sea Issue Ignored the Provisions of the United Nations Convention of the Law of the Sea and Abused the Annex to Exceed Its Jurisdiction)," *People's Daily*, July 22, 2016, 1.

87. "Feilvbin Yulun Pengji Ajinuo Zhengfu Jiang Nanhai Wenti Tijiao Zhongcai (Philippine Media Criticizes the Aquino Government for Submitting the South China Sea Issue for Arbitration)," *People's Daily*, May 15, 2016, 3.

88. "Nanfei Zishen Guoji Wenti Pinglunyuan Kanwen—Quanmian Jieshao Nanhai Wenti Lishi Jingwei, Shenke Jielu Meiguo Chashou Nanhai Wenti Shizhi (South African Senior Commentator on International Issues Publishes Article That Comprehensively Introduces the South China Sea Issue and Uncovers the US' Meddling)," *People's Daily*, May 21, 2016, 3; "Yi Guojia Daxiao Pinfu Pingpan Shifei Quzhi Huangmiu Wuzhi (It Is Absurd and Ignorant to Judge Right or Wrong Based on Countries' Sizes and Wealth),"

People's Daily, May 26, 2016, 21; "Meiguo de Hangxing Ziyou Xingdong: Shi Gongli Haishi Qiangquan? (America's Freedom of Navigation Operations: Right or Might?)," *People's Daily*, June 5, 2016, 3; "Jianada Xuezhe Pi Xifang Meiti Gei Nanhai Wenti Luantie Biaoqian (Canadian Scholar Criticizes Western Media for Labeling the South China Sea Issue Indiscriminately)," *People's Daily*, June 6, 2016, 3; "Meiguo Zuojia Ji Waijiao Zhengce Fenxi Renshi—Niuyue Shibao zai Nanhai Wenti Shang Cuo le (American Writer and Foreign Policy Analyst Ben Reynolds—The *New York Times* Is Wrong About the South China Sea)," *People's Daily*, June 16, 2016, 21; "E Waijiaobu Cheng Disanfang Shili Jieru Nanhai Wenti Zhi Hui Jiaju Jushi Jinzhang (Russia Ministry of Foreign Affairs Says That Interference By Third Parties Into the South China Sea Issue Will Only Heighten the Tensions)," *People's Daily*, June 12, 2016, 3; "Meiguo Lumang Zhi Ju Weihai Yazhou Anquan (Reckless Move By the US Endangers Asian Security)," *People's Daily*, July 9, 2016, 2; "Shuangchong Biaozhun Shi Dui Guoji Fazhi de Xiedu—Nanhai Zhongcai'an Buguo Shi Chang Zhengzhi Naoju (Double Standards Are a Desecration of International Rule of Law—The South China Sea Arbitration Was Nothing But a Political Farce)," *People's Daily*, July 15, 2016, 3.

89. "Riben Bushi Nanhai Wenti Dangshiguo Meiyou Zige Dui Zhongfang Shuosandaosi (Japan Is Not a Party Involved in the South China Sea Issue and Is Not Qualified to Make Irresponsible Remarks About China)," *People's Daily*, July 25, 2016, 3; "Ri Mei Ao Meiyou Renhe Zige Dui Bieguo Zhishouhuajiao (Japan, the US, and Australia Have No Right to Point Fingers at Other Countries)," *People's Daily*, July 28, 2016, 3.

90. "Zhongcaiting Kuoquan Lanquan Yanzhong Sunhai Guoji Fazhi (The Encroachment and Abuse of Authority By the Court of Arbitration Seriously Damages International Law)," *People's Daily*, May 11, 2016, 3; "Duo ge Guojia he Diqu Zhuanjia Xuezhe Zai Jieshou Benbao Jizhe Caifang Shi Biaoshi Nanhai Zhongcai'an Pohuai Diqu Anquan Zhixu He Duihua Jizhi (Experts and Scholars from Many Countries and Regions Said in Interviews with Our Reporter That the South China Sea Arbitration Undermined Regional Security Order and Dialogue Mechanisms)," *People's Daily*, June 30, 2016, 10; "Lanyong guojifa jiu shi chongji guoji zhixu (To Abuse International Law Is to Attack the International Order)," *People's Daily*, July 12, 2016, 3; "Suowei Zhongcai Ling Nanhai Xingshi Geng Fuza—Fang Meiguo Zishen Waijiaoguan Fu Limin (The So-Called Arbitration Makes the South China Sea Issue More Complicated—Interview with US Senior Diplomat Charles Freeman)," *People's Daily*, July 19, 2016, 3.

91. "Zhongcai Jieguo Wuyi Diqu Heping (The Arbitration Ruling Is Not Beneficial to Regional Peace)," *People's Daily*, July 21, 2016, 3; "Linshi Zhongcaiting Suowei Caijue Weixie Quyu Wending (The Makeshift Arbitral Tribunal's So-Called 'Ruling' Threatens Regional Stability)," *People's Daily*, July 25, 2016, 21; "Suowei Nanhai Zhongcai Zangsong Le Fazhi Gongyun (The So-Called South China Sea Arbitration Ruined Justice and Rule of Law)," *People's Daily*, July 29, 2016, 21.

92. Author interview, May 28, 2017, Beijing.

93. *China Daily* first reprinted the English-translated version on July 13 and then *People's Daily* reprinted the Chinese-translated version on July 25. See "Czech Expert Warns US and the Philippines Not to Play Fire in South China Sea," *China Daily*, July 13, 2016, https://www.chinadaily.com.cn/world/2016-07/13/content_26073312.htm; "Qiangzhi Zhongcai Shi Xuyi Tiaoxin (Forced Arbitration Is a Deliberate Provocation)," *People's Daily*, July 25, 2016, 3.

94. Shi Shuqin, "Feilvbin Tiqi Nanhai Zhengduan Qiangzhi Zhongcai de Yuanyin, Houguo Ji Zhongguo de Yingdui" (The Causes and Consequences of the Forced Arbitration Case Brought by the Philippines and How China Should React)," *Yingguo Yanjiu* (England Studies) 7 (2015).

95. Author interview, May 26, 2017, Beijing.

96. "Meiguo, Xuanyao Wuli Jiushi Gao Baquan! (America, Showing Off Muscles Is Practicing Hegemony!)," *People's Daily*, June 22, 2016, 2; "Meiguo Bu Yao Zai Nanhai Wenti Shang Chongzhuang Dixian (America Must Not Cross the Bottom Line on the South China Sea Issue)," *People's Daily*, July 6, 2016, 3.

97. "Xi Jinping Met with President of the European Council, Donald Tusk and President of the European Commission, Jean-Claude Juncker," *Xinhua News*, July 12, 2016, http://www.xinhuanet.com/world/2016-07/12/c_1119207979.htm. Xi made remarks on the ruling during the meeting; PRC MoFA "Statement of the Government of the People's Republic of China on China's Territorial Sovereignty and Maritime Rights and Interests in the South China Sea," July 12, 2016, http://www.fmprc.gov.cn/nanhai/eng/snhwtlcwj_1/t1379493.htm; PRC MoFA, "Statement of the Ministry of Foreign Affairs of the People's Republic of China on the Award of 12 July 2016 of the Arbitral Tribunal in the South China Sea Arbitration Established at the Request of the Republic of the Philippines," July 12, 2016, http://www.mfa.gov.cn/nanhai/chn/snhwtlcwj/t1379490.htm; The PRC National People's Congress, "Statement of the People's Republic of China National People's Congress on the Award of 12 July 2016 of the Arbitral Tribunal in the South China Sea Arbitration Established at the Unilateral Request of the Republic of the Philippines," July 14, 2016, http://www.npc.gov.cn/npc/xinwen/2016-07/14/content_1993891.htm.

98. For full text of the white paper in Chinese, see http://www.xinhuanet.com/2016-07/13/c_1119210479.htm; in English, see http://www.xinhuanet.com/english/china/2016-07/13/c_135509153_2.htm, both accessed April 13, 2018.

99. PRC MoFA, "Vice Foreign Minister Liu Zhenmin Attends Press Release of the White Paper 'China Adheres to the Position of Settling Through Negotiation the Relevant Disputes Between China and the Philippines in the South China Sea' and Answers Questions," July 13, 2016, http://www.fmprc.gov.cn/web/wjb_673085/zygy_673101/liuzhenmin_673143/xgxw_673145/t1381069.shtml.

100. "Luoshi 'Nanhai Gefang Xingwei Xuanyan' Di Shi'er Ci Gaoguan Hui Juxing (The Twelfth Senior Officials Meeting to Implement the 'Declaration on the Conduct of Parties in the South China Sea' Was Held)," *People's Daily*, June 11, 2016, 3; "ZhongMei Zhiku Nanhai Wenti Duihua zai Huashengdun Juxing (Dialogue on the South China Sea Issue by Chinese and American Think Tanks Was Held in Washington)," *People's Daily*, July 6, 2016, 1; "Wang Yi Tong Meiguo Guowuqing Keli Tong Dianhua (Wang Yi Holds Telephone Talks with Secretary of State John Kerry of US)," *People's Daily*, July 7, 2016, 21; "Wu Shengli Huijian Meiguo Haijun Zuozhan Buzhang Jiu Nanhai Wenti Shenru Jiaohuan Yijian (Wu Shengli Meets with U.S. Secretary of Naval Operations for In-Depth Exchange of Views on the South China Sea Issue)," *People's Daily*, July 19, 2016, 21; "Zhongguo he Dongmeng Guojia Waijiaobuzhang Guanyu Quanmian Youxiao Luoshi 'Nanhai Gefang Xingwei Xuanyan' de Lianhe Shengming (Joint Statement of the Foreign Ministers of China and ASEAN Member States on the Full and Effective Implementation of the Declaration on the Conduct of Parties in the South China Sea)," *People's Daily*, July 26, 2016, 21.

158 The Art of State Persuasion

101. "Jianchi Yi 'Shuanggui Silu' Chuli Nanhai Wenti—Nanhai Zhongcai'an Buguo shi chang Zhengzhi Naoju (Adhere to the 'Dual-Track Approach' in Handling the South China Sea issue—The South China Sea Arbitration Case Is Nothing But a Political Farce)," *People's Daily*, July 19, 2016, 3; "Suowei Caijue buhui Dedao Guoji Shehui Renke—ji zai Xinjiapo Juxing de 'Nanhai Wenti: Zhuanjia yu Meiti Jianmianhui' (The So-Called Ruling Will Not Be Recognized By the International Community—A Note on the 'South China Sea Issue: Meeting of Experts and Media' held in Singapore)," *People's Daily*, July 20, 2016, 3; "Pibo Miuwu Paichu Ganrao Tantao Hezuo—Nanhai Wenti yu Quyu Hezuo Fazhan Gaoduan Zhiku Xueshu Yantaohui Zongshu (Criticizing the Fallacy, Eliminating Disturbances, and Discussing About Cooperation—A Summary of the Symposium on South China Sea and Regional Cooperation and Development)," *People's Daily*, July 21, 2016, 3.

102. "Zhongguo Yizhi he Nengli de Biran Xuanze (The Inevitable Choice Due to China's Will and Capability)," *People's Daily*, June 27, 2016, 3.

103. "Waijiaobu Fayanren—Zhong Fei Nanhai Zhengyi Zhiyou Tongguo Shuangbian Tanpan Xieshang Caineng Xunqiu Zhenzheng Jiejue (Chinese MoFA Spokesperson—China-Philippines South China Sea Dispute Can Only Be Resolved Through Bilateral Negotiations and Consultations)," *People's Daily*, May 21, 2016, 3; "Zhonghua Renmin Gonghe Guo Waijiaobu Guanyu Jianchi Tongguo Shuangbian Tanpan Jiejue Zhongguo he Feilvbin zai Nanhai Youguan Zhengyi de Shengming (Statement of the Ministry of Foreign Affairs of the People's Republic of China on Adhering to Resolving Disputes between China and the Philippines in the South China Sea Through Bilateral Negotiations," *People's Daily*, June 9, 2016, 1; "Yi Jizhixing Duihua Zengxinshiyi (Building Trust Through Institutionalized Dialogues)," *People's Daily*, June 6, 2016, 3; "Tanpan Xieshang Shi Jiejue Zhengyi de Weiyi Chulu (Negotiation Is the Sole Method to Resolve the Dispute)," *People's Daily*, June 10, 2016, 3; "Tanpan Xieshang Cai Shi Jiejue Wenti zhi Dao (Negotiation Is the Exclusive Solution to the Problem)," *People's Daily*, July 21, 2016, 3.

104. PRC MoFA, "Foreign Ministry Spokesperson Lu Kang's Regular Press Conference on June 14, 2016," June 14, 2016, http://www.fmprc.gov.cn/mfa_eng/xwfw_665399/s2510_665401/2511_665403/t1372136.shtml.

105. PRC MoFA, "Yang Jiechi Gives Interview to State Media on the So-called Award by the Arbitral Tribunal for the South China Sea Arbitration," July 15, 2016, http://www.fmprc.gov.cn/mfa_eng/zxxx_662805/t1381740.shtml. These numbers, however, are a little inflated. According to Sutter and Huang 2016, China "defined support for its position in a vague way that could elicit wider international support . . . it appeared that if a government or organization stated that it preferred that territorial disputes in the South China Sea should be settled through talks with the parties concerned, that was construed by Beijing as support for its position" (61). The Center for Strategic and International Studies also keeps an "Arbitration Support Tracker" that tracks the international support on the case (https://amti.csis.org/arbitration-support-tracker/). According to the CSIS tracker, there were 31 countries who supported China's position prior to the ruling.

106. "Jiaotong Yunshu Bu Jieshao Nanhai Daojiao Wuzuo Dengta Jianshe Qingkuang zhi Chu Wo Guo Shizhong Zhuiqiu Weihu Nanhai Chuanbo Hangxing Anquan (The Ministry of Transportation Briefed on the Construction Progress of 5 Lighthouses in the South China Sea Islands and Reefs—Our Country Will Continue to Safeguard Navigation

Safety in the South China Sea)," *People's Daily*, July 11, 2016, 6; "2016 nian Zhongguo Hanghairi gonggao (An Announcement on China Maritime Day 2016)," *People's Daily*, July 11, 2016, 6; Picture news on *People's Daily*, July 18, 2016, 1; "Ganquandao Shang Pin Ganquan (Tasting Natural Spring Water on the Robert Island)," *People's Daily*, July 27, 2016, 24.

107. "Chang Wanquan Chuxi Diliuci Zhongguo-Dongmeng Guofang Buzhang Feizhengshi Huiwu (Chang Wanquan Attends the 6th China-ASEAN Defense Ministers Informal Meeting)," *People's Daily*, May 27, 2016, 2.

108. "Zhongguo he Dongmeng Guojia Waijiaobuzhang Guanyu Quanmian Youxiao Luoshi 'Nanhai Gefang Xingwei Xuanyan' de Lianhe Shengming (Joint Statement of the Foreign Ministers of China and ASEAN Member States on the Full and Effective Implementation of the Declaration on the Conduct of Parties in the South China Sea)," *People's Daily*, July 26, 2016, 21.

109. "Maixiang Gengwei Jinmi de Zhongguo-Dongmeng Mingyun Gongtongti—Dongya Hezuo Xilie Waizhang Huiyi Zongshu (Toward a Closer China-ASEAN Community of Shared Destiny—Summary of the Series of Foreign Ministers' Meetings on East Asia Cooperation)," *People's Daily*, July 27, 2016, 21; "Paichu Ganrao, Tuijin Zhongguo Dongmeng Hezuo (Eliminate Disturbances, Promote China-ASEAN Cooperation)," *People's Daily*, July 27, 2016, 21; "Wang Yi Fenbie Huijian Ri E Zaizhang he Meiguo Guowuqing (Wang Yi Meets Japanese and Russian Prime Ministers and US State Secretary Respectively)," *People's Daily*, July 27, 2016, 21.

110. *South China Sea Public Opinion Newsletter* (Nanjing: Collaborative Innovation Center of South China Sea Studies, Nanjing University, June 2016), 1; *South China Sea Public Opinion Newsletter* (Nanjing: Collaborative Innovation Center of South China Sea Studies, Nanjing University, July 2016), 1.

111. "Meiyou Shenme Neng Handong Heping Zhengyi de Liliang (Nothing Can Shake the Power of Peace and Justice)," *People's Daily*, July 13, 2016, 5; "Zhongguo Shi Nanhai Heping Wending de Zhenzheng Weihuzhe (China Is the Real Keeper of Peace and Stability in the South China Sea)," *People's Daily*, July 18, 2016, 3; "Jianchi Hezuo Gongying, Cujin Gongtong Fazhan (Adhere to Win-Win Cooperation and Promote Mutual Development)," *People's Daily*, July 18, 2016, 21.

112. Author interview, June 7, 2017, Beijing, China.

113. There are many articles of this kind. To give a few examples: "Zhongguo Zai Nanhai Duanxuxian Nei de Lishixing Quanyi Burong Wangyi he Fouding (China's Historic Rights in the South China Sea Nine-Dash Line Should Not Be Arbitrarily Discussed or Denied)," *People's Daily*, May 23, 2016, 3; "Zhongguo Yongyou Nanhai Zhudao Zhuquan de Lishi Shishi Wukezhengbian (The Historical Fact that China Has Sovereignty Over the South China Sea Islands Is Indisputable)," *People's Daily*, May 24, 2014, 3; "Zhenxiang Yongyuan Zhi You Yi Ge—Guanyu Nanhai Zhongcai'an Zhongfei Fang Lishi Zhengju de Shiyong (There Is Always Only One Truth—On the Use of Historical Evidence from the Philippines in the South China Sea Arbitration)," May 25, 2016, 3.

114. Again, articles of this kind abound. Here are just a few examples: "Feilvbin 'Qiege' Jiliang Wufa Fouding Zhongguo Nansha Qundao de Zhengtixing (The Philippines' 'Fragmentation' Ploy Cannot Deny the Integrity of China's Nansha Islands)," *People's Daily*, May 30, 2016, 3; "Yingguo Guoji Haiyangfa Zhuanjia Zhiyi Zhongcaiting Dui Nanhai Zhongcai'an Guanxiaquan (British International Maritime Law Expert Questions

160 The Art of State Persuasion

the Jurisdiction of the Arbitral Tribunal Over the South China Sea Case)," *People's Daily*, June 22, 2016, 21; "Xieshang Tanpan Shi Jiejue Nanhai Zhengduan Zuijia Fangshi—Fang Guoji Fayuan Qian Faguan Apudule Keluoma (Negotiation Is the Best Way to Resolve Disputes in the South China Sea—Interview with Former International Court of Justice Judge Abdul Koroma)," *People's Daily*, July 5, 2016, 3.

115. Zhao, "China Must Strengthen Media Counter-Measures," 53.

116. "Hanyang Lixing Baorong de Guomin Xintai (Cultivate a Rational and Inclusive National Mentality)," *People's Daily*, July 20, 2016, 5.

117. Author interview, Beijing, China, June 5, 2017.

118. Jiang and Luo, "The Internet Media and the Construction of National Identity," 60.

119. Xie Jingzhong and Jun Zhu, "Nanhai Zhongcai'an Shejiao Meiti de Yulun Fansi" (Reflections on Public Opinion on Social Media on the South China Sea Arbitration), *Xinwen Yanjiu Daokan (Journal of News Research)* 7, no. 19 (October 2016): 19–20.

120. *South China Sea Public Opinion Newsletter*, 12.

121. Xie and Zhu, "Reflections on Public Opinion on Social Media," 19–20.

122. Ibid.

123. Zhenlibu (The Truth Department), "Feifa Jihui Youxing Xinxi (Information on Illegal Gatherings and Demonstrations)," *China Digital Times*, July 18, 2016, https://goo.gl/VrRV3Z.

124. "Manila: China Set Impossible Conditions for Visit," *Associated Press News*, September 2, 2013, https://apnews.com/article/7c828474c9624391b07315716dac0731.

125. "China's Stock Market Crash . . . in 2 Minutes," *CNN*, August 27, 2015, http://money.cnn.com/2015/07/09/investing/china-crash-in-two-minutes/; "China Faces 2016 Crisis as Bad as US Mortgage Meltdown," *TheStreet*, January 3, 2016, https://www.thestreet.com/story/13407258/1/china-faces-2016-crisis-as-bad-as-u-s-mortgage-meltdown.html.

126. Author interview, May 26, 2017, Beijing.

127. Author interview, May 26, 2017, Beijing.

5

The Nonbarking Dog

The 2011 Sino-Vietnamese Cable Cutting Incidents and the 2014 Oil Rig Crisis

This chapter delves into the conspicuous silence that surrounded two similar diplomatic crises: the cable cutting incidents of 2011 and the oil rig crisis of 2014.[1] Both incidents represent key junctures in the South China Sea dispute between China and Vietnam. Unlike the media campaigns examined in the previous chapters, the Chinese state notably stayed mute on these occurrences. This peculiar absence of state-driven media campaigns begs the question: Why did the dog not bark?

Intriguingly, as outlined in Chapter 2's congruence test, these two episodes, despite having divergent state foreign policy positions and differing existing public opinions—variables that would typically dictate varied media strategies—resulted in similar silence. This provokes a deeper inquiry into the state's decision to remain silent and an investigation into the factors that could lead to such an unexpected outcome.

In this chapter we undertake a comprehensive examination, with the goal of deciphering the Chinese state's rationale for refraining from initiating media campaigns during these pivotal incidents. This exploration provides a deeper understanding of the complex interplay between state foreign policy, public opinion, and media strategy within China's larger geopolitical framework.

Our aim extends beyond merely investigating the silence. Instead, we seek to determine what this silence reveals about the overarching mechanisms of China's media campaigns and its foreign policy strategy. By rigorously analyzing these two cases and delving into the "silent dog" phenomenon in the South China Sea disputes, this chapter endeavors to illuminate the fundamental principles that shape China's strategic narrative management in international crises.

The Art of State Persuasion. Frances Yaping Wang, Oxford University Press. © Oxford University Press 2024.
DOI: 10.1093/oso/9780197757505.003.0006

The Cable-Cutting Incidents in 2011

On May 26, 2011, a confrontation erupted between three Chinese maritime surveillance vessels and the Vietnamese oil exploration ship, *Binh Minh 02*, approximately 120 nautical miles off the Vietnamese coast. The Chinese vessels proceeded to cut the seismic survey cables of the Vietnamese ship.[2] In response, the Vietnamese Ministry of Foreign Affairs (MoFA) submitted a diplomatic note to the Chinese embassy in Hanoi contending that the Chinese actions had "violated Vietnam's sovereign rights to its exclusive economic zone and continental shelf," and demanded compensation for the damages inflicted.

Two days later, the Chinese MoFA countered, asserting that Vietnam's oil exploration activities "undermine China's rights and interests, as well as jurisdiction over the South China Sea," and defended the cable-cutting actions as "regular maritime law enforcement and surveillance activities in waters under the jurisdiction of China."[3]

Reacting to China's statement, the Vietnamese MoFA dismissed China's claim that the incident occurred in disputed areas the very next day, stating, "It is neither a disputed area nor is it an area 'managed by China.' China has deliberately misled the public into thinking that it is a disputed area."[4] In response, the Chinese MoFA doubled down on their stance on May 31, declaring that the Vietnamese oil operations were "illegal," that the Chinese actions were "completely justified," and urging Vietnam to "immediately stop infringement activities and refrain from creating new troubles."[5]

On June 9, a subsequent confrontation took place in the waters off Vanguard Bank. A Chinese fishing boat, allegedly accompanied by two Chinese fishery administration vessels, ensnared the cables of a Vietnamese survey ship, *Viking II*. The Vietnamese MoFA lodged a strong protest with the Chinese embassy in Hanoi and claimed that the Chinese action was "totally intentional, thoroughly deliberated and planned." The Vietnamese MoFA reported that the Chinese fishing boat, equipped with a "specialized cable slashing device," "headed on and rammed the exploration cables of Viking II," and "was consequently trapped in Viking II's cables, jamming Viking II's operation."[6]

The Chinese MoFA responded that the Vietnamese remarks "do not tally with the facts." It blamed the second incident on armed Vietnamese ships chasing away the Chinese fishing boat, causing it to get entangled with the cables of the Vietnamese survey ship. It claimed that "the Vietnamese vessel dragged the Chinese fishing boat for more than one hour, with the latter's tail facing the front," forcing the Chinese fishermen "to cut off the fishing net so as to separate the two vessels." It accused the Vietnamese ships of "illegally" operating in waters under China's jurisdiction and "endangering" Chinese fishermen's lives, who had operated in the same waters "for generations."[7]

Beginning on June 5, Vietnamese citizens organized weekly protests on the streets of Hanoi and in front of the Chinese embassy. Meanwhile, the Chinese navy conducted two military exercises, one on June 6 in an unspecified area in the South China Sea and another from June 16–19 near China's Hainan Island. The Vietnamese navy also performed live-fire drills near its Hon Ong Island from June 13–16. The crisis began to subside when Chinese State Councilor Dai Bingguo met with Vietnamese special envoy Ho Xuan Son on June 26 in Beijing.

This meeting was presented in a highly favorable light by China Central Television (CCTV). The relationship between the two nations was depicted as one of "good friends, good neighbors, good comrades, and good partners." This portrayal largely maintained the positive tone typically adopted by CCTV when reporting on international affairs. However, uncharacteristically, the CCTV coverage did mention maritime issues and the situation in the South China Sea. It also advised the two sides to "strengthen correct guidance of public opinion, avoiding words and actions that would harm the friendship and mutual trust of the two peoples."[8]

During the brief diplomatic crisis between May 26 and June 26, 2011, China refrained from initiating a media campaign and limited commercial media coverage. The coverage by *People's Daily* on the cable-cutting incidents was virtually nonexistent. During the thirty-one-day crisis there were only two articles, none of which made the front page and one of which merely replicated the statement from the June 9 MoFA press conference.

Similarly, CCTV News, including both Network News and Evening News, completely overlooked the incidents in their broadcasts. Only the Dai-Ho meeting on June 26 was reported by both CCTV news programs. The language used was carefully calibrated and only subtly referenced the incidents, meaning only viewers who were already aware of the incidents might connect them to the specific context of the meeting. This restrained and understated approach marked a significant departure from the more assertive media campaigns seen in other diplomatic crises.

Leaked internal notices from the Information Department of the Chinese MoFA corroborate the state's intention to keep quiet on the incidents. The central government directed media outlets to adhere strictly to the Foreign Ministry's official language when reporting on the June 9 incident.[9] As a result, commercial reports on both the May 26 and June 9 incidents followed the narrative established by Xinhua's report on the Foreign Ministry's official response.

164 The Art of State Persuasion

In fact, commercial media showed remarkable restraint on this topic. Even *Global Times*, a commercial media outlet under *People's Daily* known for its hardline and nationalist articles, tempered its language under state "guidance."[10] A *Global Times* editorial on May 30 warned, "China's restraint has limits," but by June 9 the tone changed significantly, with an editorial titled "Anger Is Not the Right Way to Handle the South China Sea Dispute."[11] This inflection suggests the state was consciously avoiding the stoking of nationalist sentiments.

Andrew Chubb concurs with this assessment, positing that the Chinese government's actions following the incidents indicate a deliberate attempt to avert domestic public attention. This assertion is bolstered by the timing and content of the Chinese MoFA's statements—the initial statement was issued on a Saturday, a day traditionally associated with less public attention. The scant Chinese media coverage was merely in response to the growing international media coverage.[12]

The absence of a media campaign in this case appears to be a result of an inherent alignment between a hawkish public opinion and a hardline state policy intent. The public was impassioned and aligned with the government's hardline approach, thereby eliminating the typical need for a state-driven media campaign to steer public opinion in favor of its policies. The "dog that did not bark" can thus be explained by the fact that the state found no need to shout when the public was already voicing its support.

A chain of events had already solidified public opinion before the events of 2011 unfolded. These events included a heated discourse led by the then US Secretary of State Hillary Clinton during the ASEAN Regional Forum in July 2010, which was hosted by Vietnam. In an unexpected turn at the Forum, Clinton announced that the South China Sea issue was an American "national interest" and asserted her support for the dispute to be resolved "without coercion."[13] This declaration was viewed by Beijing as a direct "attack on China." China's Foreign Minister Yang Jiechi responded with a seven-point rebuttal, stating, among other things, that the South China Sea region had generally been peaceful, that the issue did not encompass the entirety of ASEAN, and that the freedom of navigation in the region had not been impaired.[14]

These contentious exchanges, which received extensive coverage in the Chinese domestic media, sparked the interest of the Chinese public in the dispute. Furthermore, China's alleged declaration of the South China Sea issue as a "core interest"—albeit unverified by official sources—stoked public awareness and aroused strong emotional responses.[15] These factors contributed to the pre-existing hawkish sentiment among the Chinese public ahead of the 2011 incidents.

The emotions of the Chinese public were already running high in response to the cable-cutting incidents, despite the lack of state-fueled propaganda on the issue. Even without direct state intervention, public attention to the dispute surged. As evidenced by a search of the term "South China Sea" on the BSI during June and July, daily attention to the issue swelled to an average of over 10,000, peaking at 29,000 in mid-June. This was a significant increase compared to the average of 2,773 for the period from 2011 to 2017, highlighting the dramatic escalation of public attention to the issue.[16]

Warmongering was a common theme in online discussions. For example, a *People's Daily* editorial by Zhong Sheng with the title "The Time of Using Non-Peaceful Means to Resolve Territorial Dispute Has Passed" was reposted on ifeng, a popular news portal affiliated with Phoenix TV, opening the floor for readers to post their comments. It ended up with 216 comments and 29,674 people clicked to agree or disagree with the comments. Some of the most-agreed upon user comments were the following:

"Or it should be changed to: wake up from the dream of using peaceful means to resolve dispute."

" 'The time of using non-peaceful means to resolve territorial dispute has passed' is self-deceiving non-sense. Is *People's Daily* people's newspaper? It should rather be changed to 'World Harmony Daily.' *People's Daily* at this very sensitive and critical time expressed such thoughtless, stupid comment. Do they understand how serious the consequences and outcomes will be?"

"The so-called 'restraining principle' means while you are negotiating with them, they are holding joint military exercise. Who are you restraining? The so-called time of using non-peaceful means to resolve conflict has passed! Then why the US, France and UK do not sit and talk to Gaddafi?"

"The Chinese Communist Party must not cede the islands that we inherited from our ancestors. Such an act would make it an eternal sinner."

"Negotiation needs to be backed up by strong military strength."[17]

In another striking illustration of this bellicose online sentiment, translations of a Vietnamese report claiming that Chinese warships had discharged warning shots at Vietnamese fishing vessels in the Spratly Islands became the most commented post on the Tiexue (Iron Blood) forum shortly after the May 26 incident.[18] Although Chinese authorities refuted the veracity of this report, it nonetheless stirred a wave of bellicose responses in the online public sphere.[19] On June 8, a website associated with the Vietnamese MoFA was hacked, displaying the Chinese national flag and a slogan in Chinese that declared, "The Spratlys Belong to China."[20] An article by Ambassador Wu

Jianmin, proposing more moderate views under the title "The South China Sea Dispute: Restraint is A Kind of Confidence," was lambasted on the Tianya forum.[21]

In the context of these events, online expressions of militarism were widespread and persistent, both before and throughout the duration of the crisis. Such sentiments, characterized by bellicose rhetoric and demands for assertive action, were not confined to a small section of online extremists but instead appeared to permeate a significant portion of the digital public sphere. While it remains challenging to ascertain the exact scale of this sentiment, the significant volume of interactions and endorsements these posts received points to an influential segment of public opinion that leaned toward hawkish positions.

Notably, these virtual echo-chambers, where hardline sentiments festered, were not orchestrated or amplified by state-led media campaigns, which suggests an organic and spontaneous surge in hawkish sentiments among the Chinese populace. This assertion is further reinforced by the fact that online discourse often involved criticisms of the Chinese government itself.[22]

Critics frequently described Chinese foreign policy as overly timid or even treasonous, drawing parallels between the CCP leaders and the rulers of the Qing dynasty, who are infamously remembered for their inability to fend off territorial encroachments by foreign powers, which eventually led to the collapse of their rule.

Many online users nostalgically harked back to the era of Mao Zedong, recalling China's purported victories of "defeating America twice" and "teaching India a lesson." Others linked the issue to state corruption. Sentiments like "Corrupt officials running amok, unable to fight. Let's just give the South China Sea away" were not uncommon, reflecting a deep-seated dissatisfaction with perceived weaknesses in the state's handling of the South China Sea dispute.[23]

This outpouring of spontaneous and hardline public sentiment underscores a crucial dynamic at play—a populace driven by its own nationalistic fervor, rather than state propaganda, advocating for a more assertive and hardline approach toward territorial disputes.

This hawkish public opinion naturally aligned with the government's hardline policy intent. The Chinese actions were based on precarious grounds, as both incidents occurred in marginal areas within China's nine-dash line. The nine-dash line represents China's official claim to the South China Sea but its legal standing is unclear. From a legal standpoint, the incidents took place outside of any exclusive economic zone (EEZ) that China could potentially establish under the United Nations Convention on the Law of the Sea

(UNCLOS), based on its claimed sovereignty over the Paracel and Spratly islands. Moreover, it was still a matter of debate whether these land features could generate an EEZ in the first place. On the other hand, the incidents took place within Vietnam's EEZ as determined from its coastal baseline.

In the analysis provided by Chinese experts, the Chinese actions were driven by a combination of energy security concerns and a perceived weakening of their territorial claims in the disputed areas. Some, like Ji You, argue that Beijing was worried that the establishment of oil structures in contested territories might eventually lead to Vietnam gaining de facto control. This could potentially undermine China's claims in the future before international legal bodies, thereby increasing the risk of China permanently losing these areas. The increased activity by Vietnam, thus, was perceived as an immediate threat to China's long-term strategic and resource interests in the region.[24]

The situation surrounding the June 9 cable cutting event is marked by a level of ambiguity, with both Hanoi and Beijing presenting different narratives. According to Hanoi's account the act was a premeditated, deliberate provocation by China. However, scholarly research suggests otherwise. One study reveals that the order to sever the cables was made by the Navy's Xisha Surveillance District after consultation with its higher-ups. This decision was purportedly based on concerns for the safety of the boat and its crew, which had been entangled with the Vietnamese cables and dragged for about "two hours."[25]

This narrative aligns with the official Chinese account. However, adding a layer of complexity to this situation is the fact that Vietnamese media had reported harassment of the *Viking II* by presumed Chinese vessels several days prior to the incident.[26] This raises questions about the incident's spontaneity and lends a degree of credibility to Vietnam's assertion of it being a calculated act. It also suggests that the incident may have been a culmination of escalating tensions, rather than an isolated event. Nevertheless, due to the conflicting accounts, it is challenging to definitively determine whether the cable cutting was indeed a premeditated action or a reaction to an unplanned entanglement.

Even if we were to accept Beijing's claim that the June 9 *Viking II* incident was a genuine accident, these cable-cutting occurrences form part of a larger pattern of aggressive Chinese maritime conduct. There were several developments preceding the incidents that signaled a hardening of China's stance in its territorial disputes.

On May 2, weeks prior to the first cable-cutting incident, *China Daily*, a state-run newspaper, reported a planned rapid expansion of China Marine Surveillance (CMS) forces, the state maritime law enforcement agency. The article indicated that CMS was set to recruit more than a thousand staff by the end of 2011 to strengthen the protection of the country's marine security.[27] Shortly after, on May 20, just days before the first incident, China officially put a large oil and gas drilling platform, named Hai Yang Shi You 720, into operation.[28] Further underlining this trend, on May 24, the China National Offshore Oil Corporation (CNOOC) announced the open tendering of nineteen new blocks in the South China Sea, a move that expanded China's exploration activities over a massive area of 52,006 square kilometers.[29] These activities, combined with the incidents involving cable-cutting, serve to underscore a broader pattern of assertive maritime behavior by China, suggesting a strategic shift toward a more aggressive stance in enforcing its territorial claims.

These incidents represent a trend where China displayed increasing aggression in its responses to oil exploration activities conducted by other nations bordering the South China Sea. Although the direct involvement of the People's Liberation Army (PLA) in these incidents remains ambiguous, it is evident that China's intervention was likely authorized at least at the level of the CMS.

Chubb notes that conventional Chinese law enforcement activities in similar situations were typically limited to verbal warnings, or "hailing announcements." More aggressive and ad-hoc operations, such as the cable-cutting maneuvers that occurred on May 26, would likely require special authorization.[30]

Earlier in March of the same year, there was an incident at Reed Bank,[31] and another incident occurred in 2012.[32] These events, along with the 2011 incidents, total to at least four distinct occasions when China intervened in foreign oil companies' seismic survey activities. This series of incidents suggests an emerging pattern of assertive behavior by China in its territorial disputes.

If these events were inconsistent with the broader intentions of the Chinese state, policymakers could have taken measures to restrain operational units following the initial incidents, thereby preventing subsequent confrontations. Instead, there is evidence that such actions were not only tolerated but rewarded. This is underscored by the fact that fifty members of the Chinese coast guard were awarded for the first time on July 23 for their "heroic acts" in defending China's maritime rights.[33] This acknowledgment suggests a tacit endorsement, if not an explicit encouragement, of these hardline actions on the part of the state.

Given the congruence between public opinion and state policy, the government remained discreet, maintaining strict control over overt nationalistic sentiments. This subdued media demeanor is challenging to rationalize via audience costs theory or diversionary war theory, as both conceptual frameworks would suggest that the government should have created significant commotion. The theories would predict this either as a means of wielding influence during negotiations or as a way to distract the public's focus from internal stress. However, the state did not intentionally stir up commotion, instead opting to keep silent and even restrain the commercial media.

Another alternative explanation can be derived from the endogeneity of state policy intent, in the sense that China's hardline foreign policy intent might have been the *result* of the hawkish public opinion. If that were true then the state could have been aligning its foreign policy with existing public opinion, rather than responding to an exogenous state–public alignment with an appropriate media policy. This argument can be refuted both theoretically and empirically.

In Chapter 1, I pointed out that the Chinese state is unlikely to succumb to the pressure of public opinion—it is motivated not to, and does not need to. It is motivated not to because allowing public opinion to sway policy might hurt the state's interests—damaging its external ties and limiting it to less desirable foreign options. Downs and Saunders's work shows that the Chinese government is willing to risk significant damage to its nationalist credentials to preserve its foreign policy flexibility.[34] Nor does it need to conform to public opinion because the Chinese state is capable of moving public opinion in its desired direction.

Empirically, in this particular case, the aggressive trend in Chinese maritime behavior regarding other countries' oil exploration activities became evident as early as May, if not sooner. However, public opinion did not become sensationalized until the event had transpired, in June and July. Therefore, the sequencing of events does not support an endogeneity argument. Instead, the intensification of China's maritime policy can be attributed to a worsening external environment, weakened territorial claims, and increasing concerns over energy security. Its natural alignment with the existing hawkish public opinion, therefore, was coincident, not intentional.

The question remains as to why the state did not employ certain pacification techniques, such as echoing or hardline posturing, to effectively shield itself from nationalist criticisms—especially considering that some of these criticisms directly challenge the legitimacy of the regime. This can also be explored both theoretically and empirically.

Theoretically, I addressed this counterargument in Chapter 1 by discussing the inherent risks associated with fueling an already combative public sentiment. The state could potentially trigger an unmanageable surge in nationalist fervor if it attempts to stoke these sentiments further. A balance must be struck between maintaining control and satisfying public opinion.

In the given context, the Chinese state could communicate its hardline stance through the implementation of its hardline policies. By speaking through action rather than words, the state can maintain a hardline stance without risking the escalation of nationalist sentiment to an uncontrollable level. In this way, the state retains control over the narrative and ensures that it does not unnecessarily inflame nationalist sentiment, potentially leading to widespread public unrest or unpredictable reactions.

While the Chinese state does sometimes utilize tactics that amplify nationalist sentiment to its advantage, it also shows a consistent pattern of restraint in directly stoking nationalist fervor, opting instead to communicate its positions through policy decisions and actions. This demonstrates a clear understanding of the risks associated with excessively agitating public sentiment, and an intent to maintain a level of control over the narrative.

Beijing's View on the 2014 Oil Rig Crisis: The Strategy of Silence

The Sino-Vietnamese oil rig crisis ignited on May 2, 2014, when the state-run China National Offshore Oil Corporation (CNOOC) relocated its Haiyang Shiyou 981 oil rig, a semi-submersible drilling platform commissioned in 2012 at an expense of US $1 billion, to a contested region between the two nations without prior notification to Vietnam.[35] During the crisis the rig's position was adjusted a few times, but it was generally located approximately 17 nautical miles south of the Paracel Islands—territories claimed by both nations but currently under China's control.

The rig was positioned 130 nautical miles from the Vietnamese coast and 180 nautical miles from China's Hainan Island. If one were to disregard the claims over the Paracel Islands, the rig's location would be closer to Vietnam, resting on the Vietnamese side of the equidistant line between the Vietnamese coastline and Hainan. The rig falls within the two countries' overlapping EEZs.[36]

China's placement of the oil rig in a disputed location instigated perilous maneuvers at sea from both sides, which included vessel ramming and water cannon firings. The situation was further exacerbated by large-scale, fatal riots in Vietnam, characterized by the torching and destruction of foreign-owned factories.[37] The crisis was ultimately defused on July 15, with China announcing that Haiyang Shiyou had fulfilled its mission a month earlier than planned, leading to its withdrawal from the contentious area.[38]

As was the case during the 2011 cable-cutting incidents, Chinese media remained largely silent throughout the oil rig crisis. The government deliberately enacted measures to control information, suppress coverage, and even engage in content censorship. I argue that the absence of a media campaign in this case appears to be a result of an inherent alignment between a dovish public opinion and a moderate state policy intent. The public was dispassionate and aligned with the government's moderate approach, thereby eliminating the typical need for a state-driven media campaign to steer public opinion in favor of its policies. The "dog that did not bark" can thus be explained by the fact that the state found no need to shout when the public was already standing behind it.

Despite the prevalent nationalism in China regarding the South China Sea dispute overall, public opinion toward the specific quarrel with Vietnam remained relatively tempered in 2014. The span of 2013 through the first half of 2014 was a period of calm between China and Vietnam on the South China Sea issue. Without any major maritime disruptions for a considerable duration and the Chinese state refraining from fueling nationalism concerning its disagreement with Vietnam, bilateral relations enjoyed a period of respite. This calm allowed for a temporary subsiding of nationalist sentiments, though it was understood these could be reignited.

Journalists and editors who were interviewed depicted the public sentiment before and during the crisis as being "calm," if not "detached," and "definitely less impassioned than prior to the Sino-Philippines Scarborough Shoal standoff in 2012 or the arbitration case in 2016." They generally perceived "minimal news value" in the unfolding events, barring the riots.[39]

Figure 5.1 illustrates the daily search index for the term "South China Sea" in the BSI during the year leading up to the crisis. This pre-crisis period is characterized by a stable and relatively low frequency of mentions, with an average of 1,713, punctuated by only a few minor spikes. For context, as mentioned in Chapter 4, the average search volume during noncrisis periods between January 1, 2011, and October 15, 2017, is higher at 2,773. This comparison shows a significantly reduced level of public interest in the South China Sea topic in the run-up to the crisis.

According to the *South China Sea Public Opinion Newsletter*, public attention toward the dispute was minimal in social media during the first half of 2014, with the majority of online discussions being focused solely on the disagreement with the Philippines or the involvement of the US.[40] The lukewarm public sentiment was further confirmed by reports of a mere handful

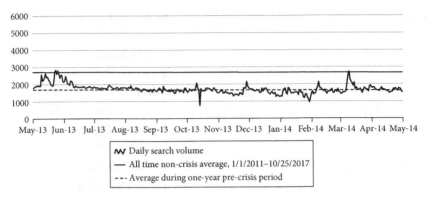

Figure 5.1 Daily Search Volume of "South China Sea" on Baidu.com During One-Year Pre-Crisis Period, May 2, 2013–May 2, 2014

of protesters turning up for a planned anti-Vietnam rally in Kunming on May 19.[41]

Despite China's seemingly provocative act of positioning the oil rig in the disputed area and engaging in hazardous confrontations with Vietnamese vessels at sea, substantial evidence suggests that Beijing maintained a moderate policy stance. The reasoning behind China's decision to move the oil rig into contested waters remains unclear and is a topic of ongoing debate among analysts.

The bilateral relationship had been on an optimistic upward trajectory since early 2013, giving Beijing seemingly little incentive to disrupt this progression. Prior to the crisis, China and Vietnam shared a fairly amicable relationship, punctuated by high-level visits from Vietnamese President Truong Tan Sang to Beijing in June 2013, and Chinese Premier Li Keqiang to Hanoi in October 2013. These diplomatic visits were characterized by reiterated commitments to maintaining peace and stability in the South China Sea. As a tangible outcome of these meetings, the China-Vietnam expert group for low-sensitivity maritime cooperation and consultation was established in December 2013, just months before the onset of the crisis.[42]

In addition to this, China engaged with ASEAN on the Implementation of the Declaration on Conduct of Parties in the South China Sea (DOC) at the tenth joint working group meeting in Singapore on March 18. Furthermore, China was in the process of developing a series of confidence-building measures under the DOC at the seventh ASEAN-China Senior Officials' Meeting on the Implementation of the DOC in Thailand on April 21. All these developments transpired just weeks before the placement of the oil rig, adding complexity to China's motivations for its subsequent actions.

The swift escalation of the situation came as a surprise to many seasoned observers, as it marked a deviation from China's previous conduct and did not seem to be the result of an impulsive decision made solely by an undisciplined CNOOC. As per the Vietnamese Ministry of Foreign Affairs (MoFA), the oil rig was defended by between "109 and 125 vessels" arranged in "three rings." This protective fleet included "4–6 warships, 2 missile frigates numbered 534 and 572 operating at 20–25 nautical miles from the oil rig, 2 pairs of minesweepers vessels numbered 840, 843 or 839, 842 (rotating daily) at about 15–25 nautical miles from the rig, and 2 pairs of fast attack ships numbered 751, 756 or 753 and an unidentified ship (rotating daily)."[43]

Shi Yinhong, a Chinese scholar, points out that the People's Liberation Army Navy (PLAN) would be the only agency capable of commanding navy warships, particularly on such a scale, indicating clear involvement of PLAN in the operation. This involvement underscores that the placement and protection of the oil rig was not a rogue decision, but instead a strategic action under the command of China's military apparatus.[44]

What, then, explains this sudden reversal in Chinese behavior toward Vietnam? The prevalent, though speculative, explanations propose a mix of factors: irrational decision-making, lack of interorganizational coordination, underestimation of Vietnam's reaction, and path dependency.[45] If these theories hold, then China's initial provocation resulted from an unintended miscalculation.

Private interviews with policy analysts close to the decision-making process disclosed that the oil rig was moved into the disputed area "without the proper consultation with the Foreign Ministry, and likely without direct involvement from the top leadership."[46] A retired government official often consulted on Vietnamese affairs corroborated this view: "Our policy (in placing the rig) in 2014 was not very stable . . . it was not a decision made by the top leadership after careful rumination."[47]

When asked on June 11 to confirm Vietnamese claims that "China had sent six warships to guard its oil rig," Chinese MoFA spokesperson Hua Chunying responded, "we have sent government vessels to the site for security."[48] The term "government vessels" would typically denote maritime law enforcement vessels, not navy ships. A similar situation occurred on June 13 with MoFA Deputy Director General of the Department of Boundary and Ocean Affairs, Yi Xianliang. When asked to verify the Vietnamese statement about China sending navy warships, Yi said, "we had to send Coast Guard ships."[49] It remains unclear, however, whether Hua and Yi were skillfully avoiding the question or were simply not informed about the navy ships' presence. The ambiguity in the Chinese officials' responses regarding the type of vessels sent to guard the oil rig indicates a potential information gap or an attempt to downplay the situation.

In late August, Vietnamese special envoy Le Hong Anh visited Beijing in an attempt to mend relations. During his discussions with senior Chinese Party officials, he emphasized, unusually, that the two parties needed to "tighten their instructions." The phrase "tighten instructions" was repeated four times in a brief two-page report of the meeting.[50] This suggests that the private explanation given to Anh involved a lack of coordination on the Chinese side, further underscoring the perceived need for clearer communication and coordinated decision-making.

A report by the Crisis Group presents a slightly different narrative, but it also reinforces the irrational decision argument. According to an interview with a "security agency-affiliated Chinese analyst," the report states, "The Central Leading Small Group on the Protection of Maritime Interests, created in 2012 and reportedly led, at least initially, directly by Xi, made the decision in the oil rig case. The foreign ministry was said to be represented by the Department of Boundary and Ocean Affairs, whose 'primary concern is sovereignty,' without Department of Asian Affairs input." Thus, the decision was made without "consultation with experts who understand Vietnam."[51]

My own interviews with individuals whom Beijing regularly consults on Vietnamese affairs indirectly confirm the last point. They stated that the placement of the rig "came as a shock," suggesting that they were not consulted on the issue.[52] The report also notes that "in internal memos, closed-door conferences, and briefings to senior officials," the prevailing view among Chinese analysts was that the decision to place the rig in disputed waters was misguided and imprudent.[53]

There also appears to have been an element of path dependency influencing the decision. In June 2012, Vietnam's state oil and gas group, PetroVietnam, invited Japanese firms for the joint development of approximately twenty oil and gas projects.[54] Around the same time, the Vietnamese Law of the Sea was passed by the Vietnamese National Assembly. In response to these actions, CNOOC invited international bids for nine oil and gas blocks.[55]

Seeing this sequence of actions and reactions, it becomes evident that the assertive moves by Vietnam invited a proportionate response from China, and that this push and pull over territorial claims had been an ongoing issue. China's actions were not isolated incidents, but rather part of a continuous pattern influenced by previous decisions and actions, a clear instance of path dependency.

This could explain why on various occasions, the Chinese MoFA spokesperson claimed that similar Chinese exploration and drilling activities had been ongoing in the same waters for "a decade," and thus, the placement of the oil rig in 2014 was simply a "natural continuation" of past activities.[56]

Hanoi reacted forcefully to the Chinese placement of the oil rig. The deputy commander/chief of staff of the Vietnam Maritime Police, Ngo Ngoc Thu, revealed that six vessels were immediately deployed to "examine and prevent the illegal intrusion of China's oil rig and the escort ships." This prompted both nations to bolster their presence near the disputed area. At the height of the standoff, over one hundred Chinese vessels and sixty Vietnamese vessels were in the area, which led to numerous severe collisions.[57]

When a phone call between Vietnam's Foreign Minister Pham Binh Minh and China's State Councilor Yang Jiechi on May 6 failed to yield any agreement, Hanoi sought support from the United Nations, ASEAN, and the United States. Vietnam circulated a note of protest against China's actions at the UN on May 7. During the 24th ASEAN Summit on May 11, Vietnam's Prime Minister Nguyen Tan Dung highlighted the incident as "a direct threat to peace, stability, maritime safety and security in the East Sea."[58]

Dung also threatened to pursue international legal action against Beijing. This warning came after the Philippines had already initiated an international arbitration case against China, as detailed in the last chapter. If Vietnam had joined this legal effort, the potential international ramifications for China could have been significantly more severe. This possibility might have influenced Beijing to adopt a more moderate foreign policy approach toward Hanoi.

The international implications of the standoff continued to grow. On May 6, the US State Department spokesperson singled out China's behavior as "provocative and unhelpful."[59] The following day, the US State Department released a press statement that condemned China's "unilateral action," describing it as "part of a broader pattern of Chinese behavior to advance its claims over disputed territory in a manner that undermines peace and stability in the region."[60] On May 21, Vietnam Foreign Minister Pham Bihn Minh called US secretary of State John Kerry to discuss the matter.[61]

Beijing's actions also held the potential to influence the Vietnamese domestic political landscape considerably. Within Vietnam, there are various political factions with differing views on how to handle relations with China. A faction within the Vietnamese government and broader society views China with suspicion, considering its actions as aggressive and hegemonic. This faction often calls for a stronger response to Chinese actions, including forging stronger alliances with other powers like the United States.

In the wake of the oil rig crisis, these anti-China sentiments could have been significantly fueled, potentially tipping the balance of power within the government toward this faction. This, in turn, could lead to an escalation of tensions, as the anti-China faction might push for more assertive actions against China, resulting in an increasingly adversarial relationship between the two countries. Consequently, this could potentially trigger regional power realignments. This provides an additional layer of complexity that may have played a part in Beijing's strategic decision to pursue a moderate policy and retreat.[62]

Taken aback by the unexpected chain of reactions and recognizing the grave risk of swaying the Vietnamese political landscape further toward the anti-China faction, Beijing needed to devise a retreat that would not damage its image. An immediate retreat was clearly undesirable, as it would project Beijing's vulnerability to both domestic and international audiences. Considering that the Vietnamese government was perceived to have tolerated, if not directly incited, riots leading to the destruction of several Chinese-owned factories and resulting in fatalities and damages, China could not afford to appear too keen on reconciliation.

State Councilor Yang Jiechi's visit to Hanoi on June 18 served as a strong signal of both sides' readiness to discuss and arrive at a peaceful resolution. The Vietnam-China Joint Steering Committee for Bilateral Cooperation, which facilitated Yang's visit to Hanoi, typically holds annual meetings, but the precise timing is decided at short notice.[63] Chinese foreign policy often makes use of seemingly routine gatherings within established multilateral or bilateral frameworks to initiate discussions on pressing matters without appearing desperate. This approach served as an ideal exit strategy for China in this situation.

Regarding Hanoi's allegations of Chinese aggression at sea, such as ramming Vietnamese ships and firing water cannons, Beijing needed to stand its ground in confrontations with Vietnamese ships in order to uphold its territorial claims and protect its vulnerable billion-dollar oil rig. The Chinese cordon was established to shield the oil rig, not to bother Vietnamese ships who arrived later than the Chinese. Even the Vietnamese MoFA spokesperson used the term "protect" when describing the actions of the Chinese vessels.[64] Given the crowded nature of the situation, with hundreds of vessels engaged in a standoff, physical altercations due to misinterpretations of intentions and incidental collisions were almost unavoidable.

Some also cite examples of economic sanctions as evidence of China's aggressive intentions toward Vietnam. Malesky and Morris-Jung state that "retail trade with China dipped noticeably in the second half of 2014,"[65] but Poh reports that "the trade account between China and Vietnam in 2014 continued to increase."[66] My own examination of data from the World Integrated

Trade Solution (WITS) and the General Statistics Office of Vietnam (GSOV) confirms Poh's observation.[67] Total retail bilateral trade increased from 50.0 billion US Dollars in 2013 to 58.6 billion in 2014, and has continued to rise since, reaching 27.8 billion in the first half of 2014 and 30.8 billion in the second half. The only dip was in tourism, but travel advisories and cancelled chartered flights were not limited to China.[68] According to Poh's interviews with Vietnamese diplomats and analysts, sanctions were expected but they were not employed or threatened. A Vietnamese analyst also told Poh that "it was his understanding that local officials in China—such as those in Yunnan and Guangxi—were 'specifically instructed' to ensure that economic interactions along the border between China and Vietnam were not affected by the dispute. These local Chinese officials . . . proactively approached their Vietnamese counterparts to ensure that economic interactions were sustained, even as bilateral tensions continued to rise."[69]

To sum up, the puzzling upward trend of the bilateral relationship until the deployment of the oil rig; the uncertainty and potential misjudgment underpinning Beijing's initial decision to deploy the oil rig; its predominantly defensive stance at sea; its subsequent attempts to deescalate the situation; and the dismissal of economic sanctions speculation all suggest that Beijing had a moderate policy intent.

Considering the subdued public opinion and Beijing's moderate policy intentions, an aggressive media campaign was not only unnecessary, but also undesired. Instead, the state decided to keep the dispute out of the public eye. Beijing still made information readily available on the dispute, partially to respond to the clamor from the Vietnamese side and partially to pre-empt the populace's exposure to it through foreign media. This accounts for why the media coverage was borderline based on the two criteria established in Chapter 2. *People's Daily* published 36 articles during the 74 days of the crisis, from May 2 to July 15, none of which were on the front page, indicating a moderate volume but no salience. Nevertheless, Beijing's reluctance to bring the dispute into the limelight is evident in four notable media features.

First, the reporting on the dispute was delayed. Anti-China protests began in Hanoi and several other cities on May 11 and escalated into violent riots on May 13 and 14. However, Xinhua News did not release any Chinese reports of the riots until midnight on May 15—a delay of almost two days. Other Chinese media outlets also exhibited caution in their coverage of the issue. They refrained from reporting on the riots until Xinhua's report was released and Foreign Minister Wang Yi officially addressed them.[70]

Second, coverage on the dispute was limited. With only 36 articles over 74 days, the volume barely exceeded the threshold for a media campaign.

China's limited coverage was primarily a reaction to Vietnam's aggressive propaganda campaign, particularly its international outreach. At a press conference on June 9, Chinese MoFA Spokesperson Hua Chunying stated: "[Vietnam is] spreading rumors around the world to vilify and hurt China unscrupulously and groundlessly. Given that, we must present the facts in front of the international community so as to set the record straight." Aside from this reactive coverage, Chinese reporting on the issue was rather sparse.

Third, dispute coverage was buried in low-traffic subsections of newspapers, a trend seen across all official media outlets and major commercial news portals.[71] On the day of the riots in Vietnam, the official websites of *People's Daily* and Xinhua News both had other headlines than the riots: "Private cars will be exempted from inspection for the first six years starting from September." Meanwhile, news about the riots was pushed down to the fourth and fifth items, respectively. This strategy reduced the visibility of the dispute, while still making information accessible for those who might have heard about it elsewhere and were actively searching for it. In this way, the CCP could dampen the issue without losing the opportunity to frame the issue to the Western media.

Fourth, the official, accusatory tone toward the Vietnamese government was softened. After the riots, Chinese MoFA Spokesperson Hua Chunying initially blamed the violence on the "Vietnamese government's indulgence and connivance toward domestic anti-China forces and criminals."[72] However, when the final official transcript was released, the language had been altered to state that "the Vietnamese side has an inescapable responsibility for the beating, smashing, looting and burning targeted at China and other countries."[73] The shift from "connivance" to "inescapable responsibility" markedly softened the accusation, demonstrating a more diplomatic approach.

These media features substantiate the four media policy directives on the dispute leaked by *China Digital Times*. On May 7, propaganda authorities instructed online media to "continue to find and delete reports on Sino-Vietnamese ship collisions and maritime standoff, and report on work progress in a timely manner."[74] A May 14 order concerning the anti-China riots directed outlets to "not report on the issue, republish foreign coverage, or allow discussion in online forums."[75] After Xinhua released the news, the directive was updated on May 15 to "use only the Xinhua copy or information from the Foreign Ministry's website."[76] On May 18, a second instruction reiterated that the media must "use Xinhua copy only."[77] My interviews with Chinese editors and journalists corroborate these leaked media directives. Editors from a hardline newspaper disclosed that after publishing a couple of articles on the dispute, they were asked to "moderate their tone."[78]

The Nonbarking Dog   **179**

It remains a topic of discussion as to why the Chinese authorities did not leverage nationalism as a tool to pressure Hanoi into accepting the fait accompli at sea. Indeed, Beijing had coercive goals during the crisis: to halt Vietnamese interference in the oil rig's exploration activities, to prevent Vietnamese ships from ramming the rig; to dissuade Hanoi from escalating the situation by appealing to international bodies such as the UN or ASEAN, or by seeking legal recourse or support from the US and other global powers; and to convince Hanoi to suppress internal nationalist sentiment and bring an end to the riots.

However, despite these coercive goals, Beijing opted not to invoke audience costs to bolster them. The public sentiment surrounding the dispute was relatively subdued, and the state refrained from stoking the flames of nationalism. This restraint in media behavior contradicts the prediction offered by audience costs theory, which suggests that the state would employ a media campaign to achieve its coercive aims.

Similarly, the lack of a media campaign also contradicts the diversionary theory. If the state had intended to distract the public from a domestic crisis, it would have launched a media campaign to shift public attention. However, the state showed restraint, choosing not to stoke nationalism or create a diversion.

One potential explanation for this could be that the Chinese government recognized the risks associated with inciting nationalism and possibly losing control of the narrative. In a volatile situation like this, where public sentiment could easily swing from one extreme to the other, it was crucial to maintain a level-headed approach. Stirring nationalist fervor could have led to unexpected backlash or even domestic instability, potentially jeopardizing the regime's long-term interests. By keeping its silence, the government might have been better able to manage the situation, maintaining domestic stability while continuing to pursue its strategic objectives.

Inciting nationalism also carries international risks. As previously discussed, China's actions could have potentially influenced Vietnam's domestic political dynamics, thereby affecting regional realignments. Given that the public was already behind its back on a moderate policy, the Chinese government did not have an incentive to shoulder these risks. Thus, by not stoking nationalism, Beijing was able to avoid creating potential political turbulence both domestically and internationally.

Conclusion

This chapter has explored two instances where media campaigns were notably absent. In both scenarios, public opinion and state policy intent were

180 The Art of State Persuasion

in harmony, thus the state had no motivation either to galvanize an already hawkish public opinion or to pacify an already tepid public sentiment. These cases defy the expectations of both the audience costs theory and the diversionary war theory, as both theories would forecast a contrary outcome—a media campaign employed for coercion or diversion.

This chapter provides a nuanced understanding of the strategic considerations a state might undertake in managing public opinion and media use during international crises. We learn that when public sentiment aligns with state policy, there may be no need for the state to deploy media campaigns to steer public opinion.

It also highlights the limitations of the audience costs theory and the diversionary war theory. These theories anticipate the state will use a media campaign for coercive or diversionary purposes. However, the cases presented in this chapter contradict those expectations, demonstrating situations where no media campaigns were launched despite clear state objectives.

The chapter also underlines the potential risks of stoking nationalism, both domestically and internationally. It shows that regardless of whether public sentiment is strong or weak, the state may opt not to fuel nationalistic fervor in order to avoid potential backlash or international political turbulence.

Finally, the chapter reinforces the (mis)alignment theory—the idea that the state's approach to media campaigns is dictated by the alignment or misalignment between public sentiment and state policy. The theory suggests that the absence of media campaigns in these cases can be attributed to the state's strategic decisions given the alignment between public sentiment and its policy intent.

Notes

1. The cable-cutting incidents, although each one a discrete event, constitute as a whole a larger dispute regarding oil exploration activities in the South China Sea. These incidents sparked weekly public protests in Vietnam and live-fire naval exercises on both sides. Hence, they are considered as one crisis in this book.
2. "VN Condemns Chinese Intrusion," VietnamNet, May 28, 2011, http://english.vietnam net.vn/en/politics/8839/vn-condemns-chinese-intrusion.html.
3. PRC MoFA, "Foreign Ministry Spokesperson Jiang Yu's Remarks on China's Maritime Law Enforcement and Surveillance on the South China Sea," May 28, 2011, http://houston. china-consulate.org/eng/fyrth/t826601.htm.
4. Vietnam MoFA, "Press Conference on Chinese Maritime Surveillance Vessel's Cutting Exploration Cable of PetroViet Nam Seismic Vessel," May 29, 2011, http://www.mofa.gov. vn/en/tt_baochi/pbnfn/ns110530220030.

The Nonbarking Dog   **181**

5. PRC MoFA, "Foreign Ministry Spokesperson Jiang Yu's Regular Press Conference on May 31, 2011," June 1, 2011, http://www.china-embassy.org/eng/fyrth/t827089.htm.

6. Vietnam MoFA, "Foreign Ministry Spokesperson Nguyen Phuong Nga Answers Question from the Media at the Press Conference on June 9, 2011 Concerning the Viking II Incident," June 9, 2011, http://www.mofa.gov.vn/en/tt_baochi/pbnfn/ns110610100618.

7. PRC MoFA, "Foreign Ministry Spokesperson Hong Lei's Remarks on Vietnamese Ships Chasing away Chinese Fishing Boats in the Waters off the Nansha Islands," June 9, 2011, http://na.china-embassy.org/eng/fyrth/t829427.htm.

8. "Dai Bingguo Huijian Yuenan Lingdaoren Teshi Hu Chunshan (Dai Bingguo Meets Vietnamese Leadership's Special Envoy Ho Xuan Son)," CCTV Xinwen Lianbo (Network News), June 26, 2011, http://tv.cntv.cn/video/C16624/b7fda32c294a45da9b0eb09c8 2d97a2b.

9. Zhenlibu (The Truth Department), "Guanyu Yuenan zai Nanhai Kaicai Youqitian deng Wenti (About Vietnam's Oil Exploration Activities in the South China Sea)," *China Digital Times*, June 10, 2011, https://goo.gl/qKvMvM.

10. Author interview, May 29, 2017, Beijing.

11. "Yuenan Nanhai Maoxian Niantou Zengjia; Zhongguo Kezhi shi you Xiandu de (Vietnam's Risky Ideas in the South China Sea Increase; China's Restraint Has Limits)," *Huangqiu Shibao* (*Global Times*), May 30, 2011; "Fennu bu shi Chuli Nanhai Zhengduan Zhengdao (Anger Is Not the Right Way to Handle the South China Sea Dispute)," *Huangqiu Shibao* (*Global Times*), June 9, 2011.

12. Andrew Chubb, "Chinese Popular Nationalism and PRC Policy in the South China Sea" (PhD diss., University of Western Australia, 2016), 469.

13. Hillary Rodham Clinton, "Remarks at Press Availability," US Department of State, https://2009-2017.state.gov/secretary/20092013clinton/rm/2010/07/145095.htm, accessed May 8, 2018.

14. PRC MoFA, "Yang Jiechi Waizhang Bochi Nanhai Wenti shang de Wailun (Foreign Minister Yang Jiechi Refutes Fallacies on the South China Sea Issue)," July 25, 2010, http://www.mfa.gov.cn/chn//pds/wjb/wjbz/zyhd/t719371.htm.

15. The whole South China Sea as a "core interest" meme was discussed in detail in Michael Swaine, "China's Assertive Behavior (Part One: On 'Core Interests')," *China Leadership Monitor* 34 (Winter 2010), https://carnegieendowment.org/2010/11/15/china-s-assertive-behavior-part-one-on-core-interests-pub-41937.

16. The BSI data did not become available until after January 1, 2011, so there is not enough data to do a similar one-year pre-crisis average index comparable to those I did on the arbitration case in 2016 in Chapter 4 and the oil rig crisis in 2014 in this chapter.

17. The original *People's Daily*'s article had the title "Meiyou Yige hao Huanjing jiu Bu Keneng Jiejue Nanhai Wenti (It Is Impossible to Solve the South China Sea Problem Without a Good Environment)." See Zhong Sheng, *People's Daily*, July 20, 2011, 3. The article was reposted with the title "Tongguo Fei Heping Shouduan Jiejue Zhengduan de Shidai yi Guoqu (The Time of Using Non-Peaceful Means to Resolve Territorial Disputes Has Passed)," at http://news.ifeng.com/mil/4/detail_2011_07/22/7876049_9.shtml, accessed May 7, 2018.

18. For the original Vietnamese report, see "Nội dung cuộc điện đàm với ngư dân (The Content of the Conversation with Fishermen)," *VN Express*, June 1, 2011, http://vnexpress.net/tin-tuc/thoi-su/tau-quan-su-trung-quoc-no-sung-ban-duoi-tau-viet-nam-2196554-p2.html.

182 The Art of State Persuasion

> For the Chinese translation and reposting on Tiexue Forum, together with the comments, see http://bbs.tiexue.net/post_5113116_1.html, accessed May 8, 2018.

19. "Waijiaobu: Zhongguo Chuan Xiang Yuenan Yumin Mingqiang Baodao Zixuwuyou (Ministry of Foreign Affairs: Chinese Ship Firing Shots at Vietnamese Fishermen Is Fabricated)," *China News*, June 4, 2011, https://news.qq.com/a/20110604/000002.htm.

20. "Yuenan Guanfang Wangzhan zao Heike Gongji, Wangye shang Chuxian Zhongguo Guoqi (Vietnamese Official Website Attacked By Hackers, the Chinese National Flag Appears on the Website)," *Global Times*, June 9, 2011, http://world.huanqiu.com/roll/2011-06/1744 628.html.

21. For the reposting and the thread of comments, see http://bbs.tianya.cn/post-worldlook-360420-1.shtml. Wu was a renowned Chinese diplomat who served as the MoFA spokesperson, ambassador to the Netherlands, Geneva, and France, as well as President of China Foreign Affairs University.

22. For examples of these harsh criticisms, see Chubb, "Chinese Popular Nationalism and PRC Policy in the South China Sea," 212–13.

23. This comment was one of many posted on a short video clip published by Phoenix TV. See "Zhongguo Wo San Wangpai, Ding Nanhai Daju (China's Three Trump Cards Will Determine the Outcome on the South China Sea)," ifeng, June 30, 2011, http://v.ifeng.com/v/sanwangpai/index.shtml#e9253db1-9ecd-4e1c-9af3-abb78271a2d4.

24. Ji You, "The PLA and Diplomacy: Unraveling Myths about the Military Role in Foreign Policy Making," *Journal of Contemporary China* 23, no. 86 (March 4, 2014): 251.

25. You, "The PLA and Diplomacy."

26. "1 More Vietnam Ship Harassed by Foreign Vessels," VietnamNet Bridge, June 1, 2011, http://english.vietnamnet.vn/fms/society/8634/1-more-vietnam-ship-harassed-by-fore ign-vessels.html.

27. *China Daily*, May 2, 2011, 2.

28. *People's Daily*, June 13, 2013, 2.

29. China National Offshore Oil Corporation (CNOOC), "Notification of First Batch of Blocks in Offshore China Available for Foreign Cooperation in Year 2011," May 24, 2011, http://www.cnooc.com.cn/art/2014/9/25/art_6241_1148001.html.

30. Chubb, "Chinese Popular Nationalism and PRC Policy in the South China Sea," 468.

31. The Reed Bank incident is a brief confrontation between two Chinese patrol boats and a Philippine survey ship on March 2, 2011. This study does not include it as a separate case, because it failed to escalate into a crisis and resembles many other similar episodes that occur frequently in the South China Sea. However, the Reed Bank incident shares a striking similarity with the subsequent Sino-Vietnamese cable-cutting incidents that happened within the same year, both of which revolved around disputes related to oil exploration activities.

32. Carlyle Thayer reports that another incident occurred on June 30, in which "Vietnamese escort vessels were able to chase off the Chinese boats." But this incident has been "kept under wraps by Vietnamese authorities." See Carlyle A. Thayer, "China's Cable Cutting: Once Is an Incident Twice Is Pattern," Background Briefing (Thayer Consultancy, June 9, 2011), 1–2, https://www.scribd.com/document/57491115/Thayer-China-s-Cable-Cutting-Once-is-an-Incident-Twice-is-a-Pattern.

33. "2011 Nian Zhongguo Haijian Dashiji (2011 China Marine Surveillance Memorabilia)," June 28, 2012, *Xinhua News*, http://guoqing.china.com.cn/2012-06/28/content_25756 969.htm.

The Nonbarking Dog   183

34. Erica Strecker Downs and Phillip C. Saunders, "Legitimacy and the Limits of Nationalism: China and the Diaoyu Islands," *International Security* 23, no. 3 (1999): 114–46.

35. This section uses materials from an article co-authored with Brantly Womack. Frances Yaping Wang and Brantly Womack, "Jawing through Crises: Chinese and Vietnamese Media Strategies in the South China Sea," *Journal of Contemporary China* 28, no. 119 (September 3, 2019): 712–28.

36. PRC MoFA, "The Operation of the HYSY 981 Drilling Rig: Vietnam's Provocation and China's Position," June 8, 2014, http://www.fmprc.gov.cn/mfa_eng/zxxx_662805/t1163 264.shtml; Vietnam MoFA, "Remarks by FM Spokesman Le Hai Binh on 4th May 2014," May 4, 2014, http://www.mofa.gov.vn/en/tt_baochi/pbnfn/ns140505232230.

37. Kate Hodal and Jonathan Kaiman, "At Least 21 Dead in Vietnam Anti-China Protests over Oil Rig," *The Guardian*, May 15, 2014, http://www.theguardian.com/world/2014/may/15/vietnam-anti-china-protests-oil-rig-dead-injured.

38. "Vietnam Anti-China Protest: Factories Burnt," *BBC News*, May 14, 2014. http://www.bbc.com/news/world-asia-27403851.

39. Author interviews, May 29, 2017; May 31, 2017; June 1, 2017.

40. Collaborative Innovation Center of South China Sea Studies at Nanjing University, *The South China Sea Public Opinion Newsletter*, January, February, March, and April 2014.

41. Brian Eyler, "The Anti-Vietnam Protest That Didn't Happen," May 19, 2014, http://www.eastbysoutheast.com/anti-vietnam-protest-didnt-happen/.

42. PRC MoFA, "China and Vietnam Held Plenary Meeting of the Governmental Delegation on Border Negotiation," December 7, 2013, http://www.fmprc.gov.cn/mfa_eng/zxxx_662 805/t1108277.shtml.

43. Vietnam MoFA, "The 6th Regular Press Conference," June 26, 2014, http://www.mofa.gov.vn/en/tt_baochi/tcbc/ns140628000810.

44. As quoted in Jane Perlez, "Vietnamese Officials Intolerant of Violence as Standoff with China Continues," *New York Times*, May 17, 2014. https://www.nytimes.com/2014/05/18/world/asia/vietnamese-officials-intolerant-of-violence-as-standoff-with-china-contin ues.html.

45. For an enumeration of these speculations, see Carlyle A. Thayer, "China's Oil Rig Gambit: South China Sea Game-Changer?," *The Diplomat*, May 12, 2014, https://thediplo mat.com/2014/05/chinas-oil-rig-gambit-south-china-sea-game-changer/.

46. Author interview, May 31, 2017, Beijing.

47. Author interview, June 2, 2017, Beijing.

48. PRC Ministry of Foreign Affairs, "Foreign Ministry Spokesperson Hua Chunying's Regular Press Conference on June 11, 2014," June 11, 2014, http://www.fmprc.gov.cn/mfa_eng/xwfw_665399/s2510_665401/t1164598.shtml.

49. "Waijiaobu Bianhaisi Fusizhang Yi Xianliang jiu Zhongjian-nan Xiangmu Juxing Chuifenghui (Deputy Director General of MoFA Department of Boundary and Oceanic Affairs Yi Xianliang Holds Briefing on Triton-south Project)," PRC MoFA Press Briefing, June 14, 2014, http://www.fmprc.gov.cn/web/wjb_673085/zzjg_673183/t1165600.shtml.

50. "Vietnam, China Agree to Restore, Develop Ties," *Nhan Dan*/VNA, August 27, 2014, http://en.nhandan.org.vn/politics/external-relations/item/2753802-na-chairman-meets-young-japanese-parliamentarians.html.

51. International Crisis Group, "Stirring Up the South China Sea (III): A Fleeting Opportunity for Calm," May 7, 2015, https://www.crisisgroup.org/asia/north-east-asia/china/stirr

184 The Art of State Persuasion

ing-south-china-sea-iii-fleeting-opportunity-calm.https://www.crisisgroup.org/asia/north-east-asia/china/stirring-south-china-sea-iii-fleeting-opportunity-calm.

52. Author interviews, June 2, 2017, Beijing; November 20, 2017, Washington, DC.

53. International Crisis Group, "Stirring up the South China Sea (III): A Fleeting Opportunity for Calm," 5.

54. "Vietnam to Propose Oil, Gas Development with Japan," *Thanh Nien News*, June 13, 2012, http://www.thanhniennews.com/business/vietnam-to-propose-oil-gas-development-with-japan-media-6807.html.

55. "CNOOC Opens Tender to Foreign Companies for 9 Oil and Gas Blocks [in Chinese]," *Tencent News*, June 26, 2012, https://news.qq.com/a/20120626/001565.htm.

56. These wordings have been mentioned at multiple occasions, for an example see PRC Ministry of Foreign Affairs, "Foreign Ministry Spokesperson Hua Chunying's Regular Press Conference on June 18, 2014," June 19, 2014, http://www.fmprc.gov.cn/mfa_eng/xwfw_665399/s2510_665401/t1166826.shtml.

57. Ngo Ngoc Thu, "The Situation on the Area with China's Illegal Drilling Rig HD981 within Vietnam's Waters," Vietnam MoFA press briefing, Hanoi, May 7, 2014; "Video shows 'Vietnamese Boat Ramming Chinese Ships' in Disputed Waters," *South China Morning Post*, June 14, 2014, http://www.scmp.com/news/china/article/1532371/beijing-accuses-vietnam-ramming-vessels-over-1500-times; Michael Green et al., "China-Vietnam Oil Rig Standoff," Countering Coercion in Maritime Asia: The Theory and Practice of Gray Zone Deterrence (Center for Strategic and International Studies, June 12, 2017), 208–9. Both sides released video clips of these collisions, accusing the other side as the aggressor. See "Waijiaobu Bianhaisi Fusizhang Yi Xianliang jiu Zhongjiannan Xiangmu Juxing Chuifenghui (Deputy Director General of MoFA Department of Boundary and Oceanic Affairs Yi Xianliang Holds Briefing on Triton-south Project)," PRC MoFA Press Briefing, June 14, 2014, http://www.fmprc.gov.cn/web/wjb_673085/zzjg_673183/t1165600.shtml.

58. Vietnam MoFA, "Regular Press Briefing by MOFA's Spokesperson Le Hai Binh On May 15, 2014," May 15, 2014, http://www.mofa.gov.vn/en/tt_baochi/pbnfn/ns140516233943.

59. Jen Psaki, "Daily Press Briefing: May 6, 2014," US Department of State, May 6, 2014, Washington, DC, https://2009-2017.state.gov/r/pa/prs/dpb/2014/05/225687.htm.

60. Jen Psaki, "Vietnam/China: Chinese Oil Rig Operations Near the Paracel Islands," May 7, 2014, Washington, DC, https://2009-2017.state.gov/r/pa/prs/ps/2014/05/225750.htm.

61. Carlyle A. Thayer, "4 Reasons China Removed Oil Rig HYSY-981 Sooner Than Planned," *The Diplomat*, July 22, 2014.

62. Author interview, June 2, 2017, Beijing.

63. PRC MoFA, "Foreign Ministry Spokesperson Hua Chunying's Regular Press Conference on June 17, 2014," June 17, 2014, http://www.fmprc.gov.cn/mfa_eng/xwfw_665399/s2510_665401/t1166317.shtml.

64. The Vietnamese MoFA spokesperson used the word "protect" when he was saying that "China used between 109 and 125 vessels to protect Haiyang Shiyou oil rig 981." Vietnam MoFA, "The 6th Regular Press Conference," June 28, 2014, http://www.mofa.gov.vn/en/tt_baochi/tcbc/ns140628000810.

65. Edmund Malesky and Jason Morris-Jung, "Vietnam in 2014: Uncertainty and Opportunity in the Wake of the HS-981 Crisis," *Asian Survey* 55, no. 1 (2015): 172.

66. Angela Poh, "The Myth of Chinese Sanctions over South China Sea Disputes," *Washington Quarterly* 40, no. 1 (2017): 153.

The Nonbarking Dog 185

67. The WITS incorporates data from the World Bank, the UNSD Commodity Trade (UN Comtrade) (UN Comtrade) database, the WTO's Integrated Data Base (IDB) and others. There is only trivial difference between the WITS data and the GSOV data. No data source is cited with the Malesky and Morris-Jung claim.

68. Poh, "The Myth of Chinese Sanctions over South China Sea Disputes," 153.

69. Poh, 154.

70. "Zhongguo Meiti Jinshen Baodao Yuenan Shitai (Chinese Media Cautious in Reporting the Vietnam Incident)," *BBC Chinese*, May 16, 2014, http://www.bbc.com/zhongwen/simp/china/2014/05/140516_china_vietnam_press.

71. Andrew Chubb, "China's Information Management in the Sino-Vietnamese Confrontation: Caution and Sophistication in the Internet Era," *China Brief* 14, no. 11 (June 4, 2014): 15, https://jamestown.org/program/chinas-information-management-in-the-sino-vietnamese-confrontation-caution-and-sophistication-in-the-internet-era/.

72. Chubb, "China's Information Management in the Sino-Vietnamese Confrontation," 16–17. Quoting from Bloomberg, May 15, 2014, https://www.bloomberg.com/news/articles/2014-05-14/anti-china-protests-in-vietnam-spur-warnings-factory-closures.

73. PRC Ministry of Foreign Affairs, "Foreign Ministry Spokesperson Hua Chunying's Regular Press Conference on May 15, 2014," May 15, 2014, http://www.fmprc.gov.cn/mfa_eng/xwfw_665399/s2510_665401/t1156451.shtml.

74. Zhenlibu (The Truth Department), "Gao Yu, Waitao Tanguan, Yuenan Haijun, he Bitebi" (Gao Yu, Fled Corrupt Officials, Vietnamese Navy and Bitcoin), *China Digital Times*, May 7, 2014, https://goo.gl/mpFi7s.

75. Zhenlibu (The Truth Department), "Zai Yue Zhongzi Qiye Bei Yuenanren Chongji" (Chinese Companies in Vietnam Were Attacked), *China Digital Times*, May 14, 2014, https://goo.gl/uT1Evq.

76. Zhenlibu (The Truth Department), "Zai Yue Qiye, Wei Pengyuan, Zhuanjiyin Liangyou, he Shenzhen Kuaibo" (Chinese Companies in Vietnam, Wei Pengyuan, Genetically Modified Grain and Oil, and Shenzhen QVOD Player), *China Digital Times*, May 15, 2014, https://goo.gl/v94Dyn.

77. Zhenlibu (The Truth Department), "Xinjiang Keshi An, Yuenan Qiye he Zhongguo de Aidashi" (Xinjiang Kashgar Incident, Factories in Vietnam, and A Chinese History of Being Bullied), *China Digital Times*, May 18, 2014, https://goo.gl/4JhQKu.

78. Author interviews, May 29, 2017, Beijing; May 31, 2017, Beijing.

6
Mobilization versus Pacification

A Textual Analysis

In this book, we have identified two types of media campaigns China employs in international conflicts: mobilization and pacification. The primary objective of mobilization campaigns is to drum up support for aggressive foreign policies and military action. In contrast, pacification campaigns are designed to soothe a disgruntled public, diminish domestic opposition to a preferred moderate policy, and circumvent mass mobilization against the regime. While both strategies may seem similar on the surface, employing concentrated high-profile media coverage to raise issue awareness and managing public opinion by carefully selecting topics and manipulating emotions, they serve fundamentally different objectives.

This chapter delves into the intricate differences between mobilization and pacification campaigns. Both types of media campaigns are characterized by a marked surge in the intensity of media coverage. Additionally, they both employ negative rhetoric to some extent, owing to the contentious nature of the disputes. Despite these commonalities, it is crucial to understand that they are distinct types of media campaigns with divergent, even opposing, foreign policy goals. Therefore, discerning between these two forms of campaigns becomes an invaluable skill for anyone seeking a deeper understanding of a state's foreign policy objectives.

Recognizing the distinctions between types of campaigns is imperative to fully grasp the foreign policy objectives of authoritarian regimes and to understand the impact of media on public opinion within these states. Traditionally, decoding the foreign policy intentions of an authoritarian state has relied on experiential knowledge, back-channel information, anecdotes, impressions, instincts, and even speculative methods akin to reading tea leaves. However, through the analysis of publicly available data, such as media text data, one can deduce an authoritarian state's foreign policy intent based on existing public opinion and types of media campaigns, employing evidence-based reasoning and logical deductions.

Considering the typical elusiveness surrounding the actions of authoritarian states, and the common tendency of states to misrepresent their intentions

The Art of State Persuasion. Frances Yaping Wang, Oxford University Press. © Oxford University Press 2024.
DOI: 10.1093/oso/9780197757505.003.0007

during foreign policy crises,[1] assessing public opinion and media campaign types offers a far more feasible approach to accurately discerning state intentions. This method relies on tangible evidence rather than speculative instinct, providing a more reliable and precise interpretation of authoritarian behavior.

To empirically differentiate between mobilization and pacification campaigns, I have compiled a dataset consisting of article texts from eleven distinct Chinese media campaigns, which are the same campaigns detected in the medium-N study in Chapter 2.[2] These campaigns span the history of Chinese interstate territorial disputes since the establishment of the People's Republic in 1949.[3] I code each campaign based on its valence, topics, and the emotions targeted for manipulation, and then compare the outcomes between mobilization and pacification campaigns. This process helps to draw a clear distinction between these two types of media campaigns.

The results of my analysis indicate that mobilization and pacification campaigns indeed exhibit differences in terms of valence, topics, and the emotions they seek to manipulate. Mobilization campaigns typically adopt a more negative valence, focusing on themes of victimhood, allegations of aggression, and perceived injustices. Conversely, pacification campaigns generally display a more positive valence, emphasizing the risks and costs associated with conflict, the legitimacy of China's claims, and the preference for diplomacy, peace, and dialogue.

In terms of emotional appeal, mobilization campaigns often employ emotive and inflammatory language, inciting strong negative emotions such as anger and hatred. On the other hand, pacification campaigns aim to soothe emotions, resorting to less intense negative emotions like sadness or fear, or even fostering positive emotions such as respect or happiness.

In the following sections, I first revisit the theoretical distinctions between mobilization and pacification campaigns as discussed in Chapter 1. Drawing from this, I formulate hypotheses suitable for text analysis. I then describe the data and methods utilized to test these hypotheses and present the results. Following a thorough discussion and evaluation of the empirical outcomes in light of the testing hypotheses, I conclude by exploring the theoretical and pragmatic implications of these results.

Distinguishing Between Mobilization and Pacification

As recollected from earlier chapters, particularly chapter 1, although both mobilization and pacification campaigns amply a particular issue by raising the volume and salience of media coverage, their motivations and methods differ significantly. Table 1.2 in Chapter 1 compares the important features of these two campaign types. Unlike mobilization campaigns, which aim to galvanize the public, pacification campaigns aim to calm and pacify the public. Pacification campaigns adopt a harsh rhetoric seemingly like that of mobilization campaigns, but solely for purposes of echoing public opinion to build social trust, or for hardline posturing to salve angry publics and prevent mass mobilization against the regime.

While mobilization might imply substantial punishments, pacification resorts to hardline posturing with either no substantive punishments or very vague ones. This strategy ensures that the posturing does not undermine the pacification objective. It allows for more flexibility and latitude for the government, while satiating a nationalist demand for a hardline position and preventing mass mobilization against the regime.

One potential hazard of hardline echoing or posturing in pacification campaigns is that it may further incite nationalist audiences or unintentionally send an escalatory signal to an adversary. Therefore, states must use tough rhetoric sparingly—essentially "softening the message."[4] States may also communicate with an opponent country via private credible channels to preempt unintended external escalation.

Additionally, states could temper the harsh rhetoric with positive framing to alleviate both domestic and international risks. Positive framing entails selecting uplifting stories, utilizing affirmative language, promoting positive emotions, and endorsing messages that are supportive of the government and condemn violence. This strategic use of positive framing can effectively temper the intensity of hardline rhetoric, ensuring the overall communication still aligns with the pacification objective.

Moreover, unlike a mobilization campaign that incites action, a pacification campaign discourages action by permitting or even promoting, venting, and censoring content that might provoke action. Social media serves as an immediate platform for individuals to vent their anger and frustration in a public forum, allowing the state to maintain control while giving the public a sense of participation and expression.

In both mobilization and pacification campaigns, different emotions are employed, each with varying intensity. Mobilization campaigns amplify emotions by eliciting potent negative and positive feelings, while pacification attempts to temper emotions by emphasizing objective facts and rational cost-benefit analysis.

Mobilization campaigns often stir potent negative emotions toward the adversary—they incite a robust sense of injustice and sadness about the situation and ignite anger and hatred toward the target nation or its people. These campaigns invoke memories of past injustices and employ vivid imagery of violence inflicted upon members of the "in-group." The opponent in mobilization campaigns is typically portrayed as an irredeemable demon who commits unforgivable atrocities and can only be eradicated.

In contrast, pacification campaigns merely echo, and modestly, existing negative emotions; the antagonist in these campaigns is depicted as a fallible villain who can potentially be redeemed and forgiven. Pacification campaigns attempt to dull these negative emotions with objective facts, usually gleaned from investigative journalism and expert knowledge. They aim to dilute negative feelings with positive emotions, such as boosting patriotism and confidence in the government, lauding the heroism of soldiers, presenting their own claim as just, and claiming the moral high ground through the espousal of peaceful resolution, restraint, and respect for international law.

Even though negative emotions are present in both mobilization and pacification campaigns, the predominant negative emotions used in each campaign type differ. Mobilization tends to provoke intense negative emotions, such as anger or hatred, to inflame or provoke, while pacification uses milder negative emotions, such as sadness or fear, merely to echo or posture.

Anger and fear represent two divergent emotions on the "approach-avoidance" dimension of emotions, corresponding to the common phrase of "fight or flight." Anger is a robust "approach" emotion that augments individuals' propensity to attribute blame, inflict harm on the offender and rectify an injustice, reduces their willingness to consider policy compromises, and is particularly effective in eliciting risky and punitive policies.[5] Conversely, fear is a powerful "avoidance" emotion that heightens people's recognition of the critical need for precautionary measures, erodes their confidence and support for dangerous initiatives, and bolsters their preference for retreat or conciliatory policies.[6] Since mobilization advocates action while pacification discourages it, anger and fear are common features of mobilization and pacification campaigns, respectively.

States also aim to delegitimize negative emotions that could potentially incite violence or induce action. Acknowledging the significant emotional underpinnings of social movements and activism, particularly anger and hatred,[7] media narratives work to delegitimize these "unhelpful" emotions by nurturing an aversion to social unrest and violence and claiming the moral high ground of civility, patriotism, and benefit to the nation.[8]

Testing Hypotheses

Drawing on the theoretical distinctions between mobilization and pacification campaigns, I have developed a set of hypotheses that can be tested using text data.[9] The hypotheses formulated here provide a useful starting point for distinguishing between the two campaign types in question. They also represent the majority of the characteristics we have described above. These hypotheses are categorized into three dimensions of text data: valence, narratives, and emotions.

Valence is a term from psychology that refers to the evaluative (positive or negative) quality of a piece of text data.[10] Valence is the most basic emotional dimension and has become a widely used value in text analysis, especially in sentiment analysis. Narrative, on the other hand, refers to the main topics or slants of media coverage. It is another important dimension of text data that can be analyzed to test hypotheses about mobilization and pacification campaigns. The third category of hypotheses focuses on emotions, which goes beyond the single positive-negative dimension of valence. This category labels a text corpus with specific types of emotions it evokes, such as happiness or anger, along with their corresponding intensities. Overall, by examining these three dimensions of text data, we can test hypotheses about the differences between mobilization and pacification campaigns.

Valence

Based on our analysis so far, mobilization campaigns consistently employ negative evaluations of their opponents. In contrast, pacification campaigns utilize negative content to echo public sentiment, but do so in moderation, often balancing it with positive framing. Therefore, the rhetoric of states should be harsher in mobilization campaigns, and milder in pacification campaigns. When we convert these concepts into the language of valence, we arrive at the following two groups of hypotheses:

H1a: Mobilization campaigns use more negative words on average than pacification campaigns.

H1b: Pacification campaigns use more positive words on average than mobilization campaigns.

H1c: Mobilization campaigns reference the opponent countries/governments more negatively than pacification campaigns.

Narratives

In mobilization campaigns, state media often portray the ingroup as victimized and accuse the outgroup of aggression. This typically involves depictions of extensive damage inflicted on ingroup members, references to past grievances, and criticism and condemnation of the other's aggression. The outgroup is also often portrayed as cruel and inhumane. Pacification campaigns also involve negative narratives such as accusations, condemnation, complaints of injustice, and laments about the situation. However, they are supplemented by positive aspects of the dispute, including messages that support the government and the status quo, and that oppose violence and unrest. Thus, we can expect significant overlap among campaigns within each campaign type in terms of the topics, angles, and aspects of the stories they cover ("within commonness"). At the same time, we should see distinctive topics and narratives that set mobilization campaigns apart from pacification campaigns ("between distinctiveness").

H2a: A substantial overlap exists in terms of top words and key topics among campaigns within each campaign type.

H2b: A considerable share of top words and key topics shared among campaigns within each campaign type exhibit distinctiveness between the two campaign types.

Emotions

Mobilization and pacification campaigns evoke different types and intensities of emotions. In mobilization campaigns, the emotions are mainly negative and intense, such as anger, hatred, and a strong sense of injustice. In contrast, pacification campaigns elicit a mix of reactive emotions, including sadness, anger, pity, fear, and a moderate sense of injustice, balanced by positive emotions.

Based on these distinctions, I propose the following hypotheses:

H3a: Mobilization campaigns utilize more negative emotions than pacification campaigns.

H3b: Pacification campaigns utilize more positive emotions than mobilization campaigns.

H3c: Among negative emotions, mobilization campaigns utilize more intense negative emotions such as hatred or anger, whereas pacification campaigns utilize milder negative emotions such as sadness or fear.

H3d: Mobilization campaigns utilize stronger emotions than pacifications campaign, either positive or negative.

Data

The primary dataset, referred to as the Chinese Media Campaigns on Territorial Disputes (CMCTD) data, comprises a total of 9,391 pertinent articles from *People's Daily*. These articles pertain to eleven media campaigns focused on six territorial disputes involving China. These campaigns represent the entirety of media campaigns initiated by China concerning its border and offshore territorial disputes since 1949. For an article to be considered "pertinent," it must primarily address the dispute rather than merely mentioning it in passing. To ensure accuracy, I conducted keyword searches for the six territorial disputes and manually excluded articles where the dispute was mentioned but not the primary subject matter.

Drawing from the assessments established in the medium-N study regarding existing public sentiment and the state's foreign policy intentions in each case, the eleven campaigns can be categorized into mobilization and pacification campaigns. Mobilization campaigns, designed to galvanize existing moderate or weak public sentiment toward a more assertive foreign policy, encompass four of the total campaigns, accounting for 8,685 articles. Conversely, pacification campaigns, intended to soothe a currently assertive public opinion to accommodate a more moderate foreign policy, make up the remaining seven campaigns and 706 articles.

Each article serves as an individual unit of observation, with their full texts utilized for text analysis.[11] Depending on the level of analysis, there are two major text corpora—one comprising of 8,685 articles from all mobilization campaigns and the other consisting of 706 articles from all pacification campaigns. Alternatively, there are eleven smaller text corpora, each containing articles from a single media campaign. Table 6.1 and Table 6.2 present the summary statistics of the CMCTD data, including each media campaign's disputing country, year, the start and end dates, duration, the number of front-page articles published on the dispute, the number of all relevant articles and their averages during each campaign.

Utilizing the CMCTD data, I created a more focused dataset called Chinese Media Campaigns Opponent-Referenced (CMCOR) data. This dataset exclusively includes five words preceding and fifteen words following terms that represent the opponent country or government. In this dataset, each mention makes up as an individual observation, comprising a maximum of 20 words.[12] The purpose of creating this data was to specifically examine the tone associated with references to the opponent country or government, enabling the evaluation of hypothesis H1c.

Table 6.1 Summary Statistics of the Four Mobilization Campaigns in the CMCTD Data

#	Case	MC Start	MC End	Duration (Days)	Front-Page Articles	All-Relevant Articles	Average Front-Page Articles	Average All-Relevant Articles
2	Sino-India 1962	6/1/1962	12/31/1963	578	346	1029	18.0	53.4
4	Sino-Soviet 1969	3/3/1969	9/21/1969	202	56	446	8.3	66.2
5	Sino-Vietnam 1974	1/12/1974	2/18/1974	37	7	12	5.7	9.7
7	Sino-Vietnam 1979	11/5/1978	3/31/1990	4164	581	7198	4.2	51.9

MC: Media Campaign.

Table 6.2 Summary Statistics of the Seven Pacification Campaigns in the CMCTD Data

#	Case	MC Start	MC End	Duration (Days)	Front-Page Articles	All-Relevant Articles	Average Front-Page Articles	Average All-Relevant Articles
10	Sino-Japan 1990	9/29/1990	10/30/1990	31	7	27	6.8	26.1
11	Sino-Japan 1996	7/25/1996	10/30/1996	97	11	113	3.4	34.9
12	Sino-Japan 2005	4/1/2005	6/1/2005	61	13	167	6.4	82.1
13	Sino-Japan 2010	9/9/2010	11/6/2010	58	2	35	1.0	18.1
16	Sino-Japan 2012	9/3/2012	10/31/2012	58	25	137	12.9	70.9
20	Sino-Philippines 2016	6/1/2016	8/1/2016	61	13	208	6.4	102.3
21	Sino-India 2017	6/27/2017	8/4/2017	38	2	19	1.6	15.0

Table 6.3 Summary Statistics of the CMCOR Data

Campaigns	Reference Markers	# of Observations (Mentions)	Average # of Mentions/Article
Sino-India 1962	印度、印度政府、尼赫鲁	13,986	13.6
Sino-Soviet 1969	苏修、苏联、沙皇	6,465	14.5
Sino-Vietnam 1974	西贡、越南、傀儡	63	5.3
Sino-Vietnam 1979	越南、苏联、越军	56,122	7.8
Sino-Japan 1990	日本、日方、日本政府	133	4.9
Sino-Japan 1996	日本、日方、日本政府	1,039	9.2
Sino-Japan 2005	日本、日方、日本政府	1,066	6.4
Sino-Japan 2010	日本、日方、日本政府	145	4.1
Sino-Japan 2012	日本、日方、日本政府	1063	7.8
Sino-Philippines 2016	菲律宾、美国、仲裁庭	2,081	10.0
Sino-India 2017	印度、印方、印军	148	7.8

Table 6.3 presents the summary statistics of the CMCOR data, including the reference markers for the opponent country or government in each campaign, the number of observations/mentions, and the average number of observations/mentions per article. To provide an illustration, Figure 6.1 offers a snapshot of the data by utilizing "苏修" (Soviet Revisionist) as a reference marker in the 1969 Sino-Soviet border conflict.

All text data then underwent a preprocessing step for word segmentation and stop words removal.[13] The cleaned data consisted of lines of words and phrases devoid of stop words. Each line corresponded to an article in the CMCTD data or to a mention of the opposing country or government in the CMCOR data.

Method

To test the hypotheses, I employ dictionary-based sentiment analysis and structural topic models (STM). Table 6.4 provides an overview of the data, methodology, and dictionaries utilized for each hypothesis.

To examine the valence-based hypotheses, I utilized the National Taiwan University Sentiment Dictionary (NTUSD) along with its augmented version, ANTUSD.[14] These dictionaries are widely employed for sentiment analysis of Chinese texts and have undergone rigorous testing, demonstrating a high level of accuracy. The NTUSD classifies words within articles as positive or negative, without considering the intensity of valence. In other words, it

	0	1	2	3	4	5	6	7	8	9	10	11	12	13	14	15	16	17	18	19	20
0	珍宝岛	无可争议	地是	中国	领土		叛徒	集团	贼喊捉贼	抗议	照会	继承	沙俄	帝国主义	衣体	推行	社会	帝国主义	侵略	政策	强盗
1	苏修	叛徒	集团	不顾	我国	政府	一再	警告	侵犯	我国	领土	领空	制造	流血事件	勾结	美帝					
2	边防战士	多名	边防部队	被迫	自卫还击	苏修	叛徒	集团	蓄意	制造	武装挑衅	事件	中国	犯下	一新	罪行	暴露	社会	帝国主义	狰狞面目	本月
3	胜利	保卫	我国	神圣	领土	苏修	叛徒	集团	一手	挑起	武装冲突	孤立	事件	苏修	我国	政府	领空	制造	流血事件	一九六七年	一月
4	一手	挑起	武装冲突	孤立	事件	苏修	叛徒	集团	不顾	我国	政府	一再	警告	侵犯	我国	领土	领空	制造	流血事件	一九六七年	一月
5	十一月	底到	一九六八	一月	五日	苏修	叛徒	集团	十八次	出动	边防军	侵入	黑龙江省	珍宝岛	以北	七里	沁岛	地区	破坏	群众	生产
6	军用飞机	侵犯	黑龙江省	领空	次数	苏修	叛徒	集团	罪行	激起	我国	军民	义愤	中国	严正	警告	苏修	叛徒	集团	无产阶级	文化大革命
7	帝国主义	社会	法西斯主	狰狞面目	暴露	苏修	叛徒	集团	罪行	激起	我国	军民	义愤	中国	严正	警告	苏修	叛徒	集团	无产阶级	文化大革命
8	新华社	三日	讯		叛徒	集团	指使	苏联	边防军	入侵	我国	领土	制造	帝国主义	侵略	政策	滔天罪行	我国	政府	苏联政府	
9	集会	强大	示威游行	愤怒	声讨	苏修	叛徒	集团	勾结	美帝	猖狂	反华	推行	社会	帝国主义	侵略	政策	滔天罪行	我国	政府	苏联政府
10	声势浩大	游行示威	队伍	高举	强烈抗议	苏修	侵犯	我国	领土	珍宝岛	誓死保卫	祖国	神圣	领土	巨幅	标语	振臂	愤怒	高呼	打倒	苏修
11	标语	振臂	愤怒	高呼	打倒	苏修	打倒	社会	帝国主义	打倒	新	沙皇	打倒	美帝	苏修	打倒	各国	反动派	军民	严正	警告
12	新	沙皇	打倒	美帝	打倒	苏修	打倒	各国	反动派	军民	严正	警告	苏修	叛徒	集团	中国	神圣	领土	不容	侵犯	一意孤行
13	各国	反动派	军民	严正	警告	苏修	叛徒	集团	中国	神圣	领土	不容	侵犯	一意孤行	挑衅	中	苏	边境	武装冲突	马克思主义	列宁主义
14	纷纷	集会	示威游行	严正	声讨	苏修	叛徒	集团	滔天罪行	结成	浩浩荡荡	队伍	四面八方	涌向	反	修路	苏联	大使馆	高呼	强烈抗议	苏修

Figure 6.1 Snapshot of the CMCOR Data Using "Soviet Revisionist" as a Reference Marker in the 1969 Sino-Soviet Border Conflict

Table 6.4 Summary of Methods for Testing Each Sets of Hypotheses

	Hypotheses	Data	Method	Dictionaries
1. Valence	H1a: Mobilization campaigns use more negative words on average than pacification campaigns. H1b: Pacification campaigns use more positive words on average than mobilization campaigns.	CMCTD	Dictionary-based Sentiment Analysis	NTUSD, and ANTUSD for robustness check
	H1c: Mobilization campaigns reference the opponent countries/governments more negatively than pacification campaigns.	CMCOR	Dictionary-based Sentiment Analysis	NTUSD, and ANTUSD for robustness check
2. Narratives	H2a: A substantial overlap exists in terms of top words and key topics among campaigns within each campaign type. H2b: A considerable share of top words and key topics shared among campaigns within each campaign type exhibit distinctiveness between the two campaign types.	CMCTD	Top words & STM	N/A
3. Emotions	H3a: Mobilization campaigns utilize more negative emotions than pacification campaigns. H3b: Pacification campaigns utilize more positive emotions than mobilization campaigns. H3c: Among negative emotions, mobilization campaigns utilize stronger negative emotions such as hatred or anger, whereas pacification campaigns utilize more moderate negative emotions such as sadness or fear. H3d: Mobilization campaigns utilize stronger emotions than pacifications campaign.	CMCTD	Dictionary-based Sentiment Analysis	DLUT Emotion Ontology

concentrates solely on the count of positive and negative words present in the text, not how positive or negative these words are. For each article, I computed the positive and negative scores by determining the proportion of positive and negative words respectively. The overall valence of each article was then evaluated by calculating the difference between these scores, yielding an aggregated score. This score gives a comprehensive measure of the article's valence. A positive (negative) aggregated score indicates a greater number of positive (negative) words compared to negative (positive) words.

On the other hand, ANTUSD not only labels words as positive or negative but also assigns each word a weight, representing the intensity of its valence. This weight ranges from -1 (most negative) to 1 (most positive). This approach echoes the NTUSD's aggregated score methodology, but integrates the intensity of the valence as a weight factor. I repeated the tests using ANTUSD as a robustness check to ensure the validity of the results.

To determine if there are any significant differences among campaigns and between campaign types, I employed statistical tests such as t-tests, analysis of variance (ANOVA), or predicted scores using linear regressions. These tests allow us to assess whether there are statistically significant variations in the scores within each campaign type and between different campaign types.

Regarding narratives, I extracted the top fifty most frequently used words for each campaign and deployed the STM to evaluate the prevalence of common and distinctive topics within and across campaign types.[15] While STM is an advanced topic model that augments the capabilities of traditional probabilistic models like latent Dirichlet allocation (LDA),[16] due to its unsupervised nature, it remains predominantly useful only for exploratory purposes. Consequently, any interpretation drawn from it necessitates complementary substantive knowledge about the media campaigns and their content for accurate inference.

For the analysis of emotions, I utilized the Dalian University of Technology (DLUT) Emotion Ontology dictionary.[17] This unique resource is the only Chinese language dictionary that applies specific emotion labels to textual content. The emotion categories in the DLUT Emotion Ontology are drawn from Ekman's six fundamental emotions, namely anger, disgust, fear, happiness, sadness, and surprise.[18] Furthermore, a category labeled "good" is included to encapsulate all positive emotions. These seven broad categories are further divided into 21 subcategories. For example, the sadness category comprises emotions such as sorrow, disappointment, guilt, and longing. Each of the 21 emotions is assigned a rating on an intensity scale that ranges from 1 to 9, where 1 denotes the weakest intensity and 9 signifies the strongest intensity.

In this study, I employed the DLUT Emotion Ontology dictionary to label emotional words according to their respective intensities. I compared the frequency of emotional words, taking into account their weighted intensities, across the seven broad emotion categories between different campaign types. I also reviewed the most prominent emotions from the 21 subcategories and contrasted them between campaign types. This approach allowed me to evaluate whether specific emotions were distinctively evoked in each campaign type.

Results and Discussion

The results provide substantial support for all the proposed hypotheses.

Valence

Table 6.5 presents the mean values for positive, negative, and aggregated sentiment scores, which were obtained by applying the NTUSD dictionary to the CMCTD dataset.

On average, articles from mobilization campaigns include roughly 28 negative words as classified by the NTUSD dictionary, about four more negative words than those in pacification campaigns (24). Conversely, articles from pacification campaigns contain around 32 positive words as per the NTUSD dictionary, which is approximately nine more positive words compared to articles in mobilization campaigns (23). These results lend credence to hypotheses H1a and H1b. Statistical significance tests, such as t-tests and ANOVA, confirm that the discrepancies in positive, negative, and aggregated scores between mobilization and pacification campaigns are all statistically significant at the 0.001 confidence level. This signifies that articles from mobilization campaigns differ significantly from those in pacification campaigns in terms of valence.

Figure 6.2 visualizes the data from Table 6.5, contrasting the mean positive, negative, and aggregated scores between mobilization and pacification campaigns. The red dots correspond to the mean scores of mobilization campaigns, while the green dots denote pacification campaigns, with the benchmarks placed along the Y-axes. Figure 6.3 presents the predicted positive, negative, and aggregated scores using a linear regression model with

Table 6.5 CMCTD Data Average NTUSD Sentiment Scores

	Mobilization Campaigns	Pacification Campaigns
Average Positive Scores	22.9	32.1
Average Negative Scores	−28.4	−23.8
Average Aggregated Scores	−0.017	0.016

200   The Art of State Persuasion

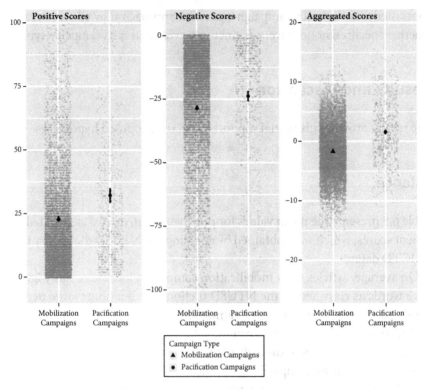

Figure 6.2   Comparison of NTUSD Sentiment Scores with Data Distribution

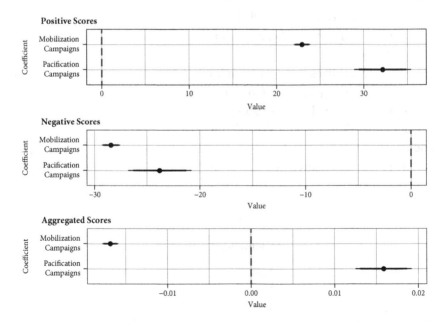

Figure 6.3   Predicted NTUSD Sentiment Scores with 95% and 90% Confidence Intervals

95 percent and 90 percent confidence intervals. Notably, none of these intervals between mobilization and pacification campaigns overlap. These visualizations confirm that mobilization campaigns are significantly more negative than pacification campaigns.

Figures 6.4 and 6.5 illustrate the NTUSD sentiment scores categorized by campaigns. Figure 6.4 displays boxplots representing the median sentiment scores and data distribution. With the only exception of the Sino-Japan dispute in 1996, all other pacification campaigns (shown in green) exhibit medians situated on the positive side of the zero line.[19] Conversely, all of the mobilization campaigns (depicted in red) display medians located on the negative side.

Figure 6.5 presents predicted sentiment scores by campaigns using linear models. Again, apart from the Japan 1996 case, all pacification campaigns are positioned on the positive side of the zero line, while all mobilization campaigns are situated on the negative side. These figures provide additional evidence supporting hypotheses H1a and H1b.

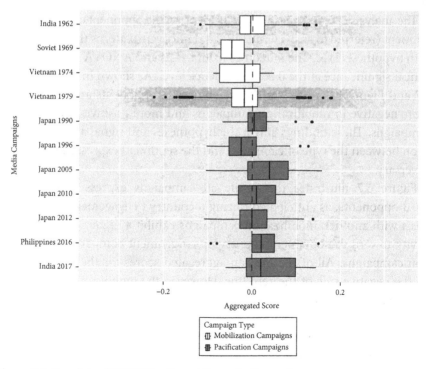

Figure 6.4 Boxplots of NTUSD Sentiment Scores by Campaigns

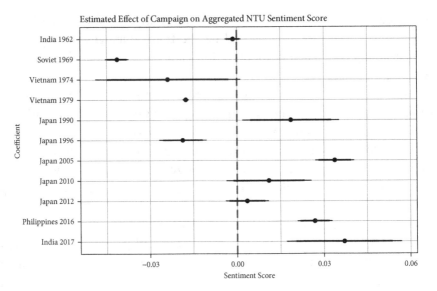

Figure 6.5 Predicted NTUSD Sentiment Scores by Campaigns

These results remain robust even when I use the ANTUSD dictionary, which takes into account the intensity of valence. Detailed results of this robustness check can be found in Appendix 5.

The analysis of texts that specifically mention the opponent country or government (referred to as the CMCOR data) uncovers patterns that correspond with hypothesis H1c. The outcomes from t-tests and ANOVA all suggest statistical significance at the 0.001 confidence level. As shown in Tables 6.6 and 6.7 and Figure 6.6, it is clear that references to opponents are considerably more negative in mobilization campaigns and more positive in pacification campaigns. These findings affirm the hypotheses and signal a strong association between the type of campaign and the sentiment expressed toward the adversary.

Figure 6.7 illustrates that while all campaigns express negativity toward opponents, as anticipated during a country's engagement in a dispute crisis with another, mobilization campaigns exhibit a higher degree of negativity toward the opponent country or government compared to pacification campaigns. All of the median aggregated scores for the campaigns sit on the negative side of the zero line. However, the mobilization campaigns, represented in red, demonstrate a higher negative score, indicating a more negative sentiment. This finding aligns with the expected pattern, indicating that mobilization campaigns tend to portray the opponent country or government in a more negative light than pacification campaigns.

It is important to highlight that the findings further corroborate a temporal differentiation elaborated in Chapter 1 and validated by the medium-N study in Chapter 2. This distinction lies between the mobilization campaigns that

Table 6.6 CMCOR Data Average NTUSD Sentiment Scores

	Mobilization Campaigns	Pacification Campaigns
Average Positive Scores	0.9	1.1
Average Negative Scores	−2.3	−1.6
Average Aggregated Scores	−0.071	−0.022

Table 6.7 CMCOR Data Average ANTUSD Sentiment Scores

	Mobilization Campaigns	Pacification Campaigns
Sentiment Scores	-0.325	0.028

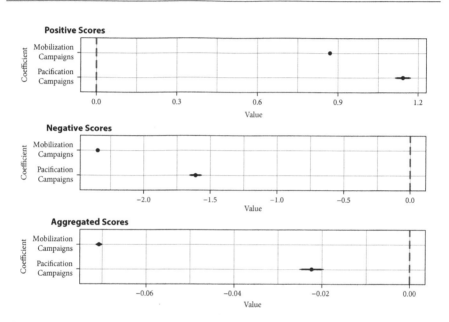

Figure 6.6 Predicted NTUSD Sentiment Scores of CMCOR Data with 95% and 90% Confidence Intervals

predominantly took place before 1980, and the pacification campaigns, which occurred mostly after 1990. This raises the question of whether the difference in valence observed here reflects a change in the reporting style of the newspaper itself rather than the reporting styles of these media campaigns.

The available evidence does not support the notion that *People's Daily* content on foreign disputes has systematically become more positive over the years. In Oksenberg and Henderson's *Research Guide to People's Daily Editorials, 1949–1975*, it is emphasized that *People's Daily* serves as the only continuous source on Chinese affairs.[20] Furthermore, An's study of *People's Daily* front page articles from 1978 to 2013 reveals a variable number of negative reports in selected years, without indicating a consistent pattern of

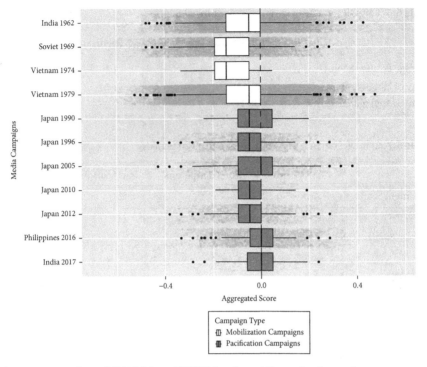

Figure 6.7 Boxplots of CMCOR Data NTUSD Sentiment Scores by Campaigns

increasing positivity.[21] Additionally, Zhao's longitudinal content analysis of *People's Daily* editorials from 1977 to 2010 indicates a greater number of critiques against local governments and specific government branches after 1989, suggesting an overall negative tone in *People's Daily* over time. However, it is important to note that these analyses cover various topics and not solely foreign policy.[22] In scrutinizing the official rhetoric specifically pertinent to foreign conflicts, the consistency of Godwin and Miller's presentation of China's warning terminology—including commonly used terms in *People's Daily*—stands the test of time.[23] For these reasons, the difference in valence observed here truly reflects disparities between the two campaign types, rather than a shift in *People's Daily* reporting style.

Narratives

Examining the most commonly used words in *People's Daily* articles offers a simple yet informative way to gauge the narratives of these campaigns. It provides insights into the topics covered, the framing of issues, and the emphasized aspects of the stories. Appendix 6 provides a complete list of fifty most frequently used words in mobilization campaigns and pacification campaigns.

In mobilization campaigns, notable top words include "invasion," "fight," "soldiers," "enemy," "self-defense," "resolutely," "military provocation," "motherland," "sovereignty," "the whole world," "United Nations," "arise," and "set out." While the use of "invasion" and "military provocation" often serves to accuse the other of aggression, terms like "self-defense," "motherland," "the whole world," and "United Nations" suggest a sense of self-righteousness in one's own position. Words like "arise," "fight," and "set out" typically imply calls for action, whereas "soldiers," "enemy," and "resolutely" hint at a militarized nature or a strong intensity in the advocated responses. These observations align with the narratives of mobilization campaigns discussed earlier.

The most common words in pacification campaigns include "territory," "sovereignty," "peace," "stability," "cooperation," "world," "dispute," "illegal," "negotiation," "safeguard," "so-called," "political," "strengthen," "two countries," "important," "severely," "hope," and "promote." While terms like "severely," "illegal," and "so-called" may be used to criticize the other party, they are significantly less intense compared to the prominent words in mobilization campaigns. Words such as "territory," "sovereignty," and "safeguard" are typically associated with defending one's own claims, but the key words like "peace," "stability," "cooperation," "negotiation," "political," "strengthen," "two countries," "important," "hope," and "promote" indicate a moderate course of action. These findings align with the narratives of pacification campaigns discussed earlier, highlighting a focus on pursuing peaceful resolutions, fostering stability, and promoting cooperative approaches.

Results from the STM provide less definitive conclusions. However, when considering these results alongside substantive knowledge of the media campaigns, several common themes within mobilization campaigns and pacification campaigns emerge as distinctive features of each campaign type. This finding offers support for hypotheses H2a and H2b, which suggest that mobilization campaigns and pacification campaigns exhibit characteristics common within their respective campaign types but distinctive between the two types.

Figures 6.8 and 6.9 present the most frequent topics of each campaign, grouped by campaign types, including their topical content (the words used within a topic) and topical prevalence (how much of a document is associated with a topic).[24] It is important to focus on the topics listed at the top of each chart with the highest topical prevalence, as they represent the most dominant topics within each campaign type.

206   The Art of State Persuasion

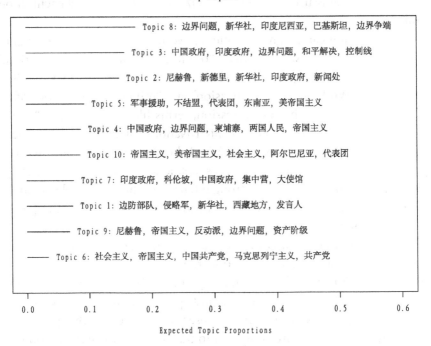

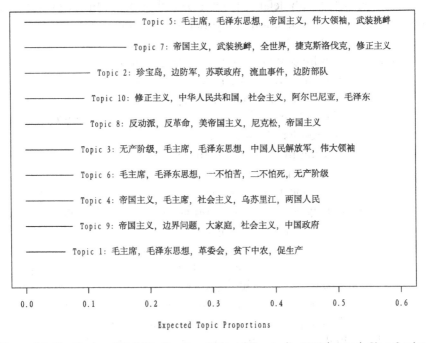

Figure 6.8 Top Topics of Mobilization Campaigns (Sino-India 1962 (upper), Sino-Soviet 1969 (lower))

Mobilization versus Pacification 207

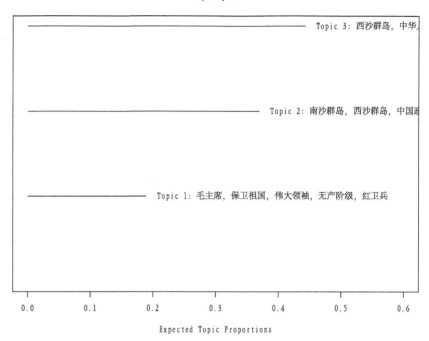

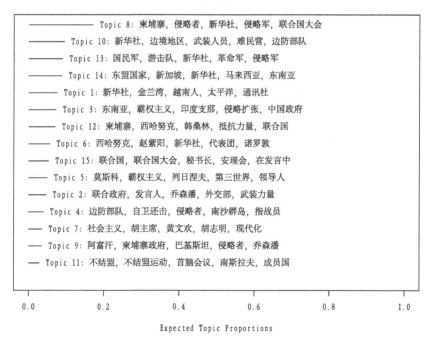

Figure 6.8 Continued (Sino-Vietnam 1974 (upper), Sino-Vietnam 1979 (lower))

208 The Art of State Persuasion

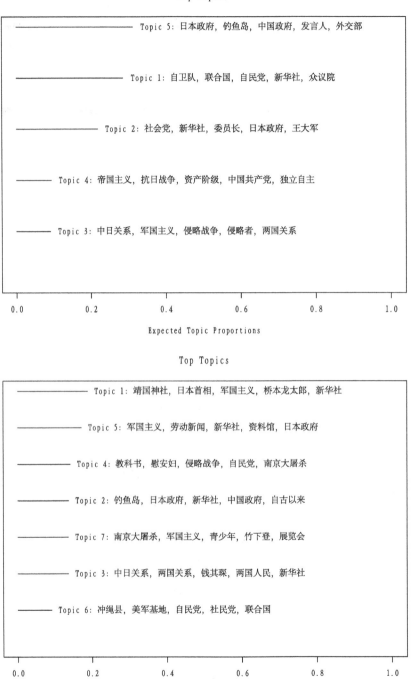

Figure 6.9 Top Topics of Pacification Campaigns (Sino-Japan 1990 (upper), Sino-Japan 1996 (lower))

Mobilization versus Pacification 209

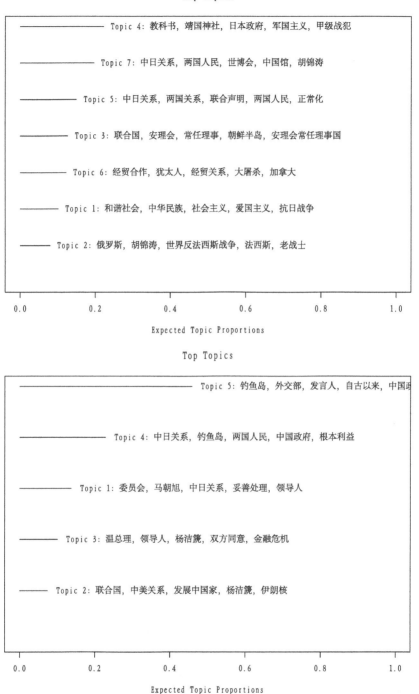

Figure 6.9 Continued (Sino-Japan 2005 (upper), Sino-Japan 2010 (lower))

210 The Art of State Persuasion

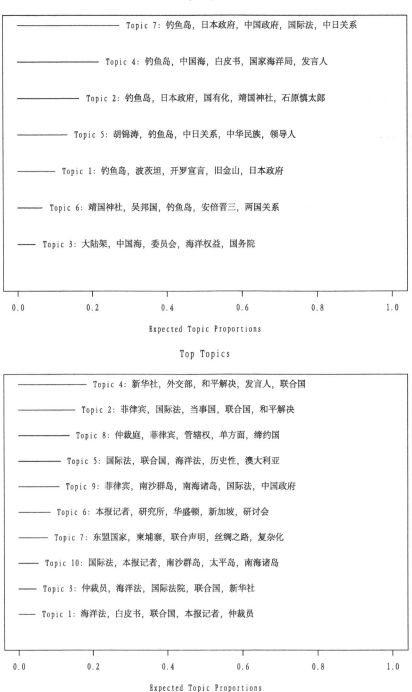

Figure 6.9 Continued (Sino-Japan 2012 (upper), Sino-Philippines 2016 (lower))

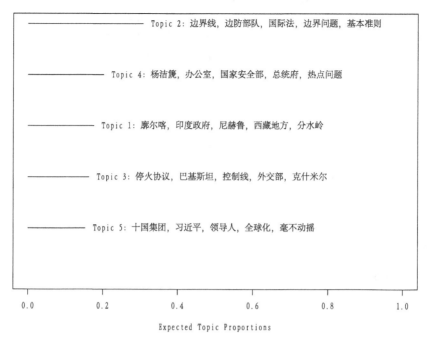

Figure 6.9 Continued (Sino-India 2017)

One common theme that emerges across the board is the territorial dispute. This includes descriptions of the disputed territory, relevant parties involved, the history and development of the dispute, incidents leading up to the current crisis, and evidence supporting one's own claim. These topics can be observed in various campaigns, such as topic eight and four in the India 1962 campaign, topic two in the Soviet 1969 campaign, topics three and two in the 1972 Vietnam campaign, topics ten and four in the Vietnam 1979 campaign, topic five in the Japan 1990 campaign, topic two in the Japan 1996 campaign, topic five in the Japan 2010 campaign, topics seven, four, and two in the Japan 2012 campaign, topics five and nine in the Philippines 2016 campaign, and topics two, one, and three in the India 2017 campaign.

It is worth noting that the Japan 2005 campaign deviates from this common theme, which aligns with our understanding that issues such as Japan's bid for UN Security Council permanent membership, controversies over history textbooks, and Japanese Cabinet members' visit to the Yasukuni Shrine assumed greater prominence in that particular campaign compared to the territorial dispute. This consistency between the identified topics and our substantive understanding of the campaign content increases our confidence in the overall accuracy of the estimation.

Two themes consistently emerge within mobilization campaigns, effectively distinguishing them from pacification campaigns. The first theme places a substantial emphasis on ideology. This theme can be seen through the recurrent mention of ideological terms and phrases, such as "socialism," "American imperialism," and "Marxist Leninism" in the sixth and tenth topics of the India 1962 campaign. Similarly, we see "Mao Zedong thought" and "revisionism" appearing in the fifth and seventh topics of the Soviet 1969 campaign, "Mao Zedong," "proletariat," and "red guards" in the first topic of the Vietnam 1974 campaign, and "socialism" and "modernization" in the seventh topic of the Vietnam 1979 campaign.

These ideological references are conspicuously absent in the pacification campaigns, highlighting their distinct nature in mobilization campaigns. While these ideological slogans may be more characteristic of the pre-reform era, they still play an essential role within the context of mobilization campaigns. Ideology, as an intellectual construct, simplifies complex global issues and presents them in starkly polarizing terms. It characteristically dichotomizes world affairs into a black-and-white narrative, thereby creating a simple and accessible narrative for the public to grasp.

In mobilization campaigns, this clear demarcation between "us" and "them" is extremely beneficial. By defining the "other" or the "enemy" in clear ideological terms, such campaigns can instill a strong sense of unity among the home public against a common adversary. This binary framing helps to stir collective emotions, ignite nationalistic fervor, and rally public sentiment toward a more assertive and uncompromising policy response.

Ideological references further solidify the moral standing of the home country, often presenting it as a beacon of virtue up against an ideologically flawed adversary. This portrayal imbues the public with a sense of righteous indignation against the enemy, thereby amplifying support for hardline policies and actions.

Moreover, by using ideological labels like "American imperialism" or "revisionism," the mobilization campaigns link the specific situation at hand to larger global or historical narratives. This broad contextualization enhances the perceived significance of the issue, further fueling the public's emotional investment and encouraging a stronger call to action.

Another prominent theme that differentiates mobilization campaigns from pacification campaigns is the heightened focus on analyzing the international situation. This thematic characteristic is reflected in the recurring topics that emerge within the text data of these campaigns. For instance, in the 1962 India campaign, topics like "(US) military aid" and "nonalignment" suggest a strategic consideration of the broader geopolitical context. In the 1969 Soviet campaign, the reference to "the whole world" and "Czechoslovakia" underscores an expansive perspective on global dynamics. Similarly, mentions of "Southeast Asia," "the Third World," and the "Non-Aligned Movement" in the 1979 Vietnam campaign demonstrate an engagement with the broader international political landscape.

While pacification campaigns occasionally address aspects of the international situation, their emphasis is significantly less pronounced compared to that in mobilization campaigns. This concentrated analysis of the global context in mobilization campaigns serves a crucial strategic purpose.

By dissecting the international scenario, mobilization campaigns aim to highlight perceived threats and potential conflicts. This detailed exposition is designed to frame the current situation as part of a broader, more complex global pattern of aggression or instability. Consequently, it reinforces a fatalistic narrative that conflict, or even war, is inevitable.

This narrative aims to instill a sense of imminent danger and urgency in the public consciousness. By presenting a more aggressive policy response as a necessary reaction to an unfavorable international climate, these campaigns seek to garner public support for hardline measures. Therefore, the analysis of the international situation functions as a strategic tool to rally public sentiment and legitimize a more assertive foreign policy.

One recurring theme that stands out distinctly in pacification campaigns is the emphasis on the importance of bilateral relationships and the advocacy for a "peaceful resolution." This theme emerges prominently in the analysis of the topical content across various pacification campaigns. For instance, in the 1996 Japan campaign, references to the "bilateral relationship" and "peoples of the two countries" underline the significance attached to interpersonal connections and the mutual relationship between the two nations. This sentiment is echoed in the 2005 Japan campaign with references to "Sino-Japan relations," "peoples of the two countries," and "normalization."

The 2010 Japan campaign further reinforces this theme, with topics like "Sino-Japan relations," "fundamental interests," "handle properly," and "both sides agree" pointing toward a consensus-driven, diplomatic approach to conflict resolution. The 2012 Japan campaign maintains a similar narrative with repeated mentions of "Sino-Japan relations" and "bilateral relationship."

The emphasis on "peaceful resolution" in the 2016 Philippines campaign and references to a "ceasefire agreement" and "globalization" in the 2017 India campaign further highlight this pacification theme. The choice of these words creates a narrative that presents peaceful resolution of conflicts as being in the best interests of all involved parties.

The emphasis on preserving bilateral relationships underscores the importance attached to long-term diplomatic ties, suggesting that they take precedence over individual disputes. The underlying message is that disputes should be approached with prudence and an aim to resolve them amicably without disrupting the overall relationship. This narrative aligns with the characteristic themes of pacification campaigns, which prioritize diplomatic negotiations and peaceful solutions over confrontational tactics.

In summary, the analysis of the top words and topics provides support for hypotheses H2a and H2b, which suggests that there is a combination of shared topics and words among campaigns within each campaign type that are also distinct between campaign types. The presence of common themes within each campaign type reinforces the notion that certain topics are consistently emphasized and associated with mobilization or pacification campaigns. At the same time, the distinctiveness of certain topics and words between campaign types highlights the specific focus and narrative strategies employed in mobilization and pacification campaigns. These findings lend further credibility to hypotheses 2 and contribute to our understanding of the unique characteristics of each campaign type.

Emotions

Figure 6.10 features a comparative bar chart that illustrates the frequency of seven broad emotion categories, each weighted by its respective intensity. This chart facilitates a clear visual comparison of these values across different campaign types, thus providing an illustrative representation of the emotional distribution within each campaign type.

When examining the seven broad emotion categories, it becomes evident that mobilization campaigns have higher scores in the "disgust" category, while pacification campaigns have higher scores in the "good" and "happy" categories, which are the three most prevalent emotions in the dataset. These findings provide support for hypotheses H3a and H3b, suggesting that mobilization campaigns elicit more negative emotions, while pacification campaigns elicit more positive emotions.

If we zoom in on negative emotions, mobilization campaigns score higher in disgust, anger, and surprise, whereas pacification campaigns score higher in sadness and fear. This evidence substantiates hypothesis H3c, which postulates that mobilization campaigns generally trigger more intense, or "approach," types of negative emotions like hatred (which closely relates to "disgust") and anger. On the other hand, pacification campaigns tend to elicit milder, or "avoidance," types of negative emotions such as sadness and fear.

Figure 6.11 showcases the six most prevalent emotions across the 21 categories for both mobilization and pacification campaigns. It is notable that while mobilization campaigns score higher in the "condemnation" category, they also show higher scores in the "praise" category. Comparing these two categories, it is clear that mobilization campaigns generally elicit

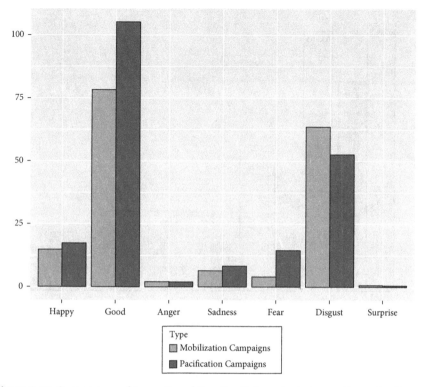

Figure 6.10 Comparison of Seven Broad Emotion Categories between Campaign Types

more intense emotions than pacification campaigns. This finding lends credence to hypothesis H3d, positing that mobilization campaigns intentionally heighten emotions by evoking both strong negative and positive sentiments. Conversely, pacification campaigns aim to temper emotions by emphasizing objective facts and minimizing emotional intensity. This data suggests that while mobilization campaigns are designed to trigger a gamut of strong emotions among the audience, pacification campaigns aim to foster a more rational, balanced perspective through a focus on factual information.

When we assess the proportion of content relating to "praise" and "condemnation" within each campaign type, we see a distinct difference. In pacification campaigns, there is a significantly higher ratio of "praise" to "condemnation" content, approximately 5:3 (51.535:32.013). This indicates that these campaigns direct more focus and effort toward content that praises or positively portrays the subject, rather than content that condemns or negatively portrays it. Conversely, mobilization campaigns show a near-equal distribution of "praise" and "condemnation" content, roughly a 1:1 ratio (65.869:63.865). This reveals that in mobilization campaigns, equal attention is given to both the positive and negative aspects of the subject matter.

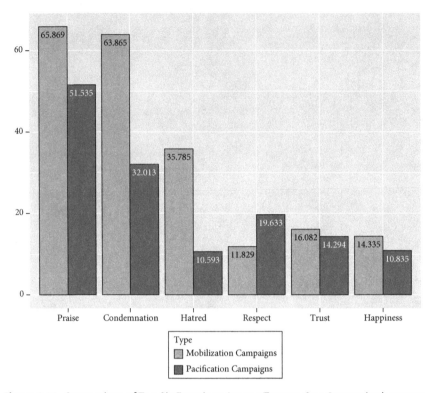

Figure 6.11 Comparison of Top Six Emotions Among Twenty-One Categories between Campaign Types

These findings align with hypotheses H3a and H3b, suggesting that pacification campaigns elicit more positive emotions through a higher proportion of praise content, whereas mobilization campaigns evoke a balanced mix of positive and negative emotions.

The chart also reveals differences in the next two emotion categories—"hatred" and "respect." Mobilization campaigns notably have higher scores in the "hatred" category, emphasizing stronger negative emotions. On the other hand, pacification campaigns yield higher scores in the "respect" category, pointing toward an emphasis on positive emotions. This pattern aligns with hypotheses H3a and H3b, supporting the idea that mobilization campaigns tend to foster stronger negative emotions such as hatred, while pacification campaigns encourage more positive emotions like respect. These results further underline the different emotional focuses of mobilization and pacification campaigns.

Conclusion

Through computer-assisted content analysis of *People's Daily* articles in mobilization and pacification campaigns, this chapter has revealed the distinct characteristics of these campaign types. Specifically, pacification campaigns exhibit a more positive valence, while mobilization campaigns tend to be more negative. Furthermore, these campaign types differ in the topics they address, encompassing both shared and distinctive themes within each category. Moreover, they employ different emotions with varying intensities—mobilization campaigns predominantly utilize stronger forms of negative emotions, while pacification campaigns incorporate more moderate forms of both positive and negative emotions.

Understanding the distinct characteristics and strategies of mobilization and pacification campaigns is vital for policymakers. The observed patterns provide insights into the framing techniques and emotional appeals used by states in shaping public opinion toward foreign policy issues. For example, if a state uses mobilization campaign strategies—emphasizing ideological differences, analyzing the international situation with a sense of urgency, and provoking intense emotions—it could signal an impending hardline stance or escalation in its foreign policy. In contrast, pacification campaigns, which prioritize bilateral relationships and advocate for peaceful resolutions, could indicate the state's intention to de-escalate conflicts and maintain stable relations.

These insights gained from studying campaign patterns could be particularly beneficial during periods of diplomatic tensions. Policymakers and analysts could employ tools such as text analysis to examine state or official media content. This would help determine whether the media campaign's intention is to mobilize the public toward a more assertive stance or to pacify and promote a more moderate approach. Understanding the intention behind these campaigns can inform diplomatic responses, allowing policymakers to respond more effectively and strategically.

Future research should consider expanding these investigations to other authoritarian regimes. Similar patterns observed in other contexts could suggest a common playbook employed by authoritarian states when dealing with foreign policy issues. This would further validate the usefulness of analyzing media campaigns as a means of understanding a state's foreign policy intentions. The more countries this research encompasses, the more useful it becomes as a tool for deciphering state intentions on a broader scale, aiding diplomatic decision-making worldwide.

218 The Art of State Persuasion

Notes

1. James D. Fearon, "Rationalist Explanations for War," *International Organization* 49, no. 3 (1995): 379–414.
2. The article texts from the three outlier cases in the medium-*N* study—the 1959 Sino-Indian border dispute, the 1988 Sino-Vietnamese clash in the Spratlys, and the 2012 Sino-Philippines Scarborough Shoal standoff—have been omitted. The rationale behind this decision is to identify patterns from verified instances of either mobilization or pacification campaigns, without introducing potential confounding factors that may distort the overall analysis.
3. Original data is available at https://doi.org/10.7910/DVN/MDNY8Z, Harvard Dataverse.
4. Susan L. Shirk, *China: Fragile Superpower* (New York: Oxford University Press, 2007).
5. James N. Druckman and Rose McDermott, "Emotion and the Framing of Risky Choice," *Political Behavior* 30, no. 3 (2008): 297–321; Deborah A. Small, Jennifer S. Lerner, and Baruch Fischhoff, "Emotion Priming and Attributions for Terrorism: Americans' Reactions in a National Field Experiment," *Political Psychology* 27, no. 2 (2006): 289–98; Michael MacKuen et al., "Civic Engagements: Resolute Partisanship or Reflective Deliberation," *American Journal of Political Science* 54, no. 2 (2010): 440–58.
6. Jennifer S. Lerner et al., "Effects of Fear and Anger on Perceived Risks of Terrorism: A National Field Experiment," *Psychological Science* 14, no. 2 (March 2003): 144–50; Druckman and McDermott, "Emotion and the Framing of Risky Choice"; MacKuen et al., "Civic Engagements"; Charles S. Carver and Eddie Harmon-Jones, "Anger Is an Approach-Related Affect: Evidence and Implications," *Psychological Bulletin* 135, no. 2 (2009): 183; Andrew J. Elliot, Andreas B. Eder, and Eddie Harmon-Jones, "Approach–Avoidance Motivation and Emotion: Convergence and Divergence," *Emotion Review* 5, no. 3 (2013): 308–11.
7. Helena Flam and Debra King, *Emotions and Social Movements* (London: Routledge, 2007); Jeff Goodwin, James M. Jasper, and Francesca Polletta, *Passionate Politics: Emotions and Social Movements* (Chicago: University of Chicago Press, 2009); James M. Jasper, "The Emotions of Protest: Affective and Reactive Emotions in and around Social Movements," *Sociological Forum* 13 (1998): 397–424.
8. Guobin Yang, "(Un) Civil Society in Digital China| Demobilizing the Emotions of Online Activism in China: A Civilizing Process," *International Journal of Communication* 11 (2017): 1945–65.
9. As not all campaign features can be tested through text analysis, and some characteristics may not even be related to texts, I have limited my hypotheses to those that could be tested with text data. For instance, in Table 1.2 of Chapter 1, features such as "2. Echoing," "3. Posturing," "4. Positive Framing," and "5. Emotions," are ideally suited for testing with text data. "1. Dictating the Discourse" is a characteristic common to both campaign types. The "6. Venting" element typically occurs on social media platforms; hence it is more appropriately tested with text data from social media posts, not text data from official media outlets such as *People's Daily*, which is the source of the compiled data used in this study.
10. Nico H. Frijda, *The Emotions* (New York: Cambridge University Press, 1986); Charles Egerton Osgood, George J. Suci, and Percy H. Tannenbaum, *The Measurement of Meaning* (Champaign: University of Illinois Press, 1957).
11. Replication files are available at https://doi.org/10.7910/DVN/WA1XQF, Harvard Dataverse.
12. To account for potential variations in how the opponent country or government was referred to in the newspaper, I identified reference markers based on the top words in each

campaign. I selected the three most frequently used reference markers for each campaign. For instance, in the case of the Sino-Soviet border conflict in 1969, I identified "Suxiu (Soviet Revisionist)," "Sulian (Soviet Union)," and "Shahuang (The Tsar)" as the reference markers based on the top words chart for that campaign. Besides, a list of stop words, such as "is," "are," is excluded prior to the extraction. Stop words are words in the Chinese language that do not convey much substantive meaning. We compiled the list of stop words based on the stop words generated by Harbin Industrial University, Sichuan University Machine Intelligence Lab, and Baidu. Considering the structure of the Chinese language, five words before and fifteen words after the reference markers are sufficiently inclusive to encompass the words related to the concept of interest (the opposing country or government), while also being restrictive enough to exclude irrelevant words. The choice of the number of words was based on pretesting. The stop words, the extraction replication files, and the extracted data can all be found in the replication files.

13. For the extraction of CMCOR data, I employed a more extensive stop word list (accessible in the replication files). For all other text data, I used R's Jieba package for segmentation and stop words removal.

14. Lun-Wei Ku and Hsin-Hsi Chen, "Mining Opinions from the Web: Beyond Relevance Retrieval," *Journal of the American Society for Information Science and Technology* 58, no. 12 (2007): 1838–50.

15. Margaret E. Roberts, Brandon M. Stewart, and Dustin Tingley, "STM: An R Package for Structural Topic Models," *Journal of Statistical Software* 91, no. 1 (2019): 1–40. In the analysis of top words, in addition to eliminating the standard stop words provided by the Jieba R package, I further excluded words that lack substantial relevance to the narratives, such as "说" (say) or "新" (new). The complete list of excluded words can be found in the replication files.

16. David M. Blei, Andrew Y. Ng, and Michael I. Jordan, "Latent Dirichlet Allocation," *Journal of Machine Learning Research* 3 (2003): 993–1022.

17. Linhong Xu et al., "Constructing the Affective Lexicon Ontology," *Journal of the China Society for Scientific and Technical Information* 27, no. 2 (2008): 180–85.

18. Paul Ekman, "An Argument for Basic Emotions," *Cognition and Emotion* 6, no. 3–4 (May 1, 1992): 169–200.

19. A careful examination of the 1996 Japan case in the case narratives in Appendix 2 reveals no notable factors that could elucidate the observed deviation. While the deviation warrants a more comprehensive case study, its inclusion within this chapter would exceed the space limitations. Nonetheless, it is important to note that despite the deviation, the overall trend exhibited in the data remains consistent with the proposed hypotheses.

20. Michel Oksenberg and Gail Henderson, *Research Guide to People's Daily Editorials, 1949–1975* (Ann Arbor: University of Michigan Press, 2020), xi.

21. Nali An, "The Research of People's Daily Discourse Change from 1978 to 2013," *China Media Report Overseas* 10, no. 3 (2014).

22. Sicong Zhao, "The People's Daily: A Longitudinal Content Analysis of Editorials from 1977–2010" (Master's thesis, Iowa State University, 2014).

23. Paul H. Godwin and Alice L. Miller, "China's Forbearance Has Limits: Chinese Threat and Retaliation Signaling and Its Implications for a Sino-American Military Confrontation," China Strategic Perspectives (Washington, DC: Center for the Study of Chinese Military Affairs, Institute for National Strategic Studies, 2013).

24. Roberts, Stewart, and Tingley, "STM," 2.

7
Extending the Argument
to Other Autocracies

The degree to which we can extrapolate our current understanding of China's media campaigns on territorial disputes and their use in managing public opinion to other authoritarian nations remains uncertain. Variations in media strategies are frequently observed in other authoritarian states, with the media sometimes amplifying and at other times, intentionally remaining silent on key issues.

For instance, in the 1930s, Imperial Japan used a propaganda campaign to rally support for its invasion of Northeast China, commanding headlines for months.[1] Similarly, during Russia's military campaign in Ukraine, the Russian media launched an aggressive propaganda campaign portraying Ukraine as a "neo-Nazi" state and justifying the invasion as a "rescue" mission to "protect" Russians and Russian-speakers from "fascist aggression."[2] Yet at the onset of the invasion, the Russian media refrained from reporting on the matter. Mainstream Russian newspapers sidestepped the elephant in the room and focused on other stories, such as President Vladimir Putin attending the opening ceremony of a new football stadium in Moscow.[3] Furthermore, the 1988 Spratlys clash between Vietnam and China had remained a taboo topic for nearly three decades in Vietnam until recently, as the clash "was vividly recalled and widely covered by Vietnam's media" on its 28th anniversary in 2016.[4]

Much like Chinese pacification campaigns, not all of these media strategies are deployed for advocating wars. An example of this is evident in the lead-up to the signing of the Iranian nuclear deal. Over a period of two years, Iranian media consistently pushed a strong anti-West narrative, dismissing the idea of seeking negotiations as a sign of weakness. They framed the deal as an act of "heroic flexibility," thus preparing the public to accept the agreement. This demonstrates the utility of media campaigns in facilitating nonconfrontational policy decisions as well.[5]

Can the misalignment theory presented in this book travel to other authoritarian countries, beyond China? Despite the diversity among autocratic

The Art of State Persuasion. Frances Yaping Wang, Oxford University Press. © Oxford University Press 2024.
DOI: 10.1093/oso/9780197757505.003.0008

polities, their propaganda systems exhibit more similarities than one might initially assume. When it comes to exerting control over media, China's practices often echo in the corridors of other authoritarian regimes around the world. China's ability to manipulate media narratives, to both pacify and mobilize public sentiment according to its foreign policy objectives, is something many autocratic states aspire to emulate.

From an operational standpoint, the tactics deployed by these regimes can be strikingly similar. They can range from stringent censorship and state-controlled media outlets to the use of social media platforms for the spread of disinformation or government-sanctioned narratives. Moreover, just like China, these regimes employ both negative and positive emotional appeals, manipulate the salience of different topics, and use both direct and indirect methods to exert influence over public opinion.

Therefore, the misalignment theory, which has been primarily applied to analyze China's media campaigns in this book, potentially holds valuable insights for understanding the media strategies of other autocratic regimes as well. The ability of these regimes to align or misalign public opinion with foreign policy intentions, as demonstrated by China, serves as an important dimension for analysis in global political communication. Hence, this theory, rooted in the study of China, may very well travel beyond its original context and find applicability in the wider spectrum of authoritarian politics.

Due to the similarities between the propaganda systems of China and Vietnam, analyzing Vietnam's perspective of the 2014 oil rig crisis provides an optimal starting point for expanding the external validity of the misalignment theory to other authoritarian states. Additionally, this case study serves as an invaluable secondary test for the scenario where public opinion is hawkish, yet state foreign policy remains moderate. Considering the counterintuitive nature of pacifying propaganda campaigns and their significant role within the overall theoretical framework, this supplementary examination is indeed warranted.

The first half of the chapter juxtaposes the Chinese propaganda system, particularly the state–society relationship which forms the central premise of the misalignment theory, with the systems of other authoritarian nations. In the second half of the chapter, we delve into an exploration of the Vietnamese propaganda system and state control, laying the groundwork for a supplementary case study—the 2014 oil rig crisis, viewed from Vietnam's perspective. The chapter concludes with a synthesis of the case study and its implications for extending the theory to other authoritarian regimes.

Comparison with Other Autocracies

Autocracy is a general category that contains many different regime types. Geddes, Wright and Frantz categorize authoritarian regimes into several subtypes: "dominant-party," "military," "personalist," "monarchic," or "hybrids of the first three." These subtypes are determined by where the control over policy, leadership selection, and security apparatus lies—in the hands of "a ruling party," "the military," "an individual dictator," "a royal family," or a combination of the first three.[6] Weeks's authoritarian regime typology further distinguishes regimes based on whether the leader is elite-constrained (nonpersonalist) or unconstrained (personalist) and whether the regime is civilian or military, yielding categories such as nonpersonalist civilian regimes ("machines"), nonpersonalist military regimes ("juntas"), personalist civilian regimes ("bosses"), and personalist military regimes ("strongmen").[7] There are also "communist ideocracies" or "revolutionary regimes" like Maoist China and Cuba, "totalitarian" regimes such as North Korea, and "post-totalitarian" regimes such as contemporary China.[8] Another subtype is "competitive authoritarianism" or "semi-authoritarianism," which are regimes that exhibit a mix of democratic façades and authoritarian traits.[9]

Regardless of who controls the central functions of the state and how it's achieved, all authoritarian regimes grapple with two fundamental issues, as highlighted by Milan Svolik—the challenge of managing the masses and the challenge of power-sharing with other elites. Whether the power is vested in political parties, the military, monarchs, ideologies, or ostensibly democratic institutions, all aim to solve these problems so that they can perpetuate authoritarian rule.[10] Central to managing the masses is media control, which is a staple in the tool kit of an authoritarian ruler. This tool is fairly consistent across different types of authoritarian regimes—news and information are tailored for mass consumption, and a prevailing political narrative is orchestrated by the ruling authority.[11]

This brings us to the first of a few shared features of authoritarian propaganda systems that help extend the Chinese experiences to other contemporary authoritarian states: direct ownership and control of state official media and the heavy influence of commercial media. Media control in different authoritarian systems does not differ substantially and may only vary in the strength and specific means adapted to each system's unique situation. After all, authoritarianism is defined as "a system that enforces strict obedience by the media to political authorities" and "is operationalized as strict control of content by the state."[12]

Extending the Argument to Other Autocracies   223

China is ranked by Freedom House as having "one of the world's most restrictive media environments," with a press freedom score of 87 out of 100 in 2016 (the higher the score, the less free the country is). This places China after 11 other countries/territories, including North Korea, Turkmenistan, Uzbekistan, Crimea, Eritrea, Cuba, Equatorial Guinea, Azerbaijan, Iran, Syria, and Bahrain. Sixty-six countries or territories' press is rated as "not free," while 73 others are considered "partly free."[13] The means of media control in China, described in Chapter 2, are mundane in other authoritarian states. These include control of finances, personnel, law, structures, administration, and coercive means. For example, surveys find that in Russia, the state-run television remains "one of the most trusted and authoritative institutions in the country."[14] The specific methods and techniques may differ, but these states often learn from each other's experiences even at a tactical level.

Second, like China, numerous authoritarian states have undergone similar developments, including media commercialization and digitization, leading to varying degrees of liberalization. Countries such as Jordan, Afghanistan, Iran, Morocco, Egypt, Singapore, Malaysia, Syria, United Arab Emirates, Qatar, and many others all experienced these global waves of commercialization and digitization.[15] While each of these countries may have distinct experiences, they fall along a spectrum of liberalization and residual authoritarianism, mirroring the pattern seen in China. Jonathan Becker describes the differences between a totalitarian media system in the Soviet Union and a neo-authoritarian media system in present-day Russia, including "the degree of relative autonomy vis-à-vis the state, the breadth of negative and positive control, the degree of pluralism and the mechanisms of control, not to mention ideological context."[16] Totalitarian systems like that of the old Soviet Union have become very rare, if not extinct. "Aside from a few outliers such as Cuba, North Korea, and Turkmenistan," today's authoritarian regimes do not seek total control of the media; instead, they pursue "effective control"—"enough for them to convey their strength and puff up their claims to legitimacy while undermining potential alternatives."[17] Maria Repnikova characterizes this relaxation of complete media control as the emergence of "semi-controlled spaces."[18]

As a result, media outlets in most contemporary authoritarian states fall within a spectrum, ranging from completely state-owned and state-run to "nominally private but in fact under government control." "Most authoritarian regimes . . . employ both their own state media and private media to do their bidding."[19] There are occasionally a few private media outlets that are considered to have a "free" spirit, with varying degrees of independence and even defiance. For example, Klein's study on Iranian commercial media reveals that some commercial media align with the state's media rhetoric up to 91 percent in terms of overlapping content and framing, while others align as little as 45 percent.[20] However, it is rare for commercial media in any authoritarian system to entirely reject the state's narrative or to openly defy a state guideline, as it would risk their closure. Faced with state pressure, commercial media have to delicately balance their daily operations between upholding journalistic standards for factual reporting, generating profit, and self-preservation. In matters of sensitive diplomacy, when these objectives conflict, they almost always prioritize self-preservation.

Third, internet censorship is prevalent globally. In 2013, the world witnessed a general decline in internet freedom, displayed in "broad surveillance, new laws controlling web content, and growing arrests of social-media users."[21] Over the past few years, numerous incidents in countries such as India, Malaysia, Thailand, and Vietnam, among others, have highlighted this growing concern. These are not isolated occurrences but part of a larger pattern indicating the extensive restrictions that various regimes are putting in place to monitor and control internet use.[22]

China sits at the forefront of internet censorship and hosts the World Internet Conference annually. Initiated by the country itself, this conference stands as a testament to China's global efforts to assert its right to regulate its own internet as per its preferences, free from foreign intervention. This forms the crux of the concept of internet sovereignty—a term coined and frequently reiterated by China during these conferences.

China's position on internet censorship, along with its sophisticated techniques, serve as a model that is being emulated worldwide. According to reports, "Beijing actively shares its expertise with other governments, including those in Belarus, Vietnam, and Zimbabwe."[23] In Vietnam, where the internet enjoys relative freedom, the government still employs various mechanisms to control content.

In Russia, a law enacted in 2013 empowers the state to shut down websites hosting content deemed inappropriate. By the close of that year, "over 20,000 websites found themselves blocked."[24] Additionally, a 2014 law mandates any website, blog, or public social-media account with daily viewership exceeding 3,000 to register with Roskomnadzor (the Russian telecommunications regulator) as a media outlet. These entities must then comply with associated regulations, including prohibitions on anonymous authorship and assuming legal responsibility for comments posted by users.[25]

Cuba, on the other hand, passed Decree Law 209 in 1996. The law stipulates that internet access "would be selective and would be granted in a regulated manner," making the country's approach toward internet usage quite restrictive as well.[26]

Fourth, like China, control strategies have become more subtle and sophisticated. The "channeling" strategy and the emphasis on positive, state-sourced content is not unique to China. Similar to China's "50 cent army," Vietnam operates a "Force 47" and Russia has a "troll army." "A reliable cast of government-approved pundits" are regularly featured on Russian mainstream televisions.[27] As of February 23, 2018, Venezuelan president Hugo Chávez boasted 4.21 million Twitter followers, some of whom were offered financial incentives to follow him.[28] During the Arab Spring, Bahraini authorities flooded social media platforms such as Twitter and Facebook with pro-regime content.[29] Russia has also embraced a media strategy prioritizing entertainment over political mobilization, aimed at diverting public attention from protests surrounding the questionable parliamentary elections in December 2011.[30]

The parallelisms between China's propaganda system and those in other contemporary authoritarian regimes worldwide should bolster our confidence in extrapolating the argument beyond China's boundaries. Similarly, Becker posits that the Russian media system is not vastly different from its counterparts in other authoritarian regimes.[31] In line with this, Lankina et al. anticipate that "Russian state-controlled media's news coverage of pivotal and highly politically sensitive events to exhibit greater similarity to the Chinese model in terms of greater levels of control over the media in their coverage of these events."[32]

Carter and Carter distinguish between the propaganda strategies of electorally constrained autocracies and their unconstrained counterparts, suggesting the former favor persuasion while the latter prefer domination.[33] I contend that these two strategies are not antithetical, but rather complementary, typically adopted in varying proportions, rather than being exclusive or categorical.

There may indeed be a difference in the extent of absurdity between the lies propagated by electorally constrained autocracies and those spun by their unconstrained counterparts. However, a clear distinction does not necessarily exist. All leaders understand that lies need to be titrated with some factual truth to be convincing. Autocrats are no exception. They understand that "to keep viewers' and readers' attention and to discourage citizens from turning to independent media, the information projected on state television screens or in newspapers has to reflect political reality at least to some extent."[34] Autocracies not constrained electorally like China also commonly adopt persuasion, which Carter and Carter characterize as "acknowledging a regime's failings" and "blending facts with advantageous fiction." Hence, persuasion is not proprietary to electorally constrained autocracies. A prominent example of this was when former Chinese Premier Wen Jiabao described China's economic growth as "uncoordinated, inefficient, unbalanced, and unsustainable" during the 2007 National People's Congress press conference. By acknowledging these issues, which were already evident and well-known, he gained credibility as an honest, clear-sighted, and competent leader who deeply cares about the welfare of his country and its economy.

This divergence from Carter and Carter's argument is partly due to the domain of international crisis news. Carter and Carter recognize that international news propaganda is "analytically distinct from its domestic counterpart," and concede that "international news propaganda across autocracies [are] more similar than domestic propaganda."[35]

In fact, Schatz and Maltseva assert that "most authoritarian regimes seek to avoid, where possible, the use of naked coercion." They categorize the authoritarian regimes as "particularly keen . . . to ration the use of overt force" and favoring persuasion as "soft authoritarian regimes."[36] Persuasion remains "central to his efforts."[37] Furthermore, soft authoritarian regimes are becoming more popular and constitute a large majority of today's authoritarian regimes. After all, naked state domination begets international isolation or even opprobrium. Countries that rely on pure state violence like North Korea and Turkmenistan are not only mocked and scorned by democracies, but also secretly distained by their autocratic peers.

The paradoxical and reciprocal relationship between the state and public opinion outlined in Chapter 1, despite being common in modern authoritarian states, is most representative of those with robust populist leanings, a phenomenon referred to as "populist authoritarianism." Populist authoritarianism, as exemplified by China, is characterized by a Maoist Mass Line ideology, abundant social capital and interpersonal trust, a widespread prevalence of political discord and public engagement, a highly responsive government, weak institutions, and strong regime support.[38]

Other authoritarian states with populist inclinations that closely resemble these attributes of China should make the most conducive cases for the application of this theory. These include, but are not limited to, China under and after Mao, Vietnam under and after Ho Chi Minh, Cuba under Castro, post-revolution Iran, present-day North Korea, Argentina under Perón, Venezuela under Chávez, Russia under Putin, and Thailand under Thaksin and Yingluck.[39]

Comparing the Vietnamese and Chinese Contexts

Vietnam and China both operate under party-state systems where the Communist Party of Vietnam (CPV) and the Chinese Communist Party of China (CCP) wield the overwhelming power in their respective country's political, economic, and social spheres. All print media in both nations are either owned by or effectively controlled by their respective Communist parties. While there is a diverse array of media outlets that are commercialized to different extents, both governments maintain efficient administrative and legal tools to regulate the media. The state oversees key personnel appointments at major media outlets, carries out daily monitoring and censorship of media content, provides both general guidelines and detailed directives regarding which issues to cover and how they should be presented, and sanctions or even imprisons journalists who violate the state's directives.

Having experienced an extended period of colonization and numerous major wars against foreign powers, Vietnam has had less opportunity for state building and economic development, arguably resulting in a weaker central control compared to China. Consequently, civil society in Vietnam is considerably more active than in China, with the internet being relatively freer.[40] Websites such as Google and the *New York Times* are accessible in Vietnam, unlike in China. Despite these variances in control level, the CPV retains organizational and legal resources to tighten media control whenever necessary.[41] For instance, Google is mandated to host its servers within Vietnam, simplifying the process for Hanoi to censor content when required.[42] Freedom House reports indicate that the Vietnamese government amplified its repression of print and online journalists in 2013, incarcerating more than double the number of writers and bloggers compared to the previous year.[43] "In September [2013], the state introduced Decree 72, which restricted all websites and social media from publishing anything that 'provides information that is against Vietnam.'"[44] According to Freedom House's 2014 rating on "Freedom of Expression and Belief," both Vietnam and China received a score of four out of sixteen, with lower scores indicating less freedom.[45]

In addition to authoritarian rule and tight media control, both countries have witnessed a rise of popular nationalism in recent years. Some scholars argue that this is a direct result of state instigation, partly intended to divert public attention away from domestic problems such as rampant corruption, escalating inequality, and sluggish economic performance following the 2008 global financial crisis.[46] Others argue that nationalism is promoted to fill the ideological vacuum and consolidate regime legitimacy after both countries loosened their Marxist-Leninist ideals to incorporate capitalist economic instruments.[47]

Defending the Fatherland: The Oil Rig Crisis through Hanoi's Lens

At the onset of the crisis, the Vietnamese government was confronted with an already hawkish public opinion, but the state sought a more moderate approach. The upsurge in Vietnamese public opinion toward China concerning the South China Sea sovereignty disputes dates back to 2007. A senior Vietnam specialist based in China indicated that anti-China protests over the issue began in 2007, when word reached Hanoi that China was contemplating upgrading Sansha County's administrative status to the prefecture level. Hanoi decided to mobilize college students to regularly protest against China's plans.[48] These orchestrated anti-China demonstrations successfully deterred Beijing from advancing the plan until June 2012, when the Vietnamese National Assembly approved the "Vietnamese Law of the Sea," staking claims to the Paracels and the Spratlys. Beijing retaliated a month later by proceeding with the Sansha City plan. These regular weekend protests heightened awareness and fueled emotions surrounding the dispute among the Vietnamese public, signifying the onset of a steady decline in Vietnamese public opinion toward China.

The hawkish public opinion toward China on the South China Sea dispute gained further momentum with the encouragement of America's "Pivot to Asia" policy. A notable event that marked this trend was a heated debate at the ASEAN Regional Forum in Hanoi in July 2010, led by then US State Secretary Hillary Clinton. The wave of nationalist sentiment in Vietnam also experienced a surge during the cable-cutting incidents in the summer of 2011. Enraged Vietnamese took to the streets once again, but this time the protests were more grassroots than state-directed, and they sustained for as long as two months. Testimonies from observers who witnessed the protests firsthand affirm that these demonstrations were spontaneous.[49]

As noted in Chapter 5, the period spanning 2013 and early 2014 was relatively calm in the context of the two countries' relationship. Although Chinese public opinion eased, the anti-China sentiment in Vietnam continued to fester. Anti-China protests reignited in the summer of 2013, highlighting the persistently genuine and intense public emotions on the issue, leading the government to suppress the rallies.[50] A Pew Global Attitudes Survey conducted from April 16 to May 8, 2014 in Vietnam, just before and at the very start of the crisis, indicates that 78 percent of respondents held unfavorable views of China, while merely 16 percent expressed favorable opinions. This starkly contrasted with the Vietnamese's overwhelming favorability toward all other major regional powers—the United States (76 percent favorable), Russia (75 percent favorable), Japan (79 percent favorable), and India (67 percent favorable).[51]

However, evidence points to a moderate foreign policy intention by the state, with a substantial disconnect between this policy intent and the prevailing public opinion. Hanoi had little incentive to escalate the tension and impair the bilateral relationship with China. The Vietnamese economy was asymmetrically dependent on China. Before the crisis, China had become Vietnam's largest trading partner, reaching approximately $50 billion total turnover in 2013.[52] China was also "the sixth-largest investor by the number of projects and fourteenth largest by the total capital (about $14.7 billion) invested, respectively."[53] Considering China's rapidly expanding appetite for overseas investment, there was immense potential for further growth in bilateral investment.

Admittedly, Hanoi's initial stance toward the public protests was ambiguous, even permissive. Vietnamese police stood by as hundreds, later thousands, of demonstrators rallied across the country and outside the Chinese embassy. They even cheered on the demonstrators by "broadcasting complaints about China's actions" using loudspeakers "atop police vans," inviting state television to document the event, and handing out banners that read "We entirely trust the party, the government and the people's army."[54] Nevertheless, Hanoi was acutely conscious of the risk that public protests could turn against them. The violent riots of May 13–14, 2014 served as a sober warning to CPV leaders that strong public opinion, if left unchecked, could spiral out of control, compromising Vietnam's national interests and directly threatening the regime. Scores of factories were damaged in the rampage, including the ones managed by South Koreans and Taiwanese. One Chinese company reported four deaths and 130 casualties.[55] The Vietnamese leadership reacted quickly, detaining 300 individuals involved in the rioting. China evacuated more than 3,000 of its citizens, and, unsurprisingly, Chinese tourism to Vietnam plummeted. As General Hoang Cong Tu from the Vietnamese Ministry of Public Security aptly stated, "they [the rioters] have seriously undermined the country's image, and such action has to be punished."[56]

While no government is tolerant of riots, the CPV had extra reasons to worry about anti-China disturbances. Hanoi knew well that anti-China sentiment could easily connect to an agenda critical of the regime. An open letter penned by sixty-one party members in late July exemplifies the linkage: on the one hand, the letter called for "liberat[ion] . . . from dependence upon China" and for the state to "promptly sue China at an international tribunal;" on the other hand, it blamed the regime for the current situation, and demanded "abandoning the erroneous policies of building socialism and decisively veering towards a national and democratic direction, focusing on a moderate transformation of the political regime from its present totalitarianism to a democratic system."[57] Senior Vietnamese analysts affiliated with a government think tank point to the internal debate and the division between the anti-China, more liberal faction led by the then Prime Minister Nguyen Tan Dung and the pro-China, more conservative faction helmed by the Party General Secretary Nguyen Phu Trong, with one balancing and checking the other.[58] This is also evident in the CPV Central Committee's ninth plenary session, held during May 8–14, shortly after the Chinese installation of the oil rig and amidst ongoing riots. "A heated debate erupted about how Vietnam should respond to China's challenge."[59] However, when the "tough on China" agenda was embraced by the same group of people who openly advocated for democratization and the overthrow of the socialist authoritarian CPV rule, the pro-China, conservative faction within the top leadership prevailed.

As the crisis unfolded, Hanoi adopted a three-tiered response: dispatching law enforcement vessels to the rig's location to protest and potentially disrupt Chinese operations; initiating bilateral negotiation channels; and mobilizing international pressure to force China to withdraw. There is only some hardline element in the first response. China charged Vietnam with ramming Chinese vessels "a total of 1,416 times," in addition to "send[ing] frogmen and other underwater agents to the area, and dropped large numbers of obstacles, including fishing nets and floating objects, in the waters."[60]

However, it remains unclear whether Vietnamese vessels were there solely to express protest, or whether they aggressively attempted to breach the Chinese cordon and disrupt Chinese operations by ramming their ships. It is reasonable to believe that there may have been ramming incidents on both sides and some accidental collisions due to the congested space. A ship's movements could also be easily misinterpreted as aggressive under such conditions. While this matter is still inconclusive, it is clear that Vietnam's presence in the disputed area was crucial in upholding its claim to the Paracels.

As Womack notes, "The method of establishing territorial claims in international law has the pernicious effect of maximizing confrontation and hostility . . . unchallenged occupation is nine-tenths of the law. Thus each has an incentive to increase its presence and to protest or oppose occupation by others, and all parties to the dispute have done both repeatedly over the past forty years."[61] Without immediate and effective protests, inaction from Vietnam could potentially be interpreted by China as Hanoi's tacit acceptance of a fait accompli. Therefore, even if the Chinese accusations were accurate, the Vietnamese actions were fundamentally defensive in nature.

Moreover, Hanoi was notably proactive in pursuing bilateral communication channels with their Chinese counterparts. According to Carlyle Thayer, "Immediately after the oil rig crisis broke out, Vietnam's leaders adopted a conciliatory diplomatic posture."[62] Hanoi requested the activation of a hotline between senior leaders, and offered to send a special envoy and pressed for a visit by its party secretary general.[63] On May 6, Vietnamese Foreign Minister Pham Binh Minh reached out to Chinese State Councilor Yang Jiechi. All things considered, Vietnam's policy was reactive and proportionate, further supporting the theory of a moderate policy intention.

Analysts indeed observed a growing rift between a nationalist public and a restrained government during the crisis—a gap between bellicose public opinion and a more moderate state policy intent. Malesky and Morris-Jung observed that "the oil rig crisis highlighted a growing gap between state leadership and the wider Vietnamese society" and highlighted an "increasing polarization between state and society."[64] Bui's examination of 570 *Thanh Nien News* articles during the crisis also revealed "some gap between the official news stories and readers' comments," and that "the public's response is arguably more emotional and more demanding of a tougher position."[65] The discrepancy between the state and the public required the CPV to align public opinion with its intended moderate policy before implementing the said policy. As a result, Hanoi adopted a pacification media campaign.

Throughout the seventy-four-day crisis, from May 2 to July 17, 2014, *Nhan Dan* (*The People*), the Vietnamese equivalent of China's *People's Daily*, published 224 articles addressing the dispute, averaging three articles each day. In instances where a media campaign is enacted, the most noticeable attribute is the seeming relevance of all content. Even an article about a beauty pageant includes statements such as contestants "call[ed] for actions to support Vietnam Government to defend its sovereignty in the East Sea and asking China to immediately withdraw its illegal Haiyang Shiyou-981 oil rig and ships off Vietnam's waters."[66] *Thanh Nien News* (*Youth News*), ranked among the top five most influential newspapers in Vietnam, published 570 articles on the subject, averaging eight articles a day.[67]

During the media campaign, Hanoi employed strong language to maintain an image of a firm stance against China to meet public expectations, though no substantive punitive measures were threatened. The pressure from nationalistic public critique was intense and real. Bui reports that readers posted comments below the news articles critiquing the government's delayed reporting of the oil rig installation and the relatively tame statements issued by the Ministry of Foreign Affairs spokesperson in the initial days of the crisis.[68] To placate the nationalistic public, the state issued sternly worded statements, denouncing China's installation of the oil rig as "brazen," "illegal," and "void," and the maneuvers of Chinese maritime patrol vessels as "aggressive" and "intimidating."[69] During the ASEAN Summit on May 11, Vietnamese Prime Minister Nguyen Tan Dung gave a high-profile pitch to fellow ASEAN leaders and chastised China's actions as a "direct threat" to regional peace and stability. These statements were extensively reported in the Vietnamese media.

However, despite the heated rhetoric, the actual policy responses indicated were notably vague and noncommittal, offering no concrete plan of action. Bui affirms that "these statements remained vague about Vietnam's likely response. For example, they stated that 'China needs to take responsibilities for its actions,' and if China continued with its aggressive behavior, 'Vietnam has to take defensive measures in response' or 'Vietnam will take appropriate measures.'"[70] When questioned whether Vietnam would follow the Philippines' example and sue China in an international court, the Foreign Ministry responded that "priority is given to negotiating disputes with neighboring countries, but does not exclude any other peaceful means."[71] Even Prime Minister Dung, the strongest advocate of this legal action, stated that "timing was crucial," indicating a considerable level of restraint.[72] Defense Minister Phung Quang Thanh's statement at the Shangri-La Dialogue on May 31 that legal action was merely "a last resort" further verifies the insubstantial nature of the firm rhetoric.[73]

The Vietnamese media adopted a broad coverage strategy for the confrontations in the disputed zone, but with a key twist. Instead of highlighting Chinese aggressiveness in the region, the media predominantly spotlighted the heroic actions of the country's maritime law enforcement officers "defending the fatherland." In Bui's content analysis of *Thanh Nien News* articles, a significant proportion were dedicated to this narrative (146 out of 570 articles, or 25.6 percent), equating to an average of two such articles each day.[74]

This positive framing strategy aimed to highlight the government's assertive response in the face of the conflict, effectively countering nationalistic criticisms. It presented a narrative of the government acting decisively in defense of the country, thereby nurturing a more pro-government nationalism among the populace. This media approach served to redirect popular anger and animosity into a form of nationalism that was supportive of the government's actions, thereby reinforcing the validity of the (mis)alignment theory.[75] The media campaign was a critical tool to reconcile the divergence between public sentiment and state policy intent by showcasing government action in a positive light, thereby mitigating public discontent and facilitating policy implementation.

To prevent exacerbating anti-China sentiments among the Vietnamese public, the government employed a tripartite strategy. First, they sought to redirect public anger toward fostering patriotism and national unity. This was evident in articles from *Thanh Nien News* that Bui analyzed, which underscored the need for national unity, applauded maritime enforcement officers, and provided aid to affected fishermen. Above all, these pieces showcased a firm belief in the government's capacity to manage the situation.[76]

Second, they astutely mirrored the public's anti-China emotions, but in a controlled manner. According to Bui, the media coverage did include anti-China rhetoric, but the most negatively charged assessments of China were largely confined to the perspectives of foreign observers and scholars.[77] This strategy allowed the government to resonate with public sentiment, offering a sense of agreement and support. However, by containing such sentiment in moderation and within foreign analyses, they minimized the risk of further inflaming nationalist emotions and causing unintended escalations with China.

Third, the government was cautious about referencing historical disputes between Vietnam and China. Bui's analysis revealed that very few articles touched upon these contentious historical events. This approach demonstrates the government's restraint in inciting domestic public emotions regarding the ongoing crisis, given the potential for historical grievances to easily spark public animosity. According to Bui, significant events like China's expulsion of Vietnamese forces from the Crescent Group in the Paracel Islands in 1974, the Johnson South Reef skirmish in 1988, and even the border war in 1979 were rarely mentioned in most news articles.[78]

In tandem with the aforementioned strategies, the state also utilized digital platforms as a public pressure release valve. Recognizing the profound impact of social media and online forums in the modern era, the government gave its citizens space to voice their frustrations and anger over the disputes with China.

The state's stance was mostly lenient, as long as the online discussions did not directly attack the Vietnamese leadership or incite anti-government actions. Such an approach helped ensure that the online space did not turn into a hotbed of subversive activities that could potentially destabilize the nation. At the same time, it provided a regulated outlet for the Vietnamese public to vent their feelings and engage in discourse about the situation, enabling them to feel heard and validated in their concerns.

All in all, these techniques align closely with the observable implications of pacification campaigns as described and validated in earlier chapters. Specifically, the Vietnamese media campaign provides a noteworthy parallel with the Sino-Philippines arbitration case detailed in Chapter 4. Observing such consistent patterns across diverse scenarios strengthens our understanding and confidence in the mechanics and strategies employed in pacification campaigns.

Audience Costs?

The audience costs theory provides a potential explanation for the Vietnamese propaganda campaign, considering Hanoi's coercive goals during the crisis, primarily to halt Chinese oil rig drilling operations and enforce its departure from the disputed area. The audience costs theory suggests that leaders who fail to fulfill public threats during a crisis face penalties from their domestic audience. Therefore, leaders make public commitments to specific courses of action to increase the political cost of backing down, which also amplifies the credibility of their threats.

To ascertain whether the Vietnamese propaganda campaign aligns with this theory during the crisis with China, two pivotal questions arise.

First, we must determine if Hanoi issued explicit public threats that Beijing would face severe consequences if it did not withdraw from the disputed area. Essentially, did Hanoi stake a public position that would make backtracking politically expensive, thus tying its own hands? If Hanoi openly threatened Beijing with substantial consequences for continued drilling activities, the audience costs theory could be applicable.

Second, the question of whether Hanoi capitalized on the potent nationalist sentiment within Vietnam during negotiations with Beijing needs to be explored. If Hanoi harnessed anti-China sentiment as a tool to rally the public, demonstrating to Beijing that failure to comply with their demands would lead to considerable political costs at home, this would also suggest a strategy consistent with the audience costs theory.

In response to the first question regarding whether Hanoi issued explicit public threats to Beijing, the answer leans toward a "no." While Hanoi did make threats, most were relatively vague and nonspecific. Statements such as "Vietnam has to take defensive measures in response" or "Vietnam will take appropriate measures" if China did not comply did not clearly outline the specific actions that Vietnam would take. These ambiguities made the threats less definitive, which did not align with the typical premises of the audience costs theory.

The only concrete threat from Hanoi was the potential of seeking international legal action. However, even this threat was not issued with unwavering determination. Hanoi's position regarding this action was often depicted as a measure of "last resort," contingent on "timing," and conveyed with an apparent preference for bilateral negotiations with Beijing.[79] This stance further illustrates the lack of clear, firm threats from Hanoi, which contradicts the audience costs theory.

By keeping their threats vague and highlighting the preference for negotiations, Vietnam avoided tying its own hands in the international arena. This allowed for more flexibility and room for maneuver in dealing with the crisis, without risking significant political cost if they needed to change their strategy.

Regarding the second question—whether Hanoi used strong nationalist sentiment as leverage in negotiations with Beijing—the answer is somewhat elusive. Complete records of conversations between leaders and diplomatic representatives from both countries are not fully available for assessment. From the information reported, however, there seems to be a general lack of evidence suggesting that domestic public opinion was strategically utilized as a bargaining tool by Hanoi.

Interestingly, the public protests, which erupted on May 11 and quickly escalated into violence by May 13, appeared to be more of a hindrance than an advantage for Hanoi. Beijing swiftly placed the blame on Hanoi for its inability to prevent the riots. China openly criticized Vietnam's miscalculation in stirring extreme nationalist sentiment, resulting in unintended repercussions. An editorial from the *Global Times* stated that Hanoi "does not know the danger of playing with extreme nationalism and does not have the ability to control violence."[80]

The fallout extended beyond Vietnam-China relations. Countries/regions including Taiwan, Singapore, Malaysia, and South Korea, whose factories were also targeted during the protests, voiced serious concerns about public safety. The escalating unrest dented investor confidence, causing Vietnamese stocks to plummet.

In light of these developments, it appears that the strong nationalist sentiment, rather than serving as leverage for Hanoi in negotiations with Beijing, instead evolved into a significant liability, undermining the application of the audience costs theory in this context.

Based on this analysis, it appears that Hanoi's strategy during the crisis does not fall neatly within the framework of the audience costs theory. One key aspect of Hanoi's approach was its preference for ambiguity and flexibility, which enabled it to adapt to the unfolding crisis. Rather than issuing clear, specific threats that would bind it to a particular course of action—and potentially expose it to significant political costs if circumstances changed—Hanoi chose to keep its options open. This approach provided Hanoi with the latitude to navigate the shifting political landscape without constraining itself to a specific path. Furthermore, rather than leveraging strong nationalist sentiment as a bargaining tool against Beijing, Hanoi found itself managing the domestic fallout of public protests. The surge in public sentiment became more of a challenge to handle rather than an asset to exploit in negotiations with Beijing.

Conclusion

This chapter broadens the pacification argument to include Vietnam, expanding the application of the misalignment theory beyond China to other authoritarian states, both theoretically and empirically. During the same oil rig crisis, the response from Vietnamese media sharply diverged from China's. Despite their similar moderate policy intent, Hanoi initiated a media campaign while Beijing largely refrained.

This stark contrast can be attributed to the differences in the prevailing public opinion in each country. Vietnam was experiencing a significant gap between state perspectives and public sentiment, which was not the case in China. This gap drove Hanoi to undertake a pacification media campaign.

The behavior of Vietnamese media during this crisis further substantiates the pacification function of a media campaign. As the campaign worked to temper public opinion, Hanoi was able to pursue a moderate foreign policy without substantial domestic constraints.

Through this strategy, Hanoi effectively managed public sentiment and navigated a complex international dispute, underscoring the potential of media campaigns as tools for public sentiment pacification in authoritarian states. This case presents a compelling application of the misalignment theory and adds a valuable dimension to our understanding of media usage in international crises under authoritarian regimes.

Notes

1. Louise Young, *Japan's Total Empire: Manchuria and the Culture of Wartime Imperialism*, vol. 8 (Berkeley: University of California Press, 1998).

Extending the Argument to Other Autocracies 237

2. Andrew Higgins, "In Ukraine, Russia Plays a Weighted Word Game," *New York Times*, April 17, 2014; Jill Dougherty, "Everyone Lies: The Ukraine Conflict and Russia's Media Transformation," August 29, 2014, https://shorensteincenter.org/everyone-lies-ukraine-conflict-russias-media-transformation/.

3. "Russian Media Report 'Invasion of Ukraine,'" *BBC News*, August 28, 2014, https://www.bbc.com/news/world-europe-28965597.

4. "Did 1988 Battle Anniversary Hint Rise in Vietnam-China Tensions?" *Asia Times*, March 23, 2016, http://www.atimes.com/did-1988-battle-anniversary-hint-rise-in-vietnam-china-tensions/.

5. Hossein Bastani, "How Iranian Media Prepared the Public for the Nuclear Deal," *The Guardian*, July 24, 2015, https://www.theguardian.com/world/iran-blog/2015/jul/24/how-iran-media-supreme-leader-prepared-the-public-nuclear-deal.

6. Barbara Geddes, Joseph Wright, and Erica Frantz, "Autocratic Breakdown and Regime Transitions: A New Data Set," *Perspectives on Politics* 12, no. 2 (June 2014): 318.

7. Jessica L. Weeks, "Strongmen and Straw Men: Authoritarian Regimes and the Initiation of International Conflict," *American Political Science Review* 106, no. 2 (2012): 326–47.

8. Steffen Kailitz, "Classifying Political Regimes Revisited: Legitimation and Durability," *Democratization* 20, no. 1 (January 1, 2013): 39–60; Steven Levitsky and Lucan Way, "The Durability of Revolutionary Regimes," *Journal of Democracy* 24, no. 3 (2013): 5–17; Juan José Linz, *Totalitarian and Authoritarian Regimes* (Boulder, CO: Lynne Rienner Publishers, 1975); Juan J. Linz and Alfred Stepan, *Problems of Democratic Transition and Consolidation: Southern Europe, South America, and Post-Communist Europe* (Baltimore: Johns Hopkins University Press, 1996).

9. Steven Levitsky and Lucan A. Way, *Competitive Authoritarianism: Hybrid Regimes After the Cold War* (New York: Cambridge University Press, 2010); Marina Ottaway, *Democracy Challenged: The Rise of Semi-Authoritarianism* (Washington, DC: Carnegie Endowment for International Peace, 2003).

10. Milan W. Svolik, *The Politics of Authoritarian Rule*, Cambridge Studies in Comparative Politics (Cambridge: Cambridge University Press, 2012).

11. Christopher Walker and Robert W. Orttung, "Breaking the News: The Role of State-Run Media," *Journal of Democracy* 25, no. 1 (January 2014): 71.

12. Jennifer Ostini and Anthony Y. H. Ostini, "Beyond the Four Theories of the Press: A New Model of National Media Systems," *Mass Communication and Society* 5, no. 1 (February 1, 2002): 47.

13. Freedom House, "Freedom of the Press 2017: Table of Country Scores," https://freedomhouse.org/report/table-country-scores-fotp-2017, accessed February 23, 2018.

14. Regina Smyth and Sarah Oates, "Mind the Gaps: Media Use and Mass Action in Russia," *Europe-Asia Studies* 67, no. 2 (February 7, 2015): 289.

15. These examples are summarized in Daniela Stockmann, "Propaganda for Sale: The Impact of Newspaper Commercialization on News Content and Public Opinion in China" (PhD diss., University of Michigan, 2007), 4–6. For further details, see Adam Jones, "From Vanguard to Vanquished? The Tabloid Press in Jordan," *Political Communication* 19, no. 2 (April 1, 2002): 171–87 (on Jordan); Shir Mohammad Rawan, "Modern Mass Media and Traditional Communication in Afghanistan," *Political Communication* 19, no. 2 (April 1, 2002): 155–70 (on Afghanistan); Garry Rodan, "Asia and the International Press: The Political Significance of Expanding Markets," *Democratization* 5, no. 2 (June 1, 1998): 125–54 (on Singapore and Malaysia); Muhammad I. Ayish, "Political Communication on

Arab World Television: Evolving Patterns," *Political Communication* 19, no. 2 (April 1, 2002): 137–54 (on Syria, UAE, and Qatar).

16. Jonathan Becker, "Lessons from Russia: A Neo-Authoritarian Media System," *European Journal of Communication* 19, no. 2 (June 1, 2004): 144.

17. Walker and Orttung, "Breaking the News," 72.

18. Maria Repnikova, "Critical Journalists in China and Russia: Encounters with Ambiguity," in *Citizens and the State in Authoritarian Regimes: Comparing China and Russia*, ed. Karrie Koesel, Valerie Bunce, and Jessica Chen Weiss (New York: Oxford University Press, 2020), 117.

19. Walker and Orttung, "Breaking the News," 71.

20. Adam Gordon Klein, "Quiet Road to War: Media Compliance and Suppressed Public Opinion in Iran" (PhD diss., Howard University, 2010).

21. Freedom House, "Freedom on the Net 2013: Despite Pushback, Internet Freedom Deteriorates," https://freedomhouse.org/report/freedom-net/freedom-net-2013, accessed February 23, 2018.

22. Sheena Chestnut Greitens, "Authoritarianism Online: What Can We Learn from Internet Data in Nondemocracies?" *PS: Political Science & Politics* 46, no. 2 (April 2013): 263.

23. Walker and Orttung, "Breaking the News," 78.

24. Freedom House, "Russia: Freedom of the Press 2016," https://freedomhouse.org/report/freedom-press/2016/russia, accessed February 23, 2018.

25. Ibid.

26. Shanthi Kalathil and Taylor C. Boas, "The Internet and State Control in Authoritarian Regimes," *First Monday*, August 6, 2001), 10, https://firstmonday.org/ojs/index.php/fm/article/download/876/785?inline=1.

27. Walker and Orttung, "Breaking the News," 81.

28. "Hugo Chávez Rewards Three-Millionth Twitter Follower with New Home," *The Guardian*, June 2, 2012.

29. Sean Aday et al., "New Media and Conflict after the Arab Spring," *United States Institute of Peace* 80 (2012): 8.

30. Walker and Orttung, "Breaking the News," 75.

31. Becker, "Lessons from Russia."

32. Tomila Lankina, Kohei Watanabe, and Yulia Netesova, "How Russian Media Control, Manipulate, and Leverage Public Discontent: Framing Protest in Autocracies," in *Citizens and the State in Authoritarian Regimes: Comparing China and Russia*, ed. Karrie Koesel, Valerie Bunce, and Jessica Chen Weiss (Oxford University Press, 2020), 140.

33. Erin Baggott Carter and Erin Carter, *Propaganda in Autocracies: Institutions, Information, and the Politics of Belief* (Cambridge; New York: Cambridge University Press, 2023). (Cambridge; New York: Cambridge University Press, 2023).

34. Lankina, Watanabe, and Netesova, "How Russian Media Control, Manipulate, and Leverage Public Discontent," 140.

35. Carter and Carter, *Propaganda in Autocracies*, 26–27.

36. Edward Schatz and Elena Maltseva, "Kazakhstan's Authoritarian 'Persuasion,'" *Post-Soviet Affairs* 28, no. 1 (January 1, 2012): 46.

37. Ibid., 47.

38. Wenfang Tang, *Populist Authoritarianism: Chinese Political Culture and Regime Sustainability* (New York: Oxford University Press, 2016).

39. These regimes are enumerated in ibid., 166.
40. These judgments are made based on the author's personal experiences and discussions with people and analysts who are familiar with both countries' political systems.
41. Broadcasting Board of Governors, "Media Use in Vietnam 2013," 2013, http://www.bbg.gov/wp-content/media/2013/12/Vietnam-research-brief-final1.pdf, accessed May 9, 2018.
42. Freedom House, "Freedom in the World 2014," 2014, https://freedomhouse.org/sites/defaul/files/2020-02/Freedom_in_the_World_2014_complete_book.pdf, 764.
43. Ibid.
44. Ibid.
45. "Freedom in the World 2014," 161, 763.
46. Le Hong Hiep, "Performance-Based Legitimacy: The Case of the Communist Party of Vietnam and Doi Moi," *Contemporary Southeast Asia: A Journal of International and Strategic Affairs* 34, no. 2 (August 22, 2012): 145–72.
47. Suisheng Zhao, *A Nation-State by Construction: Dynamics of Modern Chinese Nationalism* (Redwood City, CA: Stanford University Press, 2004); Peter Hays Gries, *China's New Nationalism: Pride, Politics, and Diplomacy* (Berkeley: University of California Press, 2004).
48. Author interview, November 20, 2017, Washington, DC.
49. Author interview, February 21, 2017, Hanoi.
50. "Rare Protest in Vietnam Raises a Call to Curb China," *New York Times*, June 3, 2013, http://www.nytimes.com/2013/06/03/world/asia/rare-protest-in-vietnam-raises-call-to-curb-china.html.
51. Pew Research Center Global Attitudes and Trends Datasets, available at http://www.pewglobal.org/datasets/. For more information on the 2014 survey in Vietnam, see http://www.pewresearch.org/methodology/international-survey-research/international-methodology/global-attitudes-survey/vietnam/2014, accessed May 9, 2018.
52. "China Remains Vietnam's Biggest Trade Partner in 2013," *Xinhua News*, January 29, 2014, http://www.chinadaily.com.cn/business/chinadata/2014-01/29/content_17264283.htm.
53. Edmund Malesky and Jason Morris-Jung, "Vietnam in 2014: Uncertainty and Opportunity in the Wake of the HS-981 Crisis," *Asian Survey* 55, no. 1 (2015): 172.
54. "Vietnam Allows Anti- China Protest over Oil Rig," *Daily Mail*, May 10, 2014, http://www.dailymail.co.uk/wires/ap/article-2625366/Vietnam-allows-anti-China-protest-oil-rig.html.
55. Gerry Mulany, "Chinese Company puts Death Toll in Vietnam Riots at 4," *New York Times*, May 21, 2014, https://sinosphere.blogs.nytimes.com/2014/05/21/chinese-company-puts-death-toll-in-vietnam-riots-at-4/.
56. Jane Perlez, "Vietnamese Officials Intolerant of Violence as Standoff with China Continues," *New York Times*, May 17, 2014, https://www.nytimes.com/2014/05/18/world/asia/vietnamese-officials-intolerant-of-violence-as-standoff-with-china-continues.html.
57. "An Open Letter by 61 Party Members to The Central Executive Committee and All Members of the Communist Party of Vietnam," July 28, 2014, https://www.journalofdemocracy.org/sites/default/files/custom_search/Letter%20from%2061%20Vietnamese%20Party%20members.pdf.
58. Author interview, February 23, 2014, Hanoi.
59. Carlyle A. Thayer, "4 Reasons China Removed Oil Rig HYSY-981 Sooner Than Planned," *The Diplomat*, July 22, 2014.

60. PRC MoFA, "The Operation of the HYSY 981 Drilling Rig: Vietnam's Provocation and China's Position," June 8, 2014, http://www.fmprc.gov.cn/mfa_eng/zxxx_662805/t1163264.shtml.

61. Brantly Womack, "The Spratlys: From Dangerous Ground to Apple of Discord," *Contemporary Southeast Asia: A Journal of International and Strategic Affairs* 33, no. 3 (2011): 373–74.

62. Thayer, "4 Reasons China Removed Oil Rig HYSY-981 Sooner Than Planned."

63. Ibid.

64. Malesky and Morris-Jung, "Vietnam in 2014," 169–70.

65. Nhung T. Bui, "Managing Anti-China Nationalism in Vietnam: Evidence from the Media during the 2014 Oil Rig Crisis," *The Pacific Review* 30, no. 2 (2017): 183.

66. "Dang Thu Thao Crowned Miss Vietnam Oceans 2014," *Nhan Dan*, May 26, 2014, http://en.nhandan.com.vn/culture/lifestyle/item/2536502-dang-thu-thao-crowned-miss-vietnam-oceans-2014.html.

67. Bui, "Managing Anti-China Nationalism in Vietnam."

68. Ibid., 180.

69. Vietnam MoFA, "Regular Press Briefing by MOFA's Spokesperson Le Hai Binh On May 15, 2014," May 15, 2014, http://www.mofa.gov.vn/en/tt_baochi/pbnfn/ns140516233943.

70. Bui, "Managing Anti-China Nationalism in Vietnam," 175.

71. Vietnam MoFA, "International Press Conference on China's Downed Drilling Rig in Vietnam's Waters," May 7, 2014, http://www.mofa.gov.vn/vi/tt_baochi/pbnfn/ns140509011156.

72. Thayer, "4 Reasons China Removed Oil Rig HYSY-981 Sooner Than Planned."

73. *Shangri_La Dialogue Report*, 13th Asia Security Summit, Singapore, 30 May—1 June 2014, International Institute for Strategic Studies, 29, https://www.iiss.org/-/media/Silos/ShangriLa/2014/Shangri-La-Dialogue-Report-2014.pdf, accessed May 9, 2018.

74. Bui, "Managing Anti-China Nationalism in Vietnam," 178.

75. Ibid., 169.

76. Ibid., 169.

77. Ibid., 179.

78. Ibid., 179.

79. These wordings were respectively expressed by Defense Minister Phung Quang Thanh, Prime Minister Nguyen Tan Dung, and Vietnam MoFA. Please refer to earlier discussion for details.

80. "Sheping: Yuenan Da Za Qiang Shao zai Shijie Mianqian Diurenxianyan (Editorial: The Beating, Smashing, Looting and Burning Shamed Vietnam in Front of the Whole World)," *Global Times*, May 16, 2014, http://opinion.huanqiu.com/editorial/2014-05/4996625.html.

Conclusion

This book embarks on a mission to elucidate when and why authoritarian states, like China, initiate domestic media campaigns on otherwise dormant foreign disputes, and how they influence public opinion via these campaigns. I have argued that media campaigns are a result of misalignment between existing public opinion and the state's preferred foreign policy. Based on how public opinion and state policy are misaligned, I have identified two distinctive types of campaigns. The first, known as a mobilization campaign, focuses on marshalling public support for a hardline policy. The second type, referred to as a pacification campaign, strives to mitigate potential public resistance to a more moderate policy.

The study sheds light on the unique domestic pressures and motivations that authoritarian leaders grapple with, and the sophisticated statecraft they employ to steer public opinion on foreign policy matters. A careful calibration of public sentiment not only bolsters regime stability but also provides greater leeway in foreign policy execution.

Moreover, the book delivers valuable insights to policymakers by providing social-scientific tools capable of deciphering the foreign policy intent of authoritarian states. By analyzing publicly available data such as media content, it is possible to gauge the underlying motivations and likely actions of these regimes. The goal is to enrich the toolkit of those engaging with authoritarian states, enabling a more nuanced interpretation of their domestic narratives and foreign policy directions.

Implications for International Relations and Comparative Politics

The misalignment theory expands upon existing domestic theories of international relations and augments the body of work emphasizing the role of public opinion. It adds the element of media control as an instrument of statecraft. Unlike previous theories that focused on how domestic factors influence a

The Art of State Persuasion. Frances Yaping Wang, Oxford University Press. © Oxford University Press 2024.
DOI: 10.1093/oso/9780197757505.003.0009

242 Conclusion

state's foreign policy, the misalignment theory also examines how states manipulate their citizens to further their foreign policy goals. This presents an interactive, rather than a one-sided, relationship. The fundamental premise is that public opinion exerts pressures and constraints on the state regarding foreign policy choices and implementation. Given these anticipated pressures and constraints, the state employs media manipulation to align public opinion with its foreign policy goals. In essence, the misalignment theory reverses the logic of conventional domestic theories of international relations.

This logic echoes the studies on threat inflation but is contextualized within an authoritarian setting. Research on threat inflation explores how states garner public support for preventive wars, such as the 2003 Iraq War, by manipulating political and media agendas to magnify external threats.[1]

However, few studies have explicitly addressed or even acknowledged an equally significant role of the media: its pacifying function. A pacifying media campaign aims to alleviate the constraints imposed by public opinion on a state's foreign policy decisions and implementations, making it particularly effective in situations marked by strong nationalist sentiment on salient international disputes. A more complete picture of how authoritarian states exploit media to serve their foreign policy needs emerges when we consider both mobilizing and pacifying functions.

In particular, the pacification mechanism of the (mis)alignment theory carries substantial implications for the audience costs theory. Pacification presents an innovative alternative, where a state publicizes a dispute not for a hands-tying, coercion-enhancing function, but as a hands-freeing strategy to emancipate itself from public constraint. In addition, pacification enriches the securitization literature by providing additional causes for, and means of, desecuritization (the opposite process of securitization, wherein an issue is constructed through a successful speech act to be a matter of security that "poses an existential threat" and "calls for urgent and exceptional measures").[2]

This book also contributes to the authoritarian public opinion literature in the field of comparative politics from the unique perspective of foreign policy. The in-depth analysis of four plus one cases bolsters our understanding of the bidirectional relationship between the state and the public in authoritarian states: while the public exerts pressure and constraints on the state, the state, in turn, can manipulate public opinion through media control to align it with its policy objectives. In essence, public opinion carries weight in authoritarian states, but its influence is not decisive; the state, while not all-powerful, has the ability to sway public opinion to serve its policy requirements.

The scope of this book broadens the conventional state–society dynamics frequently observed in domestic politics to encompass foreign policy contexts. Through empirical evidence, the book establishes that foreign policy issues present a conducive environment for the effective implementation of pacification campaigns. Certain characteristics of foreign policy issues—such as their generally lower stakes and distant impact on the majority of the public, and their relatively higher stakes for the state—allow the state propaganda to posture without losing credibility, to let people vent without losing control, and to assuage public sentiment before it becomes too entrenched. This contributes to the authoritarian public opinion literature by introducing a context where the state, despite not being almighty, emerges as the dominant agent in shaping foreign policy outcomes.

Utility to Policymakers

This book also carries significant practical implications, particularly for policymakers. Aggressive rhetoric is frequently equated with an aggressive foreign policy intent, a perception held by the public, media, intelligence community, and even state leaders. While leaders typically exercise caution in drawing such inferences, it remains essential to demystify pacification campaigns, making them more explicit and better understood.

With the burgeoning popular nationalism in many authoritarian states, pacification campaigns are increasingly employed and thus demand further study. The ability to distinguish between the two types of campaigns can aid policymakers in discerning when regimes are readying the ground for aggression or moderation. Enhanced interpretation of state intentions can minimize the miscalculations that are commonplace in crisis and conflict situations. Given the inherent opacity in authoritarian states, there is an urgent need to develop newer and more scientifically rigorous methods to discern their intentions.

Policymakers could utilize the conclusions presented in Chapter 6, alongside other non–text related distinctions summarized in Table 1.2, as a guidebook to determine if a current media campaign by an authoritarian state is of a mobilizing or pacifying nature. This is particularly beneficial for leaders engaging with authoritarian states like China.

In the event of a diplomatic crisis, if the opposing country initiates a media campaign, leaders could compile a sample of official media content for text analysis, studying valence, topics, and emotions, akin to the methods employed in Chapter 6. Policy analysts could then compare these results with the averages of past Chinese mobilization and pacification campaigns to discern the nature of the current media campaign.

If the opposing country is not China and has displayed distinct styles in its past mobilization and pacification campaigns, it would be advantageous to collect all data from its previous campaigns in a manner similar to the methodology of this book, and compute country-specific averages. These averages could then serve as more accurate benchmarks for drawing conclusions.

The classification of campaign types could be further corroborated by measuring the prevailing public opinion prior to the media campaign. An existing moderate/weak public opinion or an existing hawkish public opinion could notably boost our confidence in categorizing the campaigns as mobilization or pacification, respectively.

These calculations, leveraging open-source data, render the policymaking process concerning an opposing country's foreign policy intentions highly implementable and even replicable. It provides the best estimate using readily available data supported by robust research and evidence, rather than conjecture or speculations. For each calculation, the use of computer-assisted text analysis and language expertise would be essential.

One caveat that policy analysts should bear in mind is the possible policy changes of the opposing regime. As underscored in the medium-N study presented in this book, Chinese policymakers altered their strategy midway through a crisis in three out of twenty-one cases. Furthermore, much like any other social scientific studies, these calculations are not error-proof, as exemplified in the deviant cases featured in the medium-N study. Therefore, for all these reasons, policy analysts should weld the consideration of these calculations with other qualitative observations and intelligence.

This book also speaks directly to the ongoing policy debate concerning China's rise and the associated regional tensions in the Asia Pacific, issues that have become central to US foreign policy and national security. The findings of this book, particularly the numerous pacification campaigns China has conducted over some of its most contentious territorial disputes, compel us to reevaluate our prevailing impression of an increasingly "assertive" China.

Scholars have engaged in intense debate over the meme of a newly assertive China.[3] However, it appears that Washington has largely embraced this view, and it has since risked becoming a self-fulfilling prophecy. The lens through which we view the world often shapes what we see—a classic demonstration of confirmation bias.

The narrative presented in this book highlights that China is considerably constrained domestically. The bellicose Chinese rhetoric frequently cited in Western media is, in part, the result of selective interpretation driven by bias, and partly a reflection of China's domestic constraints. It urges us to look beyond the surface, acknowledging that not all assertiveness is a sign of aggressive intent, but might instead be a mechanism to cope with domestic constraints.

During historical moments of power transitions and fluctuations, such as the present, these perspectives could critically refine our understanding of Chinese intentions and approaches. By looking beyond the rhetoric, we may be better positioned to understand China's behavior and respond in ways that enhance rather than diminish regional stability. This understanding could lead to more nuanced and effective policies, reducing the risk of misunderstandings that could escalate into conflict.

Furthermore, recognizing the complexities of the interplay between domestic and foreign policies in authoritarian states such as China, we can anticipate policy shifts and better prepare for our interactions with such regimes. This could significantly contribute to more peaceful and constructive international relations in the Asia Pacific region, and potentially on a global scale.

Extending the Argument and Future Research

The misalignment argument could possibly extend to three areas. First, the argument's relevance and applicability to other authoritarian states warrants further examination. Chapter 7's analysis of the oil rig crisis from Vietnam's perspective extends the pacification argument to Vietnam, a country with a propaganda system strikingly similar to that of China. However, exploring its application in other authoritarian states with varying levels of media control could be fruitful.

In Chapter 7, I demonstrate that China's propaganda system differs more in scale than in nature from other states. Chinese internet censorship, for example, is emulated by other authoritarian (and sometimes nonauthoritarian) states. This should enhance our confidence in the generalizability of the argument to other authoritarian states.

State media behaviors exhibit considerable variation in interstate disputes, particularly those that frequently involve authoritarian states. Take, for example, Russia's invasion of Ukraine in 2014. Initially, state-controlled media refrained from reporting on the issue. However, once the invasion became public knowledge, Putin initiated a vigorous media campaign that depicted violent separatists as "supporters of federalization" and justified the incursion as a means of "rescuing Russians and Russian-speakers from the atrocities of Fascists."[4] In the territorial dispute between Ethiopia and Eritrea that precipitated a severe two-year war, Eritrean state television broadcasted ballads about

246 Conclusion

Badme, a disputed territory with neither strategic significance nor valuable resources.[5] Conversely, alleged border conflicts between Saudi Arabia and Yemen in the 1980s were neither confirmed by Saudi authorities nor brought to public attention.[6] Application of the misalignment theory to these intriguing cases could provide valuable insights into the political machinations of these authoritarian states, thereby enhancing our understanding of their unique dynamics.

Second, an obvious opportunity to extend the argument lies in nonterritorial foreign policy issues. The present study is confined to territorial disputes because these disputes are believed to be the most conspicuous cases to examine the control of public opinion in authoritarian regimes. When delving into a subject as relatively unexplored as this one, the most effective approach is to scrutinize cases where patterns are most noticeable and hence easily discernible. The control and manipulation of publicity become particularly pronounced in territorial disputes, making these disputes the optimal context for theory development. Thus, future research could potentially expand the argument to encompass a broader range of foreign policy issues beyond territorial disputes.

Due to the territorial focus of the study, I omitted several cases due to their nonterritorial nature; for instance, the three crises related to the Taiwan issue and recent close encounters between China and the US in the South China Sea, resulting from China's construction of artificial islands and the US's freedom of navigation operations. The Taiwan issue essentially revolves around a dispute over regimes rather than territory. The Sino-American offshore encounters were excluded as there is no territorial conflict between the two nations. However, a logical progression in this line of research would be to extend the argument to include these cases. Other nonterritorial incidents also warrant exploration, such as significant and recent Sino-American diplomatic crises like the 1999 Belgrade Embassy bombing, the 2003 EP3 incident, and the 2009 Impeccable incident.

A third intriguing avenue for future research would involve applying the argument to democracies. The selection of the authoritarian state followed the same logic outlined above, of having cases with salient media control. But this is not to say that there is no media control in democracies, even if the ways and means are certainly more subtle. The threat inflation literature provides strong evidence that this media control often occurs. But aside from inflating a threat and mobilizing the public for an aggressive foreign policy such as a preventive war, can a democracy pacify the public in the same way as autocracies do? Are there instances where democracies have successfully quelled a nationalist public to serve the purpose of a moderate foreign policy?

If such instances exist, how have democracies accomplished this feat? These are deeply compelling questions.

Finally, it is important to acknowledge the existence of numerous propaganda types beyond the two outlined in this book. While I have condensed these media strategies into two broad categories for simplicity, it should not eclipse the fact that states might adapt these models with numerous variations or even develop new ones in the future. This book also does not delve into other forms of propaganda, such as political education.

Altogether, these projects should further advance our knowledge of the triangular relationship between the public, the media, and the state in foreign policy and international relations.

Future Trends of Media Campaigns

The implementation and structure of media campaigns will continue to evolve in sync with the dynamics of authoritarian state–society relations. Authoritarian states make up the majority of today's nations. Despite persistent efforts to promote global democracy, led by the United States, democratic backsliding is occurring at a faster pace than democratization.

Over a decade after the Arab Spring, only Tunisia has transitioned into a true democracy among the involved Middle Eastern countries. Libya, Syria, and Yemen have been devastated by years of civil wars, and Egypt has become a military-backed autocracy with a popular leader. In Asia, authoritarian regimes consistently enjoy higher public support than democratic ones. Over time, authoritarian regimes have demonstrated increased adaptability and resilience. The relationship between authoritarian states and societies will increasingly conform to the prototypical, paradoxical, and reciprocal relationship outlined in Chapter 1.

Chapter 1 also outlines three assumptions for pacification: 1) existing but surmountable domestic costs; 2) the unavailability of the hard power alternative—complete blackout-type censorship; and 3) the escalating need for pacification, that is, the growth of nationalism.

As digital authoritarianism further develops with ongoing technological advancements and state learning, it is plausible that each of these conditions will become even more prevalent. Therefore, media campaigns in which states persuade through mobilization and pacification will likely become more prevalent and intricate. If we liken nationalism to a pet dragon under the control of state authorities in China, we could say that the state keeps it alive and occasionally provokes it, as long as it does not breathe fire. However, when

248 Conclusion

it does and oversteps its bounds occasionally, the state master reins it in to ensure the flames do not harm them. As such, pacification campaigns, the "magic potion" that can tame these nationalist flames, will become increasingly significant.

Notes

1. John J. Mearsheimer, "Imperial by Design," *The National Interest* 111 (2011): 16–34; Stephen M. Walt, "The Threat Monger's Handbook," *Foreign Policy*, May 4, 2009, https://foreignpol icy.com/2009/05/04/the-threatmongers-handbook/; Stephen M. Walt, "Is the Cyber Threat Overblown?," *Foreign Policy*, March30, 2010, https://foreignpolicy.com/2010/03/30/is-the-cyber-threat-overblown; Stephen M. Walt, "Threat Inflation 6.0: Does al-Shabab Really Threaten the US," *Foreign Policy*, September 26, 2013, https://foreignpolicy.com/2013/09/26/threat-inflation-6-0-does-al-shabab-really-threaten-the-u-s).

2. Barry Buzan, Ole Waever, and Jaap de Wilde, *Security: A New Framework for Analysis* (Boulder, CO: Lynne Rienner Publishers, 1998), 21; Barry Buzan and Ole Wæver, *Regions and Powers: The Structure of International Security*, Cambridge Studies in International Relations (Cambridge: Cambridge University Press, 2003), 491.

3. Michael Swaine, "China's Assertive Behavior (Part One: On 'Core Interests')," *China Leadership Monitor* 34 (Winter 2010), https://carnegieendowment.org/2010/11/15/china-s-assertive-behavior-part-one-on-core-interests-pub-41937; Alastair Iain Johnston, "How New and Assertive Is China's New Assertiveness?," *International Security* 37, no. 4 (2013): 7–48; Dingding Chen, Xiaoyu Pu, and Alastair Iain Johnston, "Debating China's Assertiveness," *International Security* 38, no. 3 (2014): 176–83; Kai He and Huiyun Feng, "Debating China's Assertiveness: Taking China's Power and Interests Seriously," *International Politics* 49, no. 5 (September 1, 2012): 633–44.

4. Andrew Higgins, "In Ukraine, Russia Plays a Weighted Word Game," *New York Times*, April 17, 2014.

5. Marc Lacey, "Badme Journal; Torn Town Changes Countries, but Not Conviction," *New York Times*, April 16, 2002, http://www.nytimes.com/2002/04/16/world/badme-journal-torn-town-changes-countries-but-not-conviction.html.

6. John B. Allcock, ed., *Border and Territorial Disputes*, 3rd ed. rev. and updated (Detroit: Longman Group, 1992).

APPENDIX 1

Coding Rules

For each case, code the two variables based on the following definitions and measurements/data.

State Foreign Policy Intent

Definition

A state's *intended* foreign policy against a foreign rival in a diplomatic crisis, which can be characterized as hardline or moderate.

Hardline (coded as "H"):

1. The unprovoked threat, display, or use of force;
2. The unprovoked threat or use of economic sanctions; or
3. Responses of larger scale or higher severity if provoked.

Moderate (coded as "M"):

1. Compromises;
2. Inaction; or
3. Passive responses of equal or lesser scale or lower severity if provoked.

Measurements and Data

1: State actions *deliberated*: records of internal deliberations, and recollections by officials and analysts with privileged policy access to the state's policy preference from archives and interviews;
2: State actions *motivated*: to be logically deduced from historical accounts of situational factors that the state faces;
3: State actions *enacted*: accounts of actual policies pursued from secondary sources.
   I ask coders to code the cases as one of four categories: "H," "M," "H→M," or "M→H." The two latter categories indicate a change in the state policy intent within the timeframe of a case. The arrow indicates the direction of the change. I also ask coders to record the categories of supporting evidence to help me understand how they reached their judgment about each case.

250 Appendix 1

Existing Public Opinion

Definition

The public's *existing* policy preference against a foreign rival in a diplomatic crisis *before* a state responds. Existing public opinion can be characterized into three categories: strong hardline preference (hawkish), strong moderate preference (dovish), and weak or no preference, possibly due to insufficient knowledge or indifference toward the issue. The terms "strong" and "weak" represent the intensity of these policy preferences. "Hardline" and "moderate" reference the content of the policy, mirroring the terminology used when discussing state policy preferences. For the purposes of this study, strong moderate (dovish) preferences and weak preferences are grouped together due to their similar effects on the overall outcome.

1. Hawkish (coded as "H")
2. Dovish or Weak (coded as "D")

Measurements and Data

1: Public opinion *perceived*:
   A) Archives and interviews: state officials' perception of public opinion before or at the beginning of a crisis.
   B) Secondary sources: historical accounts of public opinion before or at the beginning of a crisis.

2: Public opinion *measured*:
   A) Public opinion surveys: country thermometer against a rival state compared to other states before or at the beginning of a crisis. A low country thermometer can indicate a hardline policy preference, and a high thermometer a moderate policy preference.
   B) Baidu Search Index (BSI): this measures the average search volume for the main keywords related to the dispute during the twelve months preceding the crisis, compared to the all-time average. BSI serves as a useful gauge of public attention, while it does not infer the public's policy preference. Thus, a high search volume could represent either a strong hardline or a strong moderate policy preference. Conversely, a low search volume typically indicates weak public opinion.

3: Public opinion *inferred*:
   A) *Spontaneous* public demonstrations before or at the beginning of a crisis can indicate a strong hardline or a strong moderate policy preference.
   B) Social media: online expression of public opinion before or at the beginning of a crisis.
   C) Secondary sources on situational factors that could have affected public opinion, such as previous media exposure due to militarization for a strong hardline or a strong moderate policy preference, or lack of knowledge due to government censorship for a weak public opinion.

I ask coders to code the cases as one of two categories: "H" and "D." I also ask the coders to record the categories of supporting evidence to help me understand how they reached their judgment about each case. The extent of agreement was then assessed based on their ratings.

APPENDIX 2

Case Descriptions

Case #1. 1959 Sino-Indian Border Clashes at Longju and Kongka Pass

The Sino-Indian border dispute, similar to many of China's territorial disputes, stems from the historical imprints of colonialism and the absence of clear boundary demarcation. The only historical attempt at setting boundaries, the McMahon Line, was established during the 1913–1914 Simla Conference by Great Britain. However, this proposed boundary was not recognized by the then newly founded Republic of China (ROC).[1]

These unresolved issues became the key contentious points shortly after the establishment of the People's Republic of China (PRC) and India's independence. The dispute's complexity was further magnified due to the lack of administrative control in this remote region.

The Sino-Indian border dispute escalated into armed conflict for the first time in August 1959, which happened five months after the Tibetan uprising and Dalai Lama's seeking refuge in India. During this tense period, two violent incidents transpired in the disputed territory: the confrontation at Longju on August 25, and the clash at the Kongka Pass on October 21.

Public Opinion

The Sino-Indian border dispute was largely hidden from the public eye before 1959, with only a select few, including state leaders, possessing any knowledge of it. Moreover, these individuals did not feel a pressing need to address it, thereby relegating it to the sidelines. Chinese leaders maintained that the conditions were not "ripe for settlement,"[2] consistently deferring discussions on the issue. Several opportunities for negotiation were bypassed, such as during the 1953–1954 talks between China and India on trading privileges and Tibet's political status, during the mutual visits exchanged by Jawaharlal Nehru and Zhou Enlai in 1954, and when a Chinese magazine, *China Pictorial*, depicted large areas of territory claimed by India as belonging to China in 1958. The latter incident spurred Nehru to once again seek clarification from China, which was nonetheless dismissed by Beijing.

State Policy Intent

Following a minor border skirmish on August 25, 1959, China opted for a peaceful resolution to the Sino-Indian border dispute. Mao Zedong led a Politburo meeting in which it was concluded that the matter should be addressed through negotiations.[3] Wu Lengxi, who attended the meeting and was at the time the head of the Xinhua News Agency, general editor of *People's Daily*, and the Politburo's record keeper for Soviet Union relations, recalls Mao saying "Before the negotiations, [we] should suggest [to the Indian counterpart] to keep the status quo, neither side should move their troops, and random, small strife on the ground should be resolved by

252   Appendix 2

ad hoc agreements."[4] This recollection of Mao's decision is corroborated by a declassified CIA study on March 2, 1963: "By fall 1959, the Chinese leaders had decided to switch from a policy of no negotiations on an overall border settlement, coasting along on the basis of the existing status quo, to one of preliminary discussions with a view to an eventual overall settlement."[5]

Case #2. 1962 Sino-Indian Border War

In retaliation to Indian Prime Minister Jawaharlal Nehru's Forward Policy, the People's Liberation Army (PLA) initiated a major strike along the Eastern and Western sections of the Sino-Indian border on October 20, 1962. A month later, following a resounding victory, China proclaimed a ceasefire and retreated from the Eastern section.

Public Opinion

Despite the propaganda campaign in 1959, public awareness and sentiment concerning the border dispute remained confined. This can be attributed to the restrained nature of the 1959 campaign and the geographical reality that the disputed border areas were both remotely located and sparsely populated.

State Policy Intent

Although China's assault was in response to provocation and the Chinese military swiftly withdrew to the Line of Actual Control (LAC) following its victory, the preemptive nature and unprecedented scale of the attack are undeniable. Nonetheless, China's policy hardening was not an abrupt shift but was drawn out over time, encompassing several unsuccessful diplomatic attempts and a series of strong verbal warnings.[6]

Case #3. 1967 Sino-Indian Border Clashes at Nathu La and Cho La

In September and October of 1967, a sequence of military confrontations took place along the Sino-Indian border near Sikkim. These included the Nathu La clash from September 11 to 14 and the Cho La clash on October 1.

Public Opinion

The Sino-Indian border, located in a remote frontier region, had been the site of conflict in 1962 but had since faded from the public consciousness, at least among the average Chinese populace. The war had certainly brought the dispute into wider public awareness, yet few people held strong feelings about the issue. Furthermore, the specific conflict during this crisis—which was centered on the Sikkim section of the Sino-Indian border—was virtually unknown. In addition to these factors, the Chinese people in 1967 were preoccupied by the chaos of the Cultural Revolution. As Chinese domestic politics spiraled into turmoil over the summer of 1967, a public engrossed in internal political matters paid scant attention to the border dispute.

State Policy Intent

These incidents represented low-intensity militarized confrontations that were unlikely to have received authorization from the Chinese Central Military Commission (CMC).[7] This inference is drawn from General Wang Chenghan's memoir, in which he recounts his involvement in the Nathu La skirmishes of 1967.[8] Wang states that a frontline headquarters was not established until after September 11, "For the PLA, the establishment of a frontline headquarter . . . usually precedes the initiation of any authorized operation."[9] Additionally, after these incidents, Chinese Premier Zhou Enlai issued instructions to the Chinese forces to return fire only when fired upon.

Case #4. 1969 Sino-Soviet Border Conflict

The Sino-Soviet split that emerged in the late 1950s culminated in an intense border conflict in 1969 and brought the two countries to the brink of a nuclear war.

Public Opinion

Before the onset of conflict in March 1979, despite the high profile of the intensifying Sino-Soviet split, the Chinese public had limited awareness of the border dispute. Between October 1964 and February 1969, there were a total of 4,180 border incidents,[10] but these attracted almost no media attention. Prior to March 1969, the coverage of the border dispute in *People's Daily* was virtually nonexistent. Given that official media sources dominated the flow of information during this era, the Chinese public had very few alternative means of learning about the dispute, and therefore, they had little knowledge or preference on the dispute.

State Policy Intent

In response to the Soviet Union's territorial transgressions, China initially adopted an escalated response of a planned ambush on March 2, 1979. The historical consensus suggests that "it was the Chinese who initiated the March 1969 border conflict."[11] As far back as January 1968, during the Qiliqin incident, the CPC Central Military Commission (CMC) had contemplated conducting military counterattacks against the Soviets.[12] Archival records indicate that the incident on March 2 was a Chinese ambush retaliating against previous Soviet incursions on Zhenbao Island, while the event on March 15 was a calculated Chinese counterattack in response to Soviet soldiers' retaliation.

China severed direct communication between the top leaders of the two countries,[13] but it was never their intention to escalate the conflict to a total war.[14] The limited military strategy was reflected in Mao's own remarks, recalls general Chen Xilian, "We should stop here. Do not fight any more!"[15] However, the subsequent Soviet reaction exceeded Chinese leaders' expectations, and by August 1969, the threat of a Soviet nuclear strike became "real and imminent."[16] The Soviet Union probed the United States and its East European allies about a general war against China.[17] The US took steps to ready its nuclear bombers.[18] Mao was "shocked" and "nervous," prompting Chinese leaders to evacuate from Beijing. They grasped every opportunity to reduce the tension and began dialogues with their Soviet counterparts in early September, on the occasion of Ho Chi Minh's funeral.[19]

254 Appendix 2

Case #5. 1974 Sino-Vietnamese Clash in the Paracels

On January 19, 1974, the navies of China and South Vietnam engaged in a brief battle near the contested Paracel Islands. The Chinese emerged victorious and have maintained control of the Islands ever since.

Public Opinion

Prior to the clash, the Chinese public had little knowledge of the territorial dispute in the Paracel Islands.

State Policy Intent

China had strong incentives to seize the territory. The discovery of potential offshore petroleum resources in the South China Sea in the early 1970s prompted a flurry of occupation activities by littoral states. Within three years from 1971 to 1973, the Philippines seized five features and South Vietnam six.[20] Fearing a weakened claim position, China increased its physical presence around the Paracels and sought to force South Vietnam to accept the fait accompli.[21] The Chinese People's Liberation Army Navy (PLAN) and the Chinese Academy of Sciences each carried out a survey mission around the Paracels in 1970 and 1973, respectively.[22] The PLAN also built a harbor and a wharf on Wood Island in the Paracels in 1971.[23]

Restraints on military action were also loosening. By January 1974 the US had withdrawn from Vietnam, even though North Vietnam had not won the civil war. On the one hand, a battle of this nature carried a low risk of provoking US intervention, thereby minimizing the risk of escalation. On the other hand, North Vietnam was unlikely to publicly condemn the action, given that both China and North Vietnam were battling the same adversary in the south.

Despite the battle's short duration, the decision was made directly by China's top leaders. The directive was originally defensive in nature—"not to fire the first shot; fight back when attacked."[24] But as the battle developed, China quickly expanded its victory to seize three islands, and its initial defensive posture proved to be nothing but a tactic to win the moral high ground. After the battle, China drew in its missile-armed frigates in preparation for possible retaliation from Saigon. After the crisis waned, Chinese leaders took steps to consolidate China's presence on the Paracels.[25]

Case #6. 1978 Sino-Japanese Fishing Boat Incident near Senkaku/Diaoyu Islands

On April 12, 1978, just months before the conclusion of a monumental peace treaty between China and Japan, over eighty Chinese fishing boats appeared in the waters around the disputed Senkaku/Diaoyu islands and remained there for about a week.[26]

Public Opinion

Direct data on Chinese public opinion concerning the Senkaku/Diaoyu Islands dispute prior to the 1978 crisis is unavailable, but three points can provide some context. First, even though the issue had been publicized, Beijing had remained silent on the dispute for six years following the normalization of relations between the two countries in 1972.[27] *People's Daily* had not mentioned the word "Diaoyudao" since July 1972.

Second, two main issues have consistently strained Sino-Japanese relations and fostered negative sentiments among the populace: the divergent interpretations of World War II history and the territorial dispute over the Senkaku/Diaoyu Islands. The historical disagreement did not surface until 1982.[28]

Lastly, during the time of the Sino-Vietnamese border war, China was at a crucial turning point, with the chaos of the Cultural Revolution still fresh in people's minds and the nation moving toward rapid economic growth through the reform and opening-up policy. It was a period when the public would likely be particularly resistant to any policy that might destabilize the reform process.

State Policy Intent

Owing to a scarcity of data, there is no historical consensus on the causes of this incident. However, one can infer from China's subsequent actions that it did not intend for the incident to impede the signing of the Peace Treaty. In regards to the territorial dispute, China maintained a "shelving" policy, intending to postpone its resolution and even to avoid discussing it. Three days after the incident, Vice Premier Geng Biao attempted to quell Japanese protests by stating that the incident was "neither intentional nor deliberate." He added, "we should not argue over the island problem, and we should resolve that problem in the future."[29] Deng Xiaoping also canceled a major naval exercise by the PLAN that was intended as a display of power.[30] The crisis was effectively defused when Japanese Ambassador Sato Shoji and Chinese Vice Foreign Minister Han Nianlong agreed to refrain from discussing the issue again prior to concluding the Peace Treaty.[31]

Case #7. 1979 Sino-Vietnamese Border War

The Sino-Vietnamese border war in 1979 stands as the most recent major conflict that China engaged in. Set against the backdrop of the Cold War and the Sino-Soviet split, this war was a sharp departure from the previously intimate relationship shared by China and Vietnam, famously characterized by Mao Zedong and Ho Chi Minh as "comrade plus brother." This bond began to deteriorate from the mid-1970s due to several factors:

1. The Sino-Soviet split pressured Vietnam to choose between the two communist giants, China and the Soviet Union.
2. China's secret rapprochement with the US caused consternation in Hanoi, especially after Vietnam solidified its security alliance with the Soviet Union.
3. Discrimination and mistreatment of ethnic Chinese in Vietnam led to a massive exodus, further straining bilateral relations.
4. Ongoing border skirmishes and territorial disagreements brought both nations to the brink of conflict.
5. Vietnam's invasion of Cambodia, which aimed to oust the China-backed Khmer Rouge regime, was the final straw for Beijing.

Responding to these tensions, China launched a punitive invasion into Vietnam in February 1979. While the direct conflict was relatively brief, lasting only a few weeks, it marked a low point in Sino-Vietnamese relations, which took years to recover.

256   Appendix 2

Public Opinion

Before 1978, the Chinese public remained largely uninformed about the border dispute with Vietnam. Up until 1973, official media propagated an image of China's brotherly relationship with Vietnam, emphasizing China's unwavering support for Vietnam's quest for independence. Even when border skirmishes swelled to 926 in 1976, *People's Daily* made no mention of this. The Chinese people had been kept in the dark.[32]

The domestic political and economic background of the war even fueled some resistance to the war. The country, emerging from the tumultuous decade of the Cultural Revolution, initiated economic reforms and opened up to the global economy in 1978. The public was eager for economic rejuvenation and a return to normalcy. Xiaoming Zhang's analysis offers insight into this sentiment: "The newly adopted economic reform and opening-up policy brought great hope for a return to normalcy and increasing prosperity."[33] The looming threat of war threatened to destabilize these aspirations. Zhang specifically mentions the public sentiment in the border provinces of Guangxi and Yunnan: "Public opinion in these two provinces was pessimistic about Beijing's war decision. The local communities had undergone much hardship in the Cultural Revolution and had made considerable sacrifices for the Vietnamese war effort . . . these areas remained socially and economically backward. Nevertheless, citizens there hoped that economic reform—now the highest national priority—would bring peace, development, and better standards of living. The people and local governments in these two provinces seemed unenthusiastic about the Chinese attack on Vietnam and feared that the military action would conflict with the economic development agenda."[34]

These border provinces also bore the brunt of the refugee issue. As noted in the *History of Yunnan Province*, 35,342 Chinese refugees from Vietnam resettled in Yunnan by the end of 1980.[35] A border conflict risked further exacerbating the refugee situation and straining local resources.

Apathy or even resistance to the war was particularly evident among the troops. Following the mobilization orders in December 1978, many soldiers grappled with confusion, unsure of the righteousness of their cause and questioning the sudden turn in relations with Vietnam.[36] An interview with a retired government official revealed, "Voicing oppositions against the war, some offspring of government officials even used their connections to flee the military."[37]

Historical works generally confirm this lack of enthusiasm toward the war in the PLA and the public.[38] Andrew Scobell underscores the "mixed views of the public" and the "varying opinions" of the intellectuals. Foreign correspondents picked up on the lack of enthusiasm for the war and intellectually freely voiced that sentiment.[39] During a visit to Kunming in August 1979, even after the war broke, Nayan Chanda reported that he was struck by "the population's total apathy toward an exhibition in Kunming about China's victorious 'counterattack in self-defense.'"[40]

State Policy Intent

China was determined to "teach Vietnam a lesson." China's position toward Vietnam hardened as the relationship deteriorated. As the animosity grew to a breaking point rhetorically, diplomatically, economically, and militarily in the summer of 1978, and as the refugee and border negotiations failed in September, PLA generals began to contemplate a preemptive strike. Although framed as a "punitive" and "self-defense" measure, the planned attack was undeniably preemptive and escalatory in nature. The decision to proceed with the attack was debated extensively and subsequently confirmed.

The international environment was conducive to such an attack. Vietnam had grown closer to the Soviet Union, which China perceived as its primary external adversary. This alignment culminated in a formal Vietnam-Soviet alliance in November 1978. Vietnam's incursion into Cambodia the following month magnified China's sense of a geopolitical threat from the south. In a bid to counteract Soviet influence, China worked to mend ties with the United States and Japan. During Deng Xiaoping's US visit just prior to the military action, President Carter neither endorsed nor vociferously opposed China's plans. Deng, having engaged in multiple diplomatic visits beforehand, indicated to Carter that he anticipated "divided international reactions [to the attack]."[41]

The 1979 campaign represented a significant military undertaking. Seventeen Chinese regular armies were mobilized, deploying a staggering 220,000 troops.[42] Vietnamese accounts suggest even larger numbers: "Beijing fielded almost 600,000 regular troops including 11 army corps and many unattached divisions, about 700 aircraft of various kinds, almost 600 tanks and armored vehicles, and thousands of artillery pieces."[43] The conflict reached the very outskirts of Hanoi. Despite the final withdrawal, it was a massive operation on a foreign country's soil. China claimed Vietnamese provocations, but the scale of the Chinese so-called counterattack was significantly disproportionate.

Case #8. 1986 Sino-Indian Border Standoff at Sumdorong Chu

After almost twenty years of peace, the Sino-Indian border was once again a flashpoint in 1986. The trigger was India's discovery of Chinese troops occupying a seasonal Indian patrol point in the Sumdorong Chu valley. This initial friction was magnified as both nations deployed significant troops and conducted military drills in the vicinity.

Public Opinion

Eight years into China's economic reform and opening up policy, the general Chinese populace was more engrossed with economic prosperity than the distant Sino-Indian border conflict. Though the 1962 border war was still fresh in many memories, it held limited immediate concern for the majority.

State Policy Intent

The PLA's occupation of an Indian patrol point in Sumdorong Chu in May 1986 is considered by many to be the initial provocation that sparked the crisis. But from China's perspective, the establishment of the Indian patrol point, which China occupied only seasonally, was in itself an earlier breach of the status quo by Indian soldiers.[44] The patrol post established by Indian soldiers in 1984 was located in the neutral zone between the McMahon Line and the high ridge line, which had been unoccupied by either side.

Although large-scale forces were mobilized—"by May [1987], troop levels around Sumdorong Chu exceeded those at the start of the 1962 war, reaching as high as 50,000"—the Chinese deployment of forces remained proportional to India's.[45] China's deployment of troops was also "limited to one small area" and "under the pretext of military exercises."[46] This restraint signals China's intention to keep the situation under control and the state's desire to maintain the flexibility to de-escalate if the opportunity presented itself.

Some Western media outlets likened Beijing's assertive rhetoric to the discourse that preceded the 1962 conflict. A notable instance was in October 1986 when Chinese leader Deng Xiaoping, communicating through the US Defense Secretary, warned India that China might need to "teach India a lesson."[47] Yet Beijing's actions told a different story. When Indian Prime

258 Appendix 2

Minister N. D. Tiwari visited Beijing in May 1987 and brought with him a message from Indian leaders that they had no intention to "aggravate the situation," Beijing immediately agreed to withdraw troops and resume the border talks.

China was at the time still fighting a war with Vietnam (1979–1990). Launching simultaneous campaigns on two fronts would have been a precarious military strategy.

Case #9. 1988 Sino-Vietnamese Clash in the Spratlys

In March 1987, China capitalized on a UNESCO assignment to construct observation posts in the Spratlys as a foothold to enhance its influence in the region. This maneuver spurred a succession of naval standoffs between China and Vietnam, culminating in a brief skirmish near Johnson South Reef on March 14, 1988.

Public Opinion

The Chinese propaganda campaign against the Vietnamese lasted as long as the Sino-Vietnamese border war, which had been going on for nine years by 1988. The Vietnamese were consistently portrayed in a negative light, as unappreciative and malevolent. As a result, the Chinese public was hostile toward the Vietnamese, even over a dispute that was unfamiliar to most of them.

State Policy Intent

The global geopolitical landscape at the time was conducive for China's ambitions in the Spratlys. The Soviet Union was mired in its protracted conflict in Afghanistan, and the US-China relations were in a relatively benign phase. This minimized the risk of intervention by major third parties.

Given this backdrop, in 1987 China made a pivotal choice to secure a permanent footprint in the contested region.[48] Espying the UNESCO Intergovernmental Oceanographic Commission (IOC)'s global oceanic survey as a timely opening, China proactively offered to construct observation posts in the Spratlys. This veiled strategic move was aimed at amplifying its territorial claims there. Subsequently, the People's Liberation Army Navy (PLAN) undertook an extensive maritime patrol, executing its largest-ever survey expedition in the Spratlys during the summer of 1987.[49] Although the Chinese and the Vietnamese recollections are contradictory as to who fired the first shot in the battle,[50] the aftermath was unequivocal: China took control over six significant landmarks, with the Johnson South Reef among them.

Case #10. The 1990 Sino-Japanese Lighthouse Crisis

On September 29, 1990, the Japanese press reported that the Japanese Maritime Safety Agency was preparing to recognize a lighthouse built by a right-wing Japanese group on the main Diaoyu/Senkaku island as an "official navigation mark."[51] Although Taiwan protested immediately after the announcement, China did not respond until October 18 when a Ministry of Foreign Affairs spokesperson was asked about the issue at a press conference. The spokesperson denounced the recognition of the lighthouse as "a violation of China's sovereignty" and demanded that the Japanese government "immediately take effective measures to stop the activities of the ring-wing group and prevent similar events in the future."[52] On October 21, the Japanese Maritime Safety Agency repelled two dozen Taiwanese who were attempting to place a torch on the island to assert sovereignty.[53] China condemned the safety agency's actions and demanded that the Japanese government "immediately stop all violations of China's sovereignty."[54] China had also been criticizing Japan's pending Diet bill that authorized deployment of Japanese forces for overseas United Nations peacekeeping missions. On October 23, Japanese Prime Minister Toshiki Kaifu promised to adopt a "cautious attitude" in handling the lighthouse matter and dispelled the concern that Japan might send military ships to patrol the disputed islands.[55] Large anti-Japanese protests broke out in Taiwan, Hong Kong, Macao, and the United States, but China prevented similar protests.[56] News of overseas Chinese protests was also blocked in China.[57] On October 27, Chinese Vice Foreign Minister Qi Huaiyuan had an urgent meeting with the Japanese Ambassador to China, reiterating China's sovereignty claim over the islands and its willingness to shelve the dispute to be resolved by a later generation, while urging Japan to consider joint development of the area's resources.[58] Reportedly Beijing and Tokyo quietly dropped the dispute three days later.[59]

Public Opinion

The decline of Communism as a source of regime legitimacy at the end of the Cold War; China's economic difficulties in the late 1980s, including rising state enterprise losses and rural unemployment; and the international isolation that followed the 1989 Tiananmen Massacre all pushed China to pursue nationalism as an alternative source of regime legitimacy.[60] Consequently, the patriotic education campaign intensified in 1990.[61] It emphasized Japanese war crimes, which aggravated the Chinese people's negative feelings toward Japan.

Despite the media blackout, the Chinese people, especially university students, learned about the dispute from the British Broadcasting Corporation (BBC) and Voice of America.[62] They sought to express their anger through peaceful demonstrations, but were denied permissions.[63] In Beijing, students hung posters and distributed handbills that criticized the CCP for being too soft on Japan.[64]

State Policy Intent

At the time of the crisis, China grappled with internal economic challenges and external security dilemmas. Domestically, the nation was in a vulnerable state. Concurrently, Japan spearheaded initiatives to reintegrate China into the international community following the Tiananmen Square incident.[65] China was keen on ensuring that the territorial dispute did not obstruct its path to economic resurgence.

Remarkably, China refrained from commenting on Japan's official acknowledgment of the lighthouse on the contested island until nearly three weeks after the announcement, and only when prompted during a press conference. Contrary to expectations, China's reaction to the situation was measured. Rather than resorting to fiery rhetoric, China floated the idea of collaborative development of the region's resources.

Despite the eruption of protests by Chinese communities abroad, Beijing conspicuously muted domestic media coverage related to the demonstrations and stymied similar outpourings within China. In a telling move, the CCP distributed a circular to local party committees, warning that the dispute over "these economically and strategically insignificant islands should not affect friendly relations between China and Japan."[66] The CCP also issued guidance to public security officials to ban student demonstrations and increase security in university districts.[67]

260   Appendix 2

In the midst of this geopolitical tension, all economic engagements between China and Japan resumed. This included the resumption of crucial Japanese loans, instrumental in reversing China's post-Tiananmen global isolation.

Case #11. The 1996 Sino-Japanese Dispute over the Diaoyu/ Senkaku Islands

On July 14, 1996, the right-wing Japan Youth Federation (JYF) erected a makeshift lighthouse on one of the smaller islands and, ten days later, applied to the Japanese Maritime Safety Agency to recognize it as an official beacon. On July 18, a Chinese Ministry of Foreign Affairs spokesperson responded that such Japanese actions were a "serious violation to the Chinese sovereignty." "The Chinese government expresses serious concern about this and requests the Japanese government to immediately take effective measures to eliminate the resulting adverse effects."[68] On July 20, Japan declared a 200-nautical-mile exclusive economic zone (EEZ) around the islands under UNCLOS Japan had ratified in June.[69] On July 29, Japanese Prime Minister Ryutaro Hashimoto visited the Yasukuni Shrine, which commemorates those who died in service of Japan in wars, but also controversially including Japan's World War II war criminals. Although he visited "in a private capacity," the last Japanese prime minister's visit to the shrine was eleven years earlier. The Chinese Ministry of Foreign Affairs spokesperson expressed "deep regret" over this act.[70] Subsequent visits to the shrine by six Japanese cabinet members and more than eighty parliament members on August 15, the 51st anniversary of Japan's surrender in World War II, further elevated tensions.

On August 18, another Japanese right-wing group, the Senkaku Islands Defense Association, placed a wooden Japanese flag on the southern side of the main Diaoyu/Senkaku island.[71] On August 28, Japanese Foreign Minister Yukihiko Ikeda claimed that the Diaoyu/Senkaku islands "have always been Japan's territory" and "there is no need to explain."[72] The Chinese Ministry of Foreign Affairs spokesperson condemned Ikeda's remarks as "irresponsible."[73] *People's Daily* published a front-page editorial with the title: "Japan: Don't Do Stupid Things," declaring that the series of action by Japan betrayed its ambition to "take the islands as its own. This is absolutely intolerable by the Chinese people."[74] On September 9, the JYF returned to the island once again to repair the new lighthouse.

The next day, China lodged a strong protest with the Japanese government and warned that further tolerance for the right-wing group's actions "will cause serious damage to the Sino-Japanese relationship."[75] Large anti-Japanese protests erupted in Hong Kong, plans for expeditions to the islands were announced, and calls for boycotts of Japanese goods were made.[76] On September 13–14, the PLA carried out offshore military exercises near the islands off Liaoning Province, which may have been intended as warnings to Japan.[77] Tensions eased temporarily when Chinese Foreign Minister Qian Qichen met with Japanese Foreign Minister Ikeda on September 24 during the United Nations General Assembly. The two agreed that actions by the Japanese right-wingers were harmful to the bilateral relationship and should not be allowed.[78] But two days later, tensions peaked when Hong Kong activist David Chan drowned near the islands in an attempt to swim to the shore when the Japanese Maritime Safety Agency stopped his boat from landing on the islands.[79] This spurred large demonstrations once again in Hong Kong and Taiwan.[80] Chinese Premier Li Peng mentioned the dispute, particularly in his National Day reception address on October 1. He blamed the "interruption of and damage to the Sino-Japanese relationship" on "a tiny handful of right-wing forces and militarists in Japan" and urged Japan to "safeguard the overall interests of the bilateral relationship."[81] Meanwhile, Japan effectively denied the JYF's lighthouse recognition application.[82] On October 9, a second expedition by Hong Kong and Taiwanese activists was successful in planting their national flags on the islands.[83] The crisis came to an end on October 29 when

Chinese Vice Foreign Minister Tang Jiaxuan visited Tokyo. In his meeting with the Japanese Prime Minister Hashimoto, Tang requested to have the lighthouse removed but Hashimoto declined, citing legal limitations.[84] Tang settled for an agreement with Deputy Foreign Minister Shunji Yanai to freeze the issue altogether.[85]

Public Opinion

In the mid-1990s, China ramped up its patriotic education campaign. Coinciding with the 50th anniversary of World War II's conclusion in 1995, a surge of commemorative events spotlighting Japanese wartime transgressions flooded the public sphere.[86] This amplified anti-Japanese sentiments among the Chinese. Concurrently, the draft revision of US-Japan security guidelines further "provoked strong nationalistic feelings in China."[87]

An opinion poll conducted for the *China Youth Daily* in December 1995 found that 91.5 percent polled agreed that the Japanese right-wingers' erection of a lighthouse on the islands posed a serious challenge to China.[88] After Ikeda's August 28 statement, a petition by a Chinese activist for Chinese leaders to send warships to demolish the lighthouse garnered 257 signatures.[89] Throughout the course of the dispute, over 37,000 letters and petitions with more than 150,000 signatures were sent to *People's Daily* and *People's Liberation Daily*, demanding that the Chinese government act more aggressively.[90] Despite tight control of the internet by the government, more than 200 messages calling for anti-Japanese demonstrations circulated on universities' bulletin board systems (BBS).[91] Upon Chen's death, seventeen members of an anti-Japanese group wore black armbands to protest.[92] The CCP was under fire for not having a tougher position against Japan, with people handing out flyers and hanging posters that criticized the government's conciliatory policy.[93]

State Policy Intent

According to Philip Saunders's interviews with Chinese analysts in Beijing and Shanghai in 1996 and 1997, "Chinese officials were aware of negative international reactions (to its aggressive live missile firings near Taiwan in the 1995–1996 Taiwan Strait Crisis) and sought to downplay China's military capabilities for fear of driving Japan closer to the United States."[94] China also feared that impending revisions to the US-Japan alliance "might be used to cover contingencies concerning Taiwan."[95] Due to these concerns, China refrained from specifying baselines around Taiwan when it ratified the United Nations Convention on the Law of the Sea (UNCLOS) in May 1996, hoping not to trigger tensions with Japan over the Diaoyu/Senkaku Islands.[96]

Despite large protests in Hong Kong and Taiwan, Beijing prevented anti-Japanese demonstrations nationwide. The State Education Commission instructed universities in mid-September to avoid "drastic words and deeds."[97] Student rallies were banned.[98] A directive was also issued to provincial governments: "The central government is determined to prevent elements of the Hong Kong public from destroying relations between Japan and China by intensifying their criticisms of Japan."[99]

According to a 1996 CCP Central Propaganda Department circular, "The Chinese side has taken a restrained attitude in order to avoid negatively influencing normal Sino-Japanese relations and to avoid causing tension in the Asia-Pacific."[100] This is corroborated by Chinese responses in remarks and actions. In early October during vice Foreign Minister Tang Jiaxuan's visit to Tokyo, Chinese leaders pressed for a resolution of the matter and settled for a less-than-ideal agreement between the two sides.

262   Appendix 2

Case #12. 2005 Japanese History Textbook, Diaoyu/Senkaku Islands Dispute, and Japan's Bid for the UN Security Council

In April 2005, China experienced widespread anti-Japanese demonstrations that persisted for more than three weeks, with several instances turning violent. These outbursts were ignited by a confluence of contentious issues: Japan's aspiration for a permanent seat on the United Nations Security Council, its downplaying of its wartime offenses in World War II within history textbooks, ongoing tensions over the Diaoyu/Senkaku Islands, and disagreements over the exploration of natural resources in the East China Sea.

During this period, the territorial and maritime disputes stood out as prominent issues straining the Sino-Japanese relationship. In 2002, the Japanese government leased three of the Diaoyu/Senkaku Islands from their private owner, claiming that doing so could help prevent "the illegal landing of third parties."[101] Despite this claim, a number of Japanese activists landed on the islands in August 2003.[102] Chinese activists also tried to land on the islands in June and October 2003, but were turned back by Japanese patrol ships.[103] Chinese activists eventually succeeded in landing on the islands in March 2004, but were arrested by Japanese authorities. Chinese protestors burned Japanese flags outside the Japanese Embassy in Beijing. Japan released the activists on the third day "so as not to hurt the bilateral relationship with China."[104] However, the Japanese Diet subsequently unanimously passed a resolution on territorial sovereignty, which became the first Diet resolution concerning the Diaoyu/Senkaku Islands.[105] On February 9, 2005, Japan announced that it would officially recognize a lighthouse on the islands and put it under "state control." China protested and denounced this as "illegal and invalid."[106]

Around the same time, the maritime dispute in the East China Sea also became acute, with both sides taking unilateral actions. Chinese and Japanese energy companies began exploring and drilling in the East China Sea on their own. Both countries protested. Talks did not come to a resolution.[107] All of these issues, together with the rekindling of the history issue that same year, triggered the largest-ever anti-Japanese protests in China. These issues became obstacles that ultimately foiled Japan's diplomatic campaign to gain a seat on the United Nations Security Council.

Public Opinion

As previously mentioned, the Diaoyu/Senkaku Islands dispute had already been publicized even before China and Japan normalized relationship in 1972. Although the Chinese state was able to keep public emotion at bay for most of the 1970s, the rise of the history issue from 1982 onward rekindled strong public sentiment.

As shown in Table A2.1, the average thermometer toward Japan polled by the Beijing Area Study since 1999 had been worsening steadily year on year, dropping to the mid-30s just before the 2005 crisis.

An opinion poll of 2,160 Chinese adults completed jointly by Asahi Shimbun and Chinese Academy of Social Sciences on March 15–31, 2005 shows that unfavorable Chinese opinion toward Japan was as high as 64.1 percent. In comparison, unfavorable opinion toward the US was only 39.8 percent.[108]

China's "new thinking" debate surfaced in 2003 when *People's Daily* Journalist Ma Licheng published an article calling for an end to irrational anti-Japanese hatred. Both Ma and scholar Shi Yinhong, who supported Ma's viewpoint, quickly found themselves in the crosshairs of passionate nationalists.[109] Peter Hays Gries observed that sentiments against Japan had been intensifying in 2003–2004, highlighted by an unprecedented wave of anti-Japanese activities across China. As *Sing Pao Daily* noted in December 2003, "Chinese feelings of hatred for the Japanese are rising without interruption."[110]

Table A2.1 Chinese Public Thermometer toward Japan, 1999–2015 (Source: Beijing Area Study)

Survey Date	Average Thermometer Toward Japan (0–100)	Change from Previous Year
2/1999	50.3	
1/2000	47.4	−5.77%
3/2001	44.5	−6.12%
3/2002	34.9	−21.57%
3/2003	45.2	29.51%
5/2004	36.7	−18.81%
5/2005	29.9	−18.53%
5/2007	33.2	11.04%
5/2009	33	−0.60%
10/2013	31.3	−5.15%
6/2015	30	−4.15%

The intensity of public sentiment was evident in the unparalleled scale of the protests. An online petition opposing Japan's bid for the UN garnered over 22 million signatures.[111] On April 16 alone, more than 10,000 individuals gathered to protest outside the Japanese Consulate in Shanghai.[112] Analyses of these demonstrations commonly concur that the public's emotions emerged organically and authentically, with no orchestration by the government.[113]

State Policy Intent

Analysts observe that there is a large discrepancy between public opinion and the government's position on Sino-Japanese relations in the spring of 2005: "Ordinary citizens demanded a strong reaction from the state, while the Foreign Ministry followed a more lenient stance."[114] Chinese government's reactions remained largely verbal, with no substantive punishment. The MoFA spokesperson's initial response to Japan's UNSC bid that China "understands Japan's aspiration to play a greater role in international affairs" came under fire among Chinese nationalists.[115] After the protests turned violent, Beijing issued instructions to media outlets not to cover the protests and to adhere news reporting strictly to the official line.[116] On April 18, Japanese Prime Minister Koizumi "held out an olive branch to China" and requested a meeting with Chinese president Hu Jintao at the Bandung conference on April 22–24.[117] Following Koizumi's signal, Beijing began "a concerted effort" to bring an end to the protests.[118] The next day, Chinese Foreign Minister Li Zhaoxing proclaimed to the country on TV that the "only correct option" was "friendly coexistence and win-win cooperation" with Japan.[119] News reporting became highly synchronized and significantly less negative in tone "after press restrictions had been imposed by the Propaganda Department."[120] As Daniela Stockmann stresses, the commercial media, which enjoyed more credibility among ordinary Chinese, "assisted the state in appeasing angry citizens."[121] Applications to hold anti-Japanese protests over the weeklong May holiday were also denied.[122]

China's Japan policy after 2005 focused on repairing bilateral relations. "Chinese authorities censored internet forums and kept activists under surveillance during important diplomatic

264   Appendix 2

visits, restricted the size and duration of token protests on war anniversaries, and discouraged mainland and Hong Kong activists from taking protest voyages to the disputed islands."[123] Despite strong nationalist opposition, Chinese authorities also allowed Japanese participation in the Chunxiao gas field, which China had unilaterally developed in 2004.[124]

Case #13. 2010 Sino-Japanese Boat Incident near Senkaku/ Diaoyu Islands

On September 7, 2010, the Japanese Coast Guard arrested a Chinese fishing trawler captain who allegedly rammed his vessel into Japan Coast Guard ships near the Diaoyu/Senkaku Islands. Beijing demanded the immediate release of the captain. Japan released the rest of the crew but extended the captain's detention, indicating a trial based on Japanese domestic law. Tokyo also denied the existence of the territorial dispute and announced that the islands were covered by the US-Japan security alliance. Beijing gradually escalated its diplomatic rhetoric to compel Tokyo to release the captain. Japan eventually released the captain on September 25, but tensions simmered through October, with widespread nationalist protests and disturbances in both countries.

Public Opinion

By the 2010 incident, Chinese public's nationalist sensitivities toward Japan had become acute. The Beijing Area Study (BAS) shows that the Chinese public's thermometer toward Japan had stayed in the low 30s since 2005 and remained the lowest of all countries surveyed. An opinion poll conducted by Genron NPO and *China Daily* of 1,617 Chinese adults in June and July of 2010 shows that 55.9 percent of respondents had negative feelings toward Japan. This was down from 65.2 percent in 2009, but still a large majority of those polled.[125]

State Policy Intent

Before the crisis broke, the Sino-Japanese relationship was on an upward trend. Japan's governments were turning over quickly. The crisis broke under Prime Minister Naoto Kan, who took office in June 2010, but four previous prime ministers had held office for only about a year each. During preceding Prime Minister Yukio Hatoyama's term in 2009, Beijing and Tokyo continued their efforts, ongoing since 2005, to repair the relationship, which included frequent top meetings between Hatoyama and Hu Jintao. These efforts resulted in a nine-point joint communiqué between the two defense ministries on military exchanges and joint training for maritime search-and-rescue missions, a hotline between the two leaderships, and the initiation of formal talks in July 2010 to implement the 2008 gas agreement for joint exploration in the East China Sea.[126] So when the Hatoyama-Kan transition took place, Beijing took a cautiously optimistic attitude and acted quickly to shore up the progress made under Hatoyama.

At the beginning of the crisis, Beijing exercised considerable restraint. This was consistent with the improvement in the bilateral relationship and was based on Beijing's expectation that Tokyo would follow precedent and release the captain swiftly. Beijing made painstaking efforts to squelch anti-Japanese demonstrations, especially leading up to September 18, the anniversary of the Mukden Incident, which marks the beginning of Japanese invasion of China in World War II. They ordered the China Federation for Defending the Diaoyu Islands (CFDD) to drop their open letter to the Japanese government, stopped an expedition voyage from setting sail in Xiamen on September 10, disrupted anti-Japanese protests in Beijing, Nanjing, and

Changsha, interrogated activists, censored keywords online, shut down internet chat rooms, and prevented outspoken PLA media commentators from writing or talking publicly about the dispute.[127]

Beijing toughened its stance, however, when Japanese authorities extended the captain's detention on September 19. Tokyo also denied the existence of the territorial dispute, departing from their longstanding policy of ignoring the dispute, and announced that the islands were covered under the US-Japan security alliance. Beijing interpreted the Japan Coast Guard's handling of the incident as a departure from the status quo. From Beijing's perspective, Japan's previous handling of such incidents usually involved expelling or deporting the intruders. But in this case, Japanese authorities arrested and detained the captain based on Japanese domestic law. The Japanese action essentially asserted Japan's *de jure* sovereignty over the Diaoyu/ Senkaku Islands and directly challenged the status quo. Accepting the legality of these actions would compromise China's claim to the Islands. As a result, China's diplomatic rhetoric escalated from "we will closely follow the situation," to denunciations of Japan's handling of the case as "ridiculous, illegal and invalid," and statements that "Japan will reap as it has sown," and "Japan shall suffer all the consequences that arise."[128] The Chinese officials who issued the protests extended all the way up to Premier Wen Jiabao.

China pursued escalatory countermeasures. They suspended high-level exchanges with Tokyo, detained four Japanese nationals for allegedly entering a restricted military area, and imposed informal economic sanctions on tourism and rare earth mineral exports to Japan.[129] The rare earth mineral embargo is a debated topic, but the coincidence in timing is highly suspicious.[130] If it was truly intentional, it would be unprecedented in terms of the scale of retaliation. In addition, when Tokyo released the captain, instead of reciprocating and releasing the Japanese nationals to defuse the tension, Beijing demanded an apology and compensation. Analysts generally agree that China "over-reached."[131]

Case #14. 2011 Sino-Vietnamese Cable-Cutting Incidents

On May 26, 2011, three Chinese maritime surveillance vessels confronted a Vietnamese oil exploration ship *Binh Minh 02* around 120 nautical miles off the Vietnamese coast and severed its seismic survey cables.[132] The Vietnamese Foreign Ministry (MoFA) handed a diplomatic note to the Chinese embassy in Hanoi, protesting the Chinese actions that "violate Vietnam's sovereign right to its exclusive economic zone and continental shelf" and demanding compensation for the damages. The Chinese Foreign Ministry responded on May 28 that Vietnam's oil exploration activities "undermine China's rights and interests as well as jurisdiction over the South China Sea." The Chinese actions were "regular maritime law enforcement and surveillance activities in the waters under the jurisdiction of China."[133] The Vietnamese MoFA further responded the next day, repeating its earlier protest and rejecting China's claim that the incident occurred in disputed areas: "It is neither a disputed area nor is it an area 'managed by China.' China has deliberately misled the public into thinking that it is a disputed area."[134] The Chinese MoFA reiterated on May 31 that Vietnamese oil operations were "illegal," the Chinese actions were "completely justified," and Vietnam should "immediately stop infringement activities and refrain from creating new troubles."[135]

On June 9, a similar incident occurred involving a Chinese fishing boat ensnaring the cables of a Vietnamese survey ship *Viking II* in the waters off Vanguard Bank. The Chinese fishing boat was reportedly accompanied by two Chinese fishery administration vessels. The Vietnamese Foreign Ministry lodged a strong protest to the Chinese embassy in Hanoi and claimed that the Chinese action was "totally intentional, thoroughly deliberated and planned." The Vietnamese MoFA reported that the Chinese fishing boat, equipped with a "specialized cable slashing device," "headed on and rammed the exploration cables of Viking II," and "was consequently

266   Appendix 2

trapped in Viking II's cables, jamming Viking II's operation."[136] The Chinese MoFA responded that the Vietnamese remarks "do not tally with the fact." It blamed this incident on armed Vietnamese ships chasing away the Chinese fishing boat, causing it to be tangled with the cables of the Vietnamese survey ship: "The Vietnamese vessel dragged the Chinese fishing boat for more than one hour, with the latter's tail facing the front," forcing the Chinese fishermen "to cut off the fishing net so as to separate the two vessels." China accused the Vietnamese ships for "illegally" operating in waters under China's jurisdiction and "endangering" Chinese fishermen's lives, who had operated in the same waters "for generations."[137]

Public Opinion

A series of provocative events before the 2011 incidents had influenced public opinion. These include the 2009 *Impeccable* incident; the heated argument on the dispute that then-US Secretary of State Hillary Clinton spearheaded at the ASEAN Regional Forum in July 2010, hosted by Vietnam;[138] and China's alleged labeling of the South China Sea as a "core interest."[139] These events publicized the issue and fanned the Chinese public's emotions. A March 2009 US State Department cable reveals that PRC officials complained about the US's increased surveillance activities following the *Impeccable* incident and warned about the "pressure from internet users and others for the PRC government to respond."[140]

Chinese public emotions reached a sensational high, with no instigation from the state, after news of the cable-cutting incidents. Despite the absence of state propaganda on the issue, a search of the word "South China Sea" on Baidu Search Index (BSI) during June and July shows that the public attention to the issue swelled to a daily average of above 10,000 and peaked at 29,000 in mid-June, compared to the all-time average of 2,773 during noncrisis periods between 2011 and 2017.

Jingoistic comments flooded online forums and social media just before and throughout the crisis. On June 8, a Vietnamese Foreign Ministry website was hacked to display the Chinese national flag and a Chinese slogan that read "the Spratlys belong to China."[141]

Evidence also suggests that these nationalistic public expressions were spontaneous. They might have partially resulted from previous state media policies of allowing or even encouraging coverage, but they were not endogenous to state media policy in *this* crisis. The fact that the flurry of online criticism often attacked the Chinese government affirms the spontaneous and genuine nature of the hardline public opinion.[142] An article by ambassador Wu Jianmin with moderate views, "The South China Sea Dispute: Restraint is A Kind of Confidence," was lambasted on the Tianya forum.[143] Typical comments accused the Chinese foreign policy of being too soft, even traitorous, and likened it to the Qing dynasty, which collapsed following territorial encroachment by foreign powers, or reminisced about Mao's era of "defeating America twice" and "teaching India a lesson." Another line of argument linked the policy to corruption: "Corrupt officials running amok, unable to fight, let's just give the South China Sea away."[144]

State Policy Intent

Both incidents occurred in marginal areas within China's nine-dash line, but beyond any EEZ that China might have hoped to generate under UNCLOS, based on its claimed sovereignty over the Paracels or the Spratlys (although whether these land features could generate an EEZ is still debatable). But these locations do fall into Vietnam's EEZ from its coastal baseline. Given the obscure nature of the nine-dash line, Chinese actions were therefore based on precarious grounds. In Chinese experts' analysis, the Chinese actions were motivated by a mixture of concerns about energy security and the perception of declining claim strength in the disputed areas. You argues that Beijing feared that the erection of oil structures in the disputed areas might eventually lead to Vietnam's de facto control, which could be used by international legal bodies against China's claim in the future, thus increasing the risk that China would lose these areas permanently.[145] Regardless of whether these concerns were warranted or paranoid, Beijing's acts were preemptive, not reactive.

There is conflicting evidence as to whether the June 9 cable cutting was premediated and deliberate as Hanoi believed. You's sources indicate that the order was made by "the Navy's Xisha Surveillance District after consulting its superiors," but out of concern for the safety of the boat and the crew on board, given that the boat had been entangled with the Vietnamese cables and dragged for "hours."[146] This story is consistent with the Chinese official story. But curiously, the Vietnamese media had already reported on harassment of *Viking II* by suspected Chinese vessels days before the incident.[147]

Even if the June 9 *Viking II* incident were truly an accident, as Beijing claimed, the cable-cuttings were part of an aggressive trend in Chinese maritime behavior at this time. On May 2, just weeks before the first incident, *China Daily* reported that "China marine surveillance (CMS) forces will expand rapidly to better protect the country's marine security ... more than 1,000 people will join the CMS staff by the end of 2011."[148] On May 20, just days before the first incident, a mega Chinese oil and gas-drilling platform "Hai Yang Shi You 720" officially went in to operation.[149] On May 24, CNOOC announced the open tendering of nineteen new blocks in the South China Sea, covering an area of 52,006 square kilometers.[150] Chubb argues that compared to China's established practice of deterring rival claimants' energy exploration activities in the disputed area through economic threats, these actions "constitute an escalation."[151]

Although the PLA's involvement was unclear,[152] China's interference seemed to be authorized at least on the level of the CMS. Chubb points out that normal Chinese law enforcement activities in similar situations were limited to "hailing announcements." Ad hoc coercive operations, such as the severing maneuvers on May 26, would need to be authorized.[153] Together with the Reed Bank incident earlier in March[154] and a later incident in 2012, there were at least four unique incidents involving China's interference in foreign oil companies' seismic survey activities.[155] These repeated incidents constitute a pattern.[156] If the incidents happened against Chinese intentions, then Chinese policymakers would have had an opportunity to restrain the operational units after the initial incidents, to prevent the subsequent confrontations. Instead, fifty Chinese coast guards were awarded for their "heroic acts" in defending China's maritime rights on July 23 for the first time.[157]

Case #15. 2012 Sino-Philippines Scarborough Shoal Standoff

The Scarborough Shoal is a chain of reefs, rocks, and an inner lagoon in the South China Sea. China, Taiwan, and the Philippines have conflicting claims to the Shoal. On April 8, 2012, a Philippine navy frigate cornered several Chinese fishing vessels in the lagoon at the Scarborough Shoal, under suspicions of poaching. Two CMS ships soon arrived, interposing themselves between the frigate and the fishing vessels to prevent an arrest and triggering a two-month standoff between the two countries in the Shoal.

Public Opinion

Just months before the crisis began, there had been widespread awareness and strong nationalist sentiment in China about the South China Sea dispute, and especially against the

268   Appendix 2

Philippines. The strong nationalist sentiment on the South China Sea dispute was a recent phenomenon, dating from around 2009. It had drawn public attention due to heightened tensions, increased US involvement, and China's willingness to allow publicity on the dispute. In June and July 2011, China experienced a "wave of public mobilization" on the South China Sea issue.[158] A search of the term "South China Sea" in the BSI shows notable surges in June and July 2011 and a daily average index of 4,000 during the one-year pre-crisis period. For comparison, the all-time average of search volume between 2011 and 2017 is 2,773.

In an interview with journalists from South and Southeast Asia in late 2011, Chinese MoFA Director-General for Asian Affairs Luo Zhaohui commented that Chinese public opinion on the issue has left "no room for China to back off . . . The Chinese general public has been asking whether the government has been too weak and easy to bully."[159] As the news of the confrontation spread, intense public reaction flooded online forums and social media. In a published essay in *The National Interest*, Fu Ying and Wu Shicun write that "Almost instantly, images of the arrested Chinese fishermen being stripped to the waist and exposed to the scorching sun on the deck made headlines on print and digital media in China, triggering off an outcry among the Chinese general public. China was thus forced to take countermeasures."[160] The public spontaneously initiated bottom-up mobilization such as small-scale protests outside the Philippine Embassy and hacking attacks.[161]

State Policy Intent

From the very onset of the crisis, China responded disproportionately with uncompromising behavior on the sea and informal economic sanctions. The Chinese decision to send CMS ships to confront the Philippine naval frigate and to prevent the arrest of the Chinese fishermen departed from previous Chinese behavior and reflected a change toward greater aggression. Previously, China "had never attempted to impose punishment beyond diplomatic protests in response," on "a string of comparable cases of Philippine authorities detaining PRC fisherfolk at the atoll."[162] After the initial standoff, in an attempt to ease the tension, Manila withdrew the navy frigate and replaced it with a coast guard vessel and a Bureau of Fisheries and Aquatic Resources vessel.[163] But instead of reciprocating the gesture, China reinforced its presence by sending its most advanced fishery patrol ship, the *Yuzheng 310*, to join two other ships already there.[164] The number of Chinese ships in the area continued to rise and reached fourteen on May 3.[165] Both parties retreated at the threat of an oncoming typhoon, but Chinese vessels returned to the Shoal shortly thereafter, establishing a regular presence until October 2016.[166]

In terms of economic sanctions, although some scholars reject and refute the alleged banana ban that imposed tighter control due to alleged pests problem,[167] China went out of its way to publicize the travel advisory, the reduction of China Southern Airlines flights to Manila, and the fruit quarantine, all of which coincided with the crisis and were reported by *People's Daily*.[168] China Youth Travel Service, a state-owned national tourist company, also offered to reimburse tour packages.[169] Altogether, these actions suggest an unofficial sanction.

Case #16. 2012 Japanese Nationalization of Diaoyu/ Senkaku Islands

In 2012, the 40th anniversary of the normalization of China-Japan relations was overshadowed by arguably the lowest point in their relationship since its normalization. In an attempt to thwart right-wing Tokyo mayor Shintaro Ishihara from buying the contested islands and potentially instigating further provocations, the Japanese government, despite numerous warnings from China, proceeded to nationalize the islands on September 11, 2012. This move triggered the most extensive anti-Japanese demonstrations in China and led to a significant standoff between the two nations.

Public Opinion

Only two years had passed since the 2010 fishing trawler incident, and the bitter disagreement between the two nations was still vivid in the minds of many Chinese. An annual public opinion survey conducted by Genron NPO and *China Daily* in April and May 2012, just months before the onset of the 2012 crisis, revealed alarming sentiments. Over half (50.2 percent) of the Chinese respondents anticipated an impending military dispute. Negative feelings toward Japan were apparent among 64.5 percent of the Chinese respondents, a figure that compared to 65.9 percent in 2011, 55.9 percent in 2010, and 65.2 percent in 2009.[170] Recognizing the profound resentments harbored by both nations, a representative from Genron NPO who presented the data remarked, "Japan-China relations are in a very difficult situation."

State Policy Intent

As China approached a pivotal, once-in-a-decade leadership transition, the last situation it desired was an intense diplomatic crisis with the potential to ignite massive protests and jeopardize societal stability. All indications suggested that they were not seeking or anticipating this magnitude of discord. On the contrary, in anticipation of the 40th anniversary, 2011 witnessed a surge of cooperative exchanges between China and Japan, and many more were scheduled for 2012.[171] Even when China first became aware of Japan's intentions to purchase the disputed islands, their reaction was measured. While they voiced their objections to Japan's plans, they did not suspend any anniversary celebration preparations. Despite consistently voicing their strong concerns, Chinese officials consistently underscored the importance of the "larger interest" of the bilateral relationship.[172]

On September 11, when Japanese Prime Minister Noda proceeded with the acquisition just a day following President Hu's highly publicized warning, China's reaction took a sharper turn. Beyond the unusually harsh language, the immediate cancellation of the anniversary celebrations, and the suspension of high-level interactions, China's most impactful retaliatory steps were twofold: the delineation of baselines around the Islands and an upsurge in maritime patrols, aiming directly at undermining Japan's de facto control over the Islands. Concurrently, the Chinese PLA Navy and Air Force executed coordinated drills near the disputed areas.[173] Notably, China refrained from resorting to economic measures levers as it had done earlier in 2010 by restricting rare earth mineral exports, though tourism was inadvertently dampened. While the baseline move and the display of force could be considered proportionate responses to Japan's nationalization and to the earlier US-Japan joint exercises in the area, the increased maritime patrols that challenged Japan's de facto control and that persisted beyond the duration of the crisis were escalated reactions.

Case #17. 2013 Sino-Indian Border Standoff at Ladakh

In April 2013, a notable incident occurred at the Sino-Indian border, particularly around the Ladakh region. Chinese soldiers erected tents in close proximity to the Line of Actual Control

270   Appendix 2

(LAC), which is the demarcation line separating Indian-held territories from Chinese-controlled areas. This action precipitated a standoff that lasted three weeks, with troops from both India and China facing off against each other.

Public Opinion

While many were aware of the border dispute stemming from the 1962 conflict, not many held intense feelings about it in contemporary times. Following the tensions in 1986, India and China signed a series of agreements aimed at crisis management and confidence-building. These agreements significantly diminished the chances of confrontations turning hostile. Thus, by the time the 2013 crisis arose, the border dispute had been largely dormant for almost three decades. Indicative of the subdued attention to the issue, the Baidu Search Index, a measure of topic popularity on China's premier search engine, showed a mere one-year average of 207 mentions leading up to the crisis. This was barely distinct from the noncrisis average of 228 mentions recorded between January 1, 2011, and October 25, 2017.[174]

State Policy Intent

At first glance, China's decision to pitch tents in the disputed area was provocative. However, China claims that it was reacting to India's increasing infrastructure buildup near the border.[175] Notably, the Line of Actual Control (LAC) has never been distinctly demarcated. Consequently, the two nations often hold different interpretations of its precise location. The tents set up by the Chinese were positioned between what China viewed as the LAC and what India perceived as the LAC. As tensions mounted, both armies promptly initiated flag meetings, which are consultations held on the LAC or at the border by commanders from both sides, seeking a peaceful resolution.

This incident's timing was especially significant as it unfolded shortly before two crucial diplomatic events. Chinese Premier Li Keqiang was scheduled to visit India, and concurrently, India's Foreign Affairs Minister, Salman Khurshid, had planned a visit to Beijing. This backdrop added a layer of diplomatic sensitivity and urgency to the situation for a diplomatic resolution.

Case #18. 2014 Sino-Vietnamese Oil Rig Standoff

The Sino-Vietnamese oil rig crisis started on May 2, 2014, when the state-owned China National Offshore Oil Corporation (CNOOC) moved its Haiyang Shiyou 981 oil rig into a disputed maritime zone between China and Vietnam without consulting Vietnam. The rig, a semi-submersible drilling platform, had been constructed in 2012 at a hefty expense of $1 billion US dollars. Throughout the duration of the crisis, the oil rig's location underwent minor adjustments but remained situated roughly 17 nautical miles south of the Paracel Islands. These islands are claimed by both nations but are presently under China's occupation.

When assessing the positioning of the rig, it was stationed approximately 130 nautical miles from the Vietnamese coast and 180 nautical miles from China's Hainan Island. Ignoring the contested claims over the Paracel Islands, the rig's location was closer to the Vietnamese coast, situating it on Vietnam's side of the equidistance line drawn between the coasts of Vietnam and China. It was nestled within the overlapping EEZs of the two countries.[176]

China's placement of the oil rig in this location triggered dangerous actions by both sides at sea in the vicinity of the rig. They rammed vessels and fired water cannons, and in Vietnam, large-scale deadly riots led to the burning down of foreign-owned factories.[177] This high-stakes crisis eventually came to an end on July 15. China announced that the Haiyang Shiyou 981 had concluded its operations a month earlier than originally planned and subsequently withdrew the rig from the area.[178]

Public Opinion

In 2013 and the first half of 2014, the relationship between China and Vietnam regarding the South China Sea dispute was relatively stable, marked by a lack of major incidents on the sea. This period of calm was partly due to the Chinese state's decision not to fan the flames of nationalism concerning the dispute with Vietnam. As a result, nationalist sentiments subsided temporarily, though they remained easily ignitable.

Several journalists and editors who were interviewed during this period noted that public opinion and nationalist sentiment were "calm" before and during the crisis, even bordering on "aloof." They also remarked that the situation was "definitely less feverish than before the Sino-Philippines Scarborough Shoal standoff in 2012 or the arbitration case in 2016." With the exception of the riots, these interviewees generally perceived "little news value" in the ongoing events.[179]

Figure A2.1 shows the daily search index of the word "South China Sea" in the Baidu Search Index (BSI) during the one-year pre-crisis period. This period featured stable and relatively low index in comparison to other periods, with just a few mild surges, and averaged at 1,713. As mentioned, the all-time average of search volume between January 1, 2011 and October 15, 2017 is 2,773.

According to the *South China Sea Public Opinion Newsletter*, the first half of 2014 saw low levels of public attention to the South China Sea dispute on social media, with most online discussions focusing exclusively on the dispute with the Philippines or the involvement of the United States.[180] Interest in the dispute with Vietnam appeared to be minimal. For example, very few protesters turned out for a scheduled anti-Vietnam rally in Kunming on May 19.[181]

In a survey conducted by Andrew Chubb in April 2013 of 1,413 Chinese adults, the option of "sending in troops" to resolve the South China Sea issue was the second-least popular policy choice among the ten options provided, trailing the "compromise through negotiation" option by about 12 percentage points. Although a substantial percentage of respondents still found the idea of using force tolerable, it was evident that a diplomatic approach was more favored by the Chinese public.[182]

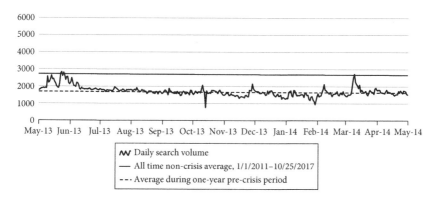

Figure A2.1 Daily Search Volume of "South China Sea" on Baidu.com During One-Year Pre-Crisis Period, May 2, 2013–May 2, 2014

272 Appendix 2

State Policy Intent

Prior to the crisis, the two countries had enjoyed a rather cordial relationship, marked by high-level visits by Vietnamese President Truong Tan Sang to Beijing in June 2013 and Chinese Premier Li Keqiang to Hanoi in October. During these visits, both sides restated their commitment to peace and stability in the South China Sea. As a concrete result of these visits, the China-Vietnam expert group for low-sensitivity maritime cooperation and consultation was established in December 2013, just months before the crisis occurred.[183] China also engaged with ASEAN on the Implementation of the Declaration on Conduct of Parties in the South China Sea (DOC) at the tenth joint working group meeting in Singapore on March 18 and was working out a number of confidence-building measures under the DOC at the seventh ASEAN-China Senior Officials' Meeting on the Implementation of the DOC in Thailand on April 21. All of these took place just weeks before the placement of the oil rig.

China's placement of the oil rig appears to be provocative, but it was likely due to unintended miscalculation. As disclosed in private interviews to policy analysts close to the decision-making, the oil rig relocation to the disputed area was "without the proper consultation with the Foreign Ministry, and likely without direct involvement of the top leadership."[184] A retired government official frequently consulted on Vietnamese affairs attests: "Our policy (in placing the rig) in 2014 was not very stable . . . it was not a decision made by the top leadership after careful rumination."[185] When asked on June 11 to confirm the Vietnamese remarks that "China has sent six warships to guard its oil rig," Chinese MoFA spokesperson Hua Chunying replied "we have sent government vessels to the site for security."[186] "Government vessels" should mean maritime law enforcement vessels, not navy ships. This happened again on June 13 with MoFA Deputy Director General of the Department of Boundary and Ocean Affairs Yi Xianliang. When asked whether the Vietnamese statement about China sending navy warships was true, Yi said, "we had to send Coast Guard ships."[187] It is not clear, however, whether Hua and Yi were skillfully deflecting the question or simply not notified of the navy ships.

In late August, Vietnamese special envoy Le Hong Anh visited Beijing in an effort to repair the relationship. Unusually, in his talks with Chinese Party seniors, he stressed that the two parties needed to "tighten their instructions." The words "tighten instructions" were repeated four times in a short two-page report of the meeting.[188] This implies that the explanation given privately to Anh involved a lack of coordination on the Chinese side. The emphasis on this phrase implies that both parties recognized the need for better communication and coordination to prevent future incidents and misunderstandings.

A Crisis Group report offers a slightly different story, but also confirms the irrational decision explanation. Based on an interview with a "security agency-affiliated Chinese analyst," the report asserts that "the Central Leading Small Group on the Protection of Maritime Interests, created in 2012 and reportedly led, at least initially, directly by Xi, made the decision in the oil rig case. The foreign ministry was said to be represented by the Department of Boundary and Ocean Affairs, whose 'primary concern is sovereignty,' without Department of Asian Affairs input." Thus, the decision was made without "consultation with experts who understand Vietnam."[189] My own interviews with individuals who are routinely consulted on Vietnamese Affairs by Beijing indirectly confirm this last point. According to them, the placement of the oil rig "came as a shock," suggesting that China's Vietnam experts were not consulted on the matter.[190] Moreover, the report also highlights that "in internal memos, closed-door conferences, and briefings to senior officials," the prevailing view among Chinese analysts was that the decision to place the rig was a mistake and ill-advised.[191]

There also appears to be an element of path dependency in the decision. In June 2012, Vietnam's state oil and gas group PetroVietnam revealed its plan to invite Japanese firms to

Appendix 2 **273**

participate in the joint development of about twenty oil and gas projects.[192] Just a few days later, the Vietnamese National Assembly passed the Vietnamese Law of the Sea. In retaliation, CNOOC invited international bids for nine oil and gas blocks.[193] This explains why the Chinese MoFA spokesperson claimed on various occasions that similar Chinese exploration and drilling activities had been ongoing for "a decade in the same waters," and that the placement of the oil rig in 2014 was only a "natural continuation" of past activities.[194]

Hanoi reacted forcefully to the Chinese placement of the oil rig. They dispatched vessels and reinforced their presence near the site, protested to Chinese leaders and formally at the UN and the ASEAN, and called upon the US to condemn the Chinese behavior. Caught off-guard by Vietnam's strong reactions and realizing the grave risk of tipping the Vietnamese domestic political scale further toward the anti-China faction, Beijing needed a face-saving retreat from the situation. An immediate retreat was certainly unappealing, as it would signal Beijing's weakness both to domestic and international audiences.

State Councilor Yang Jiechi's visit to Hanoi on June 18 is a strong signal that both sides were willing to talk and work out a peaceful solution. Yang visited Hanoi under the umbrella of the Vietnam-China Joint Steering Committee for Bilateral Cooperation, which has an established practice of meeting annually, but the specific timing of each meeting is decided on short notice.[195] It is common in Chinese foreign policy practice to use seemingly routine meetings at long-established multilateral or bilateral frameworks as a face-saving way for Beijing to initiate talks on more urgent matters without appearing too eager. From Beijing's perspective, the Vietnamese government tolerated, if not "connived" with, rioters who set aflame several Chinese-owned factories and caused deaths and damages. Therefore, China felt it deserved an apology and did not want to appear too eager to reconcile.

Beijing felt compelled to assert its authority in maritime confrontations with Vietnamese vessels to maintain its territorial claims and safeguard the precious, yet vulnerable, oil rig. In response to Hanoi's allegations of physical aggression by Chinese ships—ramming Vietnamese vessels and using water cannons—China argued that the cordon was deployed solely to defend the oil rig, not to hassle Vietnamese ships, unless their actions were misinterpreted. Interestingly, even the Vietnamese Ministry of Foreign Affairs spokesperson utilized the term "protect" when stating that "China used between 109 and 125 vessels to protect Haiyang Shiyou oil rig 981."[196] Nonetheless, this does not rule out the possibility that Chinese vessels might have wrongly perceived some harmless Vietnamese fishing boats as attempting to impede the oil rig operations and, consequently, inflicted damage. In such a congested maritime area, occasional collisions were almost unavoidable.

On possible Chinese economic sanctions, Malesky and Morris-Jung state that "retail trade with China dipped noticeably in the second half of 2014,"[197] but Poh reports that "the trade account between China and Vietnam in 2014 continued to increase."[198] My own examination of data from the World Integrated Trade Solution (WITS) and the General Statistics Office of Vietnam (GSOV) confirms Poh's observation.[199] Total retail bilateral trade increased from 50.0 billion (US dollars) in 2013 to 58.6 billion in 2014, and has continued to rise since. The second half of 2014 remained high, with 30.8 billion of the 2014 total. The only dip occurred in tourism, but travel advisories and cancelled chartered flights were not limited to China.[200] According to Poh's interviews with Vietnamese diplomats and analysts, sanctions were expected but were not employed or threatened. A Vietnamese analyst also told Poh that "it was his understanding that local officials in China—such as those in Yunnan and Guangxi—were 'specifically instructed' to ensure that economic interactions along the border between China and Vietnam were not affected by the dispute. These local Chinese officials . . . proactively approached their Vietnamese counterparts to ensure that economic interactions were sustained, even as bilateral tensions continued to rise."[201]

Case #19. 2014 Sino-Indian Border Standoff at Ladakh

In September 2014, a tense standoff occurred between Chinese and Indian soldiers in the Ladakh region. The chain of events began with India's construction of an irrigation canal near the Line of Actual Control (LAC), which was met with protest from China. As a result, the Indian side halted the construction. Tensions escalated when Indian troops erected an observation hut along the LAC, prompting China to dispatch troops to the area, equipped with cranes and bulldozers for road building. The standoff involved hundreds of soldiers from both countries and led India's army chief to cancel a foreign trip in order to monitor the situation. The tension also cast a shadow over Chinese President Xi Jinping's visit to New Delhi.[202]

Public Opinion

Despite the militarization of the dispute in 2013, it only attracted and sustained limited attention within a small circle of experts and keen observers. The Baidu Search Index shows a pre-crisis one-year average of a mere 192 mentions, compared to the all-time noncrisis average of 228.

State Policy Intent

China's public response to the standoff was remarkably measured. China's Ministry of Defense spokesperson Geng Yansheng said "the Sino-Indian border has not been fully demarcated. The rise of individual circumstances is thus unavoidable, but will not affect the overall friendly cooperation between the two countries."[203] The fact that confrontations at the border impaired the effectiveness of Xi's visit and left him embarrassed suggests that he did not intend to escalate the tension.

Case #20. 2016 International Tribunal Ruling of Sino-Philippines Arbitration

On January 22, 2013, the Philippine government initiated an international arbitration case against China over maritime rights in the South China Sea. On February 19, 2013, China rejected the arbitration and announced that it would neither accept nor participate in it. Despite Beijing's repeated protests, the case moved forward. On June 29, 2016, a ruling was imminent. The court announced its plan to issue the award on July 12, which spurred a diplomatic crisis. On July 12, the award was published, ruling largely in favor of the Philippines and against China.

Public Opinion

Throughout the year of 2015 and into the first half of 2016, a chain of reactions between the US and China reached a crisis level regarding China's land reclamation activities and the US Freedom of Navigation Operations (FONOPs) in the South China Sea. The tension was accompanied by a rancorous debate about who was actually militarizing the South China Sea, featuring a harsh tit-for-tat rhetoric between high-level officials from China and America at prominent international arenas such as the Shangri-La Dialogue, the APEC summit, and the ASEAN summits. These were captured by media with sensational headlines. In their *National*

Appendix 2   **275**

Interest article in May 2016, Fu Ying and Wu Shicun assessed Chinese public opinion to be "enraged" with "sustained attention."[204] This increased awareness was not about the Sino-Philippines arbitration per se, but the Philippines is a US ally and these issues are thus closely related.

The Beijing Area Study (BAS) survey carried out between April 10 and June 30, 2015 ranked the Philippines second lowest in country thermometers (36 out of 100), only after Japan (30 out of 100). Baidu Search Index (BSI) shows an average of about 4,000 in the search index for the word "South China Sea" during the one-year period before the start of the crisis, with several surges throughout the period. As a point of reference, the average of such searches during the entire period of available BSI data is 2,773.

The court's announcement sparked an enormous and spontaneous public outcry on the internet. From July 1–20, the number of relevant microblog posts soared to over five million, mostly on China's leading microblog Sina Weibo.[205] Large-scale protests were anticipated but preempted by the government, and the security of the Philippine Embassy in Beijing was strengthened. Scattered protests occurred in a number of cities, with people standing outside Kentucky Fried Chicken restaurants to condemn the US's involvement and call for a boycott.[206] A scholar observes that, right before the release of the award, "many people swore by war . . . once the ruling turns out to be unfavorable to China, street protests would almost certainly be expected; people might even attack the Philippine and the American Embassies."[207]

State Policy Intent

Interviews with scholars privy to policymaking processes reveal that Beijing, from the outset, desired a swift resolution to the issue.[208] After careful consideration of the advantages and disadvantages, and consultations with international law experts, Beijing chose not to participate in nor accept the arbitration. Throughout this process, Beijing showed little inclination toward punishing or threatening Manila, despite having ample opportunities to do so.[209] Instead, Beijing resorted to diplomatic efforts in an attempt to persuade the Philippines to abandon the case. As noted by Philippine Foreign Secretary Albert del Rosario, Beijing repeatedly expressed that arbitration should not be the solution to this dispute, advocating instead for bilateral consultations.[210] After these efforts proved unsuccessful, Beijing's subsequent actions were largely characterized as "reactive" and "remedial."[211]

Beijing sought diplomatic channels to resolve the issue even at the height of the crisis. In late June, for example, Beijing wasted no time in congratulating Rodrigo Duterte, who had just been sworn in as the Philippines' new president. Xi congratulated Duterte in winning the election and expressed that he was "willing to work with Duterte to push for improvement of relations between their two countries," which notably elided the ongoing arbitration.[212] After the release of the ruling, Vice Foreign Minister Liu Zhenmin remarked that China had "noted that the new Philippine government led by President Duterte was positive about resuming dialogue with China and moving forward the bilateral relationship from different aspects. We welcome that with our door widely open."[213] On August 8, Beijing sent delegates to meet Philippines' former president Fidel Ramos in Hong Kong to mend the relationship. From there, they invited President Duterte for an official visit, which occurred on October 20. President Xi met with Duterte, and the two agreed to resume direct talks on the South China Sea dispute. After Duterte's visit, China reported that the "China–Philippine relations have been turned around and put on a track of all-around improvement."[214]

Beijing also made a number of cooperative and conciliatory gestures. At the July 24 China–ASEAN Foreign Ministers' summit, right after the release of the ruling, Beijing made a concession by promising ASEAN that it would not to carry out land reclamation on the Scarborough Shoal.[215] In August, another China–ASEAN summit in China's Manzhouli resulted in a hotline

276   Appendix 2

for maritime emergencies, a Joint Statement on the Application of the Code for Unplanned Encounters at Sea in the South China Sea, and the pledge to finalize a draft for a code of conduct in the South China Sea by mid-2017.[216] As a substantive cooperative gesture, China also allowed Filipino fishermen to return to the vicinity of the Scarborough Shoal.[217]

Case #21. 2017 Sino-Indian Border Standoff near Doklam

On June 16, 2017, Chinese military road crews began to extend a road in Doklam, an area near the China-India-Bhutan trijunction that is disputed between China and Bhutan. Two days later, Indian troops entered the area and physically impeded the construction. This confrontation set off a two-month standoff between the two armies, separated by only a few hundred feet. On August 28, the two troops disengaged, and China suspended the construction.

Public Opinion

By 2017, the Sino-Indian border issue had been militarized almost every year since 2013. A few days after the Chinese MoFA confirmed the new standoff, the issue caught the public's attention on the internet.

The timing of the propaganda campaign confirms that the surge in public attention was not endogenous to the state propaganda, but genuine and spontaneous. Before the surge of public opinion near the end of June, the state media had made no noticeable propaganda efforts. The Ministry of Foreign Affairs published a short blurb on its website that confirmed the confrontation.[218] *People's Daily* reprinted the blurb the next day, in a small corner on page 21. CCTV news did not mention it. This was the extent of the coverage.

However, an online public opinion study reports that by July 1, the online discussion about the dispute had reached the "red" level of warning, the highest level in their routine monitoring of online activities.[219] Baidu Search Index shows a pre-crisis one-year average of 313, as compared to the all-time noncrisis average of 228. Official coverage did not pick up until early July, days *after* the surge of public attention and public emotions. Official media reports did not peak until after August 2, when the Chinese MoFA issued a document to clarify China's position.[220] Within twenty-four hours, *People's Daily, Xinhua News, Guangming Daily, PLA Daily*, and *Jiefang Daily* all reprinted the document in their most visible sections, and several published strongly worded editorials.[221] Interviews with Chinese journalists confirm that the Indian reporting of the issue had already gained traction online in China before the Chinese media reported on it.[222]

State Policy Intent

Based on a news report published five months after the crisis, the track construction was ordered by General Zhao Zongqi, commander of the Chinese Western Theatre Command. Zhao claimed that he had walked these tracks without much Indian confrontation for twenty years. But "As the Indian deployment has increased over the past decade, General Zhao is unwilling to accept the challenge to Chinese claims."[223]

Even though the crisis first started on June 18, the Chinese side did not publicize it until June 26 when the PRC MoFA and the Ministry of Defense confirmed the issue and voiced protests. Besides, this occurred right before important political events dictated the Chinese interest in not letting this get out of hand. The BRICS summit was about to take place in early September, with India as a participant. The 19th Party Congress, which announced the establishment of the next Chinese leadership, was also scheduled for the fall. As a result, China suspended its road construction in the disputed area, which had provoked the Indian intervention in the first place.

Analysts do not agree about whether the Chinese compromise to end the crisis was only temporary and tactical. After the crisis ended, there were reports that China continued and allegedly even increased its military presence in the area, and satellite images indicated that China might have been seeking alternative routes to South Doklam,[224] but Indian Prime Minister Modi's visit to China and meeting with Xi Jinping in April 2018 was acclaimed as historic in the bilateral relationship, and relative peace has been maintained to this day.[225]

Notes

1. Alastair Lamb, *The McMahon Line: A Study in the Relations Between India, China, and Tibet, 1904 to 1914. 2 Volumes.* (London: Routledge & Kegan Paul; Toronto: University of Toronto Press, 1966).
2. Nianlong Han, ed., *Dangdai Zhongguo Waijiao (Contemporary China's Diplomacy)* (Beijing: Shehui Kexue Chubanshe (China Social Sciences Press), 1987), 218.
3. Lengxi Wu, *Shi Nian Lunzhan, 1956–1966, Zhong Su Guanxi Huiyilu, (10-Year Polemical War, 1956–1966, A Memoir of Sino-Soviet Relations)*, vol. I (Beijing: Zhongyang Wenxian Chubanshe (Central Party Literature Press), 1999), 209.
4. Wu, *Shi Nian Lunzhan*, I:212.
5. Central Intelligence Agency, "The Sino-Indian Border Dispute: Section 1: 1950–59," March 2, 1963, www.archieve.claudearpi.net/maintenance/uploaded_pics/polo-07.pdf.
6. For detailed account of the hardening process of China's policy, see N. Maxwell, *India's China War*, First edition (New York: Random House, 2000); John W. Garver, "China's Decision for War with India in 1962," in *New Directions in the Study of China's Foreign Policy*, ed. Alastair Iain Johnston and Robert S. Ross (Redwood City, CA: Stanford University Press, 2004), 107–11.
7. M. Taylor Fravel, *Strong Borders, Secure Nation: Cooperation and Conflict in China's Territorial Disputes* (Princeton, NJ: Princeton University Press, 2008), 199.
8. Chenghan Wang, *Wang Chenghan Huiyilu (Wang Chenghan's Memoir)* (Beijing: Jiefangjun Chubanshe (People's Liberation Army Publishing House), 2004), 482.
9. Fravel, *Strong Borders, Secure Nation*, 2008, 199.
10. Yang Guihua, "1969 Nian Zhenbaodao Ziwei Fanjizhan" (Zhenbao Island Self-Defense Counterattack in 1969), *People's Daily*, July 4, 2002, http://www.people.com.cn/GB/junshi/192/8559/8564/20020704/768476.html.
11. Kuisong Yang, "The Sino-Soviet Border Clash of 1969: From Zhenbao Island to Sino-American Rapprochement," *Cold War History* 1, no. 1 (August 2000): 27–28.
12. Ibid.
13. Ibid., 36.
14. Ibid, 22.; Interview 40, June 8, 2017, Beijing.
15. Interview records with Chen Xilian, July 1995, cited in Yang, "The Sino-Soviet Border Clash of 1969," 30.
16. Yang, "The Sino-Soviet Border Clash of 1969."
17. Ibid., 34.

278 Appendix 2

18. W. Burr and J. Kimball, "Nixon's Secret Nuclear Alert: Vietnam War Diplomacy and the Joint Chiefs of Staff Readiness Test, October 1969," *Cold War History* 3, no. 2 (January 1, 2003): 113.

19. Yang, "The Sino-Soviet Border Clash of 1969," 34, 36, 37.

20. Dieter Heinzig, *Disputed Islands in the South China Sea: Paracels, Spratlys, Pratas, Macclesfield Bank* (Wiesbaden: Otto Harrassowitz, 1976), 32.

21. Heinzig, *Disputed Islands in the South China Sea*, 34; Fravel, *Strong Borders, Secure Nation*, 2008, 281.

22. John W. Garver, "China's Push Through the South China Sea: The Interaction of Bureaucratic and National Interests," *The China Quarterly* 132 (December 1992): 1000–1; State Oceanic Administration, *Zhongguo Haiyang Nianjian (China Ocean Yearbook)* (Beijing: State Oceanic Administration, 1986), 404.

23. Garver, "China's Push Through the South China Sea," 1001.

24. Zhaoxin Li, "Wo Suo Jingli de Xisha Haizhan (The Paracels Sea Battle I Experienced)," *Dangshi Bocai (Extensive Collection of the Party History)*, no. 7 (2009): 34. Li was a cryptographer working in the intelligence section of the South Sea Fleet headquarters.

25. Huaqing Liu, *Liu Huaqing Huiyilu (Liu Huaqing's Memoirs)* (Beijing: Jiefangjun Chubanshe (People's Liberation Army Publishing House), 2007), 338–43. Liu was PLA Navy's deputy chief of staff, appointed to take charge of garrisoning the Paracels after the 1974 battle.

26. For details of the incident, see Daniel Tretiak, "The Sino-Japanese Treaty of 1978: The Senkaku Incident Prelude," *Asian Survey* 18, no. 12 (December 1, 1978): 1235–49.

27. The dispute received much media exposure when the US turned over the administrative rights of the Islands to Japan in May 1972.

28. Yinan He, "National Mythmaking and the Problems of History in Sino-Japanese Relations," in *Japan's Relations with China: Facing a Rising Power*, ed. Peng Er Lam (London: Routledge, 2006), 69–91.

29. US Foreign Broadcast Information Service (FBIS) Daily Report: People's Republic of China, April 17, 1978, A6–8.

30. David Bachman, "Structure and Process in the Making of Chinese Foreign Policy," in *China and the World*, ed. Samuel S. Kim (Boulder, CO: Westview Press, 1998), 40–41.

31. FBIS Daily Report: People's Republic of China, May 11, 1978, A17–18.

32. Li Min, *ZhongYue Zhanzheng Shinian (Ten Years of the Sino-Vietnamese War)* (Chengdu: Sichuan daxue, 1993), 2.

33. Xiaoming Zhang, *Deng Xiaoping's Long War: The Military Conflict Between China and Vietnam, 1979–1991* (Chapel Hill: University of North Carolina Press, 2015), 40.

34. Ibid., 85.

35. Yunnan Province Foreign Affairs Office, *Yunnan Province History: Foreign Affairs History* (Kunming: Yunnan Renmin Chubanshe (Yunnan People's Publishing House), 1996), 149.

36. General Office of the General Political Department, ed., *ZhongYue Bianjing Ziwei Huanji Zuozhan Zhengzhi Gongzuo Jingyan Xuanbian (Compilation of Experiences of Political Work during the Counterattack in Self-Defense on the Sino-Vietnamese Border)*, vol. 1 (Beijing: Zhongguo Renmin Jiefangjun Zongzhengzhibu Bangongting (Chinese Liberation Army General Political Department, 1980), 7.

37. Author interview, June 2017, Beijing.

38. Zhang, *Deng Xiaoping's Long War*, 67; Nayan Chanda, *Brother Enemy: The War after the War* (New York: Collier Books, 1986); Andrew Scobell, *China's Use of Military Force: Beyond the Great Wall and the Long March* (New York: Cambridge University Press, 2003), 140.

Appendix 2 **279**

39. Scobell, *China's Use of Military Force*, 140.
40. Ibid., 361.
41. Zhang, *Deng Xiaoping's Long War*, 61.
42. Min, *Zhong Yue Zhanzheng Shinian (Ten Years of the Sino-Vietnamese War)*, 19.
43. Truong-Chinh, "The Vietnamese people are determined to defeat any aggressive schemes of Chinese expansionism and hegemonism," *Nhan Dan*, February 17, 1982. Truong-Chinh was a member of the Communist Party of Vietnam (CPV) Politburo and President of the Council of State.
44. Mira Sinha Bhattacharjea, "India-China: The Year of Two Possibilities," in *Yearbook on India's Foreign Policy, 1985–86*, ed. Satish Kumar (New Delhi: SAGE Publications, 1988), 152, 156.
45. Fravel, *Strong Borders, Secure Nation*, 200–201.
46. Ibid., 200–201.
47. Maninder Dabas, "The Story of the Sumdorong Chu Standoff—When India Avoided War with China Through Sheer Diplomacy," *India Times*, August 20, 2016, http://www.indiati mes.com/news/the-story-of-the-sumdorong-chu-standoff-when-india-avoided-war-with-china-through-sheer-diplomacy-260266.html.
48. Fravel, *Strong Borders, Secure Nation*, 288–92.
49. Garver, "China's Push Through the South China Sea"; Zhang Liangfu, *Nansha Qundao Dashiji (Chronology of the Spratly Islands)* (Beijing: Haiyang Chubanshe (China Ocean Press), 1996), 120–21.
50. For Chinese accounts of the battle, see Xiaohui Yang, "Chongfan Lishi: Zongyue Chiguajiao Haizhan (Return to History: The Sino-Vietnamese Johnson South Reef Battle)," *Shehui Guancha (Social Outlook)* 10 (2014): 66–68; Yongbing Wang, "Chiguajiao Dengluzhan (Johnson South Reef Battle)," *Jiancha Fengyun (Prosecutorial View)* 21 (2015): 77–79. For Vietnamese accounts, see "Deadly Fight Against Chinese for Gac Ma Reef Remembered," *TN News*, March 14, 2013, http://www.thanhniennews.com/society/deadly-fight-against-chinese-for-gac-ma-reef-remembered-3235.html; and "Vietnamese Soldiers Remember 1988 Spratlys Battle against Chinese," *Thanh Nien News*, March 14, 2016, http://www.thanhniennews.com/politics/vietnamese-soldiers-remember-1988-spratlys-battle-agai nst-chinese-60161.html.
51. Kyodo, September 29, 1990, in FBIS Daily Report: East Asia, October 2, 1990, 11–12.
52. "Waijiaobu Fanyanren Fabiao Tanhua: Diaoyu Dao shi Zhongguo Guyou Lingtu (Ministry of Foreign Affairs Spokesperson Releases Statement: Diaoyu Islands Are An Inseparable Part of the Chinese Territory)," *People's Daily*, October 19, 1990, 1.
53. Chien-peng Chung, *Domestic Politics, International Bargaining and China's Territorial Disputes* (London: Routledge, 2004), 42–43.
54. "Waijiaobu Fayanren Chongshen: Diaoyu Dao shi Zhongguo Guyou Lingtu (Ministry of Foreign Affairs Spokesperson Reiterates: Diaoyu Islands Are an Inseparable Part of the Chinese Territory)," *People's Daily*, October 23, 1990, 1.
55. Kyodo, October 24, 1990, in FBIS Daily Report: East Asia, October 24, 1990, 2.
56. "Senkaku Islands: A Sporting Effort," *Economist*, October 27, 1990, 37; "Protests Continue," *South China Morning Post*, October 29, 1990, 1–2; "Diaoyu Islands Campaign Called 'Ruse,'" *South China Morning Post*, October 26, 1990, 2; "Beijing Turns A Blind Eye," *South China Morning Post*, October 31, 1990, 15.
57. "Bowing to Japanese Yen Has Angered the Masses," *Cheng Ming*, November 1, 1990, 6–7, in FBIS Daily Report: China, November 5, 1990, 7.

280 Appendix 2

58. "Qi Huaiyuan Jinji Yuejian Riben Zhuhua Dashi (Qi Huaiyuan Makes an Urgent Appointment with the Japanese Ambassador to China)," *People's Daily*, October 28, 1990, 1.

59. "Islands Row 'Heading for Peaceful End," *South China Morning Post*, October 30, 1990, 9.

60. Erica Strecker Downs and Phillip C. Saunders, "Legitimacy and the Limits of Nationalism: China and the Diaoyu Islands," *International Security* 23, no. 3 (1999): 127–28.

61. Suisheng Zhao, "A State-Led Nationalism: The Patriotic Education Campaignin Post-Tiananmen in China," *Communist and Post-Communist Studies* 31, no. 3 (1998): 287–302; James Reilly, *Strong Society, Smart State: The Rise of Public Opinion in China's Japan Policy* (New York: Columbia University Press, 2011), 102.

62. Downs and Saunders, "Legitimacy and the Limits of Nationalism," 130.

63. "Beijing Turns A Blind Eye."

64. "Intellectuals Criticize Government," *Hong Kong Standard*, October 31, 1990, 6; "We Want Diaoyu Islands; We Do Not Want Japanese Yen," *Cheng Ming*, November 1, 1990, 8–9, in FBIS Daily Report: China, November 2, 1990, 7.

65. Kazuhiko Togo, *Rekishi to gaiko: Yasukuni, Ajia, Toky saiban* (Tokyo: Kodansha, 2008), 190. Quoted in Jessica C. Weiss, *Powerful Patriots: Nationalist Protest in China's Foreign Relations* (New York: Oxford University Press, 2014), 107.

66. "Bowing to Japanese Yen." Quoted in Downs and Saunders, "Legitimacy and the Limits of Nationalism," 131.

67. Ibid.

68. "Ministry of Foreign Affairs Spokesperson Answers Journalists' Questions," *People's Daily*, July 19, 1996, 4.

69. "Japanese Maritime Zone to Become Controversial Reality," Agence France-Presse, July 19, 1996.

70. "Qiaoben Canbai Jingguo Shenshe, Zhongguo Zhengfu Shenbiao Yihan (Hashimoto Visited Yasukuni Shrine, Chinese Government Expressed Regret)," *People's Daily*, July 30, 1990, 1.

71. "Riben Bie Gan Chun Shi (Japan: Don't Do Stupid Things)," *People's Daily*, August 30, 1996, 1.

72. Ibid.

73. "China Blasts Ikeda's Remarks on Senkaku Islands," *Kyodo News Service*, August 29, 1996.

74. "Riben Bie Gan Chun Shi (Japan: Don't Do Stupid Things)," *People's Daily*, August 30, 1996, 1.

75. "Waijiaobu Fayanren Biaoshi Zhongguo Qianglie Kangyi Riben Youyi Fenzi Zai Deng Diaoyudao (Ministry of Foreign Affairs Expresses Strong Protests to the Japanese Right-Wingers Returning to the Daiyu Islands)," *People's Daily*, September 11, 1.

76. "Hong Kong Patriotic Compatriots Are Justified in Defending Diaoyu Islands," *Ta Kung Pao*, September 9, 1996. Quoted in Antoine Roth, "Conflict Dynamics in Sino-Japanese Relations: The Case of the Senkaku/Diaoyu Islands Dispute" (Master's thesis, George Washington University, 2013), 25.

77. "Party Leaders, Generals to Discuss Diaoyu Islands at Plenum," *Hong Kong Standard*, September 23, 1996, 1. Quoted in Downs and Saunders, "Legitimacy and the Limits of Nationalism," 134.

78. "Qian Qichen Huijian Riben Waixiang Chongshen Diaoyudao Zigu Jiushi Zhongguo Lingtu (Qian Qichen Met with Japanese Foreign Minister and Reiterates Diaoyu Islands Have Been Chinese Territory Since Ancient Times)," *People's Daily*, September 26, 1996, 6.

Appendix 2   **281**

79. "Xianggang Gejie Daonian Gangshi Guwen Chen Yuxiang (Hong Kong People Mourns Hong Kong Affairs Counsel David Chan)," *People's Daily*, October 1, 1996, 2.

80. "Democrats Start Week of Action over Diaoyu Islands," *Hong Kong Standard*, October 1, 1996, p. 3. Quoted in Downs and Saunders, "Legitimacy and the Limits of Nationalism," 135.

81. "Zai Qingzhu Zhonghua Renmin Gongheguo Chengli Sishiqi Zhounian Zhaodaihui shang de Jianghua (Speech at the Reception to Celebrate the 47th Anniversary of the Founding of the People's Republic of China," *People's Daily*, October 1, 1996, 1.

82. "Senkaku no dotai ninka shinsei, horyu seishiki kettei Ikeda gaisho, Chugoku ni tentatsu e" (FM Ikeda Communicates to China the Formal Decision to Defer the Application for Recognition of the Senkaku Lighthouse), *Asahi Shimbun*, October 4, 1996. Quoted in Roth, "Conflict Dynamics in Sino-Japanese Relations," 26.

83. "Diaoyu Activists Storm Japanese Consulate," *South China Morning Post*, October 10, 1996, p. 1. Quoted in Downs and Saunders, "Legitimacy and the Limits of Nationalism," 135.

84. Senkaku shoto no dotai tekkyo, To · Chugoku gaimu jikan ga yosei" (Chinese Vice FM Tang Requests the Demolition of the Senkaku Lighthouse), *Asahi Shimbun*, October 30, 1996. Quoted in Roth, "Conflict Dynamics in Sino-Japanese Relations," 26.

85. "Senkaku mondai, Nihon gawa no honne ha toketsu chinseika nerau—nicchu jikankyu kyogi" (Japan-China Vice Ministerial Conference: The Japanese Side's True Intention Is to Quiet Down and Freeze the Senkaku Issue), *Asahi Shimbun*, October 30, 1996. Quoted in Roth, "Conflict Dynamics in Sino-Japanese Relations," 27.

86. Zhao, "A State-Led Nationalism," 287.

87. Downs and Saunders, "Legitimacy and the Limits of Nationalism," 132.

88. "Youth Polled on Japan's Invasion of China," February 16, 1997, *Xinhua News*, in WNC. Quoted in Downs and Saunders, "Legitimacy and the Limits of Nationalism," 127.

89. Kyodo, September 2, 1996, in WNC. Quoted in Downs and Saunders, "Legitimacy and the Limits of Nationalism," 133.

90. "Army, Civilians Call Jiang Zemin to Account," *Cheng Ming*, October 1, 1996, 6–8, in WNC.

91. "Chinese Protest Finds a Path on the Internet," *Washington Post*, September 17, 1996, A9.

92. "Tong Zeng Reveals that Protect Diaoyu Activities Are Still Being Carried Out on the Mainland," *Hsin Pao*, October 1, 1996, 10, in WNC.

93. Downs and Saunders, "Legitimacy and the Limits of Nationalism," 138–39.

94. Ibid., 132.

95. Weiss, *Powerful Patriots*, 104.

96. Downs and Saunders, "Legitimacy and the Limits of Nationalism," 132.

97. "State Education Commission Sends a Message to Institutions of Higher Education Nationwide Warning Them Against Too-Drastic Words and Deeds," *Ming Pao*, September 17, 1996, A4, in WNC.

98. "Jiang Issues Campus Gap Order on Diaoyu Incident," *Hong Kong Standard*, September 17, 1996, 1.

99. "Beijing Moves to Keep Lid on Protests," *Daily Yomiuri*, October 7, 1996, p. 1, in LEXIS/NEXIS. Quoted in Downs and Saunders, "Legitimacy and the Limits of Nationalism," 138.

100. Zhao, "A State-Led Nationalism," 274.

101. "Japan's Lease of Disputed Senkaku Islands Fuels 'Ire' from China, Taiwan," *Mainichi Shimbun*, January 3, 2003.

102. Weiss, *Powerful Patriots*, 129.

282 Appendix 2

103. "Chinese Protesters leave after Nearing Isles Disputed with Japan," *Kyodo News Agency*, June 23, 2003; "Determined to Defend Diaoyu Islands," *China Daily*, October 10, 2003.

104. "Japan Deported Chinese Protesters under Political Pressure," *Japan Economic Newswire*, April 1, 2004.

105. Yinan He, "History, Chinese Nationalism and the Emerging Sino–Japanese Conflict," *Journal of Contemporary China* 16, no. 50 (February 1, 2007): 15.

106. "Waijiaobu Fayanren Da Jizhe Wen (Ministry of Foreign Affairs Spokesperson Press Conference))," *People's Daily*, February 10, 2005, 2.

107. Richard Bush, "China-Japan Tensions, 1995–2006: Why They Happened, What To Do," Brookings Policy Paper No. 16, June 2009.

108. "Dong-A Ilbo Opinion Poll: Special Research on Chinese Attitudes toward Japan and Other Nations," April 26, 2005. Quoted in Mindy L. Kotler, Naotaka Sugawara, and Tetsuya Yamada, "Chinese and Japanese Public Opinion: Search for Moral Security," *Asian Perspective* 31, no. 1 (2007): 100.

109. Peter Hays Gries, "China's 'New Thinking' on Japan," *The China Quarterly*, no. 184 (2005): 831–50.

110. "Wangmin Hu Taohui Zhongguoren Zunyan (Netizens Call for a Restoration of Respect for the Chinese People)," *Sing Pao Daily*, November 1, 2003. Quoted in Gries, "China's 'New Thinking' on Japan," 844.

111. "22 Million Chinese Seek to Block Japan's Bid to Join U.N. Council," *New York Times*, March 31, 2005, http://www.nytimes.com/2005/03/31/international/asia/22-million-chinese-seek-to-block-japans-bid-to-join-un.html.

112. Edward Cody, "New Anti-Japanese Protests Erupt in China," *Washington Post*, April 16, 2005, http://www.washingtonpost.com/wp-dyn/articles/A58567-2005Apr16.html.

113. See, for example, Weiss, *Powerful Patriots*; Yue-him Tam, "Who Engineered the Anti-Japanese Protests in 2005," *Macalester International* 18, no. 25 (Spring 2007): 281–99.

114. Daniela Stockmann, "Who Believes Propaganda? Media Effects during the Anti-Japanese Protests in Beijing," *The China Quarterly* 202 (2010): 270. Weiss also quoted a senior researcher at the China Institutes of Contemporary International Relations that "there was such a large gap between the phrase 'we understand Japan's aspiration' and the public mindset at the time." See Jessica C. Weiss, "Powerful Patriots: Nationalism, Diplomacy, and the Strategic Logic of Anti-Foreign Protest" (PhD diss., University of California, San Diego, 2008), 139.

115. Weiss, *Powerful Patriots*, 139.

116. Stockmann, "Who Believes Propaganda?," 277.

117. Agence France-Presse, April 18, 2005. Quoted in Weiss, *Powerful Patriots*, 136.

118. Weiss, *Powerful Patriots*, 136.

119. Xinhua News Service, April 19, 2005, FBIS translation. Quoted in Weiss, *Powerful Patriots*, 136.

120. Stockmann, "Who Believes Propaganda?," 278.

121. Ibid., 286.

122. Weiss, *Powerful Patriots*, 149.

123. Ibid., 163.

124. "Gas Field Deal Signals China's PR challenge," *Nikkei Weekly*, July 7, 2008.

125. "On the Results of the 6th Japan-China Joint Opinion Survey," Genron NPO and *China Daily*, August 12, 2010, http://www.beijing-tokyoforum.net/index.php?option=

com_content&view=article&id=669:on-the-results-of-the-6th-japan-china-joint-opin ion-survey&catid=141:20106&Itemid=159.

126. "Chinese and Japanese Defence Departments' Joint Press Communique," *Xinhua News Service*, November 27, 2009; "Premiers Answer Calls for Direct Hotline," *Global Times*, June 1, 2010; "China, Japan Resume Gas Talks; Two PMs Also Discuss Naval Concerns and North Korea; They Agree to Set Up Hotline," *Straits Times*, June 1, 2010.

127. Weiss, *Powerful Patriots*, 170–72; Alastair Iain Johnston, "How New and Assertive Is China's New Assertiveness?," *International Security* 37, no. 4 (2013): 27.

128. "Ministry of Foreign Affairs Holds Regular Press Conference," *People's Daily*, September 10, 2010, p. 3; "China's Dai Bingguo Urges Japan to Release Detained Crewmen," *Xinhua News Service*, September 12, 2010; Mari Yamaguchi, "China Postpones Official's Visit to Japan amid Row," *Associated Press*, September 14, 2010; "Illegal Detention of Chinese Trawler's Captain Harms Chinese Public's Trust in Japan," *People's Daily (English Version)*, September 21, 2010.

129. Tania Branigan, "Relations between China and Japan worsen over filming of military targets," *The Guardian*, September 23, 2010, https://www.theguardian.com/world/2010/ sep/23/china-japan-relations-video-filming; Keith Bradsher, "Amid Tension, China Blocks Vital Exports to Japan," *New York Times*, September 22, 2010, http://www.nytimes. com/2010/09/23/business/global/23rare.html?mcubz=0.

130. Iain Johnston argues that there is a lack of pattern in the embargo. If there were an embargo, "it was a very ragged one affecting rare earths and different Japanese ports differently" (Johnston, "How New and Assertive Is China's New Assertiveness?" 25.).

131. See, for example, Mike Mochizuki, "China Over-Reached," *The Oriental Economist* 78, no. 10 (2010).

132. "VN Condemns Chinese Intrusion," VietnamNet, May 28, 2011, http://english.vietnam net.vn/en/politics/8839/vn-condemns-chinese-intrusion.html.

133. Consulate-General of the People's Republic of China in Houston, "Foreign Ministry Spokesperson Jiang Yu's Remarks on China's Maritime Law Enforcement and Surveillance on the South China Sea" (Beijing: Ministry of Foreign Affairs of the People's Republic of China (PRC MoFA), May 28, 2011), http://houston.china-consulate.org/eng/fyrth/t826 601.htm.

134. Vietnam Ministry of Foreign Affairs (Vietnam MoFA), "Press Conference on Chinese Maritime Surveillance Vessel's Cutting Exploration Cable of PetroViet Nam Seismic Vessel" (Hanoi: Vietnam MoFA, May 29, 2011), http://www.mofa.gov.vn/en/tt_baochi/ pbnfn/ns110530220030.

135. Embassy of the People's Republic of China in the United States of America, "Foreign Ministry Spokesperson Jiang Yu's Regular Press Conference on May 31, 2011" (Beijing: PRC MoFA, June 1, 2011), http://www.china-embassy.org/eng/fyrth/t827 089.htm.

136. Vietnam MoFA, "Foreign Ministry Spokesperson Nguyen Phuong Nga Answers Question from the Media at the Press Conference on June 9, 2011 Concerning the Viking II Incident" (Hanoi: Vietnam MoFA, June 9, 2011), http://www.mofa.gov.vn/en/tt_baochi/ pbnfn/ns110610100618.

137. Embassy of the People's Republic of China in the Republic of Namibia, "Foreign Ministry Spokesperson Hong Lei's Remarks on Vietnamese Ships Chasing away Chinese Fishing Boats in the Waters off the Nansha Islands" (Beijing: PRC MoFA, June 9, 2011), http:// na.china-embassy.org/eng/fyrth/t829427.htm.

284 Appendix 2

138. PRC MoFA, "Yang Jiechi Waizhang Bochi Nanhai Wenti Shang de Wailun (Foreign Minister Yang Jiechi Refutes Fallacies on the South China Sea Issue)" (Beijing: PRC MoFA, July 25, 2010), http://www.mfa.gov.cn/chn//pds/wjb/wjbz/zyhd/t719371.htm.

139. See Michael Swaine, "China's Assertive Behavior (Part One: On 'Core Interests')," *China Leadership Monitor* 34 (Winter 2010), https://carnegieendowment.org/2010/11/15/china-s-assertive-behavior-part-one-on-core-interests-pub-41937. The whole South China Sea as a core interest meme was discussed in detail.

140. "China Seeks Reduction in Surveillance Ship Activity for Successful Summit," US State Department cable #09BEIJING781, March 25, 2009, Wikileaks, https://wikileaks.org/plusd/cables/09BEIJING781_a.html.

141. "Yuenan Guanfang Wangzhan zao Heike Gongji, Wangye shang Chuxian Zhongguo Guoqi" (Vietnamese Official Website Attacked By Hackers, the Chinese National Flag Appears on the Website), *Global Times*, June 9, 2011, http://world.huanqiu.com/roll/2011-06/1744628.html.

142. For examples of these harsh criticisms, see Andrew Chubb, "Chinese Popular Nationalism and PRC Policy in the South China Sea" (PhD diss., University of Western Australia, 2016), 212–13.

143. For the reposting and the thread of comments, see http://bbs.tianya.cn/post-worldlook-360420-1.shtml, accessed May 8, 2018. Wu was a renowned Chinese diplomat who served as the MoFA spokesperson, Ambassador to the Netherlands, Geneva, and France, as well as President of China Foreign Affairs University.

144. This comment was one of many posted on a short video clip published by Phoenix TV. See "Zhongguo Wo San Wangpai, Ding Nanhai Daju (China's Three Trump Cards Will Determine the Outcome on the South China Sea)," ifeng, June 30, 2011, http://v.ifeng.com/v/sanwangpai/index.shtml#e9253db1-9ecd-4e1c-9af3-abb78271a2d4.

145. Ji You, "The PLA and Diplomacy: Unraveling Myths about the Military Role in Foreign Policy Making," *Journal of Contemporary China* 23, no. 86 (March 4, 2014): 251.

146. Ibid., 251.

147. "1 More Vietnam Ship Harassed By Foreign Vessels," VietnamNet Bridge, June 1, 2011, http://english.vietnamnet.vn/fms/society/8634/1-more-vietnam-ship-harassed-by-foreign-vessels.html.

148. Wang Qian, "Maritime Surveillance Forces Will Expand," *China Daily*, May 2, 2011, 2, http://www.chinadaily.com.cn/china/2011-05/02/content_12429245.htm.

149. "Hai Yang Shi You 720 Wutanchuan gei Nanhai Zuo 'Heci' Jiancha (Hai Yang Shi You 720 Gives 'MRI' Scans to the South China Sea)," *People's Daily*, June 13, 2013, 2, http://cpc.people.com.cn/n/2013/0613/c83083-21821325.html.

150. "Notification of First Batch of Blocks in Offshore China Available for Foreign Cooperation in Year 2011," China National Offshore Oil Corporation (CNOOC), May 24, 2011, http://www.cnooc.com.cn/art/2014/9/25/art_6241_1148001.html.

151. Chubb, "Chinese Popular Nationalism and PRC Policy in the South China Sea," 232.

152. China's Defense Minister Liang Guanglie claimed no involvement of the PLA in the May 26 incident at the Shangri-La Dialogue on June 3–5, 2011 in Singapore.

153. Chubb, "Chinese Popular Nationalism and PRC Policy in the South China Sea," 468.

154. The Reed Bank incident is a brief confrontation between two Chinese patrol boats and a Philippine survey ship on March 2, 2011. This study does not include it as a separate case, because it failed to escalate into a crisis and resembles many other similar episodes that occur frequently in the South China Sea. It is, however, similar to the Sino-Vietnamese

cable-cutting incidents that followed within the same year, so in a way it is still covered by this analysis.

155. Carlyle Thayer reports that another incident occurred on June 30, in which "Vietnamese escort vessels were able to chase off the Chinese boats." But this incident has been "kept under wraps by Vietnamese authorities." See Carlyle A. Thayer, "Background Briefing: Recent Naval Exercises in the South China Sea," Strategic Advice and Geopolitical Estimates (SAGE) International Australia, June 7, 2011, 1–5, https://www.files.ethz.ch/isn/131071/Background%20Briefing.pdf.

156. Thayer, "Background Briefing," 1–2.

157. "2011 Nian Zhongguo Haijian Da Shi Ji" (2011 China Marine Surveillance Memorabilia), Xinhua News, June 28, 2012, http://guoqing.china.com.cn/2012-06/28/content_25756 969.htm.

158. Chubb, "Chinese Popular Nationalism and PRC Policy in the South China Sea," 468. Chubb quotes Reilly's definition of a wave of mobilization as a "rapid shift in public opinion and popular emotions, growing political activism, and expanded sensationalist coverage in popular media and on the Internet," See Reilly, Strong Society, Smart State, 24.

159. "No Room to Back Off, China Says on Disputed Islands," Jakarta Post, November 10, 2012. Quoted in Chubb, "Chinese Popular Nationalism and PRC Policy in the South China Sea," 401.

160. Wu Shicun and Fu Ying, "South China Sea: How We Got to This Stage," The National Interest, May 9, 2016, https://nationalinterest.org/feature/south-china-sea-how-we-got-stage-16118.

161. Jojo Malig, "Chinese hackers attack more Philippine websites," ABC-CBN News, May 12, 2012, http://news.abs-cbn.com/nation/05/12/12/chinese-hackers-attack-more-philipp ine-websites.

162. Chubb, "Chinese Popular Nationalism and PRC Policy in the South China Sea," 283.

163. Carlyle A. Thayer, "Standoff in the South China Sea," YaleGlobal Online, June 12, 2012, http://yaleglobal.yale.edu/content/standoff-south-china-sea.

164. "Chinese Patrol Ship Yuzheng-310 Reaches Waters off Scarborough Shoal," The China Times, April 20, 2012, http://thechinatimes.com/online/2012/04/3107.html.

165. Alexis Romero, "Chinese Boats Crowding Shoal," Philippine Star, May 3, 2012, https://www.philstar.com/headlines/2012/05/03/802659/chinese-boats-crowding-shoal.

166. Jane Perlez, "Philippines and China Ease Tensions in Rift at Sea," New York Times, June 18, 2012, https://www.nytimes.com/2012/06/19/world/asia/beijing-and-manila-ease-tensions-in-south-china-sea.html; Ely Ratner, "Learning the Lessons of Scarborough Reef," The National Interest, November 21, 2013, http://nationalinterest.org/comment ary/learning-the-lessons-scarborough-reef-9442; Richard C. Paddock, "Chinese Vessels Leave Disputed Fishing Grounds in South China Sea," New York Times, October 28, 2016, http://www.nytimes.com/2016/10/29/world/asia/south-china-sea-scarborough-shoal. html?_r=0.

167. Angela Poh, "The Myth of Chinese Sanctions over South China Sea Disputes," Washington Quarterly 40, no. 1 (2017): 143–65.

168. "Guojia Zhijian Zongju dui Jinkou Feilvbin Shuiguo Jiaqiang Jianyan Jianyi" (General Administration of Quality Supervision, Inspection and Quarantine Stepping Up Quarantine of Imported Philippine Fruits), People's Daily, May 11, 2012, 4; "Guojia Lvyouju Tixing Chufei Biyao Zhongguo Youke Ying Zanhuan Fufei Lvyou" (National Tourism Administration Advises Chinese Tourists to Suspend Travel to the Philippines),

286 Appendix 2

People's Daily, May 14, 2012, 4; "Nanhang Tiaojian Fufei Hangban" (China Southern Airlines Reduces Flights to the Philippines), *People's Daily*, May 15, 2012, 10.

169. "National Tourism Administration Advises Chinese Tourists to Suspend Travel to the Philippines," 4.

170. "Half of Chinese Foresee Military Dispute with Japan, Genron NPO Opinion Poll Shows," June 28, 2012, The 8th Japan-China Public Opinion Poll, http://www.genron-npo.net/en/opinion_polls/archives/5264.html.

171. See, for example, "Japanese PM Noda Vows Not to Visit Yasukuni Shrine During Tenure," Xinhua News, September 2, 2011, http://www.chinadaily.com.cn/world/2011-09/02/content_13609646.htm; PRC MoFA, "Hu Jintao Meets with Japanese Prime Minister Yoshihiko Noda" (Beijing: PRC MoFA, November 11, 2011), http://www.fmprc.gov.cn/mfa_eng/topics_665678/hjtAPEC_665728/t877239.shtml; "Noda Calls for Early Resumption of Gas Treaty Talks with China," *Japan Times*, November 14, 2011, https://www.japantimes.co.jp/news/2011/11/14/national/noda-calls-for-early-resumption-of-gas-treaty-talks-with-china/#.WbqeK8iGNPZ; Zhang Yunbi, "Japan PM Visit, Military Exchanges Show Warming Ties," *China Daily*, December 15, 2011, http://www.chinadaily.com.cn/cndy/2011-12/15/content_14268242.htm; Li Xiaokun and Zhang Yunbi, "China, Japan Keen to Improve Ties," *China Daily*, December 27, 2011, http://usa.chinadaily.com.cn/world/2011-12/27/content_14331920.htm.

172. Tang Jiaxuan, "Uphold Larger Interest and Manage Crisis for Sound and Steady Development of China-Japan Relations," Speech at the International Seminar on the 40th Anniversary of Normalization of China-Japan Relations Organized by the Chinese Academy of Social Sciences, August 29, 2012, http://www.fmprc.gov.cn/mfa_eng/wjdt_665385/zyjh_665391/t980262.shtml.

173. Peter Ford, "China and Japan face off: Tiny islands, big dispute," *The Christian Science Monitor*, October 2, 2012, https://www.csmonitor.com/World/Asia-Pacific/2012/1002/China-and-Japan-face-off-Tiny-islands-big-dispute.

174. The search was based on the key word "Zhong Yin Bian Jing (Sino-Indian border)."

175. See Bharti Jain, "China Sore with India Bid to Build Infrastructure along LAC," *The Economic Times*, April 25, 2013, http://economictimes.indiatimes.com/news/politics/and/nation/China-sore-with-Indian-bid-to-build-infrastructure-along-LAC/articles how/19719917.cms.

176. PRC MoFA, "The Operation of the HYSY 981 Drilling Rig: Vietnam's Provocation and China's Position" (Beijing: PRC MoFA, June 8, 2014), http://www.fmprc.gov.cn/mfa_eng/zxxx_662805/t1163264.shtml; Vietnam MoFA, "Remarks by FM Spokesman Le Hai Binh on 4th May 2014" (Hanoi: Vietnam MoFA, May 4, 2014), http://www.mofa.gov.vn/en/tt_baochi/pbnfn/ns140505232230.

177. Kate Hodal and Jonathan Kaiman, "At Least 21 Dead in Vietnam Anti-China Protests over Oil Rig," *The Guardian*, May 15, 2014, http://www.theguardian.com/world/2014/may/15/vietnam-anti-china-protests-oil-rig-dead-injured.

178. "Vietnam Anti-China Protest: Factories Burnt," *BBC News*, May 14, 2014, http://www.bbc.com/news/world-asia-27403851.

179. Author interviews, May 29, 2017, May 31, 2017 and June 1, 2017, Beijing.

180. *South China Sea Public Opinion Newsletter* (Nanjing: Collaborative Innovation Center of South China Sea Studies, Nanjing University, January 2014 to April 2014)

181. Brian Eyler, "The Anti-Vietnam Protest That Didn't Happen," May 19, 2014, http://www.eastbysoutheast.com/anti-vietnam-protest-didnt-happen/.

182. Chubb, "Chinese Popular Nationalism and PRC Policy in the South China Sea," 191–92.
183. PRC MoFA, "China and Vietnam Held Plenary Meeting of the Governmental Delegation on Border Negotiation" (Beijing: PRC MoFA, December 7, 2013), http://www.fmprc.gov.cn/mfa_eng/zxxx_662805/t1108277.shtml.
184. Author interview, May 31, 2017, Beijing.
185. Author interview, June 2, 2017, Beijing.
186. PRC MoFA, "Foreign Ministry Spokesperson Hua Chunying's Regular Press Conference on June 11, 2014" (Beijing: PRC MoFA, June 11, 2014), http://www.fmprc.gov.cn/mfa_eng/xwfw_665399/s2510_665401/t1164598.shtml.
187. PRC MoFA, "Waijiaobu Bianhaisi Fusizhang Yi Xianliang jiu Zhongjiannan Xiangmu Juxing Chuifenghui" (Deputy Director General of the Department of Boundary and Ocean Affairs Yi Xianliang's Press Conference on the Zhongjiannan Project) (Beijing: PRC MoFA, June 14, 2014), http://www.fmprc.gov.cn/web/wjb_673085/zzjg_673183/t1165600.shtml.
188. "Vietnam, China Agree to Restore, Develop Ties," *Nhan Dan*, August 27, 2014, http://en.nhandan.org.vn/politics/external-relations/item/2753802-na-chairman-meets-young-japanese-parliamentarians.html.
189. International Crisis Group, "Stirring up the South China Sea (III): A Fleeting Opportunity for Calm," May 7, 2015, 10, https://www.crisisgroup.org/asia/north-east-asia/china/stirring-south-china-sea-iii-fleeting-opportunity-calm.https://www.crisisgroup.org/asia/north-east-asia/china/stirring-south-china-sea-iii-fleeting-opportunity-calm.
190. Author interviews, June 2, 2017, Beijing, and November 20, 2017, Washington, DC.
191. International Crisis Group, "Stirring up the South China Sea (III): A Fleeting Opportunity for Calm," 5.
192. "Vietnam to Propose Oil, Gas Development with Japan," Thanh Nien News, June 13, 2012, http://www.thanhniennews.com/business/vietnam-to-propose-oil-gas-development-with-japan-media-6807.html.
193. "Zhonghaiyou zai Nanhai Kaifang Jiuge Qukuai yu Waiguo Gongsi Hezuo Kaifang" (CNOOC Opens Tender to Foreign Companies for 9 Oil and Gas Blocks), *Tencent News*, June 26, 2012, https://news.qq.com/a/20120626/001565.htm.
194. These wordings have been mentioned at multiple occasions, for example see PRC MoFA, "Foreign Ministry Spokesperson Hua Chunying's Regular Press Conference on June 18, 2014" (Beijing: PRC MoFA, June 19, 2014), http://www.fmprc.gov.cn/mfa_eng/xwfw_665399/s2510_665401/t1166826.shtml.
195. PRC MoFA, "Foreign Ministry Spokesperson Hua Chunying's Regular Press Conference on June 17, 2014" (Beijing: PRC MoFA, June 17, 2014), http://www.fmprc.gov.cn/mfa_eng/xwfw_665399/s2510_665401/t1166317.shtml.
196. Vietnam MoFA, "The 6th Regular Press Conference" (Hanoi: Vietnam MoFA, June 28, 2014), http://www.mofa.gov.vn/en/tt_baochi/tcbc/ns140628000810.
197. Edmund Malesky and Jason Morris-Jung, "Vietnam in 2014: Uncertainty and Opportunity in the Wake of the HS-981 Crisis," *Asian Survey* 55, no. 1 (2015): 172.
198. Poh, "The Myth of Chinese Sanctions over South China Sea Disputes," 153.
199. The WITS incorporates data from the World Bank, the UNSD Commodity Trade (UN Comtrade) (UN Comtrade) database, the WTO's Integrated Data Base (IDB) and others. There is only trivial difference between the WITS data and the GSOV data. No data source is cited with the Malesky and Morris-Jung claim.
200. Poh, "The Myth of Chinese Sanctions over South China Sea Disputes," 153.

288 Appendix 2

201. Ibid., 154.
202. Hari Kumar, "India: Standoff with China Eases," *New York Times*, September 27, 2014, https://www.nytimes.com/2014/09/27/world/asia/india-china-ladakh-dispute.html; Sanjeev Miglani, "Insight: With Canal and Hut, India Stands Up to China on Disputed Frontier," *Reuters*, September 25, 2014, https://in.reuters.com/article/india-china-modi-chumar-army-ladakh/insight-with-canal-and-hut-india-stands-up-to-china-on-dispu ted-frontier-idINKCN0HJ2FU20140924.
203. PRC Ministry of Defense, "Zhongyin Shuangfang Youxiao Guankong Bianjing Diqu Jushi (Effective Control of the Sino-Indian Border)," September 25, 2014, http://news.mod.gov. cn/headlines/2014-09/25/content_4539874.htm.
204. Wu and Fu, "South China Sea."
205. Yesha Jiang and Jiaojiang Luo, "Hulianwang Meijie Zhiyu Guojia Rentong de Goujian: Yi Nanhai Zhongcai'an Yuqing Chuanbo Wei Li (The Internet Media and the Construction of National Identity—Using the South China Sea Arbitration Case as an Example)," *Xinwenjie (The News World)* 24 (2016).
206. Austin Ramzy, "KFC Targeted in Protests Over South China Sea," *New York Times*, July 19, 2016, https://www.nytimes.com/2016/07/20/world/asia/south-china-sea-protests-kfc.html.
207. Zhao Jinsong, "Ying Jiajin Yulun Yingdui 'Feilvbin Nanhai Zhongcai'an'" (China Must Strengthen Media Counter-Measures Against the Philippines' South China Sea Arbitration Case), *Gonggong Waijiao Jikan* (*Public Diplomacy Quarterly*), No. 2 (2016).
208. Author interviews, Beijing, China, May 29, 2017.
209. Author interviews, Beijing, China, May 26, 2017 and May 29, 2017.
210. Lally Weymouth, "Interview with Albert del Rosario: You Will Have Chaos and Anarchy," *Foreign Policy*, October 5, 2015, https://foreignpolicy.com/2015/10/05/you-will-have-chaos-and-anarchy-albert-del-rosario-philippines-south-china-sea/.
211. Author interviews, Beijing, China, May 26, 2017 and May 29, 2017.
212. "Xi Congratulates new Philippine President on Inauguration," Xinhua News, June 30, 2016, http://www.xinhuanet.com/english/2016-06/30/c_135478948.htm.
213. Consulate-General of the People's Republic of China in Chicago, "Foreign Ministry Spokesperson Lu Kang's Regular Press Conference on July 14, 2016" (Beijing: Ministry of Foreign Affairs of the People's Republic of China (PRC MoFA), July 14, 2016), http://www. chinaconsulatechicago.org/eng/fyrth/t1381622.htm.
214. PRC MoFA, "Foreign Ministry Spokesperson Hua Chunying's Regular Press Conference on May 19" (Beijing: PRC MoFA, July 14, 2016), http://www.fmprc.gov.cn/mfa_eng/xwfw _665399/s2510_665401/t1463588.shtml.
215. PRC MoFA, "Joint Statement of the Foreign Ministers of ASEAN Member States and China on the Full and Effective Implementation of the Declaration on the Conduct of Parties in the South China Sea" (Beijing: PRC MoFA, July 25, 2016), http://www.fmprc. gov.cn/nanhai/eng/zcfg_1/t1384245.htm.
216. PRC MoFA, "The 13th Senior Officials' Meeting on the Implementation of the DOC Held in Manzhouli, Inner Mongolia" (Beijing: PRC MoFA, August 16, 2016), http://www. fmprc.gov.cn/nanhai/eng/wjbxw_1/t1389619.htm.
217. "Filipino Fisherman Back in Disputed South China Sea Shoal after Duterte's Beijing Pivot," *South China Morning Post*, October 30, 2016, http://www.scmp.com/news/asia/southe ast-asia/article/2041371/filipino-fisherman-back-disputed-south-china-sea-shoal.

218. PRC MoFA, "Foreign Ministry Spokesperson Geng Shuang's Remarks on Indian Border Troops Overstepping China-India Boundary at Sikkim Section" (Beijing: PRC MoFA, June 26, 2017), http://www.fmprc.gov.cn/mfa_eng/xwfw_665399/s2510_665401/t1473280.shtml.

219. "The Sino-Indian Standoff for Nearly 30 Days—A Most Comprehensive Public Opinion Analysis," Qingbo Yuqing (*Qingbo Public Opinion*), July 7, 2017, http://home.gsdata.cn/news-report/articles/1881.html.

220. PRC MoFA, "The Facts and China's Position Concerning the Indian Border Troops' Crossing of the China-India Boundary in the Sikkim Sector into the Chinese Territory" (Beijing: PRC MoFA, August 2, 2017), http://news.xinhuanet.com/english/2017-08/02/c_136494625.htm.

221. For the editorials, see Zhong Sheng, "Jielu Yinjun Feifa Yuejie Zhenxiang" (Exposing the Truth of the Illegal Border Transgression by the Indian Army), *People's Daily*, August 4, 2017, 3; Wu Liming, "Gei Yindu de Sandian 'Zhonggao' (Three Pieces of Advice to India)," Xinhua News, http://news.xinhuanet.com/world/2017-08/03/c_1121427634.htm, accessed April 29, 2020; Jun Sheng, "Zhongguo Lingtu Zhuquan Jueburong Qinfan" (China's Territorial Sovereignty Inviolable), *PLA Daily*, August 3, 2017, 4; "Yin Ying Liji Wutiaojian Chehui Yuejie Budui (India Should Withdraw Its Transgressive Troops Immediately and Unconditionally)," *Jiefang Daily*, August 3, 2017, 3.

222. Author interviews, January 18, 2018, Beijing.

223. "Five Months on, Understanding Doklam 'Disengagement,' a Few Other Issues," *Indian Express*, January 22, 2018, https://indianexpress.com/article/explained/five-months-on-understanding-doklam-disengagement-a-few-other-issues-india-china-5033943/.

224. "China Quietly & Cleverly Finds a New Route to S. Doklam, 7 Months After India Stopped It," *The Print*, March 19, 2018, https://theprint.in/defence/china-quietly-finds-new-route-to-s-doklam-7-months-after-india-stopped-it/43070/.

225. Given the recent nature of this case, any assessment will naturally be approached with caution due to the limited evidence available. Regardless of how the case is initially interpreted, it should be reassessed as new evidence emerges.

APPENDIX 3

Borderline Media Campaigns

The media coverage on four cases (#9, #13, #15, and #18) hovers near the established quantitative benchmarks for media campaigns—namely two front-page articles and ten relevant articles per month. Closer examination reveals that a media campaign was indeed present during the 1988 Sino-Vietnamese clash in the Spratlys, but not in the 2014 Sino-Vietnamese Oil Rig Standoff.

The 1988 media campaign was part of a larger effort, and the specific campaign related to the Spratlys clash had lower volume because the state determined that further coverage of this specific dispute was unnecessary within the wider context of the war. Conversely, the 2014 standoff saw no deliberate state efforts to highlight the dispute. The state allowed moderate commercial media coverage, but even without state intervention, the provocative events naturally attracted considerable media attention.

The media campaigns during the 2010 Sino-Japanese Boat Incident near the Senkaku/Diaoyu Islands and the 2012 Sino-Philippines Scarborough Shoal Standoff provide an intriguing mix of media amplification and censorship. These two cases showcase complex media strategies that deftly navigate the boundaries of defined media campaigns, illustrating the state's tactical use of media as an instrument to both incite and manage public sentiment.

Case #9. 1988 Sino-Vietnamese Clash in the Spratlys

The media coverage is on the border of media campaign benchmarks. There was salience but no volume. *People's Daily* published seven front-page articles in a short period of 65 days, but only a total of 10 articles. In other words, despite the significant number of articles in salient places, other spaces in the newspapers were not predominantly about the dispute.

This case is atypical because it occurred in the middle of a major war—the Sino-Vietnamese border war, and the war's accompanying, decade-long media campaign. The media was preoccupied by the larger war effort. Additional volume of general articles about this particular dispute may have been deemed unnecessary in the larger context of the war.

Case #13. 2010 Sino-Japanese Boat Incident near Senkaku/Diaoyu Islands

During the 57 days of the crisis, *People's Daily* published a total of 31 articles on the dispute, only two of which appeared in the front pages. These numbers bordered on the benchmarks for a media campaign. There was volume, but no salience.

Further investigation reveals that China did make conscious efforts to publicize the dispute, yet with clear reservations. In addition to *People's Daily*'s reporting, CCTV's flagship primetime news program, Xinwen Lianbo (Network News), covered the dispute on four evenings between September 13 and October 5, 2010. This was unusual since the program rarely covered foreign disputes. But the coverage on the September 18 public events commemorating the Japanese

292 Appendix 3

invasion in World War II failed to mention the ongoing territorial crisis. A leaked policy directive on *China Digital Times* confirms that this was intentional. The directive told media outlets to report the commemoration events as "business as usual" and "[they] should not be connected to the recent incident involving the arrest of the fishing boat crew."[1] CCTV 10 p.m. Wanjian Xinwen (Evening News) had more coverage of the dispute, broadcasting events on eleven out of twenty nights between September 11 and September 30. CCTV also featured the issue in its "Xin Shiye (New Horizon)" program on October 20 and 21.[2]

Several leaked state directives dated between September 10 and October 19 summarize the state's three main media policies. First, the state ordered the media to use the Xinhua copies only, and not to conduct their own interviews or report their own stories.[3] This was validated by the fact that 14 of the 31 *People's Daily* articles were copies of Ministry of Foreign Affairs (MoFA) statements. Second, the state instructed the media not to place this reportage on prominent sections or during prime times.[4] This could explain the small number of front-page articles and the dearth of primetime TV coverage. Third, the state did not allow online discussions or comments, and requested that any inciting or action-driven posts be censored.[5]

Case #15. 2012 Sino-Philippines Scarborough Shoal Standoff

This was again a borderline campaign. During the 53 days of the crisis, *People's Daily* published a total of 64 articles on the topic, with only one article on the front page. That one front-page article was on the launch of a deep-water drilling rig Hai Yang Shi You 981 in the South China Sea, rather than direct coverage of the crisis. These numbers border the criteria established for a media campaign. There was volume, but no salience.

On closer inspection, I find that Beijing did make deliberate efforts to publicize the dispute. However, like the Sino-Japanese fishing boat incident in 2010, the media efforts were lukewarm. During the crisis, the Chinese MoFA had twenty-nine press conferences addressing the issue. Many of the questions at these press conferences were pre-arranged. The state media reporting mirrored MoFA statements. CCTV Network News did not mention the standoff, but CCTV Evening News broadcast the issue every other night from April 11 to 18. Vice Foreign Minister Fu Ying delivered a stern message to the Philippine Embassy Charge D'affaires on May 7, accusing the Philippines of making "serious mistakes" and threatening that China has "made all preparations to respond to any escalation of the situation by the Philippine side."[6] The message was publicized on the MoFA website the next day and a flurry of media reports followed. On May 8, CCTV covered the issue again in the 10pm Evening News and featured the issue in its "Huanqiu Shixian (Global View)" program with expert commentators.[7] *People's Daily* published four articles on May 9. Although none was on the front page, these articles did consume half of an entire page three. *China Youth Daily*, *PLA Daily* and *China Newsweek* all had headlines on the dispute in the following days. To sum up, media coverage was comprehensive, but there was little on front pages or in prime time. Although leaked policy directives are not available, we can tell from reporting patterns that this was a lukewarm media campaign with clear reservations, if it counts as a campaign at all.

Case #18. 2014 Sino-Vietnamese Oil Rig Standoff

See detailed case study in Chapter 5.

Notes

1. Zhenlibu (The Truth Department), "Diaoyudao Zhuangchuan Shijian (Diaoyu Islands Boat Collision Incident)," *China Digital Times*, September 17, 2010, https://goo.gl/nCFyAH.
2. "Xunhang Diaoyudao (Patrolling the Diaoyu Islands)," Xinshiye (New Horizon), CCTV, October 20 and 21, 2010, http://tv.cntv.cn/video/C22733/fa3ef7a9ae6e45ad6cc07d8e9f53b f1d and http://tv.cntv.cn/video/C22733/f6af12a02f3946e406f6a6892e7dffd2.
3. Zhenlibu (The Truth Department), "Guanyu Diaoyudao Zhongri Yuchuan Jiufen Shijian (About the Sino-Japanese Boat Incident near Diaoyu Islands)," *China Digital Times*, September 10, 2010, https://goo.gl/1ZCpBc.
4. Zhenlibu (The Truth Department), "Guanyu Rifang Renyuan Shanchuang Wo Junshi Jinqu (About Japanese Citizens Illegally Entering Restricted Military Area)," *China Digital Times*, September 30, 2010, https://goo.gl/is5UnK.
5. Zhenlibu (The Truth Department), "Guanyu Riben Fanghuai Wo Bei Kouya Chuanzhang Yi Shi (About Japan Releasing Detained Chinese Captain)," *China Digital Times*, September 24, 2010, https://goo.gl/8UQuLh.
6. "Waijiaobu Fubuzhang Fu Ying jiu Huangyandao Shijian Zaici Yuejian Feilvbin Zhuhua Shiguan Lingshi Daiban (Vice Foreign Minister Fu Ying met with Charge D'affaires of the Philippine Embassy in China Again over the Incident at Huangyan Island)," https://www.fmprc.gov.cn/web/zyxw/t929746.shtml, accessed March 12, 2019.
7. "Zhuanjia Jianyi Baoli Xingdong Huiying Feilvbin dui Huangyandao Gaiming Chaibiao (Experts Recommend Violent Response to Philippines Changing of Huangyan Island's Name and Demolishing the Markers)," Huanqiu Shixian (Global View), CCTV, May 9, 2012, https://news.qq.com/a/20120509/000261.htm.

APPENDIX 4

Deviant Cases

Contrary to the expectations of the misalignment theory, all three deviant cases were predicted to lack media campaigns due to the alignment between the state and society. Yet media campaigns were observed in each of these cases. This document provides an in-depth analysis of the three deviant cases, seeking possible explanations for the existence of media campaigns despite the anticipated alignment.

Case #1. 1959 Sino-Indian Border Clashes at Longju and Kongka Pass

Based on the case description, the case was evaluated by raters as having weak public opinion and moderate state policy intent. According to the logic of the (mis)alignment theory, given the alignment between the public and the state, the state should not have pursued a media campaign. However, contrary to the theoretical expectation, the Chinese state did indeed initiate a media campaign, albeit a short-lived one.

Table A4.1 displays the number of relevant articles in the *People's Daily* during the 1959 campaign, including several months before and after for contextual comparison. By applying the operational definition of a media campaign—a minimum of two front-page articles and ten

Table A4.1 Number of *People's Daily* Front-Page and All-Relevant Articles during the 1959 Sino-Indian Border Dispute

Year	Month	No. of Front-Page Articles	No. of All Articles
1959	Mar	0	0
1959	Apr	3	0
1959	May	2	1
1959	Jun	1	0
1959	Jul	0	0
1959	Aug	0	0
1959	Sep	10	62
1959	Oct	3	8
1959	Nov	4	21
1959	Dec	1	8
1960	Jan	1	8
1960	Feb	0	3

296   Appendix 4

articles on any page per month, with a one-month lapse permitted—it can be inferred that the campaign lasted from September through November.

In September, *People's Daily* published an impressive 62 articles related to the topic, with 19 gracing the front pages. However, a significant drop in the number of articles was observed from September to October. October fails to meet the minimum requirement of articles on any page, thus it is considered a lapse month. The numbers in November saw a minor increase but fell short of the September volume and signaled the end of the campaign. Thus, the campaign overall was moderate and brief, with a cumulative total of 91 articles, including 17 front-page features, across a span of 77 days.

Why did the Chinese government propagandize the issue, even when the public was aligned with its moderate policy preference? First, it is important to note that China had been remarkably quiet for nearly half a year, even as an aggressive India media campaign attacked it from March onward, after the Tibetan uprising and the Dalai Lama's flight to India. Nevertheless, as shown in Table A4.1, *People's Daily* published only sparse articles on the subject. In a conversation between Chinese Vice Minister Zeng Yongquan and Charge d'Affaires of the Soviet Embassy in China, S. Antonov, Antonov commented that "China kept silent even though the whole world was fussing about it."[1]

Second, the Chinese media campaign in reaction to the Indian one was brief and geared toward clarifying China's position on the issue. Wu Lengxi reveals that "the Party's original intention was not to use the border incident to accuse India. We did not want to make a great deal of it. But India publicized it first, then slandered China, and accused China of being an 'invader,' whipping up an anti-China wave around the World. This forces us to respond; we cannot but debate with Nehru . . . This is against our will, but out of necessity."[2] In Wu's recollection, Mao quickly brought the campaign to a stop and said, "Before putting it to a stop, we should publish an editorial . . . to clarify that our engagement in this debate is *against our will*. The debate has its benefits—it can present both sides' positions and expose the truth on the border issue. But we do not want to continue the debate; we still hope to resolve the issue through negotiations."[3]

Third, with the Sino-Soviet split and the Soviet's siding with India on the dispute, China faced an increasingly hostile environment. Chinese leaders' threat perception changed around September 1959 as two incidents elevated the salience of the dispute. With India's media campaign, the pressure for China to respond reached a tipping point. And during this time, it became clear that the Soviet Union was siding with India. The first sign was a Soviet News Agency TASS statement that did not incorporate the Chinese opinion.[4] Moscow's attitude became clear when Khrushchev visited China on October 2 and criticized China's role in the dispute.[5] These factors augured a worsening security environment for China. Under these circumstances, China felt the need to prepare the public for an increasingly hostile environment, despite its moderate policy intention.

While the case outcome is not what the theory predicts, the fact that the Chinese campaign was an extremely delayed and restrained one and that the Chinese government felt the need to prepare the public for an increasingly hostile environment are consistent with the fundamental logic of the (mis)alignment theory.

Case #9. 1988 Sino-Vietnamese Clash in the Spratlys

The case was evaluated by raters as having hawkish public opinion and hardline state policy intent. Given the alignment, what could have motivated a media campaign, albeit an ambiguous one amidst a larger war? China's domestic situation might explain this exceptional case. The Chinese government faced an existential legitimacy crisis in 1987 and 1988. Economically, China's failed price reform had led to an unprecedented inflation crisis. Retail prices went up by 7.3 percent in 1987 and some cities had double-digit inflation. Price increases, especially on

Appendix 4   **297**

food items, were steeper in 1988.[6] China's state-owned enterprise (SOE) reform also faced severe challenges. SOE profit losses surged sharply in the second half of the 1980s. Politically, the democracy movement continued to grow, often challenging the Socialist ideology. Liberal intelligentsia became increasingly dissatisfied with the progress of political reform. Divisions between liberal reformists and conservatists, as they crystallized, continued to corrode elite unity. In the midst of these political trends, the 1986 student protest caused the abrupt leadership transition from Hu Yaobang to Zhao Ziyang, which sowed the seeds for the 1989 Tiananmen Massacre that shocked the world. With this legitimacy crisis at home, a diversionary explanation is highly plausible: the Chinese government used the foreign crisis as a diversion, however brief, away from its domestic troubles.

The case indeed satisfies the observable implications of the diversionary theory listed in Chapter 1. First, there was a domestic crisis. Second, the domestic crisis posed an existential threat to the survival of the Communist regime. Third, since the clash was offshore and brief, the foreign crisis was relatively easy to keep under control. Finally, the economic and political problems were not out in the open for discussion. There were only occasional innuendos; for example, articles that described government policies to stabilize prices and deepen reform, and commentaries opposing "bourgeois liberalization" and "total westernization." However, there was little to no direct coverage of either the economic or the political crisis. Only careful observers adept at reading between the lines might have gleaned the gravity of the situation.

Case #15. 2012 Sino-Philippines Scarborough Shoal Standoff

Some might argue by a diversionary logic that the state propaganda on the Scarborough Shoal standoff was to distract from the developing Bo Xilai scandal, which involved corruption charges against and the downfall of former party chief of Chongqing Province and a member of the Politburo, Bo Xilai. Nonetheless, since China had cheaper and easier ways to accomplish that goal if it wanted to, it is hard to believe that the Chinese government created the whole standoff or escalated the tension and embraced the risks involved just to divert public attention away from the Bo Xilai scandal. Besides, the fact that the state did not avoid publicizing the Bo Xilai scandal, and even featured the story in more prominent places than the Scarborough Shoal standoff, defies the diversionary logic. On April 11—the same day the Scarborough Shoal standoff was made public—*People's Daily* featured on its front page news of the Politburo's decision to try Bo Xilai, whereas it made no mention of the Scarborough Shoal crisis until the next day, on page three.[7] CCTV Network News, which did not mention the Scarborough Shoal crisis at all as it was unfolding, devoted a substantial amount of time to the Politburo's decision on Bo Xilai.[8]

The Chinese propaganda might be explained by the audience costs theory in this case. The case satisfies some observable implications of the audience costs theory listed in Chapter 1. First, negotiation to resolve the standoff was started on April 19, suspended by the Philippines on April 27, and reopened again on May 10. Throughout this period, China might have been using the harsh public rhetoric and public attention for coercive purposes—first to coerce the Philippine navy to back off, and then to stop the Philippines from involving the US and from stoking domestic nationalism, and also to urge the Philippines to return to the negotiations after the talk was suspended. Second, these demands were made public. *People's Daily* published commentaries and Chinese MoFA statements calling the Philippine navy ship to stop harassing Chinese fishing boats and leave the Scarborough Shoal, demanding the Philippine government be "consistent in words and deeds" and "restore peace and tranquility" in the disputed area.[9] The Chinese MoFA spokesperson Liu Weimin requested on April 27 that the Philippines "earnestly respect China's territorial sovereignty, and refrain from taking actions that aggravate and complicate matters."[10] *People's Daily* also cited a scholar's remark that the Philippines'

298 Appendix 4

actions would only lower the "possibility of a peaceful resolution," which served as an informal warning.[11]

However, other observable implications of an audience costs theory were not apparent. Some of these demands were specific but did not have clear deadlines. Only a few threats were made public and the only one mentioned above was insinuated through a quotation from a scholar; it was not voiced unambiguously and certainly could not hold the government accountable for implementation. There was little evidence that Manila believed at all that Beijing's hands were tied. The reserved nature of the media campaign also suggests limits on the extent to which a state is willing to engage audience costs, even if an audience costs logic might apply. This lends support to existing challenges to the audience costs theory in that the state rarely burns its bridges entirely.[12]

Notes

1. "Memorandum of Conversation Between Chinese Vice Foreign Minister Zeng Yongquan and Charge d'Affaires of the Embassy of the Soviet Union in China S. Antonov," September 10, 1959, History and Public Policy Program Digital Archive, PRC FMA 109-00873-12, 76–79, obtained by Dai Chaowu and translated by 7Brands, http://digitalarchive.wilsoncen ter.org/document/114757, accessed August 15, 2023.

2. Lengxi Wu, *Shi Nian Lunzhan, 1956–1966, Zhong Su Guanxi Huiyilu, (10-Year Polemical War, 1956–1966, A Memoir of Sino-Soviet Relations)*, vol. I (Beijing: Zhongyang Wenxian Chubanshe (Central Party Literature Press), 1999), 214.

3. Wu, *Shi Nian Lunzhan*, 215.

4. "Memorandum of Conversation Between Chinese Vice Foreign Minister Zeng Yongquan and Charge d'Affaires of the Embassy of the Soviet Union in China S. Antonov," 1959; also see Wu, *Shi Nian Lunzhan*, 213–14.

5. "Discussion between N.S. Khrushchev and Mao Zedong," 1959, Archive of the President of the Russian Federation (APRF), f. 52, op. 1, d. 499, ll. 1–33, copy in Volkogonov Collection, Manuscript Division, Library of Congress, Washington, DC, History and Public Policy Program Digital Archive, http://digitalarchive.wilsoncenter.org/document/112088, accessed August 15, 2023.

6. "China Economy Called Troubled Despite Reforms: Inflation Rages as Leaders Debate Future, CIA Says," *Los Angeles Times*, May 2, 1988, https://www.latimes.com/archives/la-xpm-1988-05-02-fi-1430-story.html.

7. "Firmly Support the Party Central Committee's Correct Decision," *People's Daily*, April 11, 2012, 1; "Zhongguo Haijianchuan Zhizhi Fei Junjian Saorao Wo Yuchuan (Chinese Marine Surveillance Ships Stops Philippine Naval Vessel Harassing Chinese Fishing Boats)," *People's Daily*, April 12, 2012, 3.

8. For CCTV Network News transcript on April 11, 2012, see http://cctv.cntv.cn/lm/xinwe nlianbo/20120411.shtml, accessed May 30, 2018.

9. "Chinese Maritime Surveillance Ship Stops Philippine Warships from Harassing Our Fishing Boats," 3; "Xiwang Feilvbin Yanxing Yizhi, shi Huangyandao Haiyu Huifu Heping Anning (Hope the Philippines' Words and Deeds Will Be Consistent to Restore Peace and Tranquility in the Scaborough Shoal Area)," *People's Daily*, May 1, 2012, 3.

10. "2012 Nian 4 Yue 27 Ri Waijiaobu Fayanren Liu Weimin Juxing Lixing Jizhehui (Ministry of Foreign Affairs Spokesperson Liu Weimin Holds Regular Press Conference on April 27,

2012)," Ministry of Foreign Affairs, April 27, 2012, https://www.mfa.gov.cn/web/fyrbt_673 021/jzhsl_673025/t927033.shtml.

11. "Fei Fang Judong Zhineng Jiangdi 'Shixian Heping Jiejue de Kenengxing' (The Philippines' Action Will Only Lower the 'Possibility of a Peaceful Resolution of the Incident')," *People's Daily*, May 9, 2012, 3.

12. Jack Snyder and Erica D. Borghard, "The Cost of Empty Threats: A Penny, Not a Pound," *American Political Science Review* 105, no. 3 (2011): 437–56; Marc Trachtenberg, "Audience Costs: An Historical Analysis," *Security Studies* 21, no. 1 (January 1, 2012): 3–42.

APPENDIX 5

Robustness Check Using the ANTUSD Dictionary

The results remain robust even when utilizing the ANTUSD dictionary, which incorporates valence intensity. This is demonstrated in Table A5.1 and Figures A5.1, A5.2, A5.3, and A5.4 presented below, where the overall trends remain consistent. Pacification campaigns exhibit significantly higher positive sentiment scores compared to mobilization campaigns, scoring 8.4 in contrast to 2.9. The confidence intervals clearly indicate a substantial difference between the two campaign types, establishing statistical significance. While the Sino-Indian border war in 1962 stands out as another exception among individual campaigns, the overall trend persists, with pacification campaigns consistently displaying more positive sentiment scores. These findings support and reinforce our initial hypotheses, suggesting that pacification and mobilization campaigns indeed differ in their valence.

Table A5.1 CMCTD Data Average ANTUSD Sentiment Scores

	Mobilization Campaigns	Pacification Campaigns
Sentiment Scores	2.9	8.4

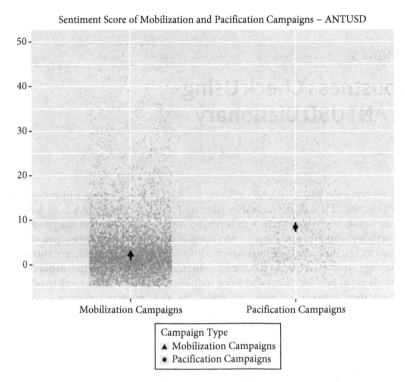

Figure A5.1 Comparison of ANTUSD Sentiment Scores with Data Distribution

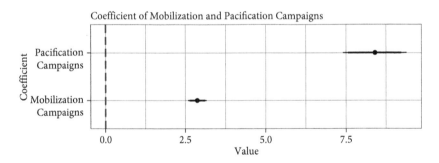

Figure A5.2 Predicted ANTUSD Sentiment Scores with 95% and 90% Confidence Intervals

Appendix 5   303

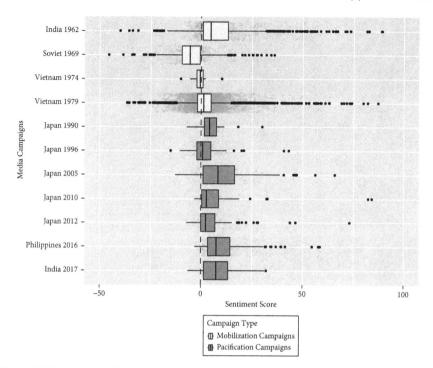

Figure A5.3 Boxplots of ANTUSD Sentiment Scores by Campaigns

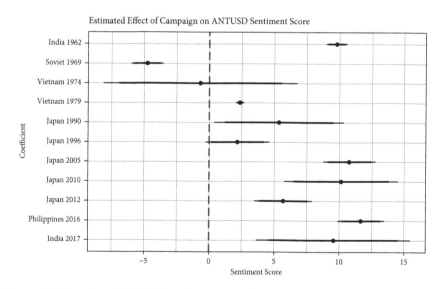

Figure A5.4 Predicted ANTUSD Sentiment Scores by Campaigns

APPENDIX 6

Fifty Most Frequent Words for Mobilization Campaigns and Pacification Campaigns

Figures A6.1 and A6.2 present the fifty most frequently occurring words in mobilization and pacification campaigns, respectively. These tables offer a valuable glimpse into the prominent themes and content found within these campaigns. The common words within each campaign type that convey specific themes, frames, or angles are bolded.

India 1962			Soviet 1969			Vietnam 1974			Vietnam 1979		
Word	Frequency	Percentage	Word	Frequency	Percentage	Word	Frequency	Percentage	Word	Frequency	Percentage
印度	10899	5.5%	苏修	4355	4.7%	西贡	54	4.0%	越南	47032	4.9%
中国	9779	4.9%	人民	3405	3.7%	中国	38	2.8%	柬埔寨	39758	4.1%
人民	5136	2.6%	中国	3228	3.5%	西沙群岛	34	2.5%	问题	14248	1.5%
中印	4522	2.3%	叛徒	2473	2.7%	领土	33	2.5%	人民	13524	1.4%
印度政府	3075	1.5%	集团	2399	2.6%	当局	31	2.3%	中国	13102	1.4%
国家	2744	1.4%	革命	2283	2.5%	南越	23	1.7%	苏联	13027	1.3%
中国政府	2415	1.2%	毛主席	1800	1.9%	主权	22	1.6%	泰国	12453	1.3%
边界问题	2334	1.2%	苏联	1512	1.6%	岛屿	21	1.6%	国家	10659	1.1%
美国	2179	1.1%	帝国主义	1307	1.4%	傀儡	21	1.6%	当局	7967	0.8%
帝国主义	1991	1.0%	领土	1196	1.3%	南沙群岛	21	1.6%	新华社	7688	0.8%
和平	1955	1.0%	沙皇	1058	1.1%	民	20	1.5%	越军	7419	0.8%
尼赫鲁	1903	1.0%	毛泽东思想	962	1.0%	艇	19	1.4%	军队	6980	0.7%
边界	1889	0.9%	伟大	956	1.0%	战斗	18	1.3%	民主	6571	0.7%
问题	1707	0.9%	反华	911	1.0%	集团	16	1.2%	会议	6225	0.6%
方面	1629	0.8%	无产阶级	903	1.0%	侵犯	16	1.2%	国际	6048	0.6%
边境	1592	0.8%	侵略	853	0.9%	渔民	15	1.1%	记者	5153	0.5%
建议	1592	0.8%	社会	829	0.9%	声明	14	1.0%	解决	5145	0.5%
解决	1578	0.8%	珍宝岛	760	0.8%	中华人民共和国	13	1.0%	侵略	5136	0.5%
谈判	1527	0.8%	武装挑衅	650	0.7%	革命	11	0.8%	地区	5128	0.5%
没有	1525	0.8%	修	644	0.7%	毛主席	11	0.8%	支持	5125	0.5%
总理	1522	0.8%	世界	627	0.7%	先锋	11	0.8%	和平	5043	0.5%
斗争	1503	0.8%	苏	622	0.7%	战士	11	0.8%	指出	4855	0.5%
新华社	1302	0.7%	社会主义	602	0.7%	中国政府	11	0.8%	难民	4486	0.5%
军队	1270	0.6%	美帝	563	0.6%	代表	10	0.7%	联合国	4476	0.5%
会议	1261	0.6%	伟大领袖	551	0.6%	舰艇	10	0.7%	没有	4362	0.5%
地区	1258	0.6%	斗争	540	0.6%	遣返	10	0.7%	报道	4102	0.4%
提出	1251	0.6%	侵犯	525	0.6%	谴责	10	0.7%	总理	3940	0.4%
社会主义	1249	0.6%	广大	521	0.6%	自卫	10	0.7%	美国	3876	0.4%
世界	1223	0.6%	胜利	518	0.6%	军队	9	0.7%	东盟	3837	0.4%
政府	1217	0.6%	起来	489	0.5%	立场	8	0.6%	世界	3830	0.4%
亚非	1215	0.6%	武装	489	0.5%	水兵	8	0.6%	要求	3769	0.4%
侵略	1191	0.6%	坚决	476	0.5%	岛	7	0.5%	继续	3753	0.4%
指出	1148	0.6%	国家	462	0.5%	非法	7	0.5%	撤军	3736	0.4%
和平解决	1140	0.6%	指出	460	0.5%	海上	7	0.5%	柬	3681	0.4%
政策	1119	0.6%	敌人	456	0.5%	军事挑衅	7	0.5%	政治	3638	0.4%
要求	1115	0.6%	战士	450	0.5%	民兵	7	0.5%	东南亚	3626	0.4%
边防部队	1105	0.6%	修正主义	448	0.5%	企图	7	0.5%	北京	3598	0.4%
支持	1092	0.5%	教导	447	0.5%	新华社	7	0.5%	发展	3594	0.4%
领土	1061	0.5%	挑衅	438	0.5%	战中	7	0.5%	方面	3507	0.4%
美帝国主义	1059	0.5%	反动派	435	0.5%	保卫祖国	6	0.4%	民柬	3473	0.4%
冲突	1052	0.5%	美帝国主义	434	0.5%	出动	6	0.4%	经济	3459	0.4%
华侨	1005	0.5%	地区	423	0.5%	东沙群岛	6	0.4%	代表	3437	0.4%
双方	1003	0.5%	文化大革命	393	0.4%	坚持	6	0.4%	举行	3422	0.4%
亚洲	980	0.5%	祖国	393	0.4%	评论	6	0.4%	部队	3419	0.4%
声明	966	0.5%	战舰	392	0.4%	入侵	6	0.4%	边境	3411	0.4%
团结	956	0.5%	彻底	384	0.4%	逃遁	6	0.4%	敌人	3355	0.3%
代表	949	0.5%	勾结	355	0.4%	张元林	6	0.4%	西哈努克	3349	0.3%
表示	940	0.5%	群众	345	0.4%	中华人民共和国外交部	6	0.4%	外长	3267	0.3%
采取	908	0.5%	同志	341	0.4%	中沙群岛	6	0.4%	曼谷	3185	0.3%
继续	895	0.4%	全世界	340	0.4%				斗争	3138	0.3%

Figure A6.1 Fifty Most Frequent Words for Mobilization Campaigns

Japan 2005			Japan 2010			Japan 2012			Philippines 2016			India 2017		
Word	Frequency	Percentage	Word	Frequency	Percentage	Word	Frequency	Percentage	Word	Frequency	Percentage	Word	Frequency	Percentage
日本	1103	3.6%	中国	256	4.9%	中国	1016	4.9%	中国	2264	5.5%	中国	132	4.5%
中国	826	2.7%	钓鱼岛	125	2.4%	钓鱼岛	977	4.7%	南海	2195	5.3%	印度	123	4.2%
历史	574	1.9%	发展	116	2.2%	日本	965	4.6%	仲裁	1171	2.8%	边界	97	3.3%
发展	567	1.9%	日方	103	2.0%	领土	391	1.9%	问题	1007	2.4%	锡金	75	2.5%
人民	406	1.3%	日本	89	1.7%	主权	332	1.6%	菲律宾	998	2.4%	国家	74	2.5%
问题	371	1.2%	问题	68	1.3%	问题	313	1.5%	仲裁庭	802	1.9%	金砖	70	2.4%
国家	307	1.0%	温总理	65	1.2%	岛屿	245	1.2%	国际	723	1.8%	中印	58	2.0%
中日关系	271	0.9%	领土	59	1.1%	历史	207	1.0%	公约	711	1.7%	条约	57	1.9%
两国	258	0.8%	关系	55	1.1%	发展	190	0.9%	解决	703	1.7%	领土	55	1.9%
和平	238	0.8%	国家	53	1.0%	国家	190	0.9%	美国	633	1.5%	印方	55	1.9%
世界	215	0.7%	表示	52	1.0%	附属	188	0.9%	国家	621	1.5%	越界	54	1.8%
合作	206	0.7%	附属	52	1.0%	日方	166	0.8%	争端	577	1.4%	地区	46	1.6%
亚洲	201	0.7%	合作	52	1.0%	国际	155	0.7%	国际法	570	1.4%	边界线	44	1.5%
关系	200	0.7%	两国	47	0.9%	海域	153	0.7%	主权	512	1.2%	边防部队	40	1.4%
重要	196	0.6%	主权	47	0.9%	岛	138	0.7%	裁决	473	1.1%	安全	39	1.3%
友好	195	0.6%	和平	42	0.8%	表示	137	0.7%	争议	466	1.1%	国际	38	1.3%
表示	183	0.6%	诺贝尔	40	0.8%	维护	135	0.6%	领土	435	1.1%	发展	33	1.1%
双方	177	0.6%	渔船	39	0.7%	美国	120	0.6%	地区	415	1.0%	会议	31	1.1%
战争	169	0.6%	非法	38	0.7%	人民	120	0.6%	表示	407	1.0%	经济	31	1.1%
经济	168	0.6%	维护	38	0.7%	中国政府	114	0.5%	和平	405	1.0%	表示	27	0.9%
教科书	167	0.5%	国际	38	0.7%	记者	108	0.5%	谈判	404	1.0%	合作	27	0.9%
社会	167	0.5%	中日关系	38	0.7%	和平	104	0.5%	案	396	1.0%	不丹	26	0.9%
记者	164	0.5%	记者	37	0.7%	台湾	90	0.4%	临时	377	0.9%	世界	26	0.9%
稳定	155	0.5%	美国	37	0.7%	合作	86	0.4%	所谓	347	0.8%	非法	25	0.8%
胜利	151	0.5%	和平	37	0.7%	立场	86	0.4%	海洋	344	0.8%	主权	25	0.8%
国际	150	0.5%	双方	35	0.7%	非法	85	0.4%	联合国	305	0.7%	维护	24	0.8%
没有	119	0.4%	推动	35	0.7%	购	84	0.4%	维护	301	0.7%	军队	24	0.8%
二战	116	0.4%	岛屿	33	0.6%	没有	84	0.4%	接受	294	0.7%	印军	23	0.8%
小泉	115	0.4%	海域	32	0.6%	关系	81	0.4%	没有	289	0.7%	政治	23	0.8%
德国	114	0.4%	战略	31	0.6%	严重	80	0.4%	海洋法	283	0.7%	确定	21	0.7%
两国人民	113	0.4%	领导人	31	0.6%	侵犯	79	0.4%	中菲	268	0.6%	双方	21	0.7%
成为	111	0.4%	事件	31	0.6%	领海	78	0.4%	立场	260	0.6%	推动	19	0.6%
日方	111	0.4%	渔民	30	0.6%	所谓	78	0.4%	稳定	253	0.6%	记者	18	0.6%
政治	111	0.4%	严重	29	0.6%	波茨坦	77	0.4%	岛礁	249	0.6%	进入	18	0.6%
侵略	110	0.4%	船长	29	0.6%	中日关系	77	0.4%	发展	240	0.6%	领导人	18	0.6%
日本政府	108	0.4%	所谓	29	0.6%	公告	73	0.4%	南沙群岛	235	0.6%	行为	18	0.6%
日中	106	0.3%	政治	29	0.6%	经济	73	0.4%	法律	233	0.6%	洞朗	17	0.6%
维护	105	0.3%	重要	29	0.6%	巡航	73	0.4%	权利	231	0.6%	会晤	17	0.6%
美国	103	0.3%	会议	26	0.5%	开罗宣言	72	0.3%	认为	230	0.6%	军队	17	0.6%
认为	102	0.3%	外交部	26	0.5%	固有	71	0.3%	协商	227	0.5%	解决	16	0.5%
胡锦涛	101	0.3%	委员会	25	0.5%	琉球	71	0.3%	单方面	211	0.5%	习近平	16	0.5%
民族	101	0.3%	经济	25	0.5%	世界	71	0.3%	合作	209	0.5%	十国集团	16	0.5%
两国关系	100	0.3%	稳定	25	0.5%	行为	70	0.3%	关系	203	0.5%	要求	16	0.5%
应该	93	0.3%	北京	24	0.5%	中国海	70	0.3%	相关	200	0.5%	英	16	0.5%
北京	92	0.3%	加强	23	0.4%	认为	69	0.3%	方式	199	0.5%	藏印	15	0.5%
欧洲	92	0.3%	希望	23	0.4%	秩序	69	0.3%	行为	198	0.5%	关系	15	0.5%
希望	92	0.3%	中国政府	23	0.4%	重要	69	0.3%	支持	196	0.5%	国际法	15	0.5%
精神	89	0.3%	世界	23	0.4%	两国	68	0.3%	东盟	195	0.5%	加强	15	0.5%
主席	89	0.3%	发言人	22	0.4%	坚决	67	0.3%	提起	193	0.5%	两国	15	0.5%
促进	88	0.3%	和平奖	22	0.4%				南海诸岛	190	0.5%	重要	15	0.5%
提出	88	0.3%	立场	22	0.4%							总理	15	0.5%
			认为	22	0.4%									
			西方	22	0.4%									
			严重	22	0.4%									
			杨洁篪	22	0.4%									
			不能	21	0.4%									
			促进	21	0.4%									
			固有	21	0.4%									
			会晤	21	0.4%									
			两国关系	21	0.4%									
			挪威	21	0.4%									
			取得	21	0.4%									
			抓扣	21	0.4%									

Figure A6.2 Fifty Most Frequent Words for Pacification Campaigns

Bibliography

Aday, Sean, Henry Farrell, Marc Lynch, John Sides, and Deen Freelon. "New Media and Conflict after the Arab Spring." *United States Institute of Peace* 80 (2012): 1–24.

Allcock, John B., ed. *Border and Territorial Disputes*. 3rd ed. rev. and updated. Detroit: Longman Group, 1992.

Allison, Graham T., and Morton H. Halperin. "Bureaucratic Politics: A Paradigm and Some Policy Implications." *World Politics: A Quarterly Journal of International Relations* 24 (Spring 1972): 40–79.

Almond, Gabriel Abraham. *The American People and Foreign Policy*. Westport, CT: Praeger, 1960.

An, Nali. "The Research of People's Daily Discourse Change from 1978 to 2013." *China Media Report Overseas* 10, no. 3 (2014).

An, Seon-Kyoung, and Karla K. Gower. "How Do the News Media Frame Crises? A Content Analysis of Crisis News Coverage." *Public Relations Review* 35, no. 2 (2009): 107–12.

Arrow, Kenneth J. *Social Choice and Individual Values*. Vol. 12. New Haven, CT: Yale University Press, 2012.

Ayish, Muhammad I. "Political Communication on Arab World Television: Evolving Patterns." *Political Communication* 19, no. 2 (April 1, 2002): 137–54.

Bachman, David. "Structure and Process in the Making of Chinese Foreign Policy." In *China and the World*, edited by Samuel S. Kim, xx–xx. Boulder, CO: Westview Press, 1998.

Bandurski, David. "How Officials Can Spin the Media." China Media Project, June 19, 2010. http://chinamediaproject.org/2010/06/19/how-officials-can-spin-the-media/.

Bandurski, David. "Taming the Flood: How China's Leaders 'Guide' Public Opinion." *ChinaFile*, July 20, 2015. http://www.chinafile.com/reporting-opinion/media/taming-flood.

Bastani, Hossein. "How Iranian Media Prepared the Public for the Nuclear Deal." *The Guardian*, July 24, 2015. https://www.theguardian.com/world/iran-blog/2015/jul/24/how-iran-media-supreme-leader-prepared-the-public-nuclear-deal.

Baum, Matthew A., and Philip B. K. Potter. "The Relationships between Mass Media, Public Opinion, and Foreign Policy: Toward a Theoretical Synthesis." *Annual Review of Political Science* 11 (2008): 39–65.

Baumgartner, Frank R., and Bryan D. Jones. *Agendas and Instability in American Politics*. Chicago: University of Chicago Press, 2010.

Becker, Jonathan. "Lessons from Russia: A Neo-Authoritarian Media System." *European Journal of Communication* 19, no. 2 (June 1, 2004): 139–63.

Berkowitz, Leonard. "Some Effects of Thoughts on Anti-and Prosocial Influences of Media Events: A Cognitive-Neoassociation Analysis." *Psychological Bulletin* 95, no. 3 (1984): 410.

Bhattacharjea, Mira Sinha. "India-China: The Year of Two Possibilities." In *Yearbook on India's Foreign Policy, 1985–86*, edited by Satish Kumar, xx–xx. New Delhi: SAGE Publications, 1988.

Blei, David M., Andrew Y. Ng, and Michael I. Jordan. "Latent Dirichlet Allocation." *Journal of Machine Learning Research* 3 (2003): 993–1022.

Bodensteiner, Carol A. "Predicting Public and Media Attention Span for Social Issues." *Public Relations Quarterly* 40, no. 2 (1995): 14.

Brady, Anne-Marie. *Marketing Dictatorship: Propaganda and Thought Work in Contemporary China*. Lanham, MD: Rowman & Littlefield, 2008.

308 Bibliography

Brady, Anne-Marie, and Juntao Wang. "China's Strengthened New Order and the Role of Propaganda." *Journal of Contemporary China* 18, no. 62 (November 1, 2009): 767–88.

Brecher, Michael. "State Behavior in International Crisis: A Model." *Journal of Conflict Resolution* 23, no. 3 (1979): 446–80.

Breckler, Steven J. "Empirical Validation of Affect, Behavior, and Cognition as Distinct Components of Attitude." *Journal of Personality and Social Psychology* 47, no. 6 (1984): 1191.

Brown, Noel, and Craig Deegan. "The Public Disclosure of Environmental Performance Information - A Dual Test of Media Agenda Setting Theory and Legitimacy Theory." *Accounting and Business Research* 29, no. 1 (1998): 21–41.

Bui, Nhung T. "Managing Anti-China Nationalism in Vietnam: Evidence from the Media during the 2014 Oil Rig Crisis." *The Pacific Review* 30, no. 2 (2017): 169–87.

Bunn, Matthew. "Reimagining Repression: New Censorship Theory and After." *History and Theory* 54, no. 1 (2015): 25–44.

Burr, W., and J. Kimball. "Nixon's Secret Nuclear Alert: Vietnam War Diplomacy and the Joint Chiefs of Staff Readiness Test, October 1969." *Cold War History* 3, no. 2 (January 1, 2003): 113–56.

Bush, Sarah Sunn, Aaron Erlich, Lauren Prather, and Yael Zeira. "The Effects of Authoritarian Iconography: An Experimental Test." *Comparative Political Studies* 49, no. 13 (2016): 1704–38.

Buzan, Barry, and Ole Wæver. *Regions and Powers: The Structure of International Security.* Cambridge: Cambridge University Press, 2003.

Buzan, Barry, Ole Waever, and Jaap de Wilde. *Security: A New Framework for Analysis.* Boulder, CO: Lynne Rienner Publishers, 1998.

Cairns, Christopher, and Allen Carlson. "Real-World Islands in a Social Media Sea: Nationalism and Censorship on Weibo during the 2012 Diaoyu/Senkaku Crisis." *The China Quarterly* 225 (2016): 23–49.

Carter, Erin Baggott, and Brett L. Carter. *Propaganda in Autocracies: Institutions, Information, and the Politics of Belief.* Cambridge; New York: Cambridge University Press, 2023.

Carver, Charles S., and Eddie Harmon-Jones. "Anger Is an Approach-Related Affect: Evidence and Implications." *Psychological Bulletin* 135, no. 2 (2009): 183–204.

Central Intelligence Agency. "The Sino-Indian Border Dispute: Section 1: 1950–59." March 2, 1963. Staff study. www.archieve.claudearpi.net/maintenance/uploaded_pics/polo-07.pdf.

Chan, Irene, and Mingjiang Li. "New Chinese Leadership, New Policy in the South China Sea Dispute?" *Journal of Chinese Political Science* 20, no. 1 (March 1, 2015): 35–50.

Chanda, Nayan. *Brother Enemy: The War after the War.* New York: Collier Books, 1986.

Chang, Julian. "The Mechanics of State Propaganda: The People's Republic of China and the Soviet Union in the 1950s." In *New Perspectives on State Socialism in China,* edited by Timothy Chee and Tony Saich, 76–124. Armonk, NY: M. E. Sharpe, 1997.

Chen, Dingding, Xiaoyu Pu, and Alastair Iain Johnston. "Debating China's Assertiveness." *International Security* 38, no. 3 (2014): 176–83.

Chen, Jidong, Jennifer Pan, and Yiqing Xu. "Sources of Authoritarian Responsiveness: A Field Experiment in China." *American Journal of Political Science* 60, no. 2 (2016): 383–400.

Chen, Jidong, and Yiqing Xu. "Why Do Authoritarian Regimes Allow Citizens to Voice Opinions Publicly?" *Journal of Politics* 79, no. 3 (2017): 792–803.

Chen, King C. *China's War with Vietnam, 1979: Issues, Decisions, and Implications.* Stanford, CA: Hoover Institution Press, 1987.

Chen, Xi. *Social Protest and Contentious Authoritarianism in China.* Cambridge: Cambridge University Press, 2012.

Chen, Xueyi, and Tianjian Shi. "Media Effects on Political Confidence and Trust in the PRC in the Post Tiananmen Period." *East Asia* 19 (September 1, 2001): 84–118.

Bibliography 309

China National Offshore Oil Corporation (CNOOC). "Notification of First Batch of Blocks in Offshore China Available for Foreign Cooperation in Year 2011." May 24, 2011. http://www.cnooc.com.cn/art/2014/9/25/art_6241_1148001.html.

Christensen, Thomas J. *Useful Adversaries: Grand Strategy, Domestic Mobilization, and Sino-American Conflict, 1947–1958.* Princeton, NJ: Princeton University Press, 1996.

Chubb, Andrew. "China's Information Management in the Sino-Vietnamese Confrontation: Caution and Sophistication in the Internet Era." *China Brief* 14, no. 11 (June 4, 2014). https://jamestown.org/program/chinas-information-management-in-the-sino-vietnamese-confrontation-caution-and-sophistication-in-the-internet-era/.

Chubb, Andrew. "Chinese Popular Nationalism and PRC Policy in the South China Sea." PhD diss., University of Western Australia, 2016.

Chubb, Andrew. "Propaganda, Not Policy: Explaining the PLA's 'Hawkish Faction.'" *China Brief* 13, no. 15 (2013).

Chubb, Andrew, and Frances Yaping Wang. "Authoritarian Propaganda Campaigns on Foreign Affairs: Four Birds with One Stone." *International Studies Quarterly* 67, no. 3 (2023). https://doi.org/10.1093/isq/sqad047.

Chung, Chien-peng. *Domestic Politics, International Bargaining and China's Territorial Disputes.* London: Routledge, 2004.

Creemers, Rogier. "Cyber China: Upgrading Propaganda, Public Opinion Work and Social Management for the Twenty-First Century." *Journal of Contemporary China* 26, no. 103 (January 2, 2017): 85–100.

Crespi, Irving. *The Public Opinion Process: How the People Speak.* London: Routledge, 2013.

Deese, James, and Roger A. Kaufman. "Serial Effects in Recall of Unorganized and Sequentially Organized Verbal Material." *Journal of Experimental Psychology* 54, no. 3 (1957): 180.

Dickson, Bruce J. *The Dictator's Dilemma: The Chinese Communist Party's Strategy for Survival.* New York: Oxford University Press, 2016.

Dimitrov, Martin K. "What the Party Wanted to Know: Citizen Complaints as a 'Barometer of Public Opinion' in Communist Bulgaria." *East European Politics and Societies* 28, no. 2 (May 1, 2014): 271–95.

Dougherty, Jill. "Everyone Lies: The Ukraine Conflict and Russia's Media Transformation." August 29, 2014. Shorenstein Center, Harvard Kennedy School. https://shorensteincenter.org/everyone-lies-ukraine-conflict-russias-media-transformation/.

Downs, Anthony. "Up and Down with Ecology: The 'Issue-Attention Cycle." *The Public*, 1972.

Downs, Erica Strecker, and Phillip C. Saunders. "Legitimacy and the Limits of Nationalism: China and the Diaoyu Islands." *International Security* 23, no. 3 (1999): 114–46.

Druckman, James N., and Rose McDermott. "Emotion and the Framing of Risky Choice." *Political Behavior* 30, no. 3 (2008): 297–321.

Duiker, William J. *China and Vietnam: The Roots of Conflict.* Vol. 1. Berkeley: Institute of East Asian Studies, 1986.

Ebon, Martin. *The Soviet Propaganda Machine.* New York: McGraw-Hill, 1987.

Ekman, Paul. "An Argument for Basic Emotions." *Cognition and Emotion* 6, no. 3–4 (May 1, 1992): 169–200.

Elliot, Andrew J., Andreas B. Eder, and Eddie Harmon-Jones. "Approach–Avoidance Motivation and Emotion: Convergence and Divergence." *Emotion Review* 5, no. 3 (2013): 308–11.

Esarey, Ashley. "Cornering the Market: State Strategies for Controlling China's Commercial Media." *Asian Perspective* 29, no. 4 (2005): 37–83.

Esarey, Ashley, Daniela Stockmann, and Jie Zhang. "Support for Propaganda: Chinese Perceptions of Public Service Advertising." *Journal of Contemporary China* 26, no. 103 (January 2, 2017): 101–17.

Fearon, James D. "Domestic Political Audiences and the Escalation of International Disputes." *American Political Science Review* 88, no. 3 (1994): 577–92.

310 Bibliography

Fearon, James D. "Rationalist Explanations for War." *International Organization* 49, no. 3 (1995): 379–414.

Fearon, James D. "Signaling Foreign Policy Interests Tying Hands versus Sinking Costs." *Journal of Conflict Resolution* 41, no. 1 (1997): 68–90.

Fewsmith, Joseph, and Stanley Rosen. "The Domestic Context of Chinese Foreign Policy: Does 'Public Opinion' Matter?" In *The Making of Chinese Foreign and Security Policy in the Era of Reform, 1978–2000*, edited by David M. Lampton, 151–87. Redwood City, CA: Stanford University Press, 1978.

Flam, Helena, and Debra King. *Emotions and Social Movements*. London: Routledge, 2007.

Fravel, M. Taylor. *Strong Borders, Secure Nation: Cooperation and Conflict in China's Territorial Disputes*. Princeton, NJ: Princeton University Press, 2008.

Frijda, Nico H. *The Emotions*. New York: Cambridge University Press, 1986.

Fu Ying, Wu Shicun. "South China Sea: How We Got to This Stage." *The National Interest*, May 9, 2016. https://nationalinterest.org/feature/south-china-sea-how-we-got-stage-16118.

Garver, John W. "China's Decision for War with India in 1962." In *New Directions in the Study of China's Foreign Policy*, edited by Alastair Iain Johnston and Robert S. Ross, xx–xx. Redwood City, CA: Stanford University Press, 2004.

Garver, John W. "China's Push Through the South China Sea: The Interaction of Bureaucratic and National Interests." *The China Quarterly* 132 (December 1992): 999–1028.

Gates, Robert M. *Duty: Memoirs of a Secretary at War*. New York: Vintage, 2015.

Geddes, Barbara. "What Do We Know About Democratization After Twenty Years?" *Annual Review of Political Science* 2, no. 1 (1999): 115–44.

Geddes, Barbara, Joseph Wright, and Erica Frantz. "Autocratic Breakdown and Regime Transitions: A New Data Set." *Perspectives on Politics* 12, no. 2 (June 2014): 313–31.

Geddes, Barbara, and John Zaller. "Sources of Popular Support for Authoritarian Regimes." *American Journal of Political Science* 33, no. 2 (1989): 319–47.

General Office of the General Political Department, ed. *ZhongYue Bianjing Ziwei Huanji Zuozhan Zhengzhi Gongzuo Jingyan Xuanbian (Compilation of Experiences of Political Work during the Counterattack in Self-Defense on the Sino-Vietnamese Border)*. Vol. 1. Beijing: Zhongguo Renmin Jiefangjun Zongzhengzhibu Bangongting (Chinese Liberation Army General Political Department), 1980.

Geng, Biao. "Geng Blao's Report on the Situation of the Indochinese Peninsula." *Journal of Contemporary Asia* 11, no. 3 (January 1, 1981): 379–91.

Gentzkow, Matthew, and Jesse M. Shapiro. "Media Bias and Reputation." *Journal of Political Economy* 114, no. 2 (April 1, 2006): 280–316.

George, Alexander L. *Propaganda Analysis: A Study of Inferences Made from Nazi Propaganda in World War II*. Evanston, IL: Row, Peterson & Co., 1959.

George, Alexander L., and Andrew Bennett. *Case Studies and Theory Development in the Social Sciences*. Cambridge, MA: MIT Press, 2005.

Godwin, Paul H., and Alice L. Miller. "China's Forbearance Has Limits: Chinese Threat and Retaliation Signaling and Its Implications for a Sino-American Military Confrontation." China Strategic Perspectives. Washington, DC: Center for the Study of Chinese Military Affairs, Institute for National Strategic Studies, 2013.

Goldstein, Joshua S. *Winning the War on War: The Decline of Armed Conflict Worldwide*. New York: Penguin, 2011.

Goodwin, Jeff, James M. Jasper, and Francesca Polletta. *Passionate Politics: Emotions and Social Movements*. Chicago: University of Chicago Press, 2009.

Gorman, Patrick. "Red Guard 2.0: Nationalist Flesh Search in China." *Journal of Contemporary China* 26, no. 104 (March 4, 2017): 183–98.

Goscha, Christopher. *Vietnam: A New History*. New York: Basic Books, 2016.

Green, Michael, Kathleen Hicks, Zack Cooper, John Schaus, and Jake Douglas. "China-Vietnam Oil Rig Standoff." In *Countering Coercion in Maritime Asia: The Theory and Practice of Gray Zone Deterrence*. Washington, DC: Center for Strategic and International Studies, June 12, 2017.

Greitens, Sheena Chestnut. "Authoritarianism Online: What Can We Learn from Internet Data in Nondemocracies?" *PS: Political Science & Politics* 46, no. 2 (April 2013): 262–70.

Gries, Peter Hays. *China's New Nationalism: Pride, Politics, and Diplomacy*. Berkeley: University of California Press, 2004.

Gries, Peter Hays. "China's 'New Thinking' on Japan." *The China Quarterly*, no. 184 (2005): 831–50.

Gunther, Albert C., Richard M. Perloff, and Yariv Tsfati. "Public Opinion and the Third-Person Effect." In *The SAGE Handbook of Public Opinion Research*, edited by Wolfgang Donsbach and Michael Traugott, 184–91. London: SAGE Publications, 2008.

Guo, Ming, ed. *ZhongYue Guanxi Yanbian Sishinian (Forty-Year Evolution of the Sino-Vietnamese Relations)*. Nanning: Guangxi Renmin Chubanshe (Guangxi People's Publishing House), 1992.

Hallgren, Kevin A. "Computing Inter-Rater Reliability for Observational Data: An Overview and Tutorial." *Tutorials in Quantitative Methods for Psychology* 8, no. 1 (2012): 23–34.

Han, Nianlong, ed. *Dangdai Zhongguo Waijiao (Contemporary China's Diplomacy)*. Beijing: Shehui Kexue Chubanshe (China Social Sciences Press), 1987.

Han, Rongbin. "Defending the Authoritarian Regime Online: China's 'Voluntary Fifty-Cent Army.'" *The China Quarterly* 224 (December 2015): 1006–25.

Harwit, Eric, and Duncan Clark. "Shaping the Internet in China: Evolution of Political Control over Network Infrastructure and Content." *Asian Survey* 41, no. 3 (2001): 377–408.

Hassid, Jonathan Henry. "Pressing Back: The Struggle for Control over China's Journalists." PhD diss., University of California, Berkeley, 2010.

Hassid, Jonathan. "Safety Valve or Pressure Cooker? Blogs in Chinese Political Life." *Journal of Communication* 62, no. 2 (2012): 212–30.

Havel, Vaclav, and Václav Havel. *The Power of the Powerless: Citizens Against the State in Central-Eastern Europe*. Armonk, NY: M. E. Sharpe, 1985.

He, Kai, and Huiyun Feng. "Debating China's Assertiveness: Taking China's Power and Interests Seriously." *International Politics* 49, no. 5 (September 1, 2012): 633–44.

He, Yinan. "History, Chinese Nationalism and the Emerging Sino–Japanese Conflict." *Journal of Contemporary China* 16, no. 50 (February 1, 2007): 1–24.

He, Yinan. "National Mythmaking and the Problems of History in Sino-Japanese Relations." In *Japan's Relations with China: Facing a Rising Power*, edited by Peng Er Lam, 69–91. London: Routledge, 2006.

Heinzig, Dieter. *Disputed Islands in the South China Sea: Paracels, Spratlys, Pratas, Macclesfield Bank*. Wiesbaden: Otto Harrassowitz, 1976.

Hensel, Paul R., and Sara M. Mitchell. "The Issue Correlates of War (ICOW) Project Issue Data Set: Territorial Claims Data." Harvard Dataverse, March 17, 2011. https://doi.org/10.7910/DVN/E6PSGZ.

Hensel, Paul R., Michael E. Allison, and Ahmed Khanani. "Territorial Integrity Treaties and Armed Conflict over Territory." *Conflict Management and Peace Science* 26, no. 2 (2009): 120–43.

Herman, Edward S., and Noam Chomsky. *Manufacturing Consent: The Political Economy of the Mass Media*. New York: Pantheon, 2002.

Hersh, Seymour. *The Price of Power: Kissinger in the Nixon White House*. New York: Simon & Schuster, 2013.

312 Bibliography

Hiep, Le Hong. "Performance-Based Legitimacy: The Case of the Communist Party of Vietnam and Doi Moi." *Contemporary Southeast Asia: A Journal of International and Strategic Affairs* 34, no. 2 (August 22, 2012): 145–72.

Higgins, Andrew. "In Ukraine, Russia Plays a Weighted Word Game." *New York Times*, April 17, 2014.

Hoang, Van Hoan. *YueZhong Zhandou de Youyi Shishi Burong Waiqu (The Reality of the Sino-Vietnamese Friendship in Fighting Ought Not to Be Distorted)*. Beijing: Renmin Publishing House, 1979.

Holsti, Ole R. "Public Opinion and Foreign Policy: Challenges to the Almond-Lippmann Consensus." *International Studies Quarterly* 36, no. 4 (1992): 439–66.

Hood, Steven J. *Dragons Entangled: Indochina and the China-Vietnam War*. Armonk, NY: M. E. Sharpe, 1993.

Hopf, Ted. "Common-Sense Constructivism and Hegemony in World Politics." *International Organization* 67, no. 2 (April 2013): 317–54.

Hopf, Ted. *Reconstructing the Cold War: The Early Years, 1945–1958*. New York: Oxford University Press, 2012.

Houn, Franklin W. *To Change a Nation*. Charleston, SC: BiblioLife, 1961.

Huang, Haifeng. "The Pathology of Hard Propaganda." *Journal of Politics* 80, no. 3 (2018): 1034–38.

Huang, Haifeng. "Propaganda as Signaling." *Comparative Politics* 47, no. 4 (2015): 419–44.

Huth, Paul K., and Todd L. Allee. *The Democratic Peace and Territorial Conflict in the Twentieth Century*. Cambridge: Cambridge University Press, 2002.

Huysmans, Jef. "Migrants as a Security Problem: Dangers of 'Securitizing' Societal Issues." In *Migration and European Integration: The Dynamics of Inclusion and Exclusion*, edited by Robert Miles and Dietrich Thränhardt, 53–72. London: Pinter Publishers, 1995.

Inkeles, Alex. *Public Opinion in Soviet Russia: A Study in Mass Persuasion*. Cambridge, MA: Harvard University Press, 2013.

International Crisis Group. "Stirring Up the South China Sea (III): A Fleeting Opportunity for Calm." May 7, 2015. International Crisis Group. https://www.crisisgroup.org/asia/north-east-asia/china/stirring-south-china-sea-iii-fleeting-opportunity-calm.https://www.crisisgroup.org/asia/north-east-asia/china/stirring-south-china-sea-iii-fleeting-opportunity-calm.

Jasper, James M. "The Emotions of Protest: Affective and Reactive Emotions in and around Social Movements." In *Sociological Forum*, 13:397–424. Springer, 1998.

Jiang, Feng, Xiaochun Ma, and Yishan Dou. *Yangyong Jiangjun Zhuan (Biography of General Yang Yong)*. Beijing: Jiefangjun, 1991.

Jiang, Min. "The Co-Evolution of the Internet, (Un)Civil Society & Authoritarianism in China." In *The Internet, Social Media, and a Changing China*, edited by Jacques deLisle, Avery Goldstein, and Guobin Yang, 28–48. Philadelphia: University of Pennsylvania Press, 2016.

Jiang, Yesha, and Jiaojiang Luo. "Hulianwang Meijie Zhiyu Guojia Rentong de Goujian: Yi Nanhai Zhongcai'an Yuqing Chuanbo Wei Li (The Internet Media and the Construction of National Identity—Using the South China Sea Arbitration Case as an Example)." *Xinwenjie (The News World)* 24 (2016).

Johnston, Alastair Iain. "Chinese Middle Class Attitudes Towards International Affairs: Nascent Liberalization?" *The China Quarterly*, no. 179 (2004): 603–28.

Johnston, Alastair Iain. "How New and Assertive Is China's New Assertiveness?" *International Security* 37, no. 4 (2013): 7–48.

Jones, Adam. "From Vanguard to Vanquished? The Tabloid Press in Jordan." *Political Communication* 19, no. 2 (April 1, 2002): 171–87.

Jones, Daniel M., Stuart A. Bremer, and J. David Singer. "Militarized Interstate Disputes, 1816–1992: Rationale, Coding Rules, and Empirical Patterns." *Conflict Management and Peace Science* 15, no. 2 (1996): 163–213.

Jowett, Garth S., and Victoria O'Donnell. *Propaganda & Persuasion*. 6th ed. Thousand Oaks, CA: SAGE Publications, 2014.

Kailitz, Steffen. "Classifying Political Regimes Revisited: Legitimation and Durability." *Democratization* 20, no. 1 (January 1, 2013): 39–60.

Kalathil, Shanthi, and Taylor C. Boas. "The Internet and State Control in Authoritarian Regimes." *First Monday*, August 6, 2001. https://firstmonday.org/ojs/index.php/fm/article/download/876/785?inline=1.

Katz, Andrew Z. "Public Opinion and Foreign Policy: The Nixon Administration and the Pursuit of Peace with Honor in Vietnam." *Presidential Studies Quarterly* 27, no. 3 (1997): 496–513.

Kecskemeti, Paul. "Propaganda." In *Handbook of Communication*, edited by Ithiel D. Pool, Wilbur Schramm, F. W. Frey, and N. Maccoby, 844–865. Chicago: Rand McNally, 1973.

Kenez, Peter. *The Birth of the Propaganda State: Soviet Methods of Mass Mobilization, 1917–1929*. New York: Cambridge University Press, 1985.

Kennedy, John James. "Maintaining Popular Support for the Chinese Communist Party: The Influence of Education and the State-Controlled Media." *Political Studies* 57, no. 3 (2009): 517–36.

Kepplinger, Hans Mathias. "Effects of the News Media on Public Opinion." In *The SAGE Handbook of Public Opinion Research*, by Wolfgang Donsbach and Michael Traugott, 192–204. London: SAGE Publications, 2008.

Khoo, Nicholas. *Collateral Damage: Sino-Soviet Rivalry and the Termination of the Sino-Vietnamese Alliance*. New York: Columbia University Press, 2011.

King, Gary, Jennifer Pan, and Margaret E. Roberts. "How Censorship in China Allows Government Criticism but Silences Collective Expression." *American Political Science Review* 107, no. 2 (2013): 326–43.

King, Gary, Jennifer Pan, and Margaret E. Roberts. "How the Chinese Government Fabricates Social Media Posts for Strategic Distraction, Not Engaged Argument." *American Political Science Review* 111, no. 3 (2017): 484–501.

Klein, Adam Gordon. "Quiet Road to War: Media Compliance and Suppressed Public Opinion in Iran." PhD diss., Howard University, 2010.

Kotler, Mindy L., Naotaka Sugawara, and Tetsuya Yamada. "Chinese and Japanese Public Opinion: Search for Moral Security." *Asian Perspective* 31, no. 1 (2007): 93–125.

Krebs, Ronald R. *Narrative and The Making of US National Security*. Vol. 138. New York: Cambridge University Press, 2015.

Ku, Lun-Wei, and Hsin-Hsi Chen. "Mining Opinions from the Web: Beyond Relevance Retrieval." *Journal of the American Society for Information Science and Technology* 58, no. 12 (2007): 1838–50.

Lacey, Marc. "Badme Journal; Torn Town Changes Countries, But Not Conviction." *New York Times*, April 16, 2002. http://www.nytimes.com/2002/04/16/world/badme-journal-torn-town-changes-countries-but-not-conviction.html.

Lamb, Alastair. *The McMahon Line: A Study in the Relations Between India, China, and Tibet, 1904 to 1914. 2 Volumes*. London: Routledge & Kegan Paul; Toronto: University of Toronto Press, 1966.

Lankina, Tomila, Kohei Watanabe, and Yulia Netesova. "How Russian Media Control, Manipulate, and Leverage Public Discontent: Framing Protest in Autocracies." In *Citizens and the State in Authoritarian Regimes: Comparing China and Russia*, edited by Karrie Koesel, Valerie Bunce, and Jessica Chen Weiss, 137–64. New York: Oxford University Press, 2020.

Lazarsfeld, Paul F., Bernard Berelson, and Hazel Gaudet. *The People's Choice: How the Voter Makes Up His Mind in a Presidential Campaign, Legacy Edition*. New York: Columbia University Press, 1968.

314 Bibliography

Lerner, Jennifer S., Roxana M. Gonzalez, Deborah A. Small, and Baruch Fischhoff. "Effects of Fear and Anger on Perceived Risks of Terrorism: A National Field Experiment." *Psychological Science* 14, no. 2 (March 2003): 144–50.

Levitsky, Steven, and Lucan A. Way. *Competitive Authoritarianism: Hybrid Regimes After the Cold War*. New York: Cambridge University Press, 2010.

Levitsky, Steven, and Lucan Way. "The Durability of Revolutionary Regimes." *Journal of Democracy* 24, no. 3 (2013): 5–17.

Li, Jiazhong. "ZhongYue Bianjie Tanpan Pianduan Huiyi (Recollection of the Sino-Vietnamese Border Negotiation)." *Zhonggong Dangshi Ziliao (CCP History Material)*, no. 1 (2005): 58–67.

Li, Zhaoxin. "Wo Suo Jingli de Xisha Haizhan (The Paracels Sea Battle I Experienced)." *Dangshi Bocai (Extensive Collection of the Party History)*, no. 7 (2009): 33–36.

Lifton, Robert Jay. *Thought Reform and the Psychology of Totalism: A Study of "Brainwashing" in China*. Chapel Hill: University of North Carolina Press, 1961.

Linz, Juan José. *Totalitarian and Authoritarian Regimes*. Boulder, CO: Lynne Rienner Publishers, 1975.

Linz, Juan J., and Alfred Stepan. *Problems of Democratic Transition and Consolidation: Southern Europe, South America, and Post-Communist Europe*. Baltimore: Johns Hopkins University Press, 1996.

Lippmann, Walter. *Public Opinion*. New York: Macmillian, 1922.

Liu, Alan P. L. *Communications and National Integration in Communist China*. Berkeley: University of California Press, 1975.

Liu, Huaqing. *Liu Huaqing Huiyilu (Liu Huaqing's Memoirs)*. Beijing: Jiefangjun Chubanshe (People's Liberation Army Publishing House), 2007.

Lobell, Steven E., Norrin M. Ripsman, and Jeffrey W. Taliaferro, eds. *Neoclassical Realism, the State, and Foreign Policy*. Cambridge: Cambridge University Press, 2009.

Lorentzen, Peter. "China's Strategic Censorship." *American Journal of Political Science* 58, no. 2 (April 1, 2014): 402–14.

Lorentzen, Peter L. "Regularizing Rioting: Permitting Public Protest in An Authoritarian Regime." *Quarterly Journal of Political Science* 8, no. 2 (2013): 127–58.

Lynch, Daniel C. *After the Propaganda State: Media, Politics, and "Thought Work" in Reformed China*. Redwood City, CA: Stanford University Press, 1999.

MacKuen, Michael, Jennifer Wolak, Luke Keele, and George E. Marcus. "Civic Engagements: Resolute Partisanship or Reflective Deliberation." *American Journal of Political Science* 54, no. 2 (2010): 440–58.

Maddux, William W., Elizabeth Mullen, and Adam D. Galinsky. "Chameleons Bake Bigger Pies and Take Bigger Pieces: Strategic Behavioral Mimicry Facilitates Negotiation Outcomes." *Journal of Experimental Social Psychology* 44, no. 2 (2008): 461–68.

Malesky, Edmund, and Jason Morris-Jung. "Vietnam in 2014: Uncertainty and Opportunity in the Wake of the HS-981 Crisis." *Asian Survey* 55, no. 1 (2015): 165–73.

Malesky, Edmund, and Paul Schuler. "Nodding or Needling: Analyzing Delegate Responsiveness in an Authoritarian Parliament." *American Political Science Review* 104, no. 3 (2010): 482–502.

Manion, Melanie. "Authoritarian Parochialism: Local Congressional Representation in China." *The China Quarterly* 218 (2014): 311–38.

Mann, James. *About Face: A History of America's Curious Relationship with China, from Nixon to Clinton*. Washington, DC: National Geographic Books, 2000.

Mao, Zedong. "Some Questions Concerning Methods of Leadership." In *Selected Works of Mao Zedong (Mao Zedong Wenji)*, Vol. 3. Beijing: Foreign Languages Press, 1967.

Maxwell, N. *India's China War*. New York: Random House, 2000.

McCombs, M. E., and A. Reynolds. "News Influence on Our Pictures of the World." In *Media Effects: Advances in Theory and Research*, edited by J. Bryant and D. Zillmann, 1–18. Mahwah, NJ: Lawrence Erlbaum Associates, 2002.

Bibliography 315

McCombs, Maxwell E., and Donald L. Shaw. "The Agenda-Setting Function of Mass Media." *Public Opinion Quarterly* 36, no. 2 (1972): 176–87.

Mearsheimer, John J. "Can China Rise Peacefully?" *The National Interest*, October 25, 2014. https://nationalinterest.org/commentary/can-china-rise-peacefully-10204.

Mearsheimer, John J. "Imperial by Design." *The National Interest*, no. 111 (2011): 16–34.

Mearsheimer, John J. *The Tragedy of Great Power Politics*. New York: Norton, 2001.

Meng, Tianguang, Jennifer Pan, and Ping Yang. "Conditional Receptivity to Citizen Participation: Evidence from A Survey Experiment in China." *Comparative Political Studies* 50, no. 4 (2017): 399–433.

Miller, Blake Andrew Phillip. "Automatic Detection of Comment Propaganda in Chinese Media." April 21, 2016. https://ssrn.com/abstract=2738325 or http://dx.doi.org/10.2139/ssrn.2738325.

Min, Li. *ZhongYue Zhanzheng Shinian (Ten Years of the Sino-Vietnamese War)*. Chengdu: Sichuan Daxue (Sichuan University Press), 1993.

Morgenthau, Hans. *Politics Among Nations: The Struggle for Peace and Power*. New York: Knopf, 1948.

Morozov, Evgeny. *The Net Delusion: The Dark Side of Internet Freedom*. PublicAffairs, 2012.

Murdock, Bennet B. "The Serial Position Effect of Free Recall." *Journal of Experimental Psychology* 64, no. 5 (1962): 482–488.

Nathan, Andrew J., and Andrew Scobell. *China's Search for Security*. New York: Columbia University Press, 2012.

National Bureau of Statistics of China. *China Statistical Yearbook 2016*. Beijing: China Statistics Press, 2016.

Nelson, Thomas E., Zoe M. Oxley, and Rosalee A. Clawson. "Toward a Psychology of Framing Effects." *Political Behavior* 19, no. 3 (September 1, 1997): 221–46.

O'Brien, Kevin J., and Lianjiang Li. *Rightful Resistance in Rural China*. Cambridge: Cambridge University Press, 2006.

Oksenberg, Michel, and Gail Henderson. *Research Guide to People's Daily Editorials, 1949–1975*. Ann Arbor: University of Michigan Press, 2020.

Ong, Rebecca. "Online Vigilante Justice Chinese Style and Privacy in China." *Information & Communications Technology Law* 21, no. 2 (June 1, 2012): 127–45.

Osgood, Charles Egerton, George J. Suci, and Percy H. Tannenbaum. *The Measurement of Meaning*. Champaign: University of Illinois Press, 1957.

Ostini, Jennifer, and Anthony Y. H. Ostini. "Beyond the Four Theories of the Press: A New Model of National Media Systems." *Mass Communication and Society* 5, no. 1 (February 1, 2002): 41–56.

Ottaway, Marina. *Democracy Challenged: The Rise of Semi-Authoritarianism*. Washington, DC: Carnegie Endowment for International Peace, 2003.

Palmer, Glenn, Vito D'Orazio, Michael R. Kenwick, and Roseanne W. McManus. "Updating the Militarized Interstate Dispute Data: A Response to Gibler, Miller, and Little." *International Studies Quarterly* 64, no. 2 (June 1, 2020): 469–75.

Path, Kosal. "Sino-Vietnamese Relations, 1950–1978: From Cooperation to Conflict." PhD diss., University of Southern California, 2008.

Perry, Elizabeth. "Moving The Masses: Emotion Work In The Chinese Revolution." *Mobilization: An International Quarterly* 7, no. 2 (June 1, 2002): 111–28.

Pinker, Steven. *The Better Angels of Our Nature: Why Violence Has Declined*. New York: Viking, 2011.

Poh, Angela. "The Myth of Chinese Sanctions over South China Sea Disputes." *Washington Quarterly* 40, no. 1 (2017): 143–65.

Political Teaching Office of PLA Nanjing Advanced Infantry School. "ZhongYue Bianjing Ziwei Huanji Zuozhan Zhengzhi Gongzuo Jingyan Xuanbian (Selected Experiences of

316   Bibliography

Political Work during the Counterattack in Self-Defense on the Sino-Vietnamese Border)." Nanjing: Nanjing Junqu Gaoji Bubing Xuexiao, 1979.

Powlick, Philip J., and Andrew Z. Katz. "Defining the American Public Opinion/Foreign Policy Nexus." *Mershon International Studies Review* 42, no. Supplement_1 (May 1, 1998): 29–61.

Quek, Kai, and Alastair Iain Johnston. "Can China Back Down? Crisis De-Escalation in the Shadow of Popular Opposition." *International Security* 42, no. 3 (2018): 7–36.

Rawan, Shir Mohammad. "Modern Mass Media and Traditional Communication in Afghanistan." *Political Communication* 19, no. 2 (April 1, 2002): 155–70.

Reilly, James. *Strong Society, Smart State: The Rise of Public Opinion in China's Japan Policy*. New York: Columbia University Press, 2011.

Repnikova, Maria. "Critical Journalists in China and Russia: Encounters with Ambiguity." In *Citizens and the State in Authoritarian Regimes: Comparing China and Russia*, edited by Karrie Koesel, Valerie Bunce, and Jessica Chen Weiss, 117–36. New York: Oxford University Press, 2020.

Repnikova, Maria. *Media Politics in China: Improvising Power under Authoritarianism*. Cambridge: Cambridge University Press, 2017.

Repnikova, Maria, and Kecheng Fang. "Authoritarian Participatory Persuasion 2.0: Netizens as Thought Work Collaborators in China." *Journal of Contemporary China* 27, no. 113 (2018): 1–17.

Risse, Thomas. "'Let's Argue!': Communicative Action in World Politics." *International Organization* 54, no. 1 (2000): 1–39.

Roberts, Margaret E., Brandon M. Stewart, and Dustin Tingley. "Stm: An R Package for Structural Topic Models." *Journal of Statistical Software* 91, no. 1 (2019): 1–40.

Rød, Espen Geelmuyden, and Nils B Weidmann. "Empowering Activists or Autocrats? The Internet in Authoritarian Regimes." *Journal of Peace Research* 52, no. 3 (May 1, 2015): 338–51.

Rodan, Garry. "Asia and the International Press: The Political Significance of Expanding Markets." *Democratization* 5, no. 2 (June 1, 1998): 125–54.

Roe, Paul. "Securitization and Minority Rights: Conditions of Desecuritization." *Security Dialogue* 35, no. 3 (2004): 279–94.

Ross, Robert S. *The Indochina Tangle: China's Vietnam Policy, 1975–1979*. New York: Columbia University Press, 1988.

Roth, Antoine. "Conflict Dynamics in Sino-Japanese Relations: The Case of the Senkaku/Diaoyu Islands Dispute." MA thesis, George Washington University, 2013.

Roth-Ey, Kristin, and Larissa Zakharova. "Communications and Media in the USSR and Eastern Europe." *Cahiers Du Monde Russe. Russie - Empire Russe - Union Soviétique et États Indépendants* 56, no. 56/2–3 (April 17, 2015): 273–89.

Russett, Bruce M. *Controlling the Sword: The Democratic Governance of National Security*. Cambridge, MA: Harvard University Press, 1990.

Schatz, Edward, and Elena Maltseva. "Kazakhstan's Authoritarian 'Persuasion.'" *Post-Soviet Affairs* 28, no. 1 (January 1, 2012): 45–65.

Scheufele, Dietram A., and David Tewksbury. "Framing, Agenda Setting, and Priming: The Evolution of Three Media Effects Models." *Journal of Communication* 57, no. 1 (2007): 9–20.

Schlæger, Jesper, and Min Jiang. "Official Microblogging and Social Management by Local Governments in China." *China Information* 28, no. 2 (July 1, 2014): 189–213.

Schoenhals, Michael. *Doing Things with Words in Chinese Politics: Five Studies*. Berkeley: Center for Chinese Studies, Institute of East Asian Studies, University of California, 1992.

Schultz, Kenneth A. *Democracy and Coercive Diplomacy*. Vol. 76. New York: Cambridge University Press, 2001.

Schurmann, Franz. *Ideology and Organization in Communist China*. Berkeley: University of California Press, 1971.

Bibliography 317

Schweller, Randall L. "Neoclassical Realism and State Mobilization: Expansionist Ideology in the Age of Mass Politics." In *Neoclassical Realism, the State, and Foreign Policy*, edited by Steven E. Lobell, Norrin M. Ripsman, and Jeffrey W. Taliaferro, 227–50. Cambridge: Cambridge University Press, 2009.

Scobell, Andrew. *China's Use of Military Force: Beyond the Great Wall and the Long March.* New York: Cambridge University Press, 2003.

Shambaugh, David. "China's Propaganda System: Institutions, Processes and Efficacy." *The China Journal*, no. 57 (2007): 25–58.

Shirk, Susan L. *China: Fragile Superpower.* New York: Oxford University Press, 2007.

Small, Deborah A., Jennifer S. Lerner, and Baruch Fischhoff. "Emotion Priming and Attributions for Terrorism: Americans' Reactions in a National Field Experiment." *Political Psychology* 27, no. 2 (2006): 289–98.

Smith, Alastair. "Diversionary Foreign Policy in Democratic Systems." *International Studies Quarterly* 40, no. 1 (1996): 133–53.

Smith, Tom W. "Is There Real Opinion Change?" *International Journal of Public Opinion Research* 6, no. 2 (1994): 187–203.

Smyth, Regina, and Sarah Oates. "Mind the Gaps: Media Use and Mass Action in Russia." *Europe-Asia Studies* 67, no. 2 (February 7, 2015): 285–305.

Snyder, Jack, and Erica D. Borghard. "The Cost of Empty Threats: A Penny, Not a Pound." *American Political Science Review* 105, no. 3 (2011): 437–56.

Speier, Hans. "Morale and Propaganda." In *Propaganda in War and Crisis: Materials for American Policy*, edited by Daniel Lerner, 3–25. New York: G. W. Stewart, 1951.

State Oceanic Administration. *Zhongguo Haiyang Nianjian (China Ocean Yearbook).* Beijing: State Oceanic Administration, 1986.

Stern, Rachel E., and Jonathan Hassid. "Amplifying Silence: Uncertainty and Control Parables in Contemporary China." *Comparative Political Studies* 45, no. 10 (October 1, 2012): 1230–54.

Stockmann, Daniela. *Media Commercialization and Authoritarian Rule in China.* New York: Cambridge University Press, 2013.

Stockmann, Daniela. "Propaganda for Sale: The Impact of Newspaper Commercialization on News Content and Public Opinion in China." PhD diss., University of Michigan, 2007.

Stockmann, Daniela. "Who Believes Propaganda? Media Effects during the Anti-Japanese Protests in Beijing." *The China Quarterly* 202 (2010): 269–89.

Stockmann, Daniela, and Mary E. Gallagher. "Remote Control: How the Media Sustain Authoritarian Rule in China." *Comparative Political Studies* 44, no. 4 (April 1, 2011): 436–67.

Stoll, Richard J. "The Guns of November: Presidential Reelections and the Use of Force, 1947–82." *Journal of Conflict Resolution* 28 (1984): 231–46.

Straubhaar, Joseph, Robert LaRose, and Lucinda Davenport. *Media Now: Understanding Media, Culture, and Technology.* Boston: Cengage Learning, 2013.

Sullivan, Jonathan, and Lei Xie. "Environmental Activism, Social Networks and the Internet." *The China Quarterly* 198 (June 2009): 422–32.

Svolik, Milan W. *The Politics of Authoritarian Rule.* Cambridge Studies in Comparative Politics. Cambridge: Cambridge University Press, 2012.

Swaine, Michael. "China's Assertive Behavior (Part One: On 'Core Interests')." *China Leadership Monitor* 34 (Winter 2011).

Tam, Yue-him. "Who Engineered the Anti-Japanese Protests in 2005." *Macalester International* 18, no. 25 (Spring 2007): 281–99.

Tang, Jiaxuan. *Zhongguo Waijiao Cidian (The Chinese Dictionary of Diplomacy).* Beijing: Shijie Zhishi Chubanshe (World Affairs Press), 2000.

Tang, Wenfang. *Populist Authoritarianism: Chinese Political Culture and Regime Sustainability.* New York: Oxford University Press, 2016.

318 Bibliography

Taubman, Geoffry. "A Not-So World Wide Web: The Internet, China, and the Challenges to Nondemocratic Rule." *Political Communication* 15, no. 2 (April 1, 1998): 255–72.

Thayer, Carlyle A. "4 Reasons China Removed Oil Rig HYSY-981 Sooner Than Planned." *The Diplomat*, July 22, 2014.

Thayer, Carlyle A. "Background Briefing: Recent Naval Exercises in the South China Sea." Strategic Advice and Geopolitical Estimates (SAGE) International Australia, June 7, 2011, 1–5, https://www.files.ethz.ch/isn/131071/Background%20Briefing.pdf.

Thayer, Carlyle A. "China's Cable Cutting: Once Is an Incident Twice Is Pattern." Background briefing. Thayer Consultancy, June 9, 2011. https://www.scribd.com/document/57491115/Thayer-China-s-Cable-Cutting-Once-is-an-Incident-Twice-is-a-Pattern.

Thayer, Carlyle A. "China's Oil Rig Gambit: South China Sea Game-Changer?" *The Diplomat*, May 12, 2014. https://thediplomat.com/2014/05/chinas-oil-rig-gambit-south-china-sea-game-changer/.

Thayer, Carlyle A. "Standoff in the South China Sea." *YaleGlobal Online*, June 12, 2012. http://yaleglobal.yale.edu/content/standoff-south-china-sea.

The Public Opinion Monitoring Office, People.com. "2013 Nian Zhongguo Hulianwang Yuqing Fenxi Baogao [Analysis on Internet-Based Public Opinion in China in 2013]." In *Blue Book of China's Society - Analysis and Forecast of Chinese Society 2014*, edited by Peilin Li, Guangjin Chen, and Yi Zhang, 215–238. Beijing: Shehui Kexue Wenxian Chubanshe (Social Science Academic Press), 2013.

Thornton, Patricia M. "Retrofitting the Steel Frame: From Mobilizing the Masses to Surveying the Public." In *Mao's Invisible Hand: The Political Foundations of Adaptive Governance in China*, edited by E. J. Perry and S. Heilmann, 237–68. Cambridge, MA: Harvard University Asia Center, 2011.

Tir, Jaroslav. "Territorial Diversion: Diversionary Theory of War and Territorial Conflict." *Journal of Politics* 72, no. 2 (April 2010): 413–25.

Tourangeau, Roger, and Mirta Galešić. "Conceptions of Attitudes and Opinions." In *The SAGE Handbook of Public Opinion Research*, edited by Wolfgang Donsbach and Michael Traugott, 141–54. London: SAGE Publications, 2008.

Trachtenberg, Marc. "Audience Costs: An Historical Analysis." *Security Studies* 21, no. 1 (January 1, 2012): 3–42.

Tretiak, Daniel. "The Sino-Japanese Treaty of 1978: The Senkaku Incident Prelude." *Asian Survey* 18, no. 12 (December 1, 1978): 1235–49.

Truex, Rory. "Consultative Authoritarianism and Its Limits." *Comparative Political Studies* 50, no. 3 (2017): 329–61.

Tsai, Wen-Hsuan. "How 'Networked Authoritarianism' Was Operationalized in China: Methods and Procedures of Public Opinion Control." *Journal of Contemporary China* 25, no. 101 (September 2, 2016): 731–44.

Tversky, A., and D. Kahneman. "The Framing of Decisions and the Psychology of Choice." *Science* 211, no. 4481 (January 30, 1981): 453–58.

Tversky, Amos, and Daniel Kahneman. "Availability: A Heuristic for Judging Frequency and Probability." *Cognitive Psychology* 5, no. 2 (1973): 207–32.

Tversky, Amos, and Daniel Kahneman. "Judgment under Uncertainty: Heuristics and Biases." *Science* 185, no. 4157 (September 27, 1974): 1124–31.

US Department of State. "China Seeks Reduction in Surveillance Ship Activity for Successful Summit." March 25, 2009, https://wikileaks.org/plusd/cables/09BEIJING781_a.html.

Wæver, Ole. " Securitization and Desecuritization." In *On Security*, edited by Ronnie D. Lipschutz, 46–86. New York: Columbia University Press, 1995.

Walker, Christopher, and Robert W. Orttung. "Breaking the News: The Role of State-Run Media." *Journal of Democracy* 25, no. 1 (January 2014): 71–85.

Wallace, Jeremy L. "Information Politics in Dictatorships." In *Emerging Trends in the Social and Behavioral Sciences*, 1–11. New York: Wiley, 2015.

Walt, Stephen M. "Is the Cyber Threat Overblown?" *Foreign Policy* 30 (2010). https://foreignpolicy.com/2010/03/30/is-the-cyber-threat-overblown/.

Walt, Stephen M. "Threat Inflation 6.0: Does al-Shabab Really Threaten the US." *Foreign Policy* 26 (2013). https://foreignpolicy.com/2013/09/26/threat-inflation-6-0-does-al-shabab-really-threaten-the-u-s/.

Walt, Stephen M. "The Threat Monger's Handbook." *Foreign Policy* 4 (2009).

Waltz, Kenneth N. *Theory of International Politics*. Long Grove, IL: Waveland Press, 1979.

Wang, Chenghan. *Wang Chenghan Huiyilu (Wang Chenghan's Memoir)*. Beijing: Jiefangjun Chubanshe (People's Liberation Army Publishing House), 2004.

Wang, Frances Yaping, and Brantly Womack. "Jawing through Crises: Chinese and Vietnamese Media Strategies in the South China Sea." *Journal of Contemporary China* 28, no. 119 (September 3, 2019): 712–28.

Wang, Yongbing. "Chiguajiao Dengluzhan (Johnson South Reef Battle)." *Jiancha Fengyun (Prosecutorial View)* 21 (2015): 77–79.

Weaver, David H. *Media Agenda-Setting in a Presidential Election: Issues, Images, and Interest*. Westport, CT: Praeger, 1981.

Wedeen, Lisa. *Ambiguities of Domination: Politics, Rhetoric, and Symbols in Contemporary Syria*. Chicago: University of Chicago Press, 1999.

Weeks, Jessica L. "Autocratic Audience Costs: Regime Type and Signaling Resolve." *International Organization* 62, no. 1 (2008): 35–64.

Weeks, Jessica L. *Dictators at War and Peace*. Ithaca, NY: Cornell University Press, 2014.

Weeks, Jessica L. "Strongmen and Straw Men: Authoritarian Regimes and the Initiation of International Conflict." *American Political Science Review* 106, no. 2 (2012): 326–47.

Weimann, Gabriel. "The Influentials: Back to the Concept of Opinion Leaders?" *The Public Opinion Quarterly* 55, no. 2 (1991): 267–79.

Weiss, Jessica C. "Authoritarian Signaling, Mass Audiences, and Nationalist Protest in China." *International Organization* 67, no. 1 (2013): 1–35.

Weiss, Jessica C. "Powerful Patriots: Nationalism, Diplomacy, and the Strategic Logic of Anti-Foreign Protest." PhD diss., University of California, San Diego, 2008.

Weiss, Jessica C. *Powerful Patriots: Nationalist Protest in China's Foreign Relations*. New York: Oxford University Press, 2014.

Weiss, Jessica C., and Allan Dafoe. "Authoritarian Audiences, Rhetoric, and Propaganda in International Crises: Evidence from China." *International Studies Quarterly* 63, no. 4 (December 1, 2019): 963–73.

Welch, David. *The Third Reich: Politics and Propaganda*. New York: Routledge, 2008.

Weller, Robert P. "Responsive Authoritarianism and Blind-Eye Governance in China." In *Socialism Vanquished, Socialism Challenged*, edited by Nina Bandelj and Dorothy J. Solinger, 83–100. New York: Oxford University Press, 2012.

White House. "National Security Strategy of the United States of America." Washington, DC, December 2017. https://www.whitehouse.gov/wp-content/uploads/2017/12/NSS-Final-12-18-2017-0905-2.pdf.

Whyte, Martin King. *Small Groups and Political Rituals in China*. Berkeley: University of California Press, 1983.

Wilson, Francis G. "Concepts of Public Opinion." *The American Political Science Review* 27, no. 3 (1933): 371–91.

Womack, Brantly. *China and Vietnam: The Politics of Asymmetry*. New York: Cambridge University Press, 2006.

Womack, Brantly. "The Spratlys: From Dangerous Ground to Apple of Discord." *Contemporary Southeast Asia: A Journal of International and Strategic Affairs* 33, no. 3 (2011): 370–87.

320 Bibliography

Woodside, Alexander. "Nationalism and Poverty in the Breakdown of Sino-Vietnamese Relations." *Pacific Affairs* 52, no. 3 (1979): 381–409.

Wu, Lengxi. *Shi Nian Lunzhan, 1956-1966, Zhong Su Guanxi Huiyilu, (10-Year Polemical War, 1956-1966, A Memoir of Sino-Soviet Relations)*. Vol. I. Beijing: Zhongyang Wenxian Chubanshe (Central Party Literature Press), 1999.

Xu, Guangchun. "Jiang Zemin Xinwen Sixiang de Hexin Neirong (The Core Ideas of Jiang Zemin's Thoughts on Media)." *Xinwen Zhanxian (News Frontline)*, no. 2 (2004).

Xu, Linhong, Hongfei Lin, Yu Pan, Hui Ren, and Jianmei Chen. "Constructing the Affective Lexicon Ontology." *Journal of the China Society for Scientific and Technical Information* 27, no. 2 (2008): 180–85.

Yang, Guobin. *The Power of the Internet in China: Citizen Activism Online*. New York: Columbia University Press, 2009.

Yang, Guobin. "(Un) Civil Society in Digital China| Demobilizing the Emotions of Online Activism in China: A Civilizing Process." *International Journal of Communication* 11 (2017): 1945–65.

Yang, Guobin, and Min Jiang. "The Networked Practice of Online Political Satire in China: Between Ritual and Resistance." *International Communication Gazette* 77, no. 3 (April 1, 2015): 215–31.

Yang, Kuisong. "The Sino-Soviet Border Clash of 1969: From Zhenbao Island to Sino-American Rapprochement." *Cold War History* 1, no. 1 (August 2000): 21–52.

Yang, Qing, and Wenfang Tang. "Exploring the Sources of Institutional Trust in China: Culture, Mobilization, or Performance?" *Asian Politics & Policy* 2, no. 3 (2010): 415–36.

Yang, Xiaohui. "Chongfan Lishi: Zongyue Chiguajiao Haizhan (Return to History: The Sino-Vietnamese Johnson South Reef Battle)." *Shehui Guancha (Social Outlook)* 10 (2014): 66–68.

You, Ji. "The PLA and Diplomacy: Unraveling Myths about the Military Role in Foreign Policy Making." *Journal of Contemporary China* 23, no. 86 (March 4, 2014): 236–54.

Young, Louise. *Japan's Total Empire: Manchuria and the Culture of Wartime Imperialism*. Vol. 8. Berkeley: University of California Press, 1998.

Yu, Frederick T. C. *Mass Persuasion in Communist China*. Westport, CT: Praeger, 1964.

Yunnan Province Foreign Affairs Office. *Yunnan Province History: Foreign Affairs History*. 53 vols. Kunming: Yunnan Renmin Chubanshe (Yunnan People's Publishing House), 1996.

Zakaria, Fareed. *From Wealth to Power: The Unusual Origins of America's World Role*. Princeton, NJ: Princeton University Press, 1999.

Zhai, Qiang. *China and the Vietnam Wars, 1950-1975*. Chapel Hill: University of North Carolina Press, 2000.

Zhang, Liangfu. *Nansha Qundao Dashiji (Chronology of the Spratly Islands)*. Beijing: Haiyang Chubanshe (China Ocean Press), 1996.

Zhang, Xiaoming. *Deng Xiaoping's Long War: The Military Conflict Between China and Vietnam, 1979-1991*. Chapel Hill: University of North Carolina Press, 2015.

Zhao, Sicong. "The People's Daily: A Longitudinal Content Analysis of Editorials from 1977–2010." Master's thesis, Iowa State University, 2014.

Zhao, Suisheng. "A State-Led Nationalism: The Patriotic Education Campaignin Post-Tiananmen in China." *Communist and Post-Communist Studies* 31, no. 3 (1998): 287–302.

Zhao, Suisheng. "Foreign Policy Implications of Chinese Nationalism Revisited: The Strident Turn." *Journal of Contemporary China* 22, no. 82 (2013): 535–53.

Zhao, Suisheng. *A Nation-State by Construction: Dynamics of Modern Chinese Nationalism*. Redwood City, CA: Stanford University Press, 2004.

Zhonggong Zhongyang Wenxian Yanjiu Shi (Party Documents Research Office of the CPC Central Committee). "Zhongguo Gongchandang Hongjun Disijun Dijiuci Daibiao Dahui Jueyi'an (Resolution of the Chinese Communist Party the Fourth Red Army Nineth Plenary Meeting)." In *Selected Works of Mao Zedong (Mao Zedong Wenji)*, 87–99. Beijing: Renmin Chubanshe (People's Publishing House), 1993.

Zhou, Deli. *Xu Shiyou de Zuihou Yizhan (The Last Battle of Xu Shiyou)*. Nanjing: Jiangsu Renmin Chubanshe (Jiangsu People's Publishing House), 1990.

Zhou, Deli. *Yige Gaoji Canmouzhang de Zishu (Personal Recollections of a High-Ranking Chief of Staff)*. Nanjing: Nanjing Chubanshe (Nanjing Publishing House), 1992.

Zhou, Junlun, ed. *Nie Rongzhen Nianpu (Chronicles of Nie Rongzhen)*. Beijing: Renmin Chubanshe (People's Publishing House), 1999.

Zhu, Jiamu. *Chen Yun Nianpu (Chronicles of Chen Yun)*. Beijing Zhongyang Wenxian Chubanshe (Central Party Literature Press), 2000.

Zhu, Jian-Hua. "Information Availability, Source Credibility, and Audience Sophistication: Factors Conditioning the Effects of Communist Propaganda in China." PhD diss., Indiana University, 1990.

Index

For the benefit of digital users, indexed terms that span two pages (e.g., 52–53) may, on occasion, appear on only one of those pages.

Tables and figures are indicated by *t* and *f* following the page number

About Face (Brzezinski), 100
activism, 189
ADIZ. *See* air defense identification zone
agenda-setting, 32
air defense identification zone (ADIZ), 141
anger, 189
anti-foreign nationalism, 28
anti-Japan nationalism, 50
Antonov, S., 296
ANTUSD dictionary, 195–98, 301
ANTUSD sentiment scores, 203*t*, 302*f*, 303*f*
approach-avoidance dimension of emotions, 33, 189
Aquino, Benigno, III, 147
Arab Spring, 225, 247
Arrow, Kenneth, 32–33
artificial islands, 130
Arunachal Pradesh, 67
ASEAN. *See* Association of Southeast Asian Nations
ASEAN-China Senior Officials' Meeting on the Implementation of the DOC, 172
ASEAN Foreign Ministers' summit, 275–76
ASEAN Regional Forum of 2010, 164, 228, 266
Association of Southeast Asian Nations (ASEAN), 127–28, 143, 146–47, 272, 273
South China Sea and, 172
astroturfing, 9, 41
audience costs
alternative explanations and, 146–48
observable implications of, 55–56
pacification mechanisms and, 54–55, 242
Scarborough Shoal standoff and, 298
Sino-Philippines arbitration case and, 146–48
Vietnam propaganda campaigns and, 234–36

audience cost theory, 8, 40, 52–54, 147
public awareness and, 54
trade-off in, 54
authoritarianism
digital, 247–48
fundamental issues for, 222
marketization impact on, 72
persuasion and, 226
popular nationalism and, 243
populist, 226
regime typology for, 222
authoritarian states
feedback mechanisms missing in, 14
foreign policymaking and, 7
media campaigns and, 5–6
media tactics of, 10, 221
misalignment theory and, 220–21
misrepresentation of intentions by, 186–87
nationalism and, 50–51
propaganda functions and, 23
public opinion and foreign policy relationship in, 130
public opinion groups and, 13–14
public opinion strategies of, 8, 9
regime legitimacy and, 131
state-society relations in, 25–29
territorial disputes and, 10
autocracies
comparison of, 222–26
defining, 222
propaganda strategies and, 9
public opinion and, 26–29
state-society alignment importance to, 24–30
availability heuristic, 32

Badme, 245–46

324 Index

Bahrain, 223
  social media and, 225
Baidu Search Index (BSI), 125*f*, 125, 126, 165, 171, 266, 267–68, 271, 275, 276
"barking without biting" phenomena, 2–3, 8, 132–46
BAS. *See* Beijing Area Study
BBC. *See* British Broadcasting Corporation
Becker, Jonathan, 223, 225
Beijing Area Study (BAS), 125, 275
Belgrade embassy bombing, 39, 43, 51, 246
binary framings, 212
Binh Minh 02 (ship), 162, 265
Bo Xilai, 297
Brady, Anne-Marie, 72
brainwashing, 68–69
Brecher, Michael, 11, 12
British Broadcasting Corporation (BBC), 259
Brzezinski, Zbigniew, 100
BSI. *See* Baidu Search Index

cable-cutting incidents, 87, 161, 162–70, 228, 265–67
Cambodia, 94, 108, 110, 255, 256–57
Carter, Ashton, 124–25
Carter, Brett, 9
Carter, Erin, 9
Carter, Jimmy, 100, 256–57
CATI. *See* computer-assisted telephone interviewing
CCP. *See* Chinese Communist Party
CCTV. *See* China Central Television
CCTV News, 163, 297
censorship, 7–8, 10, 131–32, 171
  autocracies and, 2, 5, 9
  channeling and, 72
  hard power and, 34–35, 36, 46, 52
  internet, 224, 245
  internet control and, 70
  media amplification and, 2, 80
  media control and, 75
  opinion management and, 9
  pacification and, 188
  self-, 75
  soft power and, 35
  state autonomy and, 28–29
  venting and, 43–44
  Vietnam and, 227
Central Intelligence Agency (CIA), 99, 100
Central Leading Group for Internet Security and Informatization, 71

Central Leading Group on Propaganda and Ideological Work, 73–74
Central Leading Small Group on the Protection of Maritime Interests, 174, 272
Central Military Commission (CMC), 92, 96, 102–3, 253
Central Propaganda Department (CPD), 73–74, 75–76, 104–5, 146, 261
  KFC demonstrations and, 131–32
Central Work Conference, 111–12
CFDD. *See* China Federation for Defending the Diaoyu Islands
Chai Zemin, 100
Chan, David, 260–61
Chanda, Nayan, 256
Chang Wanquan, 143
channeling public opinion (*yulun yindao*), 71–72
Chávez, Hugo, 225
Chen Xilian, 253
Chen Yun, 110–11, 112
China
  censorship in, 224
  Dalai Lama and, 67
  diplomatic crises and media campaigns, 6
  Freedom House on media environment in, 223
  information control in, 35
  intensification of maritime policy of, 169
  internet in, 69, 72, 224
  land reclamation activities, 124–25, 126, 129
  media control and, 7–8, 10
  media coverage of territorial crises in, 75–76
  media use in interstate disputes, 1–2
  nationalism in, 7–8, 227–28
  nine-dash line claim by, 122–23, 127, 166–67
  nonacceptance and nonparticipation in arbitration case, 122–23, 127–28
  policy intents of, 169
  propaganda system development in, 68–73
  propaganda system of, 221, 225
  propaganda system operations in, 73–75
  public relations responses, 135*t*
  public sentiment toward other nations in, 125
  reform in, 69
  SOE reform in, 296–97

studying diplomatic crises and, 10–11
Vietnam border with, 95
Vietnam diplomatic relations with, 172, 174, 176, 231, 273
Vietnam overflights by, 99
Vietnam refugees in, 103, 256
China-ASEAN Defense Ministers Informal Meeting, 143
China-ASEAN Foreign Ministers' summit, 129
China Can Say No, 69–70
China Central Television (CCTV), 78, 138, 291–92
cable-cutting incidents and, 163
China Daily (newspaper), 167–68
China Digital Times, 75, 178, 291–92
China Federation for Defending the Diaoyu Islands (CFDD), 264–65
China: Fragile Superpower (Shirk), 35
China Marine Surveillance (CMS), 167–68, 267, 268
China National Offshore Oil Corporation (CNOOC), 167–68, 170, 173, 174, 267, 270, 272–73
China Pictorial (magazine), 251
China Youth Daily, 261
Chinese Communist Party (CCP), 9, 22, 227
criticisms of foreign policy of, 166
internal political guidelines within, 102
"mass line" tradition in, 27
news reporting control by, 75
propaganda guidelines, 104–5
public opinion control and, 28–29
on Sino-Japanese lighthouse crisis, 259
state media and, 73
Chinese Media Campaigns on Territorial Disputes data (CMCTD data), 192–95, 193*t*, 194*t*, 199
Chinese Media Campaigns Opponent-Referenced data (CMCOR data), 192, 195*t*, 196*f*, 202, 203*t*, 204*f*
Cho La clash, 252–53
Christensen, Thomas, 31
Chubb, Andrew, 164, 271
CIA. *See* Central Intelligence Agency
civil society, 70
in Vietnam, 227
Clinton, Hillary, 164, 228, 266
CMC. *See* Central Military Commission
CMCOR data. *See* Chinese Media Campaigns Opponent-Referenced data

CMCTCD data. *See* Chinese Media Campaigns on Territorial Disputes data
CMS. *See* China Marine Surveillance
CNOOC. *See* China National Offshore Oil Corporation
Cohen, Jerome, 127
commercialization, 223
Communist Party of Vietnam (CPV), 227, 229–30
comparative politics, misalignment theory implications for, 241–43
computer-assisted telephone interviewing (CATI), 124
conflict reduction measures, 51
constructivist strategy, 42–43
costly signals, 8
Council for Mutual Economic Assistance, 94
COVID-19 pandemic, 10
CPD. *See* Central Propaganda Department
CPV. *See* Communist Party of Vietnam
Crescent Group, 233
crisis coverage, 41–42
Crisis Group, 174, 272
Cuba, 27, 92, 102–3, 106, 222, 223
internet in, 224–25
Cui Tiankai, 134–36
Cultural Revolution, 97, 101, 110–11, 252
Cybersecurity Law, 71
Cyberspace Administration of China, 71
Czech Republic, 139

Dai Bingguo, 134–36, 141–42, 163
Dalai Lama, 67, 296
Dalian University of Technology (DLUT), 198
damage control approaches, 131
Declaration on Conduct of Parties in the South China Sea (DOC), 172, 272
deconstructivist strategy, 42–43
de-escalation, 8
media campaigns and, 4
media frames and, 9
delegitimization, of emotions, 40–41, 42, 133, 144
demobilization, emotional, 9
democracy
feedback mechanisms of, 14
misalignment theory and, 246–47
Den, Hideo, 16n.3
Deng Xiaoping, 69, 95–96, 99–100, 108, 110–11, 255, 256–58

326　Index

Deng Yingchao, 110–11
Department of Asian Affairs, 174, 272
Department of Boundary and Ocean
　Affairs, 174
desecuritization, 34, 42–43, 242
Diaoyu/Senkaku Islands dispute, 1–2, 11, 34–
　35, 50, 80, 254–55, 260–61, 262–64
　boat incident and, 291–92
　Japanese nationalization of, 268–69
　lighthouse crisis and, 258–59
Dickson, Bruck, 35
dictating discourse, 37, 37*t*, 133
digital authoritarianism, 247–48
digital media, 36
digitization, 223
diplomacy, 29–30, 187, 223–24
　secret, 51
diplomatic crises, 77*t*
　China and studying, 10–11
　defining, 11
　manufacturing to shape public opinion, 48
　media campaigns and, 6, 48
　misalignment theory testing in, 76–86
　predicted and actual outcomes of, 83*t*
　statistics for media coverage of, 79*t*
discourse
　dictating, 37, 133
　elite tension with popular, 24
　pacification and, 4
diversionary theory, 31, 52–53
　alternative explanations and, 110–
　　12, 146–48
　observable implications of, 53, 110–11
　Scarborough Shoal standoff and, 297
　Sino-Philippines arbitration case
　　and, 146–48
DLUT. *See* Dalian University of Technology
DLUT Emotion Ontology dictionary, 198–99
DOC. *See* Declaration on Conduct of Parties
　in the South China Sea
Doklam, 276–77
domestic crisis
　arbitration crisis and, 148
　diversionary theory and, 53
Duterte, Rodrigo, 123, 128, 129, 275

echo effect, 38, 133
echoing, 37*t*, 38, 39, 46, 137, 138–39, 188
EEZs. *See* exclusive economic zones
Egypt, 247
elite discourse, 24

emotional demobilization, 9
emotions
　approach-avoidance dimension of, 33, 189
　campaign tactics and, 37*t*, 40–41, 42, 133
　delegitimizing negative, 189
　hypotheses focusing on, 190
　media campaigns and, 191, 214–16
　mobilization campaigns and, 33, 46, 187,
　　188, 191
　pacification campaigns and, 187, 189, 191
　promotion of positive, 144
Encomienda, Alberto, 138
EP3 incident of 2003, 246
equifinality, 52–53
Eritrea, 245–46
Ethiopia, 245–46
Evening News (Wanjian Xinwen), 291–92
exclusive economic zones (EEZs), 124, 162,
　166–67, 260, 266–67, 270
　overlapping, 170
extremists
　militarist sentiments and, 166
　public opinion and, 13–14

Facebook, 225
Fair Deal program, 31
fear, 189
Fearon, James, 8, 14–15
50 cent army, 71, 225
FONOPS. *See* Freedom of Navigation
　Operations
Force 47, 225
Foreign Affairs Leading Group, 73–74
foreign media, 133
　state silence and, 37–38
foreign policy
　domestic mobilization impact on, 30–31
　moderate, 36
　nonterritorial issues in, 246
　public opinion and, 49, 130
Foreign Policy (magazine), 147
foreign policy intent, 12–15
foreign policymaking
　authoritarian states and, 7
　public opinion and, 7, 24–25
framing, 32, 33, 40–41, 46, 133, 142–43,
　188, 232–33
　binary, 212
　crisis coverage and, 41–42
　positive, 37*t*
Freedom House, 223, 227

Freedom of Navigation Operations (FONOPS), 122, 124–25, 126, 246, 274–75
Fu Ying, 122, 129, 146–47, 268, 274–75, 292

Gang of Four, 110–11
Gates, Robert, 100
General Statistics Office of Vietnam (GSOV), 176–77, 273
Geng Biao, 92, 102–3, 255
Genron NPO, 269
George, Alexander, 6–7
Global Times, 135*t*, 235
   cable-cutting incidents and, 164
   surveys by, 124
Google, 227
grassroots support, 27, 228. *See also* astroturfing
Great Firewall, 70
Great Leap Forward program, 31
Gries, Peter, 26, 262
GSOV. *See* General Statistics Office of Vietnam
Guangming Daily, 110–11
guiding public opinion (*yulun daoxiang*), 71–72
Gulf of Tonkin, 99
Gunther, Albert, 14

Hainan Island, 170
Hai Yang Shi You 720 drilling platform, 167–68, 267
Hai Yang Shi You 981 drilling platform, 170, 231, 270–71, 273, 292
Han Nianlong, 255
hardline echoing, 188
hardline posturing, 39, 40, 133, 188
hard power, 34–35, 36, 46, 52
hard propaganda, 34–36
Hashimoto, Ryutaro, 260–61
Hatoyama, Yukio, 264
Hoang Cong Tu, 229
Ho Chi Minh, 96–97, 255
homeland disputes, 19n.33
Hong Lei, 122–23, 133–34
Hopf, Ted, 24
Hua Chunying, 135*t*, 173–74, 177–78
Hua Guofeng, 110–11
Hu Jintao, 27, 71–72, 263, 264, 269
Hu Yaobang, 110–11, 296–97

ICJ. *See* International Court of Justice

ideological references, 212
Ikeda, Yukihiko, 260
Impeccable incident, 246, 266
India, 67
   Dalai Lama and, 67, 296
   Soviet Union and, 296
information
   access to, 38
   voids or delays in, 133
information control, 35, 37–38
intercoder reliability, 81
Intergovernmental Oceanographic Commission (IOC), 258
International Court of Justice (ICJ), 138
international law, 137
international media, 1
international relations
   audience costs theories and, 8, 147
   media campaigns and interpreting, 6, 11
   misalignment theory implications for, 241–43
   pacification campaigns and, 8
international security
   media campaigns and, 6
   state-society alignment and, 24–25
International Tribunal on the Law of the Sea (ITLOS), 127, 138, 274–76
internet
   censorship of, 224, 245
   control of, 70, 71
   in Cuba, 224–25
   emergence of, 69
   in Iran, 72
   public opinion and, 27
   repressive uses of, 72
   in Russia, 224
   trolls in, 71, 225
interstate disputes, 187
   media use in, 1–2
   state media behaviors and, 245–46
intrastate disputes, 19n.33
IOC. *See* Intergovernmental Oceanographic Commission
Iran
   commercial media in, 223–24
   internet in, 72
   liberalization and, 223
   nuclear deal, 2–3, 220
Iraq War, 31, 242
Ishihara, Shintaro, 268–69
issue attention cycle hypothesis, 40

328 Index

Issue Correlates of War data, 15
ITLOS. *See* International Tribunal on the Law of the Sea

James Shoal, 1
Japan
    BAS survey on, 125
    Diaoyu/Senkaku Islands nationalization by, 268–69
    history textbooks in, 262–64
    propaganda in Imperial era, 220
    UN Security Council bid, 262–64
Japanese Maritime Safety Agency, 258–59, 260–61
Japan Youth Federation (JYF), 260–61
Jiang Zemin, 71–72
Johnson South Reef skirmish, 233
Johnston, Iain, 13–14
Journal of Red Flag, 110–11
JYF. *See* Japan Youth Federation

Kaifu, Toshiki, 258–59
Kan, Naoto, 264
Kapunan, Rod, 137–38
Katz, Andrew, 11
Kennedy, John, 56–57
Kentucky Fried Chicken (KFC), 126, 131–32, 275
Kerry, John, 141–42, 175
KFC. *See* Kentucky Fried Chicken
Khmer Rouge, 94, 255
Kim Jong-un, 26
Kongka Pass, 251, 295–96
Koroma, Abdul Gadire, 144
Krebs, Ronald R., 6
Krejčí, Oskar, 139

LAC. *See* Line of Actual Control
Ladakh, 269–70, 274
land reclamation projects, 124–25, 126, 129
language
    in mobilization and pacification campaigns, 5
    politics and, 6
    positive, 143
Laos, 94, 143
latent Dirichlet allocation (LDA), 198
latent public opinion, 13
LDA. *See* latent Dirichlet allocation
Le Duan, 93, 98–99
Le Hong Anh, 174, 272

Liang Qichao, 43
Liao Chengzhi, 16n.3
Liaoning Province, 260–61
liberal-democratic tradition, accountability and, 25
liberalization, 223
Libya, 247
Li Keqiang, 172, 272
Line of Actual Control (LAC), 252, 269–70, 274
Li Peng, 260–61
Lippmann-Almond consensus, 25
Liu Shaoqi, 96–97, 110–11
Liu Weimin, 297–98
Liu Yunshan, 22
Liu Zhenmin, 128, 141, 275
Li Wei, 28
Li Xiannian, 98, 99
Li Zhaoxing, 263
Longju and Kongka Pass clashes, 295–96
Lu Kang, 134–36, 142–43
Luo Zhaohui, 268
Lynch, Daniel, 70

Malaysia, 99–100
    James Shoal and, 1
    liberalization and, 223
    South China Sea and, 121
Ma Licheng, 262
Manila Standard (newspaper), 137–38
"manufacturing consent" propaganda model, 36
Maoist media control, 69
Mao Zedong, 31, 77–78, 93, 96–97, 110–11, 166, 251–52, 266, 296
    death of, 101
    propaganda and, 68
    Sino-Soviet border conflict and, 253
    Vietnam and, 255
marketization, 69
    authoritarianism and, 72
Marshall Plan, 94
Marxism, 110–11
Mass Line ideology, 226
mass media
    control of, 10
    filters distorting, 36
    media campaigns in, 3, 5–6
mass persuasion, 37
    tactics of, 40–41
McMahon Line, 251, 257

Index **329**

Mearsheimer, John, 24, 31
media
  agenda-setting and, 32
  alternative sources, 133
  in authoritarian states, 223
  filters distorting, 36
  foreign, 37–38, 133
  framing role of, 33
  international, 1
  liberalization and credibility of, 39
  priming role of, 32
  privatization in, 69
media campaigns, 186
  audience costs and, 8, 53–54
  authoritarian states and, 5–6
  "barking dog" puzzles in use of, 1–3
  borderline, 291
  classifying types of, 244
  crises and occurrence of, 11
  damage control approaches in, 131
  data on, 192–95
  decision tree for, 58, 58f
  diplomatic crises and, 6, 48
  distinctions between types of, 186
  effects of, 55–57
  emotions and, 191, 214–16
  future trends of, 247–48
  identifying, 78
  mobilization and alignment of, 30–34
  narratives and, 190–91, 204–14
  pacification and alignment of, 34–44
  policy interpretation and, 6
  reasons for using, 3–5
  results and discussion on, 199–216
  significance of, 5–7
  Sino-Philippines arbitration crisis
    and, 133–34
  as strategic state actions, 22
  testing hypotheses on, 189–91
  testing methods for, 195–99
  theoretical assumptions and time
    associations of, 46–48
  types of, 3–5
  United States documents on, 6
  valence and, 190, 199–204
media control, 10, 222
  Maoist, 69
  in Vietnam, 227
media coverage
  of oil rig crisis, 177–78
  during Scarborough Shoal crisis, 133

Sino-Philippines arbitration crisis
  and, 132–46
  statistics for, in diplomatic crises, 79t
  of territorial crises, 75–76
micro-blogs, 69, 126, 275
Militarized Interstate Disputes (MID), 14–15
Ministry of Foreign Affairs (MoFA), 122–23, 134
  Department of Boundary and Ocean
    Affairs, 174
  on Ikeda remarks, 260
  on Japan UNSC bid, 263
Min Jiang, 70
mirroring, 233
misalignments
  other authoritarian states and, 220–21
  types of, 22
misalignment theory, 15–16, 23t, 67
  alternative explanations and, 52–55
  assumptions of, 46, 47
  democracy and, 246–47
  extending argument for and future
    research directions, 245–47
  international relations and comparative
    politics implications of, 241–43
  logical challenges for, 48–52
  testing in diplomatic crises, 76–86
  typical case selection for, 86–88, 87t
  utility to policymakers of, 243–45
mobilization
  Christensen two-level model for, 31
  foreign policy importance of domestic, 30–31
  media campaign alignment and, 30–34
mobilization campaigns, 3–5, 186, 241
  emotions and, 33, 46, 187, 188, 189,
    191, 214–16
  exogenous or endogenous, 48–49
  ideological references and, 212
  misalignments and, 22–23
  narratives and, 190–91
  observable implications of, 45, 109, 110
  pacification distinguished from, 187–89
  PLA and, 105
  reduced use of, 47
  sentiment scores in, 301, 302f, 303f
  Sino-Vietnamese border war and, 101–10
  tactics of, 37t
  themes in, 206f, 212–13
  "us"-"them" demarcations in, 212
  valence, topics, and emotions of, 187
  valence and, 190
  words used in, 205, 305

330 Index

moderate policy intentions, 6–7, 177
  pacification campaigns and, 36
MoFA. *See* Ministry of Foreign Affairs
Morozov, Evgeny, 7
Mukden Incident, 264–65

narratives, 190–91
  controlling, 37
  defining, 190
  delegitimizing negative emotions
    and, 189
  results and discussion for, 204–14
Nathu La clash, 252–53
National Conferences of Propaganda
  Department Directors, 73–74
The National Interest, 268, 274–75
nationalism, 227–28
  anti-foreign, 28
  anti-Japan, 50
  authoritarian states and, 50–51
  in China, 7–8
  growth of, 69–70
  as negotiating leverage, 235
  popular, 243
  positive framing and, 232–33
  risks of inciting, 179
  South China Sea and, 171
  state-funded trolls for, 71
National Propaganda Thought Work
  Meeting, 71–72, 73–74
National Taiwan University Sentiment
  Dictionary (NTUSD), 195–98, 199,
  200*f*, 201, 201*f*, 202*f*, 203*t*, 204*f*
Nazis, 9, 68
  domestic propaganda by, 6–7
Negroponte, John D., 141–42
Nehru, Jawaharlal, 251, 252
neo-authoritarian media systems, 223
Network News (Xinwen Lianbo), 291–92
"New Horizon (Xin Shiye)" (television
  program), 291–92
New York Times (newspaper), 227
Ngo Ngoc Thu, 175
Nguyen Phu Trong, 229–30
Nguyen Tan Dung, 175, 229–30, 231–32
Nhan Dan (The People) (newspaper), 231
nine-dash line claim, 122–23, 127, 166–67
Nixon, Richard, 93
nonterritorial foreign policy issues, 246
NTUSD. *See* National Taiwan University
  Sentiment Dictionary

nuclear weapons, 47

Obama, Barack, 124–25
objectivist strategy, 42–43
opinion formation, 13
opinion management, 9
Ouyang Yujing, 133–34

pacification campaigns, 3–5, 186, 241,
  242, 243
  emotions and, 189, 191, 214–16
  ideological references and, 212
  mechanisms of, 36–44
  media campaign alignment and, 34–44
  misalignments and, 22–23
  mobilization distinguished from, 187–89
  moderate policy intentions and, 36
  narratives and, 190–91
  observable implications of, 45–46
  positive framing in, 188
  posturing in, 188
  sentiment scores in, 301, 302*f*, 303*f*
  Sino-Philippines arbitration crisis and, 133
  state-society alignment and, 29–30
  tactics of, 36, 37, 37*t*, 38, 39, 40–41, 42, 43
  themes in, 208*f*, 212–13
  unintended external consequences of, 51
  valence, topics, and emotions of, 187
  valence and, 190
  words used in, 205, 305
pacification mechanisms, 36–44
  audience costs and, 54–55, 242
Paracel Islands, 170, 228, 230, 233,
  254, 266–67
participatory digital persuasion, 9
patriotism, 144
The People (Nhan Dan) (newspaper), 231
People's Daily, 16n.3, 22, 77–80, 84, 110–
  11, 217
  on balanced internet environment
    efforts, 41
  Bo Xilai scandal and, 297
  cable-cutting incidents and, 163, 165
  data on articles in, 192
  Diaoyu/Senkaku Islands dispute and, 261
  narratives analysis of, 204–5
  non-Chinese experts cited in, 139, 140*t*
  on Okinawa Reversion Treaty, 50
  on patriotism, 144
  Public Opinion Monitoring Office, 9, 28
  Scarborough Shoal standoff and, 292, 297

Sino-Indian border dispute of 1959 and, 251–52, 295*t*, 296
Sino-Japanese boat incident and, 291, 292
Sino-Philippines arbitration crisis and, 132, 132*f*, 133–34, 135*t*, 137–38, 139, 141, 144, 145
Sino-Vietnamese border war and, 97, 103–4, 106–7
Sino-Vietnamese oil rig crisis and, 177, 178
Strong China Forum (quangguo luntan), 69–70, 71–72
on territorial disputes, 27
valence results and, 203–4
on Vietnam refugees, 103, 106–7
Weibo account, 145
People's Liberation Army (PLA), 128
cable-cutting incidents and, 168
campaign to improve image of, 49–50
Diaoyu/Senkaku Islands and, 260–61
General Political Department, 104–5
internal political guidelines within, 102
militia members and, 101
mobilization campaigns and, 105
Political Department, 105
Sino-India border war and, 252, 253
Sino-Vietnamese border war opinions in, 98
state media and, 73
People's Liberation Army Navy (PLAN), 255
oil rig crisis and, 173
Paracel Islands and, 254
Spratlys and, 258
Perry, Elizabeth, 49–50
persuasion
authoritarian regimes and, 226
mass, 37, 40–41
social judgment theory and, 38–39
PetroVietnam, 174
Pham Binh Minh, 175, 231
Pham Van Dong, 93, 94, 95–96, 98–99, 103
the Philippines, 87–88
BAS survey on, 125
Phoenix TV, 165
Phung Quang Thanh, 232
PLA. *See* People's Liberation Army
PLA Daily, 110–11
PLAN. *See* People's Liberation Army Navy
Poh, Angela, 176–77, 273
policy
media campaigns and interpretation of, 6

misalignment theory utility in making, 243–45
policy intent
coding rules for, 249
determining, 82
Diaoyu/Senkaku Islands dispute and, 261
endogeneity of, 169
Japanese nationalization of Diaoyu/ Senkaku islands and, 269
Sino-Indian border clashes of 1967 and, 253
Sino-Indian border disputes and, 251–52
Sino-Indian border standoff of 1986 and, 257–58
Sino-Indian border standoff of 2013, 270
Sino-Indian border war of 1962 and, 252
Sino-Japanese Boat Incident and, 255, 264–65
Sino-Japanese Diaoyu/Senkaku Islands dispute of 2005 and, 263–64
Sino-Japanese lighthouse crisis of 1990 and, 259–60
Sino-Philippines arbitration case of 2016 and, 275–76
Sino-Philippines Scarborough Shoal Standoff of 2012 and, 268
Sino-Soviet border conflict of 1969, 253
Sino-Vietnamese border war and, 256–57
Sino-Vietnamese cable-cutting incidents and, 266–67
Sino-Vietnamese oil rig crisis and, 272–73
Sino-Vietnamese Paracels clash and, 254
Sino-Vietnamese Spratly Islands clash of 1988 and, 258
Poling, Gregory, 127
politics
comparative, 241–43
language and, 6
popular discourse, 24
popular nationalism, 243
populist authoritarianism, 226
positive emotions, promotion of, 144
positive framing, 37*t*, 40–41, 46, 133, 142–43, 188, 232–33
crisis coverage and, 41–42
positive language, 143
posturing, 37*t*, 39, 40, 46, 133, 139, 188
power
hard, 34–35
soft, 9, 35
power politics, language and, 6

332 Index

power-sharing, 222
Powlick, Philip, 11
preemption, 39
primacy effect, 38
priming, 32
private channels, 188
privatization, 69
propaganda
  autocracy strategies and, 9
  decision tree for, 58, 58f
  development of Chinese system for, 68–73
  efficacy of, 56–57
  functions of, 23
  hard and soft, 34–36
  "manufacturing consent" model of, 36
  Mao Zedong and, 68
  operation of Chinese system for, 73–75
  pacifying use of, 4
  social media and delivery of, 70–71
  territorial disputes and studying, 11–12
public opinion, 12–15
  accountability and, 25
  authoritarian strategies for, 8, 9
  autocracies and, 26–29
  CCP and control over, 28–29
  changes in, 13
  coding rules for, 250
  crises engineered to shape, 48
  Diaoyu/Senkaku Islands dispute and, 261
  divergence of, 130
  emotions and manipulating, 33
  endogeneity of, 49
  foreign policy and, 49, 130
  foreign policymaking and, 7, 24–25
  interdependence with state preferences, 49
  internet and, 27
  Japanese nationalization of Diaoyu/
    Senkaku islands and, 269
  key groups in, 13–14
  latent, 13
  mobilization campaigns and, 3–4
  pacification campaigns and, 4
  perceived, 14
  policy intents and, 169
  Sino-Indian border clashes of 1967
    and, 252
  Sino-Indian border dispute and, 251
  Sino-Indian border standoff of 2013, 270
  Sino-Indian border war of 1962 and, 252
  Sino-Japanese Boat Incident and, 254–
    55, 264

Sino-Japanese Diaoyu/Senkaku Islands
  dispute of 2005 and, 262–63
Sino-Japanese lighthouse crisis of 1990
  and, 259
Sino-Philippines arbitration case of 2016
  and, 274–75
Sino-Philippines Scarborough Shoal
  Standoff of 2012 and, 267–68
Sino-Soviet border conflict of 1969, 253
Sino-Vietnamese border war and, 96–
  98, 256
Sino-Vietnamese cable-cutting incidents
  and, 266
Sino-Vietnamese oil rig crisis and, 271
Sino-Vietnamese Spratly Islands clash of
  1988 and, 258
social media and, 27
state manipulation of, 7
tacit consent and, 130–31
in United States, 25
weak, 13
Public Opinion Monitoring Office, 9, 28
Putin, Vladimir, 220

qiangguo luntan (Strong China Forum),
  69–70, 71–72
Qian Qichen, 260–61
Qi Huaiyuan, 258–59
Qiliqin incident, 253
Qing dynasty, 166, 266

rally-around-the-flag sentiments, 28, 53
Ramos, Fidel V., 129, 275
ratchet effect, 50–51, 52
rationality, encouraging, 42–43
realism, accountability and, 25
Reed Bank, 168
regime changes, supporting, 24
regime legitimacy, 131
regime survival
  audience costs theories and, 8
  pacification strategies and, 52
  state-society alignment and, 24–25
Reilly, James, 7
Repnikova, Maria, 7, 69, 223
resonance, 38–39
Richardson, John, 141–42
rollback, 24
del Rosario, Albert, 121, 147, 275
rumors
  information gaps and, 133

Index

state silence and, 37–38
Russia, 220, 245–46
  internet in, 224
  media system in, 225
  neo-authoritarian media system in, 223
  troll army, 225

SAGE Handbook of Public Opinion Research, 12
Sansha City, 228
SARS. *See* Severe Acute Respiratory Syndrome
Sato Shoji, 255
Saudi Arabia, 245–46
Saunders, Philip, 261
Scarborough Shoal, land reclamation and, 129
Scarborough Shoal Standoff of 2012, 80, 84, 121, 130, 171, 267–68, 292, 297–98
  media coverage during, 133
Schweller, Randall, 30–31
Scobell, Andrew, 98
secret diplomacy, 51
securitization, 31, 242
self-censorship, 75
semi-controlled spaces, 223
sentiment scores, 301, 302*f*, 303*f*
Severe Acute Respiratory Syndrome (SARS), 72
Shangri-La Dialogue, 124–25, 135*t*, 232, 274–75
Shirk, Susan, 7, 13–14, 35, 50–51
Shi Yinhong, 262
"silent dog" phenomenon, 161
silent majority, public opinion and, 13–14
Simla Conference, 251
Sina Weibo, 145, 275
Sing Pao Daily, 262
Sino-Indian border clashes of 1967, 252–53
Sino-Indian border dispute of 1959, 82–84, 251–52, 295–96
Sino-Indian border standoff of 1986, 257–58
Sino-Indian border standoff of 2013, 269–70
Sino-Indian border standoff of 2014, 274
Sino-Indian border standoff of 2017, 276–77
Sino-Indian border war of 1962, 80, 82–84, 252
Sino-Japanese Boat Incident of 2010, 80, 254–55, 264–65, 291–92
Sino-Japanese Diaoyu/Senkaku Islands dispute of 1996, 260–61

Sino-Japanese Diaoyu/Senkaku Islands dispute of 2005, 262–64
Sino-Japanese disputes, 1–2, 24–25
Sino-Japanese Friendship Society, 16n.3
Sino-Japanese lighthouse crisis of 1990, 258–60
Sino-Philippines arbitration case of 2016, 1, 2, 22, 80, 87, 120, 121–23, 171, 274–76
  alternative explanations in, 146–48
  "barking without biting" and, 132–46
  media coverage during, 132–46, 132*f*
  misalignment in, 130–32
  public relations responses during, 135*t*
Sino-Philippines Scarborough Shoal Standoff of 2012, 80, 84, 267–68, 292, 297–98
Sino-Soviet border conflict of 1969, 253
Sino-Soviet split, 82–84, 255, 296
  Vietnam and, 93
Sino-Vietnamese border war of 1979-1990, 80, 81–82, 87, 92–93, 130, 255–57
  media themes and, 106–8
  mobilization campaign and, 101–10
  public opinion and, 96–98
  start of, 93–96
  state policy intent and, 98–101
  war preparation education objectives in, 106
Sino-Vietnamese cable-cutting incidents, 87, 161, 162–70, 228, 265–67
Sino-Vietnamese oil rig crisis, 51, 80, 87, 161, 270–73, 292
  strategy of silence and, 170–79
  from Vietnamese perspective, 228–34
Sino-Vietnamese Paracels clash, 254
Sino-Vietnamese relationship, break of, 93–96
Sino-Vietnamese Spratly Islands clash of 1988, 80, 258, 291, 296–97
Smith, Tom, 13
social identity, 24
Socialist Democratic Federation, 16n.3
social judgment theory, 38–39
social management, 27
social media
  control strategies and, 225
  emergence of, 69
  oil rig crisis and, 171–72
  propaganda delivery and, 70–71
  public opinion and, 27
  venting on, 43, 46, 145, 188
social movements, 189

334 Index

SOE. *See* state-owned enterprise
soft power, 9, 35, 52
soft propaganda, 34–36
South China Sea, 164, 246
    BSI for, 125, 125*f*, 165, 171, 266, 267–68, 271, 275
    China ADIZ in, 141
    defining, 121
    nationalism and, 171
South China Sea dispute, 1, 41–42, 87
South China Sea oil rig crisis of 2014, 2–3
South China Sea Public Opinion Newsletter, 171–72, 271
Soviet Union, 9, 68
    India and, 296
    totalitarian media system in, 223
    Vietnam and, 93, 94, 100, 108, 256–57
Spratly Islands, 1, 80, 142, 165–66, 228, 266–67, 291, 296–97
state autonomy, 28–29
state-funded nationalist trolls, 71
state media
    hierarchy of, 73, 74*f*
    variation in behaviors of, 245–46
    Xi on loyalty of, 73
state-owned enterprise (SOE)
    media outlets and, 223–24
    reforms of, 296–97
state-public gaps, narrowing, 131–32
state-society alignment, 24–30
    conditions favoring pacification campaigns and, 29–30
    regime survival and international security and, 24–25
state-society relations, in authoritarian settings, 25–29
STM. *See* structural topic models
Stockmann, Daniela, 7, 24–25, 39, 72, 263
Strong China Forum (qiangguo luntan), 69–70, 71–72
structural topic models (STM), 195, 198, 205
Sumdorong Chu, 257–58
Svolik, Milan, 222
Syria, 223, 247

tacit consent, 130–31
Taiwan, 246
Tang Jiaxuan, 260–61
Taubman, Geoffry, 70
Territorial Claims Data, 10, 15

territorial crises, 76–77
    typical Chinese media coverage of, 75–76
territorial disputes, 11–12
    authoritarian states and, 10
    results and discussion and, 211
Thanh Nien News, 231, 232, 233
third-person effect, 14
thought control, 68–69
thought reform, 68–69
thought work, 68, 70, 71–72, 73–74
threat inflation, 31, 242
Tiananmen Square incident, 259
Tibetan uprising, 296
Tiwari, N. D., 257–58
totalitarian media systems, 223
traveling propaganda teams, 68–69
Truman, Harry, 31
Truong Tan Sang, 172, 272
Truth Department directives (*zhenlibu zhiling*), 75
Tunisia, 247
24th ASEAN Summit, 175
Twitter, 225
Two Whatevers, 110–11

Ukraine, 220, 245–46
United Nations Convention on the Law of the Sea (UNCLOS), 121, 122–23, 127, 134–36, 166–67, 260, 261, 266–67
    exclusion clause, 133–34
United Nations Security Council (UNSC), 262–64
United States
    documents of, on media campaigns, 6
    FONOPS by, 122
    public opinion in, 25
    South China Sea and, 124–25, 126, 135*t*, 138, 164, 246
    symbols of presence in China, 126
    UNCLOS and, 134–36
unrest, inciting, 24
UNSC. *See* United Nations Security Council
US-Japan Okinawa Reversion Treaty, 50

valence, 190, 199–204
Vanguard Bank, 162
venting, 37*t*, 40–41, 43, 46, 133, 145, 188
verbal mimicry, 38
Vietnam, 87–88
    anti-China protests in, 228–29, 235

Index **335**

audience costs and propaganda campaigns in, 234–36
Cambodia and, 94, 108, 110, 255, 256–57
censorship and, 227
China border with, 95
China diplomatic relations with, 172, 174, 176, 231, 273
China overflights in, 99
Chinese refugees from, 103, 256
civil society in, 227
Force 47, 225
Freedom House on media environment in, 227
Laos and, 94
media campaigns by, 2–3
nationalism in, 227–28
oil exploration operations by, 162–70
Paracel Islands and, 254
propaganda systems of, 221
Sino-Soviet split and, 93, 255
Soviet Union and, 93, 94, 100, 108, 256–57
Vietnam-China Joint Steering Committee for Bilateral Cooperation, 176
Vietnamese Law of the Sea, 174, 228, 272–73
Vietnam Maritime Police, 175
Vietnam War, 93
Viking II (ship), 162, 167, 265–66, 267
Voice of America, 259

Wall Street Journal (newspaper), 147
Walt, Stephen, 31
Wang Chenghan, 253
Wang Yi, 141–42
Wang Zhen, 110–11
Wanjian Xinwen (Evening News), 291–92
weak public opinion, 13
WeChat, 145
Weeks, Jessica, 53–54
Weibo, 134–36, 145
Weiss, Jessica, 53–54
Wen Jiabao, 225–26, 265
World Integrated Trade Solution (WITS), 176–77, 273
World War II, 11
German domestic propaganda in, 6–7

Wu Jianmin, 165–66, 266
Wu Lengxi, 251–52, 296
Wu Shicun, 129, 268, 274–75

Xie Wen, 38–39
Xi Jinping, 27, 38, 70, 128, 129, 141, 174, 272, 274
Duterte and, 275
on state media loyalty, 73
Xinhua News, 132, 135*t*, 138, 163, 177, 178, 251–52
"Xin Shiye (New Horizon)" (television program), 291–92
Xinwen Lianbo (Network News), 291–92
Xisha Surveillance District, 167, 267
Xu Hong, 134

Yanai, Shunji, 127, 134–36
Yang, Guobin, 70
Yang Jiechi, 134–36, 164, 175, 176, 231, 273
Yasukuni Shrine, 211, 260
Yemen, 245–46, 247
Yi Xianliang, 173–74, 272
yulun daoxiang (guiding public opinion), 71–72
yulun yindao (channeling public opinion), 71–72
Yu the Great, 72
Yuzheng 310 (ship), 268

Zakaria, Fareed, 30–31
Zeng Yongquan, 296
Zhang, Xiaoming, 97, 256
Zhang Jianhua, 38
Zhang Yesui, 134–36
Zhao, Suisheng, 28
Zhao Qizheng, 141–42
Zhao Ziyang, 296–97
Zhao Zongqi, 276
Zhenbao Island, 253
zhenlibu zhiling (Truth Department directives), 75
Zhong Sheng, 135*t*, 137, 141, 142, 143, 144, 165
Zhou Enlai, 251, 253
Zhu Xinhua, 28